The guide is based on based on visits carried out between 2011 and 2013 by members of Pauline Hephaistos Survey Projects (PHSP). This group of researchers, reporters and visitors always includes a variety of people, some able-bodied, some wheelchair users and some disabled walkers.

Over the years PHSP has produced more than twenty access guides, and this is the fifth edition of the London one.
Our approach is to describe the barriers to access as accurately as we can, based on a visit. We allow the reader to decide about the practicality of going there.

The name is a bit of a mouthful.
Pauline arises from St Paul, and some of us come from a Christian group attached to St Paul's School in London.
The Hephaistos part of the name arises from the Greek god who was the smithy and the equivalent of Vulcan in Roman mythology. He was a son of Zeus, who was foolish enough to defend his mother, Hera, during some major family row. Zeus kicked Hephaistos off Mount Olympus and, after a long fall, he landed at the bottom and broke his leg.
In frescoes he is shown with one leg facing one way and the other turned through 90°. Hence, he has been adopted by some as the Greek god for disabled people and gave his name to a pioneering school near Reading which a number of the group attended before its closure in 1986.

We are indebted to the Trustees of the PHSP Charitable Trust, David Aubrey, Isabel Baggott and Mukesh Patel, and to:
- Naomi Chant, and various members of the Park Information Service for information about the Lee Valley Park; and
- James Grant for help with information about TfLs provisions and plans.

This guide was first published in 1984, and then in 1989, 1996 and 2003.

ISBN 978-0-9544598-3-3

Part of the Design Criteria diagram is adapted from *Designing for the Disabled* by Selwyn Goldsmith, with the kind permission of the publishers RIBA Publications Ltd.

Ring Roads
showing the River Thames
and out-of-town *Shopmobility* sites

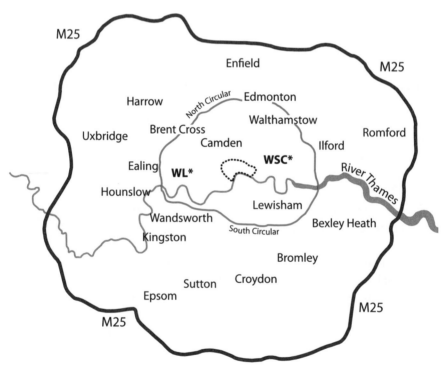

WL* Shepherds Bush (Westfield London)
WSC** Stratford (Westfield Stratford City)

Contents

*Please read the overview in the **Foreword** which discusses recent trends, and use the **Index** for individual sites / sights.*

Abbreviations

which are used throughout the book to shorten the length of the text

AA	Automobile Association
AD	Anno Domini, the year as defined in the Christian Era, and called by some the Common Era
AHL	Action on Hearing Loss
BB	blue badge for parking concessions. A Europe-wide scheme. Widened here in the guide to include any parking for marked out disabled people
BC	the year Before Christ, called by some Before the Common Era
BCF	baby change facilities
BO	box office
BSL	British sign language
BT	British Telecoms
C	Centigrade (degrees of temperature)
CAE	Centre for Accessible Environments
CBL	City Business Library
cm	centimetres
CP	car park
CPZ	controlled parking zone
CS	commentary spot on a map/plan for an audioguide
D	door width (cm)
D, ST	the door width and side transfer distance in toilets (cm)
D,W,L	the door width, cabin width, and length in a lift (cm)
DAR	Dial-a-Ride
DDA	Disability Discrimination Act
DisEnq	telephone number for enquiries by disabled people
DLF	Disabled Living Foundation
DLO	Disability Liaison Officer
DLR	Docklands Light Railway
DWP	Department of Work and Pensions
ENAT	European Network for Accessible Tourism
ETB	English Tourist Board
Ext	extension
F	Farenheit (degrees of temperature)
FAQs	frequently asked questions

FC	Football Club
GA	General admission
GF	ground floor
GFB	ground floor bedroom
GSM	Global System for Mobile Communications
h	hour/s
H&C	Hammersmith and City (underground line)
HRP	Historic Royal Palaces
IDAG	Independent Disability Advisory Group for TfL
JLE	Jubilee Line Extension (from Westminster to Stratford)
L	length (cm)
LGF	lower ground floor
LTB	London Tourist Board
M	management or administration telephone number
m	metres (similar to yards)
M25	the orbital motorway going right round Greater London
Middx	Middlesex
MSCP	multi-storey car park
NAS	National Accessible Scheme
NAT	near accessible transport, referring to accommodation
NCP	National Car Parks
NE, NW	northeast and northwest
NHS	National Health Service
NKS	RADAR National Key Scheme
NR	National Rail
O	London *Overground* (rail network)
ORNC	Old Royal Naval College
PA	personal assistant/carer/friend
PFCU	primarily for car users, referring to accommodation
PHSP	Pauline Hephaistos Survey Projects
R	tube stations where portable ramps are available
RAC	Royal Automobile Club
RADAR	Royal Association for Disability and Rehabilitation
RC	Roman Catholic
RCJ	Royal Courts of Justice
RecM	recorded message
RFH	Royal Festival Hall
RNIB	Royal National Institute of Blind People
RNID	Royal National Institute for Deaf People

SE, SW	southeast and southwest
SFTG	Step-free tube guide (available from TfL)
SIM	subscriber identification module (used in mobile phones)
SNC	Special Needs Coordinator
SOLT	Society of London Theatre
ST	side transfer space (cm) alongside a toilet
SWL	safe working load, which is the weight limit for a lift
Tel	Telephone number
TfA	Transport for all
TFA	Tourism for all
TfL	Transport for London
UG	London Underground (the tube)
UGCP	underground car park
UGF	upper ground floor
V&A	Victoria and Albert
VC	very central, referring to accommodation
VCS	Victoria Coach Station
W	width (cm)
WHS	World Heritage Site
WW	Wellcome Wing (in the Science Museum)
YHA	Youth Hostels Association
YH	Youth Hostel
YMCA	Young Men's Christian Association
YWCA	Young Women's Christian Association

16thC, 19thC etc are used for 16th century, 19th century etc.

Mathematical abbreviations

$>$	greater than
$<$	less than
$\approx$	approximately
$+$	steps up (or more than)
$-$	steps down (or attached to a floor number in a building, indicating level)

Foreword

It's a changed world

We have found that attitudes (and facilities) have changed substantially since the earlier editions of our guides, generally for the better. While there is still some way to go, particularly in connection with the question of accessible transport, people seemed increasingly aware of disability issues and of people's rights to access.

The implementation of the UK Disability Discrimination Act (DDA), has encouraged change, but its existence is a somewhat mixed blessing. Some management now takes the line "Well, we've fulfilled our statutory requirements" with the implication that it is pointless to expect something more.

It is increasingly common for people to provide facilities without the slightest idea of the how or the why. We bumped into a classic illustration of this while updating the guide. When seeing/measuring accessible toilets, we frequently found that the side transfer space was blocked by one or more, sometimes quite heavy, bins. When we drew the facility manager's attention to this and explained why the space had been provided, the most common reaction was "I had no idea how that space was used".

We now have mainly able-bodied access officers, access auditors, and contract commissioners relating to access issues. Their brief is to ensure that the provisions are 'in compliance' rather than to understand what is going on.

In addition, buildings and facilities are largely looked at in isolation (see comments below).

We are disappointed by the way that the major organisations responsible for buildings have gone about both researching and presenting access information.

This is particularly associated with the 'business model' relating to access information. People are promoting the (myth, in our view) that the reason for making places fully accessible is because there's money in it.

In our view, access, and information about it should be provided because it is a human right for people with disabilities, not because there is money to be made.

ENAT recently commented that "the profit argument is a (primitive) means to capture business people's attention and not much more. Once they have pricked up their ears you have to explain the whole story and convince them to change their mindset and their way of working, otherwise they will never succeed and customers will be disappointed - or worse.

The tourism authorities may have been seduced by their own rhetoric to some extent and it is important to note that where there are "success stories" they tend to have strong element of 'social' motivation behind them."

In addition, the ability to digitise data, and to share it via the internet, has had a profound effect on information provision. Although there is much more of it, standards relating to its collection and presentation, seem to have dropped significantly.

Websites present access information in a wide variety of ways with highly variable standards AND it is becoming much more difficult to speak to a human being if you have a query.

The funding for agencies like *Artsline* and *Tripscope* has been withdrawn, so the specialist advice provided by disabled people is not available.

Our view, based on extensive experience, is that:

- the internet has provided quick and easy links between poor quality information, where access is often assessed and described by (well meaning) able-bodied people and not by disabled people;
- internet information rarely has a date attached to it, saying when it was collected; it also rarely says what standards the providers were working to;
- transport information has been largely 'mainstreamed' and is thus provided by able-bodied people reading from a computer screen. Although they may be well meaning, it is not the same as that provided from the experience of a disabled person.

Nearly all the available information looks at individual facilities/venues. There is almost no attempt to integrate and combine practical advice on accommodation, and getting around, with that about access to the sights and places of interest.

Even professional-style organisations like *Tourism for all* (in the UK) and the *European Network for Accessible Tourism (ENAT)*, don't attempt to apply high and consistent standards to their information nor to ensure the integration mentioned above.

They simply make links to what is there, irrespective of who put it on the web, or when it was posted, and are promoting what we have described above as the 'business model'.

Another mistake is something which has increasingly happened since our last edition was published ten years ago. That is to try to integrate all the specialist information needed by people with mobility difficulties with that needed by those who are hearing or visually impaired or who maybe have learning difficulties.

This means increasingly that the research and assessment is made, and the information input, by an able-bodied person, almost certainly without direct experience of what is needed.

It seems to us that this has been the result of a well intended, but misguided, "tick box" mentality. Many of the boxes are ticked by able-bodied people, without the insights of a disabled person.

We appreciate that it's much easier to cover everyone's special needs in one document or in one place, even though the outcome may be quite confusing (because of the volume of different data included).

However, just because it's easier, doesn't make it right.

Far too little of the information is provided by those who experience the relevant challenges.

We think that information for people with visual and/or hearing impairment and for those who may be, or be with, people on the autistic spectrum, should be provided under different headings and probably in clearly different documents, either online or printed, and be provided by those with the relevant experience.

The information is of great importance, but is better supplied separately.

There is now an 'orthodox' mantra that disability is not just about wheelchairs.

While it is, of course, true that disability is not just about wheelchairs - it never has been - the mantra is being translated into, *"We don't need to do any more for wheelchair users, nor do we need to mention physical access first."*

It seems to have been forgotten that wheelchair access facilities are good for families with baby buggies and for disabled walkers, and that good wheelchair access doesn't just help a small minority .... it helps the world in general.

We have put some examples on our website under the heading Methodology where we compare our (PHSP) information, collected by those with relevant experience, and other information provided (often with goodwill) by those who do NOT have it, but who are ticking boxes and/or just running a database.

We are disappointed by the largely incomprehensible descriptions of access provided in the 'access guide' database of *DisabledGo*. We find their write-ups/database presentations to be unhelpful, and they seem to be more of an 'access audit' than an 'access guide'.
We present some comparisons between our write-ups and those of *DisabledGo* on the *Methodology* page of our website for you to make your own assessment.

In the guide, we have tried to be objective by describing what the barriers are, where they are, and how (if possible) to get around them. This approach allows people to make up their own mind as to whether or not a visit is practicable, or on how much help they might need. We have included many places where a real effort has been made to overcome barriers.
Do bear in mind, however, that inclusion in the guide doesn't imply accessibility, and what we're doing is to describe the places listed including any barriers to access.

We assume that this book will be used in conjunction with other guides and information. In particular we recommend the Eyewitness travel guide to London published by Dorling Kindersley. This contains an area by area account and uses illustrations and cut-aways which often clarify access. Readers may well have their own favourite travel guide publisher.
In addition a good street plan is essential, and if you're driving into central London, we recommend the Blue Badge User Guide. We appreciate the expense involved in buying other books and maps, but there's really no way round it.

Introduction

This book sets out to give detailed practical information about travel, accommodation, leisure activities and tourist attractions for people with mobility problems. It contains the unique *Good loo guide* covering much of central London.

If you have internet access, there will be updates on *www.accessinlondon.org*, certainly during the next two or three years, and hopefully for longer.

Those who will find the guide useful include people who use a wheelchair, those who use a stick or crutches, for whom distance is an issue, and those with young children in buggies. They include London residents, day-trippers, people visiting relatives, and, of course, visitors and tourists.

The information here is firmly based on the experiences of disabled people, and virtually every entry has been wheeled into or walked into, and measured and assessed, by one of our survey teams. The information gathering was carried out between 2011 and 2013, and what we present is a straightforward description of the 'access'.

How the guide is arranged

The guide starts with general information, and a chapter on getting around which provides the basis for visiting. There are chapters on accommodation, on the sights, shops and places of interest inside the north and south circular roads. With the focus on sport, arising from the Olympics, we have included detailed write-ups on London's major sports grounds. There is only a brief chapter on Entertainment (because good information is available elsewhere), and the key final chapter is entitled the *Good loo guide*.

The descriptions of a number of places of interest outside the north/south circular road are included on our website *www.accessinlondon.org* where there is also information about London's open-air markets and on annual events. There is additionally a detailed discussion about the drop in standards of reporting 'access' information, under Methodology.

Units and definitions

We have given measurements in centimetres (cm), and metres (m). Although these are the units increasingly being used internationally, many British people, and most Americans, still think in Imperial measures. To convert metric measurements to the more familiar Imperial units, use the following guidelines:

> 10 centimetres is about 4 inches (2.5 centimetres=1 inch)
> 1 metre is about a yard
> 1 litre is about 2 pints
> 1 kilo is about 2 pounds

Steps are listed by number, with + indicating steps up and − indicating down. Occasionally we list them as ±, in that it depends on which direction you are coming from.

The diagram titled *Design criteria* gives the approximate dimensions of a standard wheelchair. Chairs vary considerably in size so it's worth checking the exact size of yours to relate to the measurements given in the guide. With powered chairs, it's also worth checking its weight as well as adding your own weight, because some platform stairlifts have weight and size restrictions.

Movable chairs and tables

In cafés, restaurants and pubs we have not said each time that the chairs and tables are movable. It is assumed that they are movable, and therefore more convenient for chair users and for others. Where they are not movable, or if the seats and tables are high up or might cause a problem, we have said so.

Toilets

Our definition of a **wheelchair toilet** is one where the toilet is unisex; the door opens outward; the door width (D) is >70cm and the side transfer (ST) space is >70cm.

If the toilet does not quite meet these criteria, but is adapted for a chair user, then we call it an **adapted toilet**, and we give the appropriate measurements and information.

Where the cubicle is INSIDE the womens or mens toilet area, we describe them as being **wheelchair or adapted cubicles**.

Unless specified, the toilet seat is at the standard height of about 45cm.

We are aware of the need for the provision of a higher pan for those with arthritis. As toilets with higher pans are not yet widespread, we have not made a separate category.

Where we have visited and measured D and ST widths, we have included the measurements in the text.

Where we have not necessarily visited, but have good evidence of the existence of an appropriate toilet, we have referred to it as an **accessible toilet**. We did not, for example, visit all 147 accessible toilets in the new Wembley Stadium, and we haven't visited all of those on the suburban railway system.

For more information and specifications, see *Designing for Accessibility*, published by the CAE.

The main hassle we came across was the recent trend towards adding BCF to accessible toilets, making them less spacious. In addition it was common to find large nappy disposal bins placed in the ST space. When we drew this to the attention of the management, they nearly all said that they hadn't realised how a chair user might want/need to use the space.

This is an example of the dangers of mainstreaming the management of both facilities and of information, and illustrates perfectly the lack of any detailed

Design Criteria

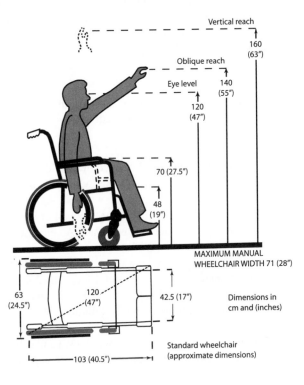

Vertical reach

160 (63")

Oblique reach

Eye level   140 (55")

120 (47")

70 (27.5")

48 (19")

MAXIMUM MANUAL
WHEELCHAIR WIDTH 71 (28")

63 (24.5")   120 (47")   42.5 (17")

Dimensions in
cm and (inches)

Standard wheelchair
(approximate dimensions)

103 (40.5")

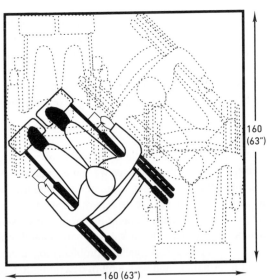

160 (63")

160 (63")

understanding of different people's needs.
Note the new facilities which are gradually being provided as *Changing places*
for people who cannot use standard accessible toilets - with enough space and
equipment, including a height adjustable changing bench and a hoist.
See *www.changing-places.org.*

Lifts

A **lift** (what might be described as a 'conventional' or 'normal' lift) is in a shaft,
with sliding doors, and a cabin which can be large or small. It goes up and down
between the floors of a building.

A **platform lift** is a rectangular vertical lift, usually to take one chair user at a
time. It often bypasses just a few steps - and may be added in a building as an
afterthought, to meet DDA requirements. Its door is normally hinged, and will
swing open outwards.

A **platform stairlift** goes up stairs at an angle (attached to the wall or banister)
and has a platform which can take a wheelchair, and occupant. An electric chair
and occupant may be too heavy, and exceed its SWL.

A **chair stairlift** goes up the stairs (attached to the wall or banister) and has a seat
into which the passenger has to transfer. This is very useful for many disabled
walkers, but for a wheelchair user, their chair has then to be carried up or down
the stairs by someone else. It is not often found in public buildings.

For lift measurements, we quote: door width (D), cabin width (W) and cabin
length (L). On this basis, you can decide whether the lift is large enough for you
to use.

A stairclimber is a free-standing and portable device to which a wheelchair may
be attached. The most common one used is a Scalomobile, but there are also
some with long caterpillar (tank-like) tracks. These devices usually need two
people to operate them, but they can enable a chair user to be helped up or down
stairs. We would comment that the only versions we've come across are not very
comfortable to use, and that only a few people are willing to operate them.

Why travel ?

If you already have travelitis (the travel bug), then you will know why so many
people do it. If you're unsure about it, then perhaps we can encourage you by
sharing our experiences. Since the 1970s, when some of our group first wanted to
travel, we have been to various parts of France, to Jersey, Norway, Germany and
Israel/Palestine, writing guides as we went. Because the group consists of both
disabled and able bodied people, we ran into all kinds of barriers and problems
that could have been divisive. In practice, we tackled problems together, and
found that, given the right information, and with a bit of determination, most

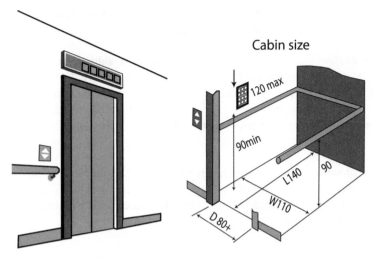

Cabin size

Passenger lift (with sliding doors)

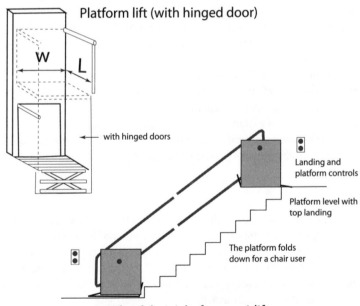

Platform lift (with hinged door)

with hinged doors

Landing and platform controls

Platform level with top landing

The platform folds down for a chair user

Wheelchair/platform stairlift

A chair stairlift is a variation for a disabled walker
(with a fold-down chair, not often found in public buildings.)

The different kinds of lifts

things were possible. We gathered this information together on a systematic basis, and have made it available via these Access guides.

Our experiences have been fun, we've learned a lot, and done things that in the normal course of events we'd never have even thought of doing. We do think that 'travel broadens the mind', and in particular it has brought us into contact with many many people. The majority have been interesting, interested and helpful, though occasionally we have met people with attitudes that were more obstructive than a spiral staircase !

Overall it has brought a series of memorable experiences. Each member of the group will have a different tale to tell. We have encountered new cultures, and seen some amazing sights. Even though there may have been a few problems and difficulties, they've been worth it.

Why London ?

There is an enormous amount to do, see and discover in London. The West End is up with Broadway in offering a variety of high class entertainment, and there are museums, galleries, sights and restaurants which match those you'll find anywhere else in the world. There are pageants, street markets, and night clubs. Although accessibility varies, there are enough historical buildings, art galleries and museums with good access to fill any itinerary.

Accessibility is something that has improved enormously during the past ten years, although to counter this there is also more attention to 'health and safety', which sometimes gets in the way of easier access.

You will find that there is an extraordinary mix of cultures and races.

You will also find that things become somewhat frantic during the morning and evening 'rush hour' on the transport system when people are getting to and from work on weekdays.

A brief history

There is no evidence that the ancient Britons settled on the site of what is now London. The Iron Age inhabitants arrived in the south-east of England around 500 BC, and one of their settlement areas was in what is now Heathrow Airport. Londinium grew after the Roman invasion in 43 AD centred on their original London Bridge which was just feet away from its current site. Now on the north side is London's high rise financial district.

After Roman rule, the Dark Ages saw London controlled by Saxon invaders, who were often in dispute with the Vikings for control of the country. This was until 1066 when William the Conqueror took over, changing Saxon England into Norman England.

London grew in both population and prestige, becoming England's most important city. The oldest parts of the Tower of London date from the late 11thC. There was a large palace and abbey at Westminster, where Chaucer and many other famous people are buried. Tudor London saw the reign of Henry VIII, whose story is best discovered at Hampton Court where he lived. The population increased rapidly. During the Stuart period, the bubonic plague hit the city, reaching its peak in 1665 with the Great Plague. London then took another purging, with the Great Fire in 1666. This is said to have been started accidentally by a baker in Pudding Lane, and the site is commemorated by a huge Doric column, known as the Monument. As part of the reconstruction, St Paul's Cathedral and many other famous churches were built.

Other centres grew and flourished outside the walls of the City, in particular to the south in Southwark. Being beyond the control of the City fathers, raffish entertainment went on here, including bear baiting, and performances of plays by Shakespear. In 1676 it had its own Great Fire, which raged for nearly a day destroying hundreds of houses and businesses.

London Bridge was built, initially at a time when the river was wider and shallower than it is now. On one of the bridges, buildings were allowed, to help pay for its upkeep. In the early 1800s a stone bridge was built, to be replaced in 1973 by the current concrete and steel construction.

The effects of the industrial revolution can be seen clearly. There are old power stations in central London. There was extensive development, including the Docklands, towards the east and this area is now being extensively redeveloped. Throughout the Georgian, Regency and Victorian eras, London grew enormously. There was a mixture of elegant housing for the wealthy, much of which remains, and of rat-infested tenements for the poor (well described by Dickens in his many novels). This reflected the success of both traders and industrialists and the human cost of that success. The less attractive parts have been, or are being, extensively rebuilt and redeveloped. The architecture of the times can be seen in many of the remaining buildings, with extensive Victorian development in outer suburban areas.

London became the capital of the British Empire, the world's largest city, and the world centre for banking and trade. Since then its relative importance has declined, but it remains one of the great capitals of the world. We hope that you have an enjoyable visit, and that the information in this guide will be helpful.

London's postcodes
If you're going to get around London, it may be helpful to know something about the way that the postcodes are arranged. They are shown on the map, and as can be seen, it's a complicated arrangement - which has grown and grown over the years.

Apart from the very central areas covered by the WC and EC codes and those designated 1, the rest of the postcodes seem to be somewhat random.

In some areas, the geographical names are organised in alphabetical order. However, the listing is further complicated because some areas have two or more alphabetical series and there appears to be little logic about the order of some of the numbers.

Places in London's outer boroughs such as Harrow, Barnet, Enfield, Ilford, Romford, Bexleyheath, Bromley, Hounslow, Richmond, Croydon, Sutton, Kingston and Uxbridge are covered by parts of twelve adjoining postcode areas (EN, IG, RM, DA, BR, TN, CR, SM, KT, TW, HA and UB).

London postcodes

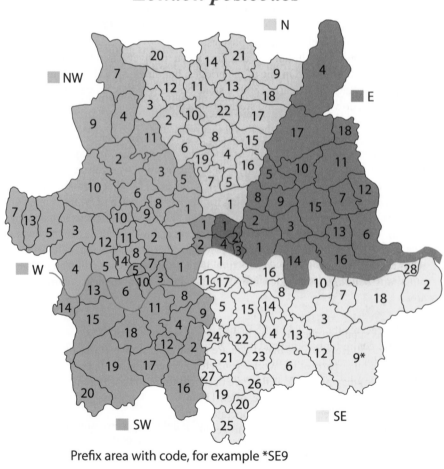

Prefix area with code, for example *SE9

E   EC   N   NW   SE   SW   W   WC

General information

This chapter covers a whole variety of topics, some of which will be primarily of interest to visitors and others which will also be useful for residents. It includes a list of companies for equipment repair and hire, and a separate list of useful contacts.

Climate

Visitors must take into account the generally mild but unpredictable weather. There are hot spells in the summer and cold periods in the winter but the forecast of 'sunshine and showers' is all too common. When packing, you should allow for chilly winds in the winter (and the possibility of snow and ice). It may rain at almost any time, but there are often good spells of several weeks when it will be dry and sunny. If you come in the summer, remember that relatively few buildings have air-conditioning, although that number is gradually increasing. The temperature can vary from 32°C/90°F right down to −11°C/10°F.

Places to go in London if it's really wet or cold include the big museums, the attractions like Madame Tussauds or the Aquarium, or some of the very big shops or covered shopping areas. There are a number of different (indoor) places around Trafalgar Square, and there's the Royal Festival Hall (RFH) on the South Bank. This is open throughout the day and has many spaces on different floors, where you can sit and read - or bring your laptop, without being forced to buy coffee. If it's fine, the parks and riverside are particularly attractive - as is Covent Garden which has street entertainment.

Drinking water and food hygiene

The level of food hygiene in Britain is generally very high. Similarly, the mains water supply is of a high standard, so that tap water and ice cubes in restaurants are safe to drink, and washed salads are safe to eat.

Electrical supply

The mains supply in the UK is an alternating current (AC) at 240 volts and 50 cycles/sec (50 Hertz). Note that if you are travelling from the USA, and possibly from some other parts of the world, your electrical equipment (battery chargers, for example) may not work as they are designed for use at a different frequency (commonly 60 Hertz) and voltage, often 110.

As a result, not all equipment will operate in the UK.

Make sure that you check on where to get hold of equipment that works before setting off.

Emergencies

In the event of accident or a serious emergency, the standard procedure is to telephone the Police, Fire Service or Ambulance by dialling **999**. That way you'll get the right help or advice. The first person you'll speak to is the operator who will ask, *'Which service do you require?'* When you then get through, you can explain what help is needed, and where you are.

A new service has been introduced for making non-emergency contact with the police by calling **101**. This should be used to report crime and other concerns that do not require an emergency response, for example if your car has been stolen or some property damaged.

Generally both doctors and dentists are available only during normal working hours. Some hospitals have a 24-hour 7-day Accident and Emergency department. If you need to collect a doctor's prescription, your nearest police station keeps a list of local pharmacies and their opening times.

Chemists (drugstores) that are open late 7 days a week include:

(the list was checked at the end of 2013)

Boots 508-520 Oxford Street, W1C 1NB (near Marble Arch, and by the junction with Park Street) *Tel:* 020 7499-6329

Bliss 5 Marble Arch, Edgware Road, Bayswater, W1H 7AP *Tel:* 020 7723-6116

Pharmacentre, 149 Edgware Road, Paddington, W2 2HU (near the junction with Sussex Gardens) *Tel:* 020 7723-2336, has a 24-hour callout and consultation service.

Boots Unit 51 Paddington Station Concourse, W2 1HB *Tel:* 020 7402-9087

Boots 114 Queensway, W2 6LS *Tel:* 020 7229-1183

Bliss 54 Willesden Lane, NW6 7SX *Tel:* 020 7624-8000

Zafash 233 Old Brompton Road, Earls Court, SW5 0EA *Tel:* 020 7373-2798

In the evening some stores/shops may use an intercom by the door to facilitate access to the pharmacy section as the rest of the shop is closed.

Equipment repair and hire

There are a number of places where it is possible to hire special equipment, including wheelchairs, and where you can buy equipment. We list here some of the principal sources, and when it was complete, we noticed that most of the providers had addresses north of the river.

For local advice, the nearest *Shopmobility* should be a good source, as should the local borough disability association. There's a list of *Shopmobility* locations later in this chapter. Alternatively, you might try the Disabled Living Foundation and look at its fact sheets.

For short periods it is possible to borrow wheelchairs and other equipment from a local branch of the **Red Cross**.

HQ address 44 Moorfields, EC2Y 9AL

Tel: 0844 871-1111   *Textphone:* 020 7562-2050
website: www.redcross.org.uk *e-mail:* information@redcross.org.uk

The following is a list of businesses providing a range of repair and/or hire facilities, and at most of them you can also purchase equipments:

Direct Mobility
Warren House, 201a Bury Street, Edmonton N9 9JE
Tel: 020 8370-7888 or 0800 092-9322
website: www.directmobility.co.uk *e-mail:* info@directmobility.co.uk
DM have a wide range of homecare products available, either for hire or to buy. These include wheelchairs, hoists, and a variety of other mobility aids.

FMS Mobility Centre
70 Victoria Road, Ruislip Manor, Middlesex, HA4 0AH
Tel: 01895 622-268
website: www.fmsmobilitycentres.com *e-mail:* info@fmsmobilitycentres.com
Provides a range of mobility aids, some of which can be hired.

GBL Wheelchair Warehouse
Unit 12, Mount Road, Hanworth, Middlesex TW13 6AR
Tel: 020 8867-2461 or 0500 901-690
website: www.gblwheelchairs.com *e-mail:* info@gblwheelchairs.com
Step-free access and **a wheelchair toilet** on-site. CP. GBL is a firm run by chair users. They offer a wide range of chairs, new, ex-demo or secondhand, and have an excellent hire or repair service. If you have a problem, give them a ring.

Independent Living Company
11 Hale Lane, Mill Hill NW7 3NU   *Tel:* 020 8931-6000
website: www.independent-living.co.uk *e-mail:* sales@independent-living.co.uk
There are 2 steps at the entrance but a portable ramp is available. Has a wide range of homecare equipment available for hire or purchase, including wheelchairs and scooters. In addition there is an extensive workshop for repairs.

Keep Able (Hearing and Mobility)
have two stores in the London area, one to the north and the other just outside the M25 to the west. These stock a wide range of mobility equipment.
They have a central communications system *Tel:* 0800 085-0688
website: www.hearingandmobility.co.uk *e-mail:* info@hearingandmobility.com
    Mill Hill
    615-619 Watford Way, Apex Corner, Mill Hill, NW7 3JN
    Staines
    11/17 Kingston Road, Staines, Middx TW18 4QX

London Wheelchair Rental
3 Bomer Close, West Drayton, Middlesex, UB7 0JP
Tel: 0800 488-0164 *website:* www.london-wheelchair-rental.com
Can provide a short-term wheelchair hire service with a range of lightweight chairs.

Medi World
444 Streatham High Road, Streatham SW16 3PX *Tel:* 020 8764-1806
website: www.mediworld.co.uk *e-mail:* sales@mediworld.co.uk
Step-free entrance. Has a wide range of homecare and mobility equipment which is available for hire or purchase.

Mobility scooter hire

Mobility scooters will be of particular interest to some - and short-term visitors may want to hire one for a few days.
They can be of enormous value to those who cannot walk far, but they vary in size (as do electric wheelchairs) and are less well accepted and understood compared with wheelchairs. There are circumstances where a long thin vehicle is less stable than a squarer wheelchair, and they certainly do not cope well with kerbs and single steps.
Not everywhere can/will accept and facilitate the use of mobility scooters, and it isn't a question which we have included in our survey when visiting buildings and facilities.
In response to a recent query to an American staying near Waterloo station who wanted to hire a mobility scooter we said "There's plenty to see within scooter distance of your hotel.
You have the whole of the South Bank (with theatre, concerts and film), including Tate Modern, and if you go across Westminster Bridge, there's Parliament Square, with Whitehall leading to Trafalgar Square etc etc You could also take a Thames Clipper (boat) to the Tower and to Greenwich, as they have recently been declared scooter friendly."
You should be able to get out and take a scooter in the back of a taxi.
Transport for All will almost certainly be able to update you about scooter use on public transport.
Possible places for scooter hire include:
Direct Mobility (see details above)

Q2db 32 Rowden Road, West Ewell, Epsom KT19 9PN
Tel: 020 8397-0197 or *mobile:* 07957 972-595
website: www.mobilityrent.co.uk *e-mail:* enquiry@q2db.co.uk

Wheelfreedom Limited
Unit 5, 271 Merton Road, SW18 5JS *Tel:* 0800 0258-005
website: www.wheelfreedom.com *e-mail:* enquiries@wheelfreedom.com
and there are some others in the listing above.

Repairs to NHS equipment

We made some enquiries about what to do if you are visiting London and you
have trouble with any equipment that may have been supplied by your local
NHS Trust. An obvious question is, 'What do I do if my wheelchair (or other
equipment) breaks down ?'
Unfortunately we didn't get any straight answers because each NHS Trust has its
own contracts for things like repairs, with different conditions. If it is something
fairly straightforward like a puncture, and you can get it repaired at modest cost,
then the thing to do is to get it fixed. Take the bill back to your own NHS Trust
Supplies office/depot, and they'll probably pay up. One thing you need to bear
in mind is that if you have to 'call out' one of the private suppliers listed here,
there may be a significant charge over and above the cost of the repair. Possibly
the best thing we can suggest is that you take with you the phone number of your
own NHS Supplies office and then, if you have a problem, at least you can ring
up and say, 'Help ! What should I do?' Alternatively, go through the NHS Trust
Supplies office nearest to where you are staying.
Organisations who have been helpful to us on various occasions are the AA and
RAC. If you are a member or are staying with a member, there may be some
simple repairs that they can help with. For wheelchair repairs a bicycle shop may
be a good place to try.

Events listings

There are numerous listings about what is happening in London. The *Evening
Standard* which is London's free evening paper, has listings, as do some of the
national dailies. It has a searchable website, *www.standard.co.uk.*
The most extensive listing of events is in *Time Out* which comes out weekly, but
now that it's free it is more difficult to find. Both the printed and web listings
tell you about theatres, restaurants, sporting, musical and special events, and
exhibitions.
Time Out London, Universal House, 251 Tottenham Court Road, W1T 7AB.
Their website is: *www.timeout.com/london Tel:* 020 7813-3000
Another good source of information is Visit London at:
www.visitlondon.com → Things to do → Whats on
There's also *The Big Issue* which is a weekly magazine which provides both an
income and hope to some of London's homeless people. It includes interesting
articles on London issues, and information about what's going on.

Maps and guides

There are literally dozens of guide books to London, all with slightly different angles and presentation. A listing here does not imply that their advice for disabled visitors or residents is particularly good, and that's why you need *Access in London* !

When choosing a guide, check the date of publication, as things change, particularly prices and opening times. There are many specialist guides to particular aspects of London and its history and life. Where relevant, we have detailed these in each chapter.

For general guides to interesting and historic places, we recommend the *Eyewitness Guide to London* published by Dorling Kindersley (DK). It includes good area maps and building cut-away's which are relevant to access. DK also publish a good *Family Guide to London* which is useful if you are coming with children.

The other guide with particularly good building cut-away's is the Michelin *Green Guide*. Other guides that we have found useful include: the *Lonely Planet London* the *Rough Guide to London* and *Time Out London*. The *Fodor London Companion* gives a comprehensive and readable background to many of the interesting places and events.

Big books that include a great deal of background information or look at the city from a different angle, include *The Times Atlas of London* which has a comprehensive borough-by-borough guide showing how each district has developed over the years, articles on famous Londoners, royal London, and sport in the capital.

There's *London The Biography* by Peter Ackroyd and published by Vintage; *Eccentric London* by Ben le Vay, published by Brandt.

Time Out publish a whole range of guides to different aspects of London life, including *London for Londoners*.

The street plans of London come in a huge variety of sizes. Some cover the whole of greater London, almost out to the M25, others cover just the central areas. They come in ring bindings, in soft covers, and in hardback.

There are four principal publishers:

* the AA for Street by Street guides;
* Collins;
* Ordnance Survey; and,
* Geographia (for the AtoZ series).

They're all good, and much depends on your choice of style, and ease of use. You can get a ring-bound, large scale street plan for central London and the Docklands area for less than £5. The one we recommend is conventionally bound, published by Collins, and called the *Superscale London atlas*.

The best place in London for finding maps and guides is:

Stanfords   12-14 Long Acre, WC2E 9LP

Tel: 020 7836-1321 *website:* www.stanfords.co.uk

Located between Covent Garden Market and Leicester Square, it is one of the largest shops in the world stocking maps and guides. +1 step from Long Acre, but step free at the back from Floral Street. The shop has been modernised and made more accessible with a lift (D75 W85 L125) to all floors.

Website sources which can be helpful in locating places include:

- *www.maps.google.co.uk* for Google maps, who now seem to be he market leaders with maps and street pictures as well as setting out routes for getting from A to B;
- *www.multimap.com* for Bing maps, which had some slightly eccentric entries in the area where PHSP has its HQ;
- *www.mylondonmap.com* has links to a tube map (though without 'access' information), and to hotels and theatres;
- *www.streetmap.co.uk* for a nicely drawn standard street plan.

These can all provide you with a local map based on a postcode, or, possibly on a street name together with the area name.

Medical and insurance issues

These notes are provided primarily for visitors to Britain.

Dealing with pre-existing medical conditions when travelling

If you want to bring medicines into the UK, you may need to check that they are licensed for use. Always carry them in labelled containers, as issued by the pharmacist. If appropriate, you might also bring a letter from your doctor giving details of the drug/s prescribed. Remember that some medicines available over-the-counter in your country may be controlled in Britain, and vice versa.

Getting advice and treatment

If you become ill while visiting Britain, you are eligible for free emergency treatment in the Accident and Emergency departments of National Health Service hospitals. However, if you are admitted to hospital as an in-patient, even from the accident and emergency department, or referred to an out-patient clinic, you will be asked to pay, unless you are a national of countries which have reciprocal health care agreements with the UK, or meet certain other criteria.

There are a number of private walk-in medical centres in central London, where you will generally have to pay for advice and/or tests. No appointment is necessary and you will normally be seen quite quickly. See the list below.

Medicentres

website: www.medicentre.co.uk *Tel:* 0845 437-0353

These are mainly for busy business people, offering medical facilities near where they work, but may also be useful to visitors. They are:

- **Bank**, 80 Cheapside, EC2V 6EE *Tel:* 020 7510-0310 with lift access;

- **near Waterloo station**, 135 Lower Marsh, SE1 7AE *Tel:* 020 7510-0305 with step-free access;
- **Paddington station**, Unit 50, W2 1HQ *Tel:* 020 7510-0312, located on the mezzanine floor above Boots, with lift access;
- **Victoria station**, (near platform 14), SW1V 1JT *Tel:* 020 7510-0314, with lift access.

People rarely travel abroad without some sort of insurance, largely because of a greater awareness of the costs involved if something unexpected happens. While you hear from time to time about legionnaire's disease, insolvent airlines, the work of pickpockets, and these days, the threat of terrorism, the risk to the individual traveller is very small indeed.

What IS important is to have good insurance cover for something which would cost a lot of money if events went badly wrong. This would include, for example, the result of injury in a traffic accident, or of an unexpected illness. You might need immediate medical treatment, and possible repatriation by air ambulance to your home country.

This has become a complicated subject, but there is a good preliminary discussion on the *Visit Britain* website, under: *www.visitbritain.com*→Travel-tips→Traveller-tips→Medical-and-health-information.

Insurance is offered as part of most travel arrangements made by agents. It is also readily available on the internet, but **for the disabled traveller there are special requirements** and if you don't do it properly, you can finish up without cover when you thought that you had it.

Much depends on whether your insurer has agreed the cover.

When our first guide *Access in Paris* was published in 1974, the insurance world proved to be very uncooperative in providing cover for disabled travellers as they were generally considered to be a bad risk ! It was not realised that very few people would want to travel abroad if they were likely to be ill. Thankfully since then much has changed and there are policies which provide good cover for the disabled traveller, although insurers are increasingly tending to 'cherry pick', offering policies only to those thought to be at lowest risk.

What you generally have to do is to answer a medical questionnaire. If your condition is stable, and you rarely need to visit your doctor, then you can say so, and issuing your policy should be straightforward.

A basic problem with any insurance is that you don't know how good your policy is until you need to make a claim. Remember that for loss and theft claims, you nearly always need to report the theft to the local police (within 24 hours) and to get a piece of paper to prove that it was reported. Similarly health/medical claims need to be thoroughly documented - and you need to consult the insurer's 24-hour telephone Helpline to ensure that you are proceeding within their guidelines. This is a little difficult if you (for example) happen to be unconscious after an accident - but the earliest possible contact with your insurers Helpline is ESSENTIAL. You need to keep copies of all receipts for money spent, and a detailed note of what happens and when it happens.

Keep a written record with you at all times of any medical condition affecting you and the generic names (not just the trade names) of any medication you are taking.

If you have a medical condition where you are dependent on taking certain medications, or if, for example, you take anticoagulants to thin your blood and prevent clotting, or if you have occasional fits, it is essential that you carry something making your condition clear to a medic or paramedic.

You may, for example, be rendered unconscious by some accident, and if the people who come to help don't know about your situation, they may not be able to provide the best treatment.

There are various ways of ensuring that the medics are informed, and that includes carrying a doctor's letter or belonging to the organisation listed below (or its equivalent in your own country).

The Medic Alert Foundation
327 Witan Court, Upper Fourth Street, Milton Keynes, MK9 1EH
Tel: 01908 951-045
website: www.medicalert.org.uk   *e-mail:* info@medicalert.org.uk
Medic-alert provides a useful service for those with medical problems that could be compounded by treatment after an accident. It is of special importance to those who have epilepsy, haemophilia, diabetes or allergies, and to those who need regular dosage of a particular drug. Membership is available for a nominal fee of £30/year. Members wear a metal emblem engraved with the telephone number of the Emergency Service and a note of the immediate medical problems of the wearer. Additional medical information is filed at the Emergency Headquarters, where the telephone is staffed 24 hours a day.

One medical/practical problem which people commonly need help with is that caused by incontinence, but with good planning, this needn't stop anyone from getting around. There are now more *Changing places* toilets around (see the *Good loo guide*). In addition, the following supplier may be of help:

Incontinence Choice
Choiceshops Ltd, Unit E, Stafford Park 18, Telford, Shropshire, TF3 3BN
Tel: 01952 913-112
website: http://www.incontinencechoice.co.uk
e-mail: incontinencechoice@choiceshops.co.uk

Price concessions

A number of places offer price reductions for chair users, blind people, and/or others on defined benefits. Sometimes, documentary evidence is required, and thus visitors would be wise to carry an appropriate doctors note.

Very often the concession offered applies to an accompanying carer/facilitator, who may get in free.

The problem is that concessions are highly capricious, and can depend as much on who's on the door as it does on official policy. The offer of price concessions for entrance is generally a well intended gesture. Just occasionally, there may be regulations which say that chair users may not enter some places without a friend or escort.

We have always taken the view that the right of access is even more important than any price concession. This essentially comes from our experiences over past years when people's rights to access have not been so widely recognised, and people have told us that 'you cannot come in'.

Because of their variability, and because they may apply to some disabled people and not to others, we have tended not to detail price concessions. Places where there are well established concessions for chair users include many historical buildings; the South Bank (National Theatre and Festival Hall complex); the Barbican; the Coliseum; Fairfield arts complex in Croydon; the Royal Opera House; the Tower Bridge Walkway and the Tower of London. There are many others, including London's buses.

There are nearly always reductions in ticket prices for children, and it is becoming increasingly common for places to offer 'family tickets', sometimes for two adults and up to three children.

Telephones

This is a subject where technology has advanced dramatically since the last edition of the guide, with the widespread use of Smartphones with internet access, in addition to the conventional mobile. While most businesses continue to have landlines, there has been a decline in their domestic use.

There's a very wide variety of provision by different companies, and the costs involved can be confusing. Watch out, in particular, for the charges made for 'special' numbers.

Unfortunately, an increasing number of organisations are using automated reply systems on their phones, so it becomes increasingly difficult to actually speak to a person.

Additionally, many queries are dealt with in call centres, which can be hundreds of km away from London, so the person answering may have no local knowledge. They can only read off the information that they have on the computer screen in front of them.

The code for London is 020 with phones in the central area being followed by a 7 and those further out followed by an 8. The 7 and 8 prefixes have recently been joined by the use of 3, following the 020 code, and thee numbers may be anywhere in London.

The inner area covers central London and Docklands numbers, while the outer area covers most subscribers more than 4 miles (6.4km) from Charing Cross. You need an eight digit number when dialling between the zones.

We set out below some of the basics of the phone numbers system. You will need to check what is built into your particular phone contract relating to the costs for calling different kinds of numbers.

See: *www.area-codes.org.uk*→uk-phone-numbering-guide, for up-to-date information.

- 0800 numbers are free if called from a landline. Many mobile operators make a charge for calls;
- an 07 number followed by any digit except '0' is usually a mobile phone number;
- **watch out for 070 codes**. They look like mobile numbers, but can cost up to 50p a minute. 070 phone numbers are intended to divert calls to the owner's location. However, because they are easy to mistake for mobile numbers, some criminals use them to try to con you into calling them and making money out of it. If you receive a missed call on your mobile from an 070 number, don't call it back – it is likely to be a scam;
- 0500 numbers are used by businesses and are free from landlines, but typically cost between 15-30p/minute from mobiles and they're not included in 'free' mobile minutes;
- 0300 numbers are not geographic, and cost the same to call as 01 or 02 phone numbers;
- 0845 numbers - many providers charge more for 0845 than 01/02/03 phone calls, but you need to look at the details in your 'phone package';
- landline phone calls on 0870 typically cost between 4.5-10p/minute for daytime calls, but again you need to look at the details in your 'phone package;
- phone numbers starting 09 are charged at a premium rate, and are the most expensive type of number to call. They are often used for TV phone-in quizzes, which at least you have a choice whether to call or not. Alarmingly, some companies use them for technical support. The most you're likely to pay from a BT landline is £1.50/minute;

The phone numbers starting 03, 0844, 0845, 0870 and 0871 aren't tied to a geographic location, so you can't tell where in the country you're calling. With the 0844, 0845, 0870 and 0871 numbers, organisations can share the profit they make from your call with network provider. With landline calls, this share

can be up to 4p/minute.
Outside London, different codes apply. If in doubt, ask the operator for advice (dial 100).

Directory enquiries

This operation has been opened up to competition, so new services are being provided from time to time, with different charges applying.
One such company is *Tel:* 118-118.
For general directory enquiries from BT, call 118-500 or use *www.192.com* for UK numbers.
For international numbers call 118-505. Note that this involves a connection charge of £1, plus a cost of £3.50/minute (from landlines).
The O2 directory enquiries number is 118-402, charged at £1/minute.
For finding business telephone numbers, probably the best way is to Google your target.

If you are ringing the UK from abroad, there will be a local code, probably 00, followed by 44 for the UK, and this REPLACES the first 0 in the London code, so to dial 020 4785-6399 from abroad, you would dial 00-44-20-4785-6399.

Hiring/renting a mobile

Once in London, the easiest way to communicate is undoubtedly with a mobile phone.
There's a good discussion of what is involved on *http://www.planetomni.com/ FAQ_sim.shtml* although note that this is written from a US perspective. If your phone can be unlocked, and works on GSM (Global System for Mobile Communications) frequencies, it should be easy to get a SIM card from one of the local providers in the UK like T-mobile or Vodafone. During your stay you simply swap your SIM card over. If this is not an option, it is also possible to buy an unlocked handset here and Carphone Warehouse is one of many suppliers.

For people who only want a mobile phone for a short period, rental/hire is an option, which should be compared with buying a pay-as-you-go one, or using your own existing phone and checking on how much it would cost to use in London. It very much depends on what you want it for, how many calls you may want to make, and how much you are prepared to spend. You may be able to hire a SIM card to put in your existing phone.
One advantage of having a mobile is that you can call ahead quite easily, and you can even call from outside a building saying that you need some assistance.
Note that this is a changing market, and we are not experts !
There are numerous suppliers, such as:
- the **Carphone Warehouse** at *www.carphonewarehouse.com Tel:* 0800 049-6250;

- **Adam Phones** offer a wide range of services at: *www.adamphones. com*→products/services→mobile consultancy→short-term-hire;
- and there are *www.fonerent.com*/about/about-us;
- *www.cellhire.co.uk*/products/uk/phone; and,
- *www.travelex.co.uk*/uk/personal/MH_default.aspx who combine currency supply with a range of other services.

Skype

Providing you have a computer with high speed Internet and a microphone, one low cost possibility for keeping in touch, is to download and use Skype, see *www. skype.com*. You can then make calls to both landline and mobile phones as well as to other people using Skype. They have both pay as you go, and subscription options, and the choice depends on how much use you make of the service. Call costs start at about 2p/min but will be higher for calls made to mobiles. Skype to Skype calls are normally free.

Easy-to-use phones

While we are not attempting to assess many of the equipment items that are available these days, one item which has become almost universally useful/ necessary is the mobile phone. Since most mobiles on the market have small buttons and a variety of add-ons that serve no purpose for many older and disabled users, we thought that some information about where to find mobiles (and other phones) that are easy to use would be helpful.

One of the unfortunate things about new technologies is that products come on to the market which people find to be really helpful, but a year or two later, there's an upgraded version which may or may not be an improvement for a particular user. Hence you will need to check on the web (or by phoning appropriate enquiry lines) to see what is currently available.

There are a number of mobile phones available with larger buttons, high contrast screens and amplified sound systems. These were first introduced by an Austrian company Emporia.

See: *www.matobmobile.co.uk Tel:* 0845 217-7712

www.emporia.co.uk→products

and: *www.rnib.org.uk*→shop→phones and mobiles→mobile phones

You may also find useful offers on this site: *www.theorder.co.uk*

For large button desk phones for landline connections have a look at:

www.uk.shopping.com→consumer electronics→landline phones→big button

The BT BIG Button 100 Corded Phone is a good example of such an instrument, but BT has a number of variations.

Textphones

Text Relay Team, c/o Internal Box 14, Telephone House,
170 Moor Lane, Preston, Lancashire PR1 1BA

Tel: 0800 7311-888   *Textphone:* 0800 500-888
website: www.textrelay.org
An estimated half a million people in the UK are unable to use a standard telephone.
Text Relay is a system which connects people using a textphone with others using a telephone or another textphone. It lets hearing and/or speech impaired people use phones to communicate through relay assistants.
If you're using a textphone (sometimes called a Minicom) or if you think the person at the other end may have a textphone, Text Relay will connect you.
When required, the relay assistants provide a text-to-voice and/or voice-to-text translation service.
To make a call from a textphone, dial 18001 + the number.
When the person you're calling answers, if they are on a telephone, they will receive an automated message informing them this is a Text Relay call and that there will be a short delay while a relay assistant joins the call.
To make a telephone call to a textphone, dial 18002 + the number
If the person you're calling picks up using a textphone, you will hear a recorded Text Relay greeting message while you wait for a relay assistant to join the call.

BT launched TextDirect In 2001, and later, Action on Hearing Loss introduced Typetalk.
The emergency number (18000) was set up in 2004.
The service was renamed Text Relay in 2009 to remove the confusion arising from the use of two names.
Text Relay is available 24 hours a day, 365 days a year. Calls are charged at your phone line standard rate. Extra costs are funded by the UK communications industry.

From April 2014 users will be able to use an Internet connected device alongside their phone for ParallelText calls, via what is being called *the Next Generation Text Service.*
Once you have installed the free app on a compatible computer, tablet or Smartphone the service will use your Internet connection, and a phone call to create a ParallelText connection between you and the service. The Internet connection will be used for the text part of the conversation while the phone call is used to set up the call, for any spoken part of the conversation, and for billing. You will thus not need a separate textphone keyboard. Once set up this service will allow you to call both textphones and telephones from your home computer, with the advantage of a full size keyboard for easier typing.

Toilets/loos

Finding suitable toilets is a serious problem for many people, and particularly for disabled people whose needs are more exacting. American readers will be used to calling them the John or the bathroom. In Britain the bathroom is the room with a bath, and not necessarily with a toilet. An informal word for toilet is 'loo', which we use from time to time in the guide.

There are far more accessible toilets around now than there were when the guide was first published. Quite a few McDonalds, Burger King, Costa Coffee, Starbucks and Pizza Hut restaurants have one, as do new shopping precincts, and an increasing number of pubs.

We include a chapter entitled the *Good Loo Guide,* which covers much of central London, and we have defined what we mean by a **wheelchair toilet**, an **adapted toilet** and an **accessible toilet** in the *Introduction* chapter.

Note the new facilities which are gradually being provided as *Changing places* for people who cannot use standard accessible toilets with enough space and equipment, including a height adjustable changing bench and a hoist. See *www. changing-places.org.*

You would be well advised to get hold of one of the special NKS (National Key Scheme or RADAR) keys which will open approximately half the accessible toilets including most of those provided by local authorities and those on rail stations.
You can get an NKS key from (among other places):
*   **the Disability Rights UK Online store** at *www.disabilityrightsuk.org*
*   **Incontinence Choice** under Bathroom and toilet aids at *www. incontinencechoice.co.uk*
*   **the Pie Guide** at *www.thepieguide.com.*

Useful organisations and contact points

There are many sources of information and who you go to depends on what you want to know. If you need advice or help, you often have to be persistent and try different contacts if your first or second enquiry does not produce a satisfactory answer. We list here some general sources and the major organisations of and for disabled people. Remember that much depends on whom you speak to. They may be new in the organisation; they may be in a hurry to do something else, or the person who really knows is in the loo. On the other hand, you'll often come across people who will go to a great deal of trouble to help.

One of the more frustrating aspects of modern life is the more extensive use in big organisations of the automatic 'multiple choice' questioning when you ring up. Often you are held in a queue with no indication of how far back you are. There is also much greater use of voice mail - which too often seems to swallow your message, and doesn't produce a response. The only advice we can give is that if the query is important, be persistent, and/or try some other way of getting an answer.

Note that more and more organisations are relying on information posted on their website. Some of these sites are comprehensive and easy to use. Others, inevitably, are slightly less user-friendly. If you're looking for more contact points or information, most sites have a links page, and you may find somewhere else that has what you need.

If a telephone number or address listed here has changed, you will almost certainly be able to get the new one from one of the other agencies listed, or via directory enquiries on 192, or one of the new services currently coming into use. Alternatively you can do an internet search.

AbilityNet
website: www.abilitynet.org.uk *e-mail:* enquries@abilitynet.org.uk
Tel: 0800 269-545 or *Tel:* 01926 312-847
With the widespread use of computer technology, there have been many developments which have been of particular value to people with disabilities. These include the use of software which enables visually impaired users to use their computers together with a wide range of other applications. AbilityNet is the leading supplier of information in this area.
Their Advice and Information Services provide free support to thousands of people every year, including free to download factsheets, telephone support and direct help from a network of over 8,000 volunteers.

Action for Blind People (AFBP), 53 Sandgate Street, Peckham, SE15 1LE
Tel: 020 7635-4800 *website:* www.afbp.org
AFBP and the RNIB (see below) have brought together their helpline services, giving people access to a wide source of knowledge and expertise from a single number.
You can call the RNIB helpline on *Tel:* 0303 123-9999 or
e-mail: helpline@rnib.org.uk

Action on Hearing Loss 19-23 Featherstone Street, EC1Y 8SL
Information line: 0808 808-0123 *Textphone:* 0808 808-9000
SMS: 0780 0000-360
Tinnitus lines: 0808 808-6666 *Textphone:* 0808 808-0007
website: www.actiononhearingloss.org.uk
e-mail: informationline@hearingloss.org.uk and
tinnitushelpline@hearingloss.org.uk
The Royal National Institute for Deaf People (RNID) was renamed in 2011 as Action on Hearing Loss (AHL). In its ongoing work, AHL wants a world where hearing loss doesn't limit or label people, where tinnitus is silenced – and where people value and look after their hearing.
It aims to promote and encourage both the alleviation and prevention of deafness.

It is mainly a service organisation, and offers care and support through both information and training. AHL has a wide range of publications including over eighty factsheets. Many are available in Braille, audio tape and large print. You can order by contacting the Information Line, or you can download some of them The RNID Typetalk service which has been the national telephone relay to enable those with hearing or speech loss to communicate is scheduled to be 'revolutionised' early in 2014, see: *www.textrelay.org*. This will take advantage of many of the new mechanisms available for making text-based calls using compatible computers, tablets or Smartphones. See the earlier writeup on Textphones and Text Relay.

Adapted Car Hire
13 High Street, Wanstead, E11 2AA *Tel:* 0845 6862-007
website: www.adaptedcarhire.co.uk *e-mail:* info@adaptedcarhire.co.uk

Adapted Vehicle Hire
Poplar House, Cowley Business Park, Cowley Road, Uxbridge, UB8 2AD
Tel: 0845 257-1670
website: www.avhltd.com *e-mail:* admin@avhltd.com
Both companies offer a range of adapted and wheelchair accessible vehicles - and are located on opposite sides of London.
Also note *www.mobility-centres.org.uk* the **Forum of Mobility Centres** who offer high quality information, advice and assessment to individuals who have a medical condition or are recovering from an accident (*Tel:* 0800 559-3636).

Age UK, Tavis House, 1-6 Tavistock Square, WC1H 9NA
Tel: 0800 169-8080; 0800 169-6565 (for the Age UK advice line)
website: www.ageuk.org.uk *e-mail:* contact@ageuk.org.uk
Age UK was formed from a merger of Age Concern and Help the Aged in 2010. It is the focal point for all voluntary groups concerned with information and services for older people. **It provides an extensive information and advice service to older people.**

Artsline are described in the chapter on *Entertainment*.

Can Be Done, Congress House, 14 Lyon Road, Harrow, HA1 2EN
Tel: 020 8907-2400
website: www.canbedone.co.uk *e-mail:* holidays@canbedone.co.uk
Can be Done is a tour operator that organises tailor-made holidays and tours for both groups and individuals. All are 'accessible'. They used to focus primarily on London, but now most of their holidays are abroad, including some really exotic and challenging destinations. They still, however, organise visits to London and are a friendly company to deal with.

Centre for Accessible Environments (CAE)

4th Floor, Holyer House, 20-21 Red Lion Court, EC4A 3EB (off Fleet Street)
Tel: 020 7822-8232 *Technical Helpline Tel:* 090 6751-6663
website: www.cae.org.uk *e-mail:* info@cae.org.uk
The CAE aims to improve access to buildings and the environment generally, working with and through architects and others. It offers information and training on the inclusive design of the built environment for disabled people. It has a useful range of publications, including *Designing for Accessibility* published as a joint venture with RIBA Publishing (Royal Institute of British Architects) and the quarterly journal *Access by Design.*
Expert information can be provided on all technical and design issues relating to access provision.

DIAL (Disability Information and Advice Lines)

Scope, 6 Market Road, Holloway, N7 9PW
Tel: 020 7619-7100 (main switchboard) and 0130 231-0123 where Scope's Helpline team will be able to direct you to the support available in your local area.
website: www.scope.org.uk/dial *e-mail:* response@scope.org.uk
The DIAL network links local disability information and advice services run by and for disabled people and now comes under the Scope umbrella (see below).

DIAL coordinates local groups offering free advice and information on all aspects of disability. Each centre is run by a group of local people with direct experience. The groups operating in the more central parts of London are:

- **POhWER**, Loman Street, Southwark, SE1 0EH *Tel:* 0300 456-2370;
- **Lambeth**, 336 Brixton Road, Stockwell, SW9 7AA *Tel:* 020 7738-5656;
- **Choice in Hackney**, 50 Hoxton Street, N1 6LP *Tel:* 020 7613-3206;
- **Wandsworth**, 64 Altenburg Gardens, Battersea, SW11 1JL *Tel:* 020 7978-7306;
- **Hammersmith and Fulham**, Greswell Street, SW6 6PX *Tel:* 020 7471-8510;
- **REAL Tower Hamlets**, 40 Southern Grove, E3 4PX *Tel:* 020 8980-2200;
- **Greenwich**, Trafalgar Road, SE10 9EQ *Tel:* 020 8305-2221;
- **Lewisham**, 2 Catford Broadway, Catford, SE6 4SP *Tel:* 020 8314-1414.

There's an extended list on the Scope website.

Disability Rights UK

Ground Floor, CAN Mezzanine, 49-51 East Road, N1 6AH
Tel: 020 7250-8181
website: www.disabilityrightsuk.org *e-mail:* enquiries@disabilityrightsuk.org
Disability Rights UK was formed in 2012 by combining the Disability Alliance, RADAR and the National Centre for Independent Living. It strengthens the voice

of disabled people and is led by people with a wide range of impairments or health conditions.

It publishes the *Disability Rights Handbook*, and the *National Keyscheme guide* to toilets using the RADAR key.

It operates a number of helplines, and can advise on many aspects of independent living. It can provide advice about dealing with the change to Personal Independence Payments (PIPs) for people who need help taking part in everyday life. These replace disability living allowance for people between the ages of 16 and 64.

Disabled Living Foundation (DLF)

Ground Floor, Landmark House, Hammersmith Bridge Road, W6 9EJ
Tel: 020 7289-6111   *Helpline:* 0300 999-0004
website: www.dlf.org.uk   *e-mails:* info@dlf.org.uk   helpline@dlf.org.uk)
The DLF works to help disabled people in aspects of ordinary life which present difficulty. It has a comprehensive information service on specialised equipment of all kinds both for the general public and for healthcare professionals. Advice is given on visual impairment, incontinence, music, sport, clothing and skin care. A publications list is available on application.

Their equipment demonstration centre is completely accessible and has **a wheelchair toilet**. It includes an accessible kitchen and a bathing and toileting area.

An appointment is necessary as you usually get shown round by an expert.
Parking is possible if you book. The display includes a special kitchen for visually impaired people. Their website is useful, and they have an excellent list of factsheets, including one on *Wheelchair hire services in the London area.*

Disabled Motoring UK (DM UK)

National Headquarters, Ashwellthorpe, Norwich, NR16 1EX
Tel: 01508 489-449
website: www.disabledmotoring.org   *e-mail:* info@disabledmotoring.org
Disabled Motoring UK is a campaigning group for disabled drivers, passengers and Blue Badge holders. It is a membership organisation with a monthly magazine. It lobbies government & businesses to improve parking, refuelling and access provision for disabled people. It is not just an organisation for drivers.

It grew out of the DDA (Disabled Drivers Association) and the DDMC (Disabled Drivers Motor Club) who joined up in 2005 to form an organisation called Mobilise. This became DM UK in 2011 as it was felt that the name more accurately reflected the aims and objectives of the charity and removed confusion with others who had similar sounding names

Disabled Persons Transport Advisory Committee (DPTAC)
website: www.gov.uk/dptac
DPTAC was set up as an independent body to advise government on the transport
needs of disabled people throughout the UK. It has produced a wide range of
reports and advice, and consults extensively with the aim of advising government
about appropriate policies to meet people's needs. Because of its wide brief, it
can also be a useful source of information.
Established in 1985, the usefulness of DPTAC was subject to review in 2013 to
improve its effectiveness. New members are due to be added in 2014.

Focus on Disability
website: www.focusondisability.org.uk *e-mail:* via the website
An excellent source of practical information, with an extensive Directory of
Organisations and Charities for Disabled People, for Carers and for the Elderly.
It is a UK website for disabled people, with information including benefits,
welfare reform, health topics and mobility information, email advice, resources
directories and independent living products. It was established by David Cross in
1999, and has all the advantages and disadvantages of web based information.

Forrester (William), 1 Belvedere Close, Guildford, Surrey, GU2 9NP
Tel: 01483 575-401 *e-mail:* wforrester@hotmail.co.uk
William is a London Registered Guide, and a round-Britain tour escort. He is a
chair user himself, and has extensive experience of organising and leading trips
and visits, both for disabled individuals and groups.
He has an MA in History from Oxford, and an Art History diploma with
distinction. William became the first *Guide of the Year* sponsored by the British
Museum. He offers tailor made tours of London using accessible transport…
in effect, independence training combined with tourism ! During this time your
plans can be discussed to make best use of your time. Alternatively, he can plan
an itinerary for you in advance.

Inclusion London
336 Brixton Road, SW9 7AA *Tel:* 020 7237-3181
website: www.inclusionlondon.co.uk
Inclusion London promotes equality for London's deaf and disabled people.
Their work is rooted in the Social Model of disability and the Cultural Model of
deafness.
They provide policy, campaigning and capacity-building support for deaf and
disabled people's organisations (DDPOs) in London.
Their Directory has an impressive list of disabled people's organisations in and
around London.

Inclusive London

Direct Enquiries Ltd, Amber House, Market Street, Bracknell, Berks, RG12 1JB

Tel: 01344 360-101 *website:* www.inclusivelondon.com

e-mail: customerservices@directenquiries.com

The information on the Inclusive London website is based on that provided by Direct Enquiries, who call themselves The Nationwide Access Register.

Direct Enquiries were recently taken over by the The MitieGroup Compliance Services who describe themselves as follows "We are a strategic outsourcing and energy services company that delivers a range of integrated facilities, energy and property services to support the buildings ...."

They are a business, not a campaigning group, and have been contracted to do work by the Mayor's office, possibly via the London Development Agency, and by other people letting contracts.

Direct Enquiries say that the register was developed in partnership with RADAR and the Employers' Forum on Disability, to provide people with information about disabled access in buildings and premises. The register has expanded to include additional information for parents such as pushchair access - which is a good development. It holds information about a variety of facilities, including hotels, pubs and tube stations.

Direct Enquiries works with all the organisations registered, and these companies provide comprehensive information about their disabled access and facilities. In other words. the information is provided principally by the buildings or facilities owner or operator, and it is not clear how much is checked by visit - nor whether any is updated.

The Register does not put the buildings in context (in our view a major flaw), and the information is presented in the form of a tick box exercise, almost certainly carried out by able-bodied people (another major flaw). It usually includes only a very limited overall description, which is not related, for example, to how do you get there, nor, very often, how big it is. It also does not say when the information was compiled.

The method of compilation explains a considerable amount of anomalous information which is presented.

For example, there is a button for *Accessible toilets*, implying that the Register has a comprehensive list of such facilities.

If you press *Accessible toilets*, and type in Trafalgar Square (a very central tourist destination), then you get a list which includes five hotels which are within 500m of the Square.

What it does not tell you is that there are two accessible toilets (NKS) in the square itself, to the left of the café. There are more in the National Gallery on the north side of the Square, at the Getty entrance (level 0) and near the café. There's another one by the cloakroom on the same level.

There are two more accessible toilets by the Crypt Café under St-Martin-in-the-Fields church. There's a further accessible toilet (NKS) in Charing Cross station.

All of these are easier to get to and to use than those in the nearby hotels - and it's quite daunting to go into a hotel where you're not staying, just to use their toilet, especially into posh five star ones.

The Inclusive London list includes three theatres, where the accessible toilet is intended only for the use of people attending a performance.

It does include one in Waterstones Bookshop on the south side of the Square, but this is presented as number 18 on the list (a long way down) although only just across the road. In finding this one, we discovered that the Inclusive London listings do NOT go in a sequence depending on distance - which we would have thought would be logical.

For information about the underground stations the website has a useful alphabetical list of all the stations, with a reasonably clear description of the access barriers. It is not clear, however, how often it is updated.

Because of the way it is presented, we think that the *Inclusive London* information is sometimes misleading, as it appears to be more authoritative than it is. It is not researched (as our information is) by visit by disabled people, but includes only that provided by business organisations registered with Direct Enquiries.

Our advice therefore is to 'use with care'. You may find some of it helpful.

Mobility Superstore
Devonshire House, 582 Honeypot Lane, Stanmore, HA7 1JS
Tel: 0845 505-5111
website: www.themobilitysuperstore.co.uk
e-mail: info@themobilitysuperstore.co.uk
The Mobility Superstore has an interesting range of goods for sale, including numerous aids in the kitchen, talking watches and easy-to-use mobile phones.

United Kingdom Disabled People's Council (UKDPC)
27 Old Gloucester Street, WC1N 3AX
website: www.ukdpc.net *e-mail:* info@ukdpc.net
The UKDPC was first established in 1981 as the British Council of Disabled People, to be the umbrella body for disabled people's organisations across the United Kingdom. It believes in, and strives for, the full inclusion of disabled people in society and the workplace.

Visit Britain
Sanctuary Buildings, 20 Great Smith Street, Westminster SW1P 3BT
Tel: 020 7578-1000 (administrative offices) *website:* www.visitbritain.com
The old/ex-**British Tourist Authority (BTA)**
The website is more about the business of tourism rather than providing useful information to the visitor. There is very little information about accessibility, and limited practical advice about where to find it. There's a page on *Guide dogs and public disabled toilets*. The message about referring to these toilets in a more

positive way hasn't reached Visit Britain yet.

The Accommodation pages lead to Accessible accommodation which highlights the National Accessible Scheme (NAS) which is almost useless in terms of finding appropriate accommodation in London, see below under Visit England. Under Transport, there's a page on *Getting around Britain with access or disabled needs*. This leads to *www.disabledtraveladvice.co.uk* which comes up with gems like "Although it has a reputation as an expensive holiday destination, London actually has a lot of cheap hotels only slightly further out, so it's worth looking for one near an accessible underground station". This comment comes under *City Breaks in London for Disabled People*, a section that was clearly put there by an able-bodied person !

What it doesn't make clear is how to find an accessible station nor does it highlight (or even mention) the *Access in London* Accommodation chapter, and the importance of location for the disabled visitor, as well as price.

Visit England

website: www.visitengland.com

It covers, predictably, places, cities, and holiday destinations to visit in England, including London.

We tried to get some useful information about Accommodation assessed under the NAS, and after some wandering, were directed to the Open Britain site. This contained very little information about accessible accommodation in London, and only 8 places were listed. Of these, there was incorrect information about several, including the Thameside YH where the 6 fully accessible rooms weren't mentioned !

We have added the NAS London results to our *Methodology* page on the website as part of a comparative case study, comparing the contents of the *Open London* guide by Time Out with our Accommodation chapter, and the NAS list.

Visit London

London & Partners, 2 More London Riverside, SE1 2RR

website: www.visitlondon.com

London & Partners run *Visit London* to promote business in London, including tourism.

A quote from their website is "Think of us as an extension of your sales and marketing team, offering comprehensive marketing, publications, networking events, trade shows and much more." "VisitLondon.com is a comprehensive guide to everything that's happening in and around London. Search hotels, attractions, travel and events and plan your perfect trip."

We comment on some of the information provided for disabled visitors in the *Foreword*, entitled *It's a changed world*. The changes aren't all good, though of course, some are. Far too much decision making and information provision is carried out by (well meaning) able-bodied people.

Accessibility information is presented on the website thus:

Home → Traveller Information → Essential Information → Accessible London and there you will find Budget Hotels, Accessible Attractions, Accessible Tours, Useful Information.

The information about us is well hidden, and you'll get there if you follow Accessible London → Useful Information → Links and Resources

You hop very quickly and easily from Accessible information to that which includes no assessment of accessibility.

The *DisabledGo* information about sites, to which you are referred, isn't easy to use, and it is unrelated to the question of where to stay, and how to get around. In our view their published information is more of a grossly over-detailed access audit of individual buildings, rather than of an easy-to-use guide. We strongly disagree with the Visit London statement that "Its access guides answer the everyday questions of disabled people, their assistants, carers, family and friends." That assessment was almost certainly written by an able-bodied person.

In inner London there are *Tourist & Travel Information Centres* as follows:

- **City of London**, St. Paul's Churchyard, EC4M 8BX, *Tel:* 020 7332-1456, located across the road from the south side of the cathedral. It is referred to in the chapter on *Places of interest* under *Inner London - City area*;

- **at several railway stations** (which provide mainly travel information), including:
  - Euston, opposite platform 10, Euston Rail Station, NW1 2HS
  - Kings Cross St Pancras, Euston Road, N1 9AL (the centre is located through brick arches at the end of St Pancras station, leading to the Underground.). This one took us quite a while to locate !;
  - Liverpool Street (towards the Underground ticket office);
  - Victoria (opposite platform 8);

- **Piccadilly Circus underground station** which can only be accessed from ground level via about 30 steps as it is in the ticket hall;

- there is a kiosk outside **Holborn underground station** in Kingsway, WC2B 6AA on weekdays;

- there's also the useful **London Visitor Centre** run by the Original Bus Tour Co at 17 Cockspur Street, Trafalgar Square, SW1Y 5BL *Tel:* 020 8877-1722. It's on the south side of the Square. It's phone is at head office in Wandsworth.

Outer London there are *Tourist & Travel Information Centres* at:

- **Greenwich**, Pepys House, 2 Cutty Sark Gardens, Greenwich, SE10 9LW *Tel:* 0870 608-2000

- **Bexley**, Central Library, Townley Road, Bexleyheath, Kent, DA6 7HJ *Tel:* 020 8303-7777

- **Swanley**, Swanley Library, London Road, Swanley, Kent, BR8 7AE *Tel:* 01322 614-660

Royal National Institute of Blind People (RNIB)
105 Judd Street, WC1H 9NE   *Tel:* 0303 123-9999
website: www.rnib.org.uk *e-mail:* helpline@rnib.org.uk
The RNIB promotes facilities for the rehabilitation, training and employment of
blind people and provides a range of braille publications. It advises on a wide
range of problems and needs.

Scope
6 Market Road, Barnsbury, N7 9PW
Tel: 020 7619-7100 *Helpline:* 0808 800-3333
website: www.scope.org.uk *e-mail:* response@scope.org.uk
Scope exists to make this country a better place for disabled people and their
families. It runs a range of services, and raises awareness of the issues that
disabled people face. It changed its name from the National Spastics Society in
1994. and now provides support, advice and information for more than a quarter
of a million disabled people and their family members each year.
It has branches all over the country. The *Disability Now* magazine seems to have
metamorphosed into an independent website *www.disabilitynow.org.uk*. We have
already mentioned the merger with the DIAL helplines.

Shape
Deane House Studios, 27 Greenwood Place, Kentish Town, NW5 1LB
Tel: 020 7424-7330 *Textphone:* 020 7424-7368
website: www.shapearts.org.uk *e-mail:* info@shapearts.org.uk
Shape is a major provider for disabled people of training in the arts, and is an
enabler of access in the widest sense.
Shape develops opportunities for disabled artists; it trains cultural institutions
to be more open to disabled people. It runs a participatory arts and development
programme and a scheme to enable groups of disabled and elderly people to
enjoy a number of arts events.

Shopmobility
National Federation of Shopmobility UK (NFSUK)
163 West Street, Fareham, Hampshire, PO16 0EF   *Tel:* 0844 4141-850
website: www.shopmobilityuk.org *e-mail:* info@shopmobilityuk.org
Shopmobility provides invaluable services and resources in a number of outer
London shopping centres (and in many other parts of the country). It tries to
ensure that disabled people have equal opportunity of access to both shops and
services. Most commonly schemes are sited in the centre of shopping areas with
adjacent BB spaces. *Shopmobility* offers scooters and both manual and powered
chairs for use, and will have valuable local knowledge.
The NFSUK exists to support and promote its affiliated Schemes to existing and
potential customers, and encourage the development of new Schemes.

Not quite all Shopmobilities are members of the Federation, and we may have included some non-members
The website includes a wealth of information, including when the schemes are open, how many parking places there are, and what they offer in the way of help.

At the end of 2013, the London Shopmobility schemes are at:

> **Bexley Heath** *Tel:* 020 8301-5237;
> **Brent Cross** *Tel:* 020 8457-4070;
> **Bromley** *Tel:* 020 8313-9292 (option 4);
> **Camden** *Tel:* 020 7482-5503;
> **Croydon** *Tel:* 020 8688 7336
> **Edmonton** *Tel:* 020 8379-1193;
> **Enfield** *Tel:* 020 8379-1193;
> **Epsom & Ewell** *Tel:* 01372-727086;
> **Harrow** *Tel:* 020 8427-1200;
> **Hounslow** *Tel:* 020 8570-3343;
> **Ilford** *Tel:* 020 8478-6864;
> **Kingston** *Tel:* 020 8547-1255;
> **Lewisham** *Tel:* 020 8297-2735;
> **Romford** *Tel:* 01708 765764 (Liberty Centre) 01708 722570 (The Brewery Centre);
> **Sutton** *Tel:* 020 8770-0691;
> **Uxbridge** *Tel:* 01895-271510;
> **Walthamstow** *Tel:* 020 8520-3366;
> **Wandsworth** *Tel:* 020 8875-9585.

Wheelchair Travel,
1 Johnston Green, Guildford, Surrey, GU2 6XS
Tel: 01483-233640 or 01483 237668
website: www.wheelchair-travel.co.uk *e-mail:* trevor@wheelchair-travel.co.uk
One of the best sources of converted vehicles for hire. Trevor Pollitt who has built-up this service over a number of years is well known to us. Wheelchair Travel has a number of adapted minibuses with either tail lifts or ramped access available for hire with or without a driver. In addition they have adapted accessible cars for a chair user plus two other people.
Their depot is deep in the heart of the country, at:
Unit 44, Martlands Estate, Smartsheath Lane, Woking, GU22 0RQ.

Wheel Get You There (24-seven)
Tel: 020 8568-3366
website: www.wheelgetyouthere.co.uk
e-mail: bookings@wheelgetyouthere.co.uk

With over 20 years experience, 24-Seven provide a minicab service with wheelchair accessible cars and minibuses. They are located near the West Middlesex University Hospital in Isleworth, west London, not far from Heathrow airport.

William Forrester *see* **Forrester (William)**

Accommodation

Accommodation in London tends to be expensive, particularly in the centre. However, the provisions have become a great deal better for the disabled visitor wanting reasonably priced accommodation, with the arrival of hotels like Holiday Inn Express, Ibis, Premier Inns, Travelodge, and Jurys Inn. In addition there are the "few frills/no frills" chains.

We have a section at the end of the chapter on low cost accommodation, including hostels, Tune hotels, easyHotels and camp sites.

Choosing where you stay is likely to result from considering a combination of location, cost, bedroom/bathroom accessibility and general hotel facilities.

There is a 'trade-off' between spending more money in the centre of London, and maybe being able to walk or wheel to many of the places you want to visit, or staying further out and travelling in - by whatever means. You can choose somewhere near an accessible tube station, and/or with BB parking. **Whatever you decide, it will be a compromise**.

One new and complicating factor is that hotel prices can now vary substantially (like airline tickets), depending on the demand for accommodation on a particular night.

It might be worth considering using two or possibly even three different hotels during your stay, to make it easier, overall, to get around and visit the places you want to get to. It's a hassle moving, but it might enable you to walk/wheel around without having to use public transport or taxis very often.

We include hotels in various price ranges, as well as campsites, and youth hostels.

Some are near accessible parts of the rail/tube/DLR lines, and a few are very central. Our data was collected mainly during 2011. Our research will be ongoing, and new information will be put on our website under *Updated information*.

We have concentrated on lower cost accommodation although we have included several four and five star hotels in particularly good locations. Virtually all have step free access and accessible rooms. Some have parking for BB holders. Some are in very central locations while others are quite close to 'accessible' train/tube/DLR stations. We have included hotels in places in/near Beckton, Croydon, Earls Court, Greenwich, Hammersmith and Stratford because of their proximity to 'accessible' rail/tube transport links. Others again will be better suited to car users (and several of the hotels do have reservable BB spaces).

They are broadly classified as:

> **VC = very central**, with a range of major sights less than 1km away
>
> **NAT** = **near accessible transport**, within 600m of an 'accessible' station for rail or tube transport (including the DLR)
>
> **PFCU** = **primarily for car users**

A few of the places we include don't quite meet those specific criteria, but are of interest for a variety of reasons, such as their provisions for disabled guests and/or their location even if more than 600m from 'accessible' transport.

The mantra which comes from TfL is that "all the buses are now accessible" but as you will see from the chapter on *Getting around* that is a somewhat over-optimistic view (based on our experience). If you can use buses easily, then, of course, more possibilities are opened up.

There are an increasing number of hotels in London which provide disabled visitors with step free access to accessible rooms, and to the other main facilities.

For chair users there's another factor, and that is the possibility of mechanical breakdown just when you want to use a stairlift. One of the hotels we visited told us that their platform stairlift was/would be out of action for some weeks as the maintenance contractor was waiting for parts. It was an object lesson which confirmed the wisdom of NOT depending on platform lifts or platform stairlifts if there is an alternative available. Similarly, intercoms often don't work when you need them.

Our advice is to remember Murphy's Law ...... *"If it can go wrong, it will ..... and it will happen at the worst possible moment ...etc"*, and therefore, for preference, to choose accommodation which has flat or ramped access, not subject to mechanical failure en route. **Similarly it is preferable to choose a hotel that has two or three lifts rather than just one, OR choose somewhere with GFBs and step-free access.**

The impact of the internet

The arrival of the internet and of web based information and booking has been a very mixed blessing. It potentially offers lower prices, and a much wider choice than conventional methods used to. However, there is less assured information than you would have got when dealing with a knowledgeable travel agent, and it is now sometimes more difficult to contact a hotel directly. Hoteliers rely more on the internet, as it is cheaper for them, and they then employ less staff to answer questions. In contacting a hotel recently through its London phone number, we found that we were speaking to someone in Germany who had NO local knowledge.

Internet booking sites commonly do not allow you to identify precisely what you want/need, nor do they define what they are offering. This is particularly true (for example) if you want to book a room with a bathroom which has a walk-in/wheel-in shower. From the website choices offered, you can rarely specify a room with twin beds or with an interconnecting room.

One slightly perverse outcome, is that with the proliferation of sites where the accessible rooms are booked on-line, IF these slightly larger rooms came to be favoured by non-disabled visitors, they could become less available to genuinely disabled guests who need the particular provisions.

We were very pleased to see that Tune hotels address this issue clearly on their website, saying that "In order to book an accessible room, you must have a disability that precludes you from staying in another room type. If you book an accessible room and do not have such a disability, we reserve the right to charge you the difference at the prevailing rate or to refuse you at check-in." We hope that others will approach this issue in a similar way.

In doing our research, we encountered serious difficulties in contacting the various chains and finding someone we could actually speak to ! *In most cases it took months, and considerable persistence on our part.* When we eventually had meetings with a chain representative they were most helpful, but the process of trying to establish contact by e-mail and then phone was ridiculously difficult. Individual customers may encounter parallel difficulties in that it can be difficult to be able to speak to a **person** who is on-site AND who knows what they are talking about ! The information given from call centres is simply based on what they can read on the screen.

It has certainly become much easier to find and book the cheapest available rooms on-line. However, when using these websites (like lastminute.com), clear and accurate information about access and about accommodation for people who have particular physical requirements is very poorly defined. There is too much reliance on the minimal (and sometimes misleading) information available on other websites.

In our view, each hotel should include a description of the facilities at the hotel much like that included here, giving real and precise information.
We include some of the experiences we had in looking at booking bargain/low-cost rooms in London on our website *www.accessinlondon.org.*

Note that most of the information on hotel/hostel websites is put in place by able-bodied people. Sometimes they don't even live in the UK and therefore have no local knowledge. It has to fit into the limited framework of the particular website (again designed by able-bodied people). The contact details usually are correct. However, what we have found is that some of the information (for example about the provisions made in 'accessible' rooms, and even about transport links) is inadequate, while some of it is downright inaccurate and/or misleading. It is almost certainly inserted from secondary sources by someone who has never come anywhere near the place, and the hotel management have not corrected it.

Other information sources

The directory of quite well researched information collected by Direct Enquiries and available at *www.inclusivelondon.com* is useful, but is undated (which is a serious omission). They have not asked the same questions that we have about the provision of wet rooms and of double vs twin beds. They have prioritised the information in a different way and the biggest drawback is that unless you already know the city well, it's not easy to coordinate the information about accommodation with distances from the major sights, and with the transport facilities.

The new *Open London* guide, written under the *Time Out* banner is very well presented, with some excellent pictures. It is a joint project between RADAR and *Tourism for All*, and has used some access audit information provided by DisabledGo. In addition there is information from the *Time Out* database. It unfortunately was not researched consistently 'by visit', and relies on presenting much of the access information in a series of symbols which are in many cases a gross oversimplification. The accommodation section has descriptions of just over twenty 4 and 5 star hotels where the room rates are commonly from £200/night upwards while listing very briefly five cheaper chain hotels. *Open London* omits to mention the Thameside youth hostel which has some of London's best facilities. It also refers to the Copthorne Tara as being 'well located' which from an access point of view it is not, while not describing the excellent provisions in its ten accessible rooms.

We suspect that the *Open London* accommodation chapter was put together by an able-bodied author who has never had to book accommodation for small groups of disabled people, or even for individuals ! It is certainly of limited help to those travelling on a tight budget.

The Access Project (PHSP) information

We collected most of the information presented here by visit. In a few instances our visit was for the previous guide edition and we updated the data by ringing up and confirming various details. Our questions are based on our experiences of travelling widely with and amongst small groups of disabled people. A few of the entries are based on information supplied by the chain representatives, based on our briefing about what we were looking for and we are most grateful to those who helped us in this way. We sent off a copy of our write-ups to everyone who is listed, so that they could confirm/correct our information.

We hope that the presentation of properly integrated information here is helpful.
It is best, if possible, to coordinate bookings and arrangements yourself using a good map, and if you can, by speaking (and/or e-mailing) directly to the hotel staff about the details which are important to you. Note the paragraph about using

Google Maps in the *Introduction* as with judicious use looking at where you're going to stay from the air, and using street view as well, can be really helpful.

In terms of the facilities for disabled guests and the choices offered at a particular hotel/hostel, much depends on when it was built and what were the prevailing 'standards' applied at that time. Until quite recently, the standard provision for an 'accessible' room was to have wider doors, a low level bath in the bathroom with grab rails, to provide space alongside the toilet for sideways transfer, and to provide a double bed. The fact that many disabled visitors would much prefer to have a wheel-in shower facility and to have the choice of double or twin beds has taken a long time to be accepted.

A number of hotels can provide a fold-up bed (which we have referred to as a z-bed) to put in the room, but there isn't always enough space to do this.

If you have particular requirements, for example about the height of the bed (for easier transfer) then it is best to negotiate directly with the hotel. Many will have small blocks to put under the bed to raise its height by several centimetres.

In describing the bedrooms we have usually quoted the width of the bedroom door first (eg D75), then the bathroom door width, and then the side transfer space alongside the toilet. We highlight whether or not the bathroom has a wheel-in shower, and whether there is a choice between a double bed and 'twins'.

Most hotel lifts can accommodate a conventional wheelchair, though if yours is particularly big/heavy then it might be worth checking with the hotel. Note that platform stairlifts frequently have a SWL (safe working load) limit which would probably preclude their use by electric chair users.

The buildings used by ALL the chains are highly variable, as they might be:
- modified office or even residential buildings;
- old/older hotels purchased from another group; or,
- 'new build', but constructed at different times, during which the standards applied have changed.

Some even have steps at the front, although we have not included any of these unless a step-free alternative has been provided. The best facilities for access are likely to be found in hotels built very recently, and/or where major refurbishment has been undertaken, but this information is unlikely to be revealed in the various website write-ups which you may look at.

The layout in the accessible rooms may depend on when the hotel was built or renovated, as the standards are continually changing. People have only recently realised that the provision of a wet room with a wheel-in/walk-in shower is appreciated by many, and that the choice between a double or of twin beds is also needed. The increasing use of zip and link beds which can make either a double bed or twins, is to be encouraged, provided that there's a thick mattress covering to go over the join.

One practical suggestion from one of our researchers for those with lack of sensation, is that:

- there is commonly a ridge down the middle of two linked mattresses, and there may be mattress buttons;
- if there isn't an adequate underblanket, it may be possible to request an additional single duvet from reception (to sleep on) thus reducing the risk of triggering a pressure sore.

Hotel design, and that of the accessible rooms

Designing for accessibility published by the CAE has many useful guidelines, but it doesn't go into detail over hotel design.

For a good overall approach, we would commend the policy outlined on the Premier Inn website *www.premierinn.com* under Disabled access. It is in the listing at the bottom of every page after Contact us; FAQs and Sitemap and is well worth reading.

From where we sit, it seems to have taken 20 or 30 years of elbow joggling and pressure from a wide range of travellers to arrive at such a statement, but the outcome is very positive. As new hotels are built and older ones renovated, the number of places providing good accessible accommodation will grow.

We have found that the requirement for accessible family rooms is not, generally, provided for particularly well in hotels. These would enable disabled parents to come with their children, and for families with one or more disabled children to get around more easily. At the moment, probably the best places to stay would be the Thameside YH or the one in the Lee Valley at Cheshunt.

There are some hotels with interconnecting rooms, though some of these only have double beds, and in our view the provision of accessible family rooms requires a little more thought and attention.

We are including two diagrams which we put together for our 2003 edition to illustrate various desirable design points. The first is a potential room layout, where the bathroom provided offers the choice between using a wheel-in shower or of using the bath (which is ideal). It highlights (by implication) the need to provide some accessible rooms with twin beds. It also highlights the need for (possibly a very small number) of rooms to have facilities for a hoist. This provision is not yet widespread, and its absence discourages and prevents some people from travelling. Note that the hoist shown in the diagram does not illustrate the possible need for help with transfer to the bath or toilet.

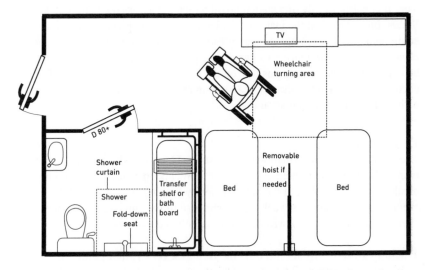

The second diagram is the plan of an accessible bathroom with a wheel-in shower, where there is plenty of room, a fold-down shower seat, and the shower area is surrounded by a flexible curtain. This is NOT a design specification, but is intended to illustrate some of the ideas and principles involved.

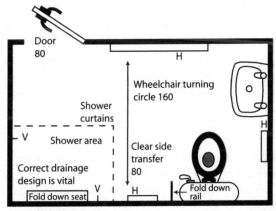

Overall dimensions 250 x 180 (150 cm min) (not drawn to scale)
H = horizontal grab bar
V = vertical grab bar
Dimensions in cm

In addition, in the many hotels not listed here with baths in their bathrooms, a provision which would be of enormous help to some is the provision of a 'bathboard'. This is a simple and inexpensive way of enabling many less able people to use a movable shower head, without having to get properly 'into' the bath. It consists simply of a slatted board which fits across the bath with two 'fixers' braced against the inside of the bath to hold it in place. It is a piece of equipment which is readily available from most of the companies listed under *Equipment repair and hire*. Alongside this provision, the shower controls must be reachable from a sitting position on the board, and room service staff must be encouraged to leave the shower head within reach. We show a bathboard on the bath in the room design diagram.

Price indicators

The indicated price information in our listing is based on the cost of a double/ twin bedded room and includes the cost of TWO people staying, including breakfast and VAT. We put the list together by looking at a booking for a Wednesday night about a week ahead, and also three months and six months ahead. A fixed datum line was needed to establish the comparisons.

The indicators below should only be used as a very rough guide for comparison purposes. They are NOT absolute prices, and when demand is low you can find bargains (ie low cost rooms) and conversely, prices can easily double or even treble, when demand is high.

£	£0-£80
££	£80-£150
£££	£150-£250
££££	£250+

The whole question of pricing has become MUCH more difficult because of the variations which depend on the demand for accommodation on a particular night, and/or on how far in advance you have booked. Variations in cost of accommodation are like those for most airline and train tickets, so that it is much more difficult to plan a visit, and to keep within a sensible budget.

We looked at room prices for all the accommodation listed in the guide, on a Wednesday, one week, and three months and six months in advance. This was to provide us with a consistent basis for making our price/cost indicators. One thing that we found was that Travelodge hotels, which can only be booked on-line, offered significantly lower prices for bookings 3-6 months in advance. As mentioned elsewhere the disabled visitors choice of room facilities is not always clear when booking on-line, but this can usually be put right by making direct contact with the hotel. Also, quoting the Travelodge example, on a heavily booked night, on that night, or just one day in advance, the room price could be as much as twice or three times that indicated here. We looked at Travelodge rooms in the ££££ bracket (on a particularly high cost night). Equally, if you can book well in advance, many of the Travelodge rooms can be booked for a price in the £ bracket.

To illustrate the variations we include a table which was on the Premier Inn website in October 2011.

Room costs at Premier Inns on different days

	Thur	Fri	Sat	Sun	Mon	Tue	Wed
London City Tower Hill	£179	£179	£179	£59	£89	£169	£159
London Tower Bridge	£159	£159	£149	£59	£128	£135	£135
London Southwark	£148	£169	£169	£69	£139	£159	£159
London City Old Street	£79	£84	£89	£59	£79	£99	£99

You may get particularly good deals at the hotels near the Excel centre when there is no major exhibition on there, or at City or Docklands hotels when business is quiet. There are also particularly good accessible rooms in the (no frills) Tune hotels, and the Liverpool Street one has thirteen of them on the GF.

We have taken the view that if you can afford to stay in the more expensive hotels, you will probably need less help and advice from us !

Contacting the hotel

If you have internet access, then the cheapest way of making contact and of asking questions is to e-mail the hotel, though if you don't get a reply, use the phone.

For people looking to telephone to make reservations and arrangements, and to check on the detailed provisions at a hotel prior to a visit, long distance call charges can get quite expensive. There are, however, an increasing number of ways to make cheap calls, but these differ in different countries. This is discussed in the chapter on *General information* under Telephones. Also, try the question on Google, and if you have friends who regularly make international calls, ask them as well.

Hotels with a hoist in the bedroom

If you need the facility of a hoist in your bedroom then three options described in more detail in the text are: the Holiday Inn Bloomsbury, the Premier Inn Stratford and the Copthorne Tara in Kensington. In addition there are:

- **The Langham London*****, 1c Portland Place, Regent Street, W1B 1JA *Tel:* 020 7636-1000, *e-mail:* lon.info@langhamhotels.com. A leading luxury hotel which has recently been refurbished and with a platform lift to bypass the steps at the entrance. There are **four accessible rooms**, each having both a wheel-in shower and a bath with rails. All are said to have a hoist. There are two Classic rooms, one Grand Executive and one Grand Junior Suite;
- **Crowne Plaza*****, Stockley Road (near Heathrow Airport), UB7 9NA. Tel: 0871 942-9140. There are **six accessible rooms**, four of which have a wheel-in shower and two a bath with grab rails. One room has a hoist to facilitate transfers.

Amongst the best facilities for value and low cost from an access viewpoint are:
- the Thameside Youth Hostel;
- for value and location, there are the Premier Inns at County Hall; Tower Bridge; by the *Anchor* pub; at Stratford; Leicester Square; Waterloo and Southwark. There's the Travelodge Covent Garden, and Holiday Inn Express at Southwark, and the Ibis at Earls Court, Euston and Stratford. In addition there are the new Tune hotels at Liverpool Street and Kings Cross; finally, for four-star ambience and exceptionally good accessible rooms there's the Copthorne Tara in Kensington, bookable at a discount through *Tourism for All.*

It is still not always easy to identify a room with the facilities you require, in a location which is convenient and at a price which you can afford, when you want to come!

Hotels

Hotels are listed by postal area, with the most central areas first ie: W1, WC1, WC2, SW1, N1, NW1, EC1, EC4 and E1, which are all north of the river, and then SE1 which is on the south bank. **Those with a number are shown on one of the hotel maps.** Others are located outside the areas covered by the maps. Since the outer postal areas do not form a consistent geographical pattern (they are organised alphabetically) our arrangement here may seem slightly illogical. The listing after SE1 is as follows: E14, E16 and E6 (all in Docklands); E15 (Stratford); SW5 (Earls Court); SW8 (Vauxhall); W8 (Kensington); SE10 (Greenwich); SW6 (Fulham); W6 (Hammersmith); Wembley; Croydon;

Heathrow; Gatwick and ending with *Low-cost accommodation*.

We have then listed the information within the various sections by price so that the cheapest places appear first, and the most expensive ones last.

The websites for the main chain hotels listed here are:

Double Tree by Hilton	*www.doubletree.hilton.com*
Fullers	*www.fullershotels.com*
Guoman	*www.guoman.com*
Holiday Inn	*www.holidayinn.com*
Holiday Inn Express	*www.hiexpress.com*
Ibis	*www.ibishotel.com*
Jurys Inn	*www.jurysinns.com*
Novotel	*www.novotel.com*
Premier Inn	*www.premierinn.com*
Sofitel	*www.sofitel.com*
Thistle	*www.thistle.com*
Travelodge	*www.travelodge.co.uk*
Tune	*www.tunehotels.com*

W1 (around Oxford Street)

1. Thistle Inn Marble Arch £££ (VC)

Bryanston Street, W1H 7EH *Tel*: 0871 376-9027
e-mail: marblearch@guomanco.uk
Located on the corner with Portman Street, and about 300m from Marble Arch.
The hotel has a clear, dated, *Access Statement* on its website.
There is a CP with 3 BB spaces in an adjacent building in Bryanston Street where a 25% discount is given to guests, but the route out involves going down quite a steep ramp (25m long and 1:6), or via ±1 steps and a very small lift. Height restriction 1.98m.
The main hotel entrance is via +4 steps and an escalator. There is a step-free route using a side entrance to the right of the main doors, where a lift (D110 W120 L175) will take you up to the 1st floor reception. The bar, restaurant and lounge are all on this level and are step-free.
The hotel has nearly 700 bedrooms. Four lifts connect the 1st floor to the bedrooms. There are **ten accessible rooms**, all with wheel-in showers. Five have twin beds and five have a double. All have an interconnecting room for use by other group or family members if required.
Wheelchair toilet (D80 ST80) on the 1st floor.

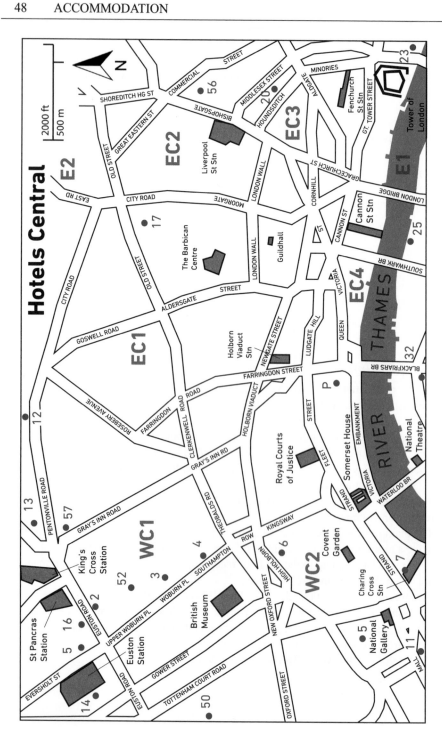

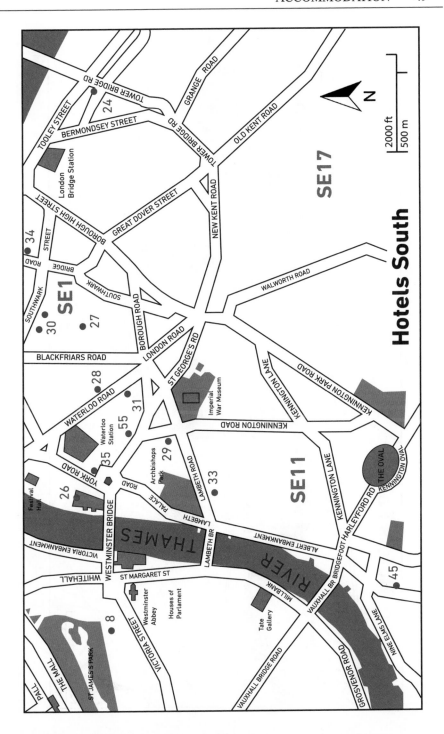

Hotels South

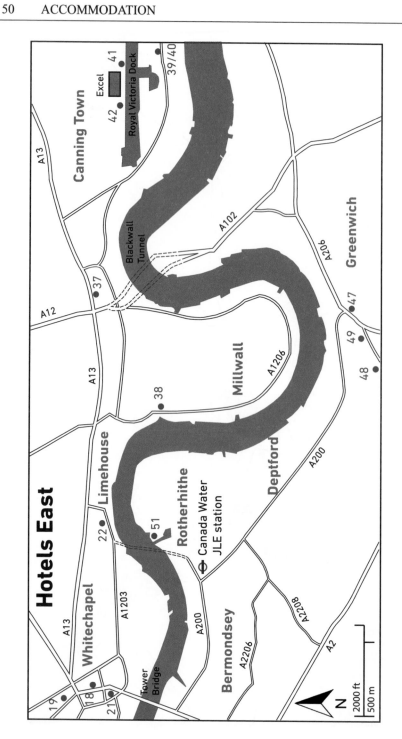

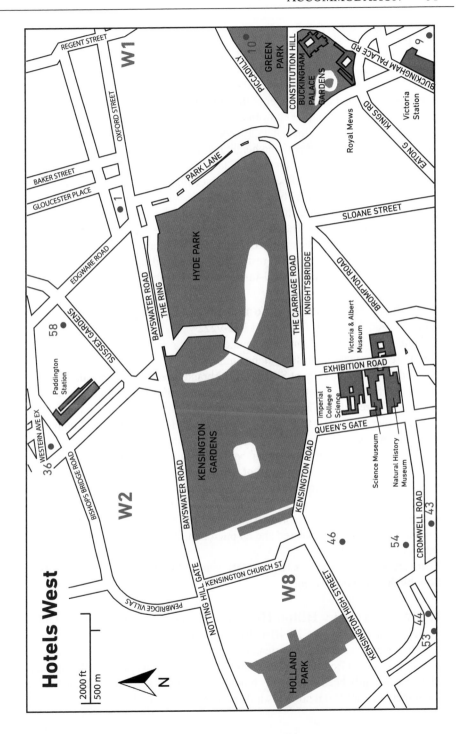

WC1 (around Bloomsbury)

2. Premier Inn London Euston ££/£££ (NAT)

1 Duke's Road, WC1H 9PJ *Tel*: 0871 527-8656

e-mail: london.euston.mti@whitbread.com

The hotel is situated on the corner with the Euston Road (south side), and near Euston station. It is about 400m from the 'accessible' St Pancras tube station. There are 4 BB spaces in the hotel CP, accessed off Duke's Road and down a slope to the LGF level. There is no height restriction for these spaces, and from them you enter the back way on the LGF taking a lift to the GF reception. We were told that parking was allocated on a 'first come' basis, which makes them of less potential value. You may be able to negotiate ! There is a step-free entrance from Duke's Road, to reception, bar and restaurant. Three lifts go to all floors. The **eleven accessible rooms** are located on floors 1-5, with one on the GF. Ten have lowered baths with grab rails and double beds. A z-bed can be provided which will restrict the space available. **The room on the GF has a bathroom with a wheel-in-shower and drop down shower seat**.

3. Holiday Inn London Bloomsbury £££ (VC)

Coram Street, WC1N 1HT *Tel*: 0871 942-9222

website: www.hilondonbloomsburyhotel.co.uk

e-mail: reservations-bloomsbury@ihg.com

Located between Marchmont Street and Herbrand Street, and alongside the Brunswick Shopping Centre. Two BB spaces are available in front of the hotel which can be reserved. There's an UGCP, managed separately, at Russell Court, 60 Coram Street, WC1H 0LP Tel: 0870 606-7050. Height restriction 2.06m and it's only open on weekdays.

Step-free from the street to reception, bar and restaurant. Three lifts go to all floors. **Eight accessible rooms**, two of which have a hoist to facilitate transfers from wheelchair to the bed, and into the bathroom. All six rooms have double beds, and low level baths with grab rails in the bathroom. Z-beds are available, and the hotel also has a portable hoist. Holiday Inn policy is that if a disabled person is travelling with a carer, and an interconnecting room is available, no extra charge is made.

There are **wheelchair toilets (D80 ST90)** with BCFs, on the GF, and on the 1st floor by the conference areas.

4. Double Tree by Hilton Hotel London - West End ££££ (VC)

92 Southampton Row, WC1B 4BH *Tel:* 020 7242-2828

e-mail: concierge@dtlondonwestend.com

Located in the old Bonnington Hotel this seven floor hotel opposite Bloomsbury Place has recently been extensively renovated. There is an UGCP run by NCP at the Imperial Hotel 100m north towards Russell Square Gardens.

Step-free entrance slightly sloped where the revolving door can be bypassed on either side. There are three lifts, two (D65 W100 L90) to the left of the reception desk, and the other, slightly bigger (D70 W80 L140) just in front of reception. As well as a bar and lounge on the GF. The restaurant is on the LGF (with +3 steps to an upper/split level) from the larger lift which will take you to a ramped alternate entrance. **Three accessible rooms** 046, 113, 118 (all seen) with the first on the GF and two on the 1st floor. All these rooms are within 50m of reception via a lift, have a toilet with ST80+ and a wheel-in shower. Room 046 has a double bed but two separate toilets while the other two rooms have twin beds. Movable ramps are available for the split level to various meeting rooms, bypassing +3. **Wheelchair toilets (D85 ST85)** on the LGF outside the lift and on the GF, while BCF are down the corridor to the right of reception en route to room 046.

Note that the lift IS quite small, and it is in some ways regrettable that during the refurbishment the number of accessible rooms was reduced from 18 to 3, although provision was made for wet rooms in the new facilities.

WC2 (around Leicester Square, and Covent Garden)

5. Premier Inn London Leicester Square (VC)
Queen's House, 1 Leicester Place, WC2H 7BP *Tel:* 0871 527-9334
e-mail: Londonleicestersquare.pi@premierinn.com
This centrally located hotel is scheduled to open in 2012.
It will have a ramp on the GF leading to two lifts. There will be step-free access to reception, and the bar/restaurant. There will be **five accessible rooms**, of which two will have a wheel-in shower. All the accessible rooms will have zip and link beds.
There will be an **accessible toilet** in the public areas. We may include a fuller description on our website under Updated information, after making a visit.
It will have step-free access to the main hotel facilities and will follow Premier Inn policy which is to include a number of **accessible rooms**. At least half of them will have a wet room with a wheel-in shower. All should have zip and link beds which can easily be separated.

6. Travelodge Covent Garden £/£££ (VC)
10 Drury Lane, WC2B 5RE *Tel:* 0871 984-6245
e-mail: londoncoventgdn.mgr@travelodge.co.uk
The hotel with more than 600 beds is (unusually) located in two separate buildings. One is on the corner of Drury Lane and Shorts Gardens, while the other is on High Holborn about 100m away. You need to go to the end of Drury Lane and then cross the road.
Each building has a reception desk, and you need to establish before coming which building you are booked into.
In terms of booking an accessible room, they have a button for saying 'please

include disabled rooms in this search', but it's not always entirely clear what you are going to get ! You therefore need to e-mail or phone the hotel to tie up the necessary details, possibly after checking the rates on-line. They normally allocate rooms as people arrive in the afternoon on a 'first come' basis, so if you need an accessible room in a particular building, you need to make this absolutely clear when you book. If you have booked an accessible room, they all have a wheel-in shower.

The Drury Lane building has more extensive facilities. The GF is elevated and approached up a longish ramp bypassing +15 steps. In addition there are split levels in the restaurant area, with a platform stairlift to bypass the steps. In the High Holborn building the bar, breakfast room and café are all together on the GF. All are step-free without the use of stairlifts, but the provisions are more limited than those in the other building, and as you will see below all the rooms there have a double bed.

There are potentially 4 BB parking spaces under the Drury Lane building, if reserved in advance. These are approached from High Holborn (which is one way, going westwards) and entered where the hotel building backs on to High Holborn (opposite the other site). The entry is marked Deliveries. There's a gate and an intercom.

In the Drury Lane building there are four lifts (D80 W160 L110), leading to **twenty-four accessible rooms**, of which 22 are twins and 2 have a double bed. All have a wet room with a wheel-in shower. Room 452 seen. The bathroom design is generally excellent, and similar to our recommended pattern (see Foreword text) with a curtain around the shower and ST >100.

In the High Holborn building there are two lifts (D80 W140 L120), leading to **eight accessible rooms**, all doubles, and all with a wet room and wheel-in shower. Room 775 seen.

There's the Holborn MSCP (run by NCP) less than 50m away, but this is probably not needed if you park under the Drury Lane building.

7. Charing Cross Hotel (a Guoman hotel) ££££ (VC)
Strand, WC2N 5HX *Tel:* 0871 376-9012
e-mail: reception.charingcross@guoman.co.uk
Built as part of Charing Cross station, it is a luxury Victorian style railway hotel which has recently been refurbished. It is located very close to Trafalgar Square. There's a comprehensive Access Statement on the website.

There is one BB space by the entrance for short term parking, and two longer term spaces may be booked in advance. There are unavoidable cobbles outside the entrance, then a large automatic sliding door. The GF has the reception and a small public bar (D82) with 1cm lip, as well as two lifts (D85 W125 L160) to all floors. The restaurant and lounge bar are on the 1st floor, to right and left of lifts respectively and are both step-free. **Two accessible rooms** (one seen), both with D85, a double bed and an interconnecting room. Bathroom D85, ST100 and a wheel-in shower. Chair users may have a problem getting to the washbasin, as there is no recess/space underneath it.

Wheelchair toilet (D85 ST110) with BCF, to left from the lounge bar on the 1st floor.

SW1 (around Victoria and Pall Mall)

8. Sanctuary House Hotel £££ (VC)

33 Tothill Street, SW1H 9LA *Tel:* 020 7799 4044

e-mail: sanctuaryhouse@fullers.co.uk

Located at the junction with Dean Farrer Street alongside the pub. About 300m from Parliament Square. Step-free to the lift (D80 W95 L130) which goes to reception on the 1st floor. All catering facilities are in the attached pub. With GF **adapted toilet (D80 ST60)** by the lift. **Two accessible bedrooms** (D85) (both seen) on the top floor, with bathroom D80 and baths and support rails. One room has a double bed and sofa bed, and the other has two single beds with more space in the bathroom. No parking on site.

9. Premier Inn London Victoria ££/£££

82-83 Eccleston Square, off 55 Gillingham Street, SW1V 1PS

Tel: 0871 527-8680 *e-mail:* londonvictoria.pi@premierinn.com

Near the junction with Belgrave Road and some 500-600m from either Victoria Station or the Coach Station. No parking facilities.

Entrance +10 steps, bypassed by a platform stairlift, to reach reception. There is an intercom at/by the bottom of the steps so that a chair user can alert reception that they want to use the platform stairlift. Two lifts go to all the floors. The restaurant is in the basement/LGF.

Five accessible rooms on the G and 1st floors. All have a double bed, and wet rooms with a wheel-in shower. A z-bed or sofa bed can be added in the room if required, but this will reduce the space available.

10. The Cavendish Hotel ££££ (VC)

81 Jermyn Street, St James's, SW1Y 6JF *Tel:* 020 7930-2111

website: www.thecavendish-london.co.uk

e-mail: info@thecavendishlondon.com

On the corner with Duke Street, the hotel has more than 200 rooms. There is valet service parking.

Step-free from the Duke Street entrance to reception. A portable ramp that can be used to access the lounge on the GF, while the bar and restaurant on the first floor are both step-free. Three lifts (D80) go to all floors. There are **three accessible rooms** (317 seen) with D80 and beds that can be split on request. Each room has a wheel-in shower with moveable seat and an adjoining room.

11. Sofitel London St James ££££ (VC)

6 Waterloo Place, SW1Y 4AN *Tel:* 020 7747-2200
e-mail: H3144@sofitel.com
On the corner with Pall Mall, and close to Trafalgar Square. No parking facility.
There is step-free access at the main entrance to reception, to the lounge/bar/
restaurant and to the lifts. **Ten accessible rooms** including some with a wheel-in
shower and some with a bath to which a bath board can be fitted.
GF accessible toilet.

N1 (around Islington)

Premier Inn London Angel Islington ££/£££

18-26 Parkfield Street, Islington, N1 0PS *Tel:* 0871 527-8558
e-mail: londonislingtongreen.pi@whitbread.com
Located opposite the junction with Bromfield Street and close to two shopping
malls between Upper Street and Liverpool Road. No parking.
Platform lift bypasses −3 steps inside the entrance. Then step-free to reception,
restaurant and lounge, and to the two lifts (D90 W130 L140).
Five accessible rooms, three with wheel-in shower and two with lowered bath
and grab rails. All have zip and link beds which can be separated. Room 201
seen, D80 ST100.
Wheelchair toilet (D80 ST80) on the GF.

12. Jurys Inn Islington ££/£££

60 Pentonville Road, N1 9LA *Tel:* 020 7282-5500
e-mail: jurysinnislington@jurysinns.com
Located about 400m north of Sadlers Wells theatre on the inner ring road, and
some 1km from the 'accessible' tube station at Kings Cross. Two BB spaces can
be reserved.
Step-free access to reception, and the bar/restaurant. **Eleven accessible rooms**,
one of which has a wheel-in shower. Two rooms have twin beds, nine have only
a double. Five have interconnecting doors to twin bedded rooms.

13. Premier Inn London King's Cross/St Pancras ££/£££ (NAT)

26-30 York Way, N1 9AA *Tel:* 0871 527-8672
e-mail: londonkingscross.pi@premierinn.com
York Way runs alongside Kings Cross station, and the hotel is very near the
junction with Caledonia Street, by The Waiting Room restaurant. No parking
facilities.
Step-free access to reception, bar and restaurant. The three lifts go to all floors.
Fourteen accessible rooms located on floors 1 - 4. These all have lowered baths
with grab rails, and double beds. A z-bed can be added in the room if required,
but this will reduce the space available.

NW1 (around Camden and Regent's Park)

14. Ibis Euston ££/£££

3 Cardington Street, NW1 2LW *Tel:* 020 7388-7777
e-mail: H0921@accor-hotels.com
Right by Euston Station, on the corner of Drummond Street and Melton Street.
The nearest accessible tube station is Kings Cross, nearly 800m away. Four BB
spaces on ground level in the staff CP can be made available on request. UCGP
attached. Flat main entrance. Step-free to reception, bar and restaurant. Two lifts
(D100 W140 L140).
Eight accessible rooms. Rooms 135 & 235 seen: D75cm, bathroom D74cm,
ST100. All have a low level bath with grab rails. They have four rooms with twin
beds, and four with a double. Some have a connecting room.
GF **accessible toilet** with a sliding door which was about to be refurbished.

15. Travelodge London Euston £/££

1-11 Grafton Place, NW1 1DJ *Tel:* 0871 984-6332
e-mail: euston@travelodge.co.uk
Located about 200m from Euston station, and just off the south end of Eversholt
Street. The nearest accessible tube station is Kings Cross, some 500m away.
There is no on-site parking.
Step-free entrance to reception, the bar and restaurant, and to the lifts.
There are **eight accessible rooms**, all with a wheel-in shower. Six have double
beds, and two have twin beds.

16. Novotel London St Pancras £££ (NAT)

100-110 Euston Road, NW1 2AJ *Tel:* 020 7666-9000
e-mail: H5309@accor.com
On the corner of Ossulston Street and right by the British Library. About 250m
from the 'accessible' tube station at St Pancras. Three BB spaces by drop off
point.
Platform lift (D80 L120) to bypass +6 steps at the entrance. Step-free to
reception, bar and restaurant and to the three lifts (D90 W140 L130). The lounge
is on a lower mezzanine level accessed from a platform lift (D80 L120).
Thirteen accessible rooms eleven of which have both a wheel-in shower and
a bath and two have just a bath. Three of the rooms have twin beds while the
remainder are doubles. Room seen D85 ST100. A hoist could be hired if needed.

EC1 (around Farringdon and Finsbury)

17. Travelodge London City Road £/££

7-12 City Road, EC1Y 1AE *Tel:* 0871 984-6333
e-mail: londoncityroad.mgr@travelodge.co.uk
Located halfway between Epworth Street and Worship Street, and just over 1km

north of parts of the City. No parking, but there is a nearby NCP (max height 1.9m) costing currently around £36/day.

The hotel is in an old building, but the entrance, and access to reception, the bar and restaurant, and to the lifts is step-free.

There are **twenty accessible rooms**, all of which have a wheel-in shower. They all have a double bed, but in some there is a separate sofa-bed, and in some the bed can be separated and made into twins.

EC4 (in the City)

P (planned) Premier Inn London Blackfriars (VC)
1-2 Dorset Rise, EC4Y 8EN *Tel:* 0871 527 9362

This centrally located hotel is scheduled to open in 2012.

It will have step-free access from the east side (Bridewell Place entrance). It will be step-free to the three lifts, and to the accessible bedrooms.

Premier Inn policy is to include a number of **accessible rooms**. At least half of them should have a wet room with a wheel-in shower. All should have zip and link beds which can easily be separated.

We will include a fuller description on our website under *Updated information*, when we have visited.

E1 (from Tower Bridge to Mile End)

18. Premier Inn London Tower Hill ££/£££ (VC)
22-24 Prescot Street, E1 8BB *Tel:* 0871 527-8646
e-mail: londoncitytowerhill.pi@premierinn.com

Located some 350m from Tower Gateway DLR station and with the Tower and Tower Bridge less than 1km away. Although there is no hotel CP, there's one BB space by a back entrance, if reserved in advance.

Step-free entrance leading to reception and the coffee lounge. There are three lifts which go to all floors. The restaurant is on the LGF.

There are **nine accessible rooms**, one on the GF and two on each of the upper floors (1-4).

Four of the bathrooms have lowered baths with grab rails and zip and link beds which can be split into two singles. The other five rooms have a double bed and a sofa bed, together with a wet room with a wheel-in-shower.

19. Ibis London City ££
5 Commercial Street, E1 6BF *Tel:* 020 7422-8400
e-mail: H5011@accor.com

Located some 200m from Aldgate East tube station (which is not accessible) in the middle of London's East End. Ideal for a visit to Petticoat Lane on a Sunday. Nearly 800m from Tower Gateway DLR station. Two designated BB spaces at the back.

There is a step-free access at the main entrance to reception, to the lounge/bar/ restaurant and the lifts to the bedrooms. **Nineteen accessible rooms** with twin beds which can be joined if requested. All the rooms have a wheel-in shower. Accessible toilet on the GF.

20. Travelodge London Liverpool Street £/££

1 Harrow Place, E1 7DB *Tel:* 0871 984-6190
e-mail: londonliverplst@travelodge.co.uk
Located about 400m from Liverpool Street station and a little over 1km north of major sights like the Tower of London and St Paul's Cathedral. This is a new build hotel, and there is step-free access to reception, the bar and restaurant, and to the lifts.
There are **eight accessible rooms** all with a double bed, and a low level bath with grab rails.

21. Travelodge London Tower Bridge £/££ (VC)

Lloyds Court, 1 Goodmans Yard, E1 8AT *Tel:* 0871 984-6388
e-mail: londontowerbrdge.mgr@travelodge.co.uk
Located on the north side of the river, and close to the Tower. Tower Gateway DLR station is about 250m away. An excellent location for sightseeing around Tower Bridge.
The entrance, and access to reception, the bar and restaurant, and to the lifts is step-free.
There are **eight accessible rooms**, two of which are twins, while the others have a double bed. All have a wheel-in shower.

22. Express by Holiday Inn Limehouse ££ (NAT)

469 The Highway, E1W 3HN *Tel:* 020 7791-3850
e-mail: reservations@exhi-limehouse.co.uk
Located about 500m from Limehouse DLR station between Heckford Street and Butcher Row. There is adjacent parking with 4 BB spaces.
Access to reception, the bar and restaurant and the two lifts is step-free.
There are **six accessible rooms**, all with a wheel-in shower and a double bed. There are interconnecting rooms and if the hotel is not full, hotel policy is to allow a carer to use this room without extra charge.
There is a GF accessible toilet.

23. Tower (a Guoman Hotel) £££ (VC)

St Katharine's Way, E1W 1LD *Tel:* 020 7481-2575
e-mail: tower@guoman.co.uk
By the northern end of Tower Bridge by the river. Relatively expensive, but well-located. On-site CP with 3 BB spaces at ground level and one in UGCP with

valet parking. Step-free access from the east with a ramp to bypass +2 steps. There are four lifts (D100 W170 L140) to the dining-room, bar and toilets on the upper foyer level. There are **wheelchair cubicles (D70 ST90)** in both the mens and womens toilets. **Three accessible rooms** with double beds and space for an additional folding bed if required. All have a wheel-in shower, and are on the 1st floor reached by lift. Room 105 seen: D85 Bathroom D85 ST125.

SE1 (around the South Bank, Bankside and Southwark)

24. Premier Inn London Tower Bridge ££ (VC)

159 Tower Bridge Road, SE1 3LP *Tel:* 0871 527-8678
e-mail: london.tower.bridge.mti@whitbread.com
Located just past Tanner Street about 500m south of the bridge. There are 10 BB spaces with step-free access to a back entrance.
Step-free entrance to reception. About 50% of seating in the bar/restaurant has a split level with one or two steps. There are three lifts. The **ten accessible rooms** all have a double bed. A z-bed is available, but it's use will restrict space in the room. The bathrooms all have a lowered bath with handrails.
Wheelchair toilet (D85 ST70) on the GF.

25. Premier Inn London Southwark ££/£££ (VC)

Bankside, 34 Park Street, SE1 9EF *Tel:* 0871 527-8676
e-mail: london.southwark.pti@whitbread.com
The hotel is attached to the Anchor Inn which is an old riverside pub, although they are run separately. The hotel entrance is in Bank End, opposite Vinopolis. Go through the arch over slightly rough paving to find the step-free entrance to reception on your left. One reservable BB space in the CP outside. The hotel has lifts which access all floors. The restaurant is located in the pub next door.
There are **three accessible rooms** all located on the GF. All have lowered baths with grab rails and double beds, though they can place a z-bed or sofa bed in the room if required, which will reduce the space available.
Breakfast is served in the Chart Room on an upper floor of the Anchor pub. This is reached from the hotel via a lift (D75 W95 L130) and a platform lift (D80 L120). There is a **wheelchair toilet (D85 ST70)** in the hotel, level with the Chart Room. The accessible parts of the pub are reached from the riverside, where there is a GF adapted toilet.

26. Premier Inn London County Hall ££/£££ (VC)

Belvedere Road, SE1 7PB *Tel:* 0871 527-8648
e-mail: reception.countyhallpi@whitbread.com
The hotel is situated in the building known as County Hall with its main entrance on the opposite side from the river and some 25m from the junction with Chicheley Street. There is a barrier on the corner to facilitate van access to the

basement area under all parts of the building. County Hall is a listed building limiting the possibility of making exterior changes. It is ideally situated for visiting the South Bank, and for getting across Westminster Bridge.

Access at the main entrance is via +15 steps, but the hotel has a Stairmate mechanical stair climbing device. It is effectively a portable inclined platform lift and the user stays in their chair while going up (or down) the steps. A bell at the bottom can be used to call the attention of the staff, but it would be worth having a mobile phone to call reception directly. There is an alternative access route via the security gate at the corner of the building, going down a ramp to reach the hotel basement. There is then lift access (under staff control). The route is a bit grotty, but facilitates entry by an electric chair user (where the chair would be too heavy for the Stairmate). Some manual chair users might prefer it as well. Note that the barrier is under the control of different management from the hotel, but someone is on duty in the little room to the left nearly all the time.

Step-free restaurant/bar and **wheelchair toilet (D70+ ST 70+)** are all on the GF. Three lifts (D85 W160 L150) link to all seven floors.

The hotel has **seventeen accessible rooms,** located on floors 2-6. Three on the 2nd floor have shower trays with lips, and one has a wet room, with a wheel-in shower. The other ten rooms have lowered baths with grab rails. All rooms have double beds, though they can place a z-bed or sofa bed in the room if required. The room with the wheel-in shower is No 238.

The hotel is very centrally located on the south bank close to the London Eye, which compensates for the hassle getting in and out.

Note the new opening of Premier Inn London Waterloo very nearby, scheduled for early 2013 (see number **35**).

27. Travelodge London Southwark £/££ (VC)

202-206 Union Street, SE1 0LH *Tel:* 0871 984-6352

e-mail: southwark.mgr@travelodge.co.uk

Located about 200m from Southwark tube station (which is accessible). It is right by the railway bridge and opposite the Lord Nelson pub. An excellent location for sightseeing.

Although there is no CP at the hotel there are three BB spaces at the back which can be reserved in advance.

The entrance, and access to reception, the bar and restaurant, and to the lifts is step-free.

There are **thirteen accessible rooms** including two with twin beds. All have a wheel-in shower.

28. Travelodge London Waterloo £/££

195-203 Waterloo Road, SE1 8UX *Tel:* 0871 984-6291

e-mail: londonwaterloo.mgr@travelodge.co.uk

Located between Barons Place and Webber Row and about 700m from Waterloo

Station. A large part of the South Bank, and also some of the major sights like Westminster Abbey and St Paul's Cathedral are less than 2km away. There are no parking facilities.

Step-free to reception, the bar and restaurant, and to the lifts. There are **fourteen accessible rooms**, all of which have zip and link beds (separable into twins), and wheel-in showers.

29. Days Hotel Waterloo ££/£££

54 Kennington Road, SE1 7BJ *Tel:* 020 7922-1331
e-mail: book@hotelwaterloo.com

Located very near the Imperial War Museum by the junction between Kennington Road and Cosser Street, near the Lambeth Road. It is nearly 1 km from Waterloo Station. CP with two surface BB spaces. Step-free entrance. Inside, the bar and restaurant are both on the GF. Two lifts (D80 W110 L140) go to all five floors. There are **two accessible rooms** on the GF, both with a wheel-in shower. One has twin beds and the other has a double. Room seen with D85 and ST150.

Adapted toilet (D85 ST65) to the left of reception. Go through the double doors to the left of the lifts and follow the corridor.

30. Holiday Inn Express Southwark ££/£££ (VC)

103 Southwark Street, SE1 0JQ *Tel:* 020 7401-2525
e-mail: info@exhisouthwark.co.uk

Located at the junction with Bear Lane and about 250m from Tate Modern. 4 BB spaces on the surface without height restriction. Main entrance +3 steps, but there's a step-free route about 30m away. You need to go round the hotel to the right and use the 'deliveries' entrance at the back. On the GF, the reception, bar and restaurant are all step-free. **Six accessible rooms** reached via the lift (D80 W120 L85). All have double beds, wheel-in showers, and interconnect with another room. Room 103 seen, D85 bathroom D75 ST100. **Wheelchair toilet (D85 ST70)** on the GF, to the left of reception and through a door. It is near the step-free entrance.

30. Premier Inn Southwark, Tate Modern (VC)

15A Great Suffolk Street, SE1 0NZ *Tel:* 0871 527 9332
e-mail: Londonsouthwarktatemodern.pi@premierinn.com

This centrally located hotel is scheduled to open in mid-2012.

It will have step-free access to reception, to the bar/restaurant area and to two lifts. There will be **six accessible rooms**, all with a wheel-in shower, and one with an interconnecting room. The beds will be zip and link.

There will be a GF **accessible toilet**. We may include a fuller description on our website under *Updated information* after making a visit.

31. H10 Hotel £££

284 Waterloo Road, SE1 8RQ *Tel:* 020 7928-4062
website: www.h10hotels.com (then choose your language)
e-mail: h10.london.waterloo@h10hotels.com
A large new-build hotel just before St George's Circus with 175 rooms. It is slightly less than 1km from Westminster Bridge. The distance to both Parliament and Tower Bridge is interestingly described in the hotel publicity leaflet as being "just a few metres" !
Two BB spaces some 25m from the entrance. Reservation essential.
The hotel has good facilities, with step-free access everywhere. Reception and bar on the GF. There are 3 lifts. Restaurant on the 1st floor. **Eight accessible bedrooms**. Five (one on each floor) are some 25m from the lift and as they are on the corner of the building are very spacious. One seen. Large bathroom (D80 ST100+) with wheel-in shower and fold-down seat. Well fitted, though without a shower curtain. All five have twin beds, and there's an interconnecting room if requested. The other three (not seen) have a smaller bathroom with a low level bath and support rails.

32. Mad Hatter £££ (VC)

3-7 Stamford Street, SE1 9NY *Tel:* 020 7401-9222
e-mail: madhatterhotel@fullers.co.uk
Behind the 19thC facade is a modern 30-bed hotel and pub. It is located near Blackfriars Bridge.
A ramp bypasses the +2 steps at the entrance. Lift (D75 W90 L130). **Three accessible rooms** (room 101 seen). All the bathrooms have a lowered bath with handrails, and limited ST space. The double beds are zip and link, and so can be converted to twins.
Wheelchair toilet (D85 ST75) on the GF near the lift. The bar and restaurant (in the pub) are step-free.

33. Novotel Waterloo £££

113 Lambeth Road, SE1 7LS *Tel:* 020 7793-1010
e-mail: H1785@accor.com
250m from the roundabout at the end of Lambeth Bridge. UGCP (max height 1.9m) with lift access.
Step-free entrance to reception lounge and bar area. Two lifts (D85 W130 L130) to all floors.
There are **ten accessible rooms** (D80 ST100+) with double beds. Half have wheel-in showers with a movable plastic chair, and the other half baths with support rails and bath boards. Rooms 524 and 124 seen. **Wheelchair toilets** on the GF and 1st floor.

34. Novotel London City South £££ (VC)

53-61 Southwark Bridge Road, SE1 9HH *Tel:* 020 7089-0400
e-mail: H3269@accor.com
Located on the corner with Thrale Street and less than 500m from Tate Modern.
Parking is available at ground level at the *All Seasons* hotel next door with no
height restriction.
There is step-free access at the main entrance to reception, bar and restaurant and
bedroom lifts. **Ten accessible rooms** all with a queen-size double bed. All have
a wheel-in shower. They are interconnected with a superior room which has a
queen bed and convertible sofa which can sleep a family of four.
There are accessible toilets on the GF in the main lobby area and on the 1st floor
in the conference area.

35. Park Plaza Westminster Bridge London £££ (VC)

200 Westminster Bridge Road, SE1 7UT *Tel:* 0844 415-6790
Reservations: 0844 415-6780 *website:* www.parkplaza.com
e-mail: ppwlres@pphe.com
The two four-star Park Plaza hotels are just across the road from each other. They
seem to be relatively competitively priced in order to achieve high occupancy
rates. Their location just south of Westminster Bridge is very good. Westminster
tube station just across the bridge is 'accessible', and there's a whole range of
interesting places nearby.
Valet parking is available.
The entrance is near the bridge, and from the downstairs foyer there are four lifts
(to the left) up to the 1st floor bypassing the escalators in front of you. The 1st
is the main floor with reception, and another group of eight lifts to the rooms at
the far end. On the 1st floor there's a spacious bar, together with a lounge and
restaurant. In the bar and lounge nearly all the furniture seems to be of the low
soft leather variety with low tables, and there are only a few higher chairs and
tables.
There are more than 1000 rooms, including some **54 accessible rooms** with a
walk-in/wheel-in shower. Each has a queen- or a king-size double bed.
There's an **accessible toilet** to the left of the bar on the 1st floor.

35. Park Plaza County Hall London £££ (VC)

1 Addington Street, SE1 7RY *Tel:* 020 7021-1800
Reservations: 020 7021-1810
website: www.parkplaza.com
e-mail: ppchres@pphe.com
See the write-up above. Addington Street is only about 150m long, with Park
Plaza hotels on both sides ! It is step-free to reception and to the GF bar. The
restaurant is on level M, reached by 3 lifts.

There are nearly 400 rooms and **more than thirty are accessible** with a walk-in/ wheel-in shower. Some have double beds, and some have twins.

There are **accessible toilets**

* on the LGF (level −1) to the left from the lift; and
* on level M, **(D85 ST70)** with BCF, immediately opposite the lift.

35. Premier Inn London Waterloo ££/£££ (VC)

At the time of writing this is a construction site, but as it is located in such a good spot we have included some basic information. It may not open until 2013.

It is situated on the corner of York Road and Addington Street, and right next to both the Park Plaza hotels listed above. It is thus in an ideal location for exploring the South Bank and just across the bridge is Westminster and Big Ben.

It is being built in the historic General Lying-in Hospital, with a new annexe attached.

It will have ramped access into reception and to the two lifts. These will give access to the bar/restaurant on the LGF with guest bedrooms on the upper floors. Guest rooms in the existing historic GLI building will be accessed via a half-flight of stairs from lift lobbies in the new building, supplemented by powered chairlifts for use by guests with wheelchairs. The accessible bedrooms will be located so as to be close to lifts and access equipment wherever possible.

Premier Inn policy is to include a number of **accessible rooms**. At least half of them should have a wet room with a wheel-in shower. All should have zip and link beds which can easily be separated.

We will include a fuller description on our website under *Updated information*, when we have visited, but we would hope that some of the accessible rooms will be reached step-free from the lifts.

W2 (around Paddington)

36. Novotel London Paddington £££/££££

3 Kingdom Street, W2 6BD *Tel:* 020 7266-6000

e-mail: H6455@accor.com

Located at the end of Kingdom Street, off Sheldon Square, and alongside the railway lines. It is about 500m from Paddington station. No parking.

Step-free to reception, the lounge/bar/restaurant and to the three lifts. There are **eleven accessible rooms**. All have a double bed and an interconnecting twin room. Seven of the rooms have walk in showers and the other four a low bath with rails.

GF **accessible toilet**.

E14 (around Canary Wharf, the Isle of Dogs and Limehouse)

37. Travelodge London Docklands £/££ (NAT)

Coriander Avenue, E14 2AA *Tel:* 0871 984-6192
e-mail: londondocklands.mgr@travelodge.co.uk
Situated on the A13 East India Dock Road, near the north end of the Blackwall
Tunnel. Approached only from the A13 westwards. It is about 300m from the
East India DLR station.
Step-free to reception, bar and restaurant. **Twelve accessible rooms** on the GF,
all with double beds (and no room for a second bed) and low level bath/shower.
Two have zipped/separable beds to make a twin. Room 004 seen, D70, bathroom
D85 ST90.
Wheelchair toilet (D85 ST85) on the GF near the bedrooms.

38. Britannia International £-£££ (NAT)

Marsh Wall, London, E14 9SJ *Tel:* 020 7712-0100 *Central/res:* 0871 474-2755
website: www.britanniahotels.com *e-mail:* reception712@britanniahotels.com
The hotel is located alongside the South Dock, and it is about 300m from the
South Quay DLR station. It's a somewhat anonymous area, but one of the
advantages of the hotel is that its prices vary enormously (by more than five
times) depending on how fully booked it is, so there are occasional bargains to be
had.
There's particularly good factual information about access on their website.
The hotel is just labelled International outside. UGCP with 2 BB spaces.
The +4 steps at the entrance are bypassed by a ramp to the left. Step-free to
reception, lounge, restaurants and the 3 lifts. There are split levels (3 or 4 steps)
to/in the main bar areas overlooking the dock, but drinks can be served in the
lounge, though the tables there are quite low.
Six accessible rooms, all with a wheel-in shower. Five twins and one double.
Wheelchair toilet (D80 ST80) with BCF on the GF, almost unsigned, to the
right of the doors into the Pizzeria. The outer door can clash with the Pizzeria
door and there's an unusual vestibule corridor inside, with the lock being on the
outer door.

E16 (around the Victoria Docks and Silvertown)

39. ETAP London City Airport £/££

North Woolwich Road, Silvertown, E16 2EE *Tel:* 020 7474-9106
e-mail: E5840@accor-hotels.com
Competitively priced, the hotel is located on right of North Woolwich Road
coming from City just after the Esso Petrol Station roundabout, and opposite
Oriental Road. It's about 600m to Pontoon Dock DLR station. On-site CP has
four BB spaces.

The website says that it is about to become an *Ibis Budget* hotel. Don't be put off because the website says '0 accessible rooms'.

Flat access to the GF which has reception desk, breakfast room and lift (D90 W105 L140) to all floors. **Four accessible rooms**, two each on first and second floors. Room seen 201: D80 BathroomD75 ST160 with handrails for wheel-in shower. The accessible rooms have twin beds. They need to be booked in advance. Check first with the hotel that an accessible room is available. Book on-line and then recheck with the hotel about the room you have been allocated. **Adapted toilet (D75 ST95 inward opening door)** on the corridor to the right past reception (staff have the key).

40. Travelodge London City Airport £/££ (NAT)

Hartmann Road, Silvertown, E16 2BZ *Tel:* 0871 984-6290
e-mail: londoncityairprt.mgr@travelodge.co.uk

Located near the junction between Connaught Road and Connaught Bridge. It is less than 600m from London City Airport DLR station.

There is a pay CP attached to the hotel at ground level with no height restriction. The entrance, and access to reception, the bar and restaurant, and to the lifts is step-free.

There are **seven accessible rooms**, all of which have a wheel-in shower.

All have a double bed, though some have sufficient space for putting in a separate z-bed.

41. Premier Inn London Docklands Excel ££ (NAT)

Excel East, Royal Victoria Dock, E16 1SL *Tel:* 0871 527-8650
e-mail: london.docklands.mti@whitbread.com

Located some 400m away from Excel East and from the Prince Regent DLR station.

10 BB spaces in the CP which is at ground level with no height restriction. Step-free to reception, bar and restaurant. Eight lifts to all floors. There are **twelve accessible rooms** on floors 1-6. All have double beds and lowered baths with grab rails. A z-bed can be put in the room but this will reduce the space available.

42. Ibis London Excel £/££ (NAT)

9 Western Gateway, Royal Victoria Dock, E16 1AB
Tel: 020 7055-2300 *e-mail:* H3655@accor.com

About 200m from the west end of the Excel Centre, and from the Custom House DLR station.

Step-free to reception, with the bar and restaurant to the right. Three lifts go to all floors.

Seventeen accessible rooms all with a wheel-in shower and all with low double beds. z-beds are available.

GF **wheelchair toilet (D100 ST100)** just before the ramp to the restaurant.

42. Novotel London Excel ££/£££ (NAT)

Western Gateway, Royal Victoria Dock, E16 1AA
Tel: 020 7540-9700 *e-mail:* H3656@accor.com
About 200m from the west end of the Excel Centre, and from the Custom House
DLR station. It is right next to the Ibis.
Using the lifts, it is step-free to reception, bar and restaurant which are all located
on the 1st floor. **Thirteen accessible rooms**, seven with a lowered bath, and six
with a walk-in/wheel-in shower. They have separable zip and link beds.

E6 (around East Ham and Beckton)

Premier Inn London Beckton ££ (NAT)

1 Woolwich Manor Way, Beckton, E6 5NT *Tel:* 0871 527-8644
e-mail: beckton.pi@premierinn.com
On the corner of Winsor Terrace and next to Beckton DLR station. The DLR
gives step-free access into Tower Gateway, Canary Wharf and Greenwich
stations, amongst others. On-site CP with 6 BB spaces.
Step-free entrance to the reception area and the restaurant, which is located next
to the main building. There is a separate annexe across the CP.
There are **six accessible rooms** all on the GF, four in the annexe and two in the
main building. One of those in the annexe has a wet room and wheel-in shower.
The rest have lowered baths with grab rails. All have a double bed, though they
can place a z-bed or sofa bed in the room if required, but this will reduce the
space available.

E15 (around Stratford)

Premier Inn London Stratford ££ (NAT)

International Square, Westfield Stratford City, Montfichet Road, E15 1AZ
Tel: 0871 527-9286 *e-mail:* londonstratford.pi@premierinn.com
The hotel is 50m from Stratford International station, and about 400m from
Stratford Regional for tube links and the DLR. The entrance is on the LGF level
of the Westfield shopping mall. There's a taxi drop-off about 50m away in CP A.
There are double automatic doors leading from the pavement into a lounge
area defined as 'ground' by the hotel. Three lifts lead to reception, the bar and
restaurant areas which are on the 1st floor. All are step-free.
It has **twenty accessible rooms**, 15 of which have a wet room with a wheel-in
shower, and the other 5 have a lowered bath with rails. All have zip and link
beds and can be converted to either twins or a double. In addition, most have an
interlinking room where other friends or family can stay. One room has a hoist to
facilitate transfer from bed to bathroom, to the shower. They are looking at ways
to extend the track to facilitate transfer to the toilet as well.
Wheelchair toilet on the 1st floor, level with the restaurant.

Holiday Inn Express London Stratford ££/£££ (NAT)

196 High Street, E15 2NE *Tel:* 020 8536-8000
e-mail: info@hiexpressstratford.co.uk
Located on the corner of Carpenters Road. The hotel has been recently extended
and so has an older part, and a newer one. There is (gated) parking for 15 cars,
with a height restriction of 2.8m, and includes 2 BB spaces. Parking costs £20/
day.
There is step-free access through the main doors or from the CP to reception,
and the bar/café. Two lifts go to all seven floors, and there are **eleven accessible
rooms**. All have an excellent wet room bathroom with a wheel-in shower,
although there's a small ridge at the entrance (to stop water from flooding out).
All also have an interconnecting room. Six of the accessible rooms in the older
part of the hotel have only a double bed. The other five newer ones have a double
bed and a separate extendable sofa-bed, effectively providing 'twin' beds.

Ibis London Stratford £/££

1A Romford Road, Stratford, E15 4LJ *Tel:* 020 8536-3700
e-mail: H3099@accor.com
Located on the corner with The Grove and about 800m from Stratford Regional
station. Parking available on site most weekends if requested, otherwise you
would need to use the Stratford Shopping Centre CPs.
Step-free access to GF area including reception, lounge and restaurant. A lift goes
to all floors. **Six accessible rooms**, all with a wheel-in shower. All have zip and
link beds which can be separated on request. Room seen had D85 with a sliding
door to the bathroom which has a wheel-in shower, and ST 100+.
Wheelchair toilet (D80 ST75) on the GF, past the bar and on the left.

SW5 (around Earls Court)

43. Premier Inn London Kensington/Earls Court ££ (NAT)

11 Knaresborough Place, SW5 0TJ *Tel:* 0871 527-8666
e-mail: londonkensington.pti@whitbread.com
The hotel is built over the railway line about 250m along Earls Court Gardens,
from the Earls Court 'accessible' tube station. It is just south of the Cromwell
Road.
No parking facilities, but the road outside has only a single yellow line.
Step-free to reception, bar and restaurant. Four lifts go to all floors. There are **five
accessible rooms** all of which have a double bed and lowered baths with grab
rails. A z-bed can be put up but this will reduce the space available.

44. Premier Inn London Kensington Olympia ££ (NAT)

22-23 Cromwell Road, SW5 9QJ *Tel:* 0871 527-8668
e-mail: londonkensingtonolympia.pi@premierinn.com
The hotel is in a Georgian style terrace on the north side of the road and about

50m from the Earls Court Road going towards Cromwell Crescent. There's an
easyHotel a few doors further along. No parking facilities.
Entrance +9 steps, bypassed by a platform stairlift getting to reception. There's an
intercom by the pavement.
The hotel is in a converted building, and the bar area is reached via a ramp. Some
parts of the restaurant can only be accessed by another platform stairlift. There
are two lifts which go to all floors. **Four accessible rooms** on the 2nd floor all
have a double bed and lowered baths with grab rails in the bathroom. A z-bed can
be put up but this will reduce the space available.

SW8 (around Vauxhall)
45. Comfort Inn Vauxhall ££
87 South Lambeth Road, SW8 1RN   *Tel:* 020 7735-9494
website: www.comfortinnvx.co.uk *e-mail:* stay@comfortinnvx.co.uk
Situated on the corner with Old South Lambeth Road, about 800m south of
Vauxhall Bridge. Small CP on-site with three BB spaces. The +3 steps at the
entrance are bypassed by a ramp. Reception, lounge, bar and restaurant all on
the GF, together with **five accessible rooms**. Room seen with D80+, bathroom
D75 and a wheel-in shower. We were told that all the rooms had a double bed and
wheel-in shower. The hotel has no portable single beds to put in a room. There is
a lift to the upper floors with non-adapted bedrooms.
Wheelchair toilet (D70+ ST70+) off the GF corridor.

W8 (around Kensington)
46. Copthorne Tara ££ (with TFA discount)
Scarsdale Place, Kensington, W8 5SR   *Tel:* 020 7937-7211
website: www.millenniumhotels.co.uk/tara
e-mail: reservations.tara@millenniumhotels.co.uk
Off Wrights Lane, about 250m from Kensington High Street. It's a bit off the
beaten track, although good for Kensington Palace, the Albert Hall and the big
museums. The nearest 'accessible' tube station is at Earls Court.
UGCP without lift access, but valet parking is available.
Flat entrance. Five lifts (D115 W190 L135). Step-free access to all facilities.
Ten accessible rooms, catering for people with a wide range of disabilities. Six
now have a wheel-in shower. Two rooms have a double bed, and six are twins.
Two single rooms (which have an interconnecting room) have a hoist to facilitate
transfer to/from the bed to the bathroom. **Wheelchair toilets (D70+ ST70+)** on
the GF and the mezzanine. It's a big hotel with long distances inside, and not very
well located, but the room adaptations are probably the best in London.
Book through *Tourism for All* (TFA) to reserve a room at a substantial discount
e-mail: info@tourismforall.org.uk or *Tel:* 0303 303 0146.
TFA membership costs about £25/year.

SE10   Greenwich

47. Ibis Greenwich ££/£££ (NAT)
30 Stockwell Street, SE10 9JN *Tel:* 020 8305-1177
e-mail: H0975@accor.com
On the corner with Greenwich High Street. It is about 250m from the Cutty Sark
DLR station and nearly 400m from the NR station. Large pay and display CP at
the back with two BB spaces.
Entrance +4 steps, bypassed by a ramp. The hotel foyer leads directly to
reception, and then into a *Café Rouge* for both eating and drinking. The **two
accessible rooms** are on the GF, with easy ramped access. Both are quite
compact, with twin beds and wheel-in showers. There's a fold-down seat, a
pull-around curtain and the shower controls are at a convenient height. ST70+ for
the toilet.
The lift (D80 W105 L135) goes to the other floors.
Wheelchair toilet (D75 ST70) to left of reception.

48. Premier Inn London Greenwich ££ (NAT)
43-81 Greenwich High Road, SE10 8JL *Tel:* 0871 527-9208
e-mail: greenwich.pi@premierinn.com
The hotel is located opposite the junction with Devonshire Drive and slightly
nearer Deptford Bridge DLR station than Greenwich train/DLR station. 1 BB
space at the front.
Step-free to reception and the bar/restaurant. Two lifts access all floors. **Eight
accessible rooms.** There are 8 universally accessible rooms. Four have lowered
baths with grab rails and four have wet rooms with a wheel-in-shower and fold
down seat with grab rails. All the beds are zip and link, which can be split into
two singles.

49. Novotel Hotel Greenwich ££/£££ (NAT)
173 Greenwich High Road, SE10 8JA *Tel:* 020 8312-6800
e-mail: H3476@accor.com
Situated right next to the main Greenwich railway station (which is accessible to
and from both platforms). It is about 500m from the centre of Greenwich.
The main entrance has large revolving doors, which can be slowed down if you
press the button with the 'wheelchair' symbol on it. There's an alternative way in
through a conventional door (W>80) to the right, but this is normally kept locked
and you'd have to use the intercom discreetely located on the wall, to contact
reception. It is step-free to reception, and the lobby, bar and restaurant areas.
There's a GF **wheelchair toilet (D80 ST80)** with BCF to the right as you come
in.
Two lifts (D80 W90 L120) lead to the upper floors where there are **eight
accessible rooms**, four have a low level bath with grab rails, and four have a

walk-in shower. The toilet has ST 70+. The rooms have zip and link beds. The accessible rooms also have interconnecting rooms, thus making a good family combination, and both sets of occupants could then access the wheel-in shower.

SW6 Fulham
Jurys Inn Chelsea Hotel ££/£££
Imperial Road, Chelsea, SW6 2GA *Tel:* 020 7411-2200
e-mail: Cei_reservations@jurysinns.com
The hotel seems to be slightly off the beaten track on the edge of an old industrial site, and near Chelsea Harbour marina and pier, with accessible boats to both Embankment and Blackfriars.
It has 172 rooms, 12 of which are accessible, and 2 have a wheel-in shower. All have double beds but a sofa-bed can be put in if requested.

Travelodge London Fulham £/££ (NAT)
290-302 North End Road, Fulham, SW6 1NQ *Tel:* 0871 984-6429
e-mail: fulham@travelodge.co.uk
Located on the corner with Haldane Road, about 400m from Fulham Broadway tube station which is 'accessible', though with a big step up into the train.
There's no on-site parking and no restaurant.
The entrance, and access to reception and the lifts, is step-free.
There are **four accessible rooms** and all have twin beds and a wheel-in shower.

W6 Hammersmith
Premier Inn London Hammersmith ££
255 King Street, W6 9LU *Tel:* 0871 527-8660
e-mail: londonhammersmith.pi@premierinn.com
Located nearly 1km from Hammersmith tube station and alongside Vencourt Place. There are 2 BB spaces at the front.
Wheelchair access is via a ramp, which leads to a lift taking you to reception on the 1st floor. The bar and restaurant are on this level. Two lifts access all 13 floors.
Three accessible rooms all have a double bed and lowered baths with grab rails in the bathroom. A z-bed can be put up but this will reduce the space available.

Holiday Inn Express Hammersmith ££/£££
124 King Street, Hammersmith, W6 0QU *Tel:* 020 8746-5100
e-mail: reservations@expresshammersmith.co.uk
The hotel is just over 500m from Hammersmith station which has lifts. Go down King Street, past the Kings Mall. It is on the right in a new mews (possibly not marked on the A-Z map), and just past Cambridge Grove and Argyle Place. Four BB spaces.
Entrance −5 steps, bypassed by a ramp. Step-free to reception, bar and restaurant

on the GF. Two lifts (D95 W100 L150) lead to **eight accessible rooms**, all double bedded and with interconnecting rooms. All have wheel-in showers. Room 101 seen: D80 bathroomD95 ST80+. The management said that the adjoining room would be free for a carer if the hotel isn't fully booked. **Wheelchair toilet (D80 ST70+)** opposite reception.

Novotel London West ££/£££ (NAT)

1 Shortlands, Hammersmith, W6 8DR *Tel:* 020 8741-1555
e-mail: H0737@accor-hotels.com
The hotel is built on an upper level terrace and is attached to a conference centre. It is less than 500m from the 'accessible' tube station at Hammersmith. There is ramped access from the Hammersmith Road, marked 'Novotel hotel & Conference Centre'. There are two other entrances:

- one just past the CP entrance in Shortlands itself and up a slight slope. The revolving door can be bypassed at the side. The two lifts (D70 W85 L110) go either to the 1st floor where you will find the reception and main hotel facilities, all step-free, or you can go down to level −1 to the CP
- the other is about 50m down Chalk Hill Road towards the CP entrance, and is on the left. There is a spacious foyer, and a reception desk which is staffed when there is a function going on. If you go straight through the foyer and turn left at the end you will find four lifts (D80 W200 L120) which will take you to the 1st floor reception and to other floors. There is a (badly) **adapted toilet (D80 ST40)** just to the left of the desk.

The UGCP has 6 BB spaces, and then lift access to either the conference centre or separately, to the hotel. For the hotel, follow the sign to the Pay Machine, and then turn right towards the door marked 'hotel entrance'. You are on floor −1. The main hotel foyer with reception, bar, restaurants and internet access points is step-free, and quite attractively laid out.

Out of more than 400 rooms only **eight are accessible** They are reached by the four lifts from the 1st floor. Room 3035 seen, which was in a far corner of the building a long way from the lift. The room, with a double bed, was quite cramped with the gap between the bed end and the furniture of just W70. It had an interconnecting door to a room with twin beds. The bathroom had, in principle, a flat access shower, but the whole facility was more suited to a disabled walker then to a chair user. The portable shower chair provided had a seat H60 (compared with the toilet with H45), so it was completely unsuitable for a chair user.

Wheelchair cubicles (D75 ST70) in the mens and womens toilets on the 1st floor. Go past the 4 lifts and turn right towards the Fitness Centre. The lock mechanism on the toilet door was extremely difficult to use, as it used a small circular wheel and needed good manual dexterity.

Wembley

Ibis Wembley £/££ (NAT)

South Way, Wembley, HA9 6BA *Tel:* 020 8453-5100

e-mail: H3141@accor.com

Across the road from Wembley Stadium NR station, and nearly 1km from Wembley Park tube station. Very close to the stadium. 5 BB spaces available at the back of the hotel.

Step-free entrance to reception, bar and 2 lifts (D90 W120 L130). Restaurant on the 1st floor. **Eleven accessible rooms** all with wheel-in showers and double beds.

Wheelchair toilet (D85 ST80) on the GF.

Hilton Wembley Plaza Hotel ££ (NAT)

Empire Way, HA9 8DS *Tel:* 020 8902-8839

e-mail: andrew.brett@hilton.com (the hotel manager in 2012)

Located at the south end of Empire Way, some 200m from Wembley Stadium NR station, and nearly 1km from Wembley Park tube station. Parking available in front of hotel.

Step-free to bar, restaurant and 3 lifts (D75 W160 L90). **Three accessible rooms**, all with D80, wheel-in showers and double beds. Room 304 seen.

We were told that this hotel would change ownership after the Olympics and might become a Holiday Inn !

Premier Inn London Wembley ££ (NAT)

151 Wembley Park Drive, HA9 8HQ *Tel:* 0871 527-8682

e-mail: londonwembley.pi@premierinn.com

At the junction with Empire Way and less than 200m from Wembley Park tube station.

8 BB spaces available directly outside entrance without height restriction.

Step-free entrance to reception, bar, restaurant and three lifts (D80 W130 L120). **Eight accessible rooms**, all with double beds, and baths with handrails. Room 120 seen, with D80 ST70.

Wheelchair toilet (D80 ST70) with BCF on the GF.

Quality Hotel ££/£££ (NAT)

Empire Way, HA9 0NH *Tel:* 020 8733-9000

e-mail: enquiries@hotels-wembley.com

Located about half way between Wembley Park tube and Wembley Stadium NR station and about 500m from each. 5 BB spaces in CP outside, without any height restriction.

Step-free to reception, bar, restaurant, and lounge. **Three accessible rooms** on the GF, all with D80, double beds, baths with handrails, and no ST space.

Wheelchair toilet (D80 ST70) with BCF by restaurant.

Croydon

Jurys Inn Croydon ££ (NAT)

Wellesley Road, Croydon, CR0 9XY *Tel:* 020 8448-6000
e-mail: jurysinncroydon@jurysinns.com
Located right by the Wellesley Road Tramline stop (a fully accessible system)
which is one stop away from East Croydon station where all the platforms are
'accessible'. Going the other way, the tram goes to the Centrale shopping entre
(quite near) or to Wimbledon which also has a fully 'accessible' station.
Step-free access to reception, and the bar/restaurant. **Ten accessible rooms**, but
only one has a wheel-in shower. All have a double bed, but some interconnect
with another room.

Premier Inn Croydon South ££ (NAT)

104 Coombe Road, Croydon, CR0 5RB *Tel:* 0871 527-8280
e-mail: croydonsouth.pi@premierinn.com
Located just over 500m from Lloyd Park Tramlink station, and about 2km from
East Croydon train station. It has a separate restaurant situated next door. The
hotel has 3 BB parking bays in front and there are a further 3 in front of the
restaurant.
The hotel has flat level entrance to the reception area. There are **two accessible
rooms** both on the GF. They have lowered baths with grab rails, and double
beds. A z-bed can be put in the room if required, but this will reduce the space
available.
The *Beefeater Grill* restaurant has step-free access and has an accessible toilet.

Heathrow

Ibis Heathrow £/££

112-114 Bath Road, Hayes, Middlesex, UB3 5AL *Tel:* 020 8759-4888
e-mail: H0794@accor.com
The only way to get to the hotel is by car, bus or taxi. There are 2 BB spaces
outside with no height restriction.
Step-free to reception, bar and restaurant. Five lifts (D100 W140 L140). **Seven
accessible rooms** (D75 bathroom D74 ST100) all with a low level bath with grab
rails. Three have twin beds, and four have a double.

Jurys Inn Hotel Heathrow ££

East Perimeter Road, Hatton Cross, Heathrow, TW6 2SQ *Tel:* 020 8266-4664
e-mail: heathrow_reservations@jurysinns.com
The hotel is just off the A30 Great SW Road, and near Hatton Cross tube station
(which is not accessible). On site CP for which charges apply.
Step-free access to reception and the lounge/bar, restaurant and lifts. It has 364

rooms, including **fourteen accessible rooms** of which just 2 have a wheel-in shower. All have a double bed, but a z-bed is available of requested.

Premier Inn Heathrow Terminal 5 ££
420 Bath Road, Longford, West Drayton, UB7 0RF *Tel:* 0871 527-9344
This hotel was scheduled to open in Spring 2012. When we have visited, we will include a fuller description on our website under *Updated information.*
It should have step-free access to the main hotel facilities and follow Premier Inn policy which is to include a number of **accessible rooms**. At least half of them will have a wet room with a wheel-in shower. All should have zip and link beds which can easily be separated.

Novotel Heathrow ££
M4 J4, Cherry Lane, West Drayton UB7 9HB *Tel:* 01895 431-431
e-mail: H1551@accor.com
Five BB parking spaces outside, with no height restriction.
There is step-free access to reception, the lounge/bar/restaurant and to the lifts to the bedrooms. **Ten accessible rooms**, five of which have twin beds, while the other five have a double bed. All have a low bath with rails.
GF accessible toilet.

Gatwick
Premier Inn Gatwick Central £
Longbridge Way, North Terminal, Crawley, RH6 0NX *Tel:* 0871 527-8406
e-mail: gatwickairport.pi@premierinn.com
Situated close to the North Terminal. 11 BB spaces at the front with no height restriction.
There is a slight slope leading to the main entrance and reception. The bar and restaurant are on the GF with level access. **Eleven accessible rooms** all of which are on the GF. All have double beds and lowered baths with grab rails. A z-bed can be put in the room if required, but this will reduce the space available.
The hotel offers a park and fly service with a bus which is suitable for wheelchair users.

Premier Inn Gatwick South £
London Road, Lowfield Heath, Crawley, RH10 9GY *Tel:* 0871 527-8408
e-mail: gatwick.air.south.pti@whitbread.com
Located about 3km south of the airport. 4 BB spaces outside, without height restriction.
There is a slope leading up to the hotel. Step-free to reception and to the restaurant next door. **Six accessible rooms** all on the GF. Two have an interconnecting room. All have lowered baths with grab rails, and double beds.

A sofa bed can be put in the room if required, but this will reduce the space available.

Premier Inn Gatwick Manor Royal £

Fleming Way, Crawley Business Centre, RH10 9DF *Tel:* 0871 527-9214
e-mail: gatwickmanorroyal.pi@premierinn.com
Nearly 4km from the airport and the train station. 7 BB spaces without height restriction.
Step-free to reception, to the restaurant and to the two lifts. **Twelve accessible rooms**. Six have lowered baths with grab rails, and zip and link beds, which can be split into two singles. The other six have wet rooms with a wheel-in-shower. These all have a double bed but a z-bed can be put in the room if required, but this will reduce the space available.

Ibis Gatwick £

London Road, County Oak, Gatwick, RH10 9GY *Tel:* 01293 590-300
e-mail: H1889@accor.com
Located within Gatwick Airport area, the hotel is a 10 to 15 minutes by bus from either Terminal. Parking is possible, including parking while you are away, obviously with an extra charge.
Step-free to reception, the bar/restaurant and the two lifts. **Ten accessible rooms**, all with a wheel-in shower. Four have twin beds and six have a double bed. **Accessible toilet** on the GF.

Borehamwood
Ibis Borehamwood £ (PFCU)

Elstree Way, WD6 1JY *Tel:* 020 8736-2600
e-mail: H6186@accor.com
Located about 20km north of central London. Elstree & Borehamwood station nearly 1km away is only accessible on one side (for southbound trains). Really only of interest to a visitor with a car, and there are 4 BB spaces with no height restriction.
Step-free to reception, and the bar/restaurant. **Six accessible rooms** with wheel-in showers and the choice of twin or double beds.

Hostels and low-cost accommodation

Low cost accommodation is of interest to many travellers and visitors who cannot afford 'businessmens prices'. Spending less on accommodation can mean that the budget for doing other things is bigger. Hence these detailed suggestions.
As discussed in the section above, there are some bargains to be had in conventional hotels. Prices vary on a seasonable basis and depend on demand.

Using a hostel or camping site can be very enjoyable, and there are some interesting places with excellent facilities for disabled visitors. There are also some "no-frills" hotels appearing with minimum staffing levels, but keeping costs low. These include the Formule One and ETAP hotels which have been around for some time, and now easyHotels and Tune hotels have appeared, offering remarkably low prices because basically all they offer is a room. Tune in particular offers low cost rooms, well equipped accessible rooms, but items like towels and/or room cleaning, involves extra charges.

Youth hostels

There are several Youth Hostels in the London area with varying degrees of accessibility. It is really only the Central London and Rotherhithe/Thameside hostels that are of interest to people with disabilities together with the hostel in the Lee Valley at Cheshunt, just outside the M25. These all provide inexpensive accommodation for both individuals and groups with accessible rooms including a wheel-in shower. Accommodation is mainly in small dormitories, which can be effectively family rooms. They are only open to members but membership is available on arrival. Opening times and charges are detailed in a booklet from the

Youth Hostel Association (YHA)
Trevelyan House,
Dimple Road, Matlock, Derbyshire, DE4 3YH,
Tel: 01629 592-600 *website:* www.yha.org.uk.

Hostels are mainly for young people but there is no age limit, and people of all ages use them. Booking is essential especially if you have specific requirements. The Thameside YH has good accessible rooms (which we have used several times). Please note that for comparison purposes **£** indicates a cost of less than £80/day for two people staying, including breakfast.

50. London Central Youth Hostel £ (VC)

104 Bolsover Street, W1W 5NU *Tel:* 0845 371-9154
website: www.yha.org.uk *e-mail:* londoncentral@yha.org.uk
A modern hostel with seven floors and 302 beds. Located between Clipstone Street and New Cavendish Street, and centrally placed some 600m to the north of Oxford Street. There are two BB spaces outside.
The 1 step at the entrance is bypassed by a ramp. The reception desk is to the left, in a large room with a bar/café, and computers/WiFi access. There is a GF **adapted toilet (D80 ST60)** nearby. There are **three accessible rooms** on the GF. **All have D80+ together with an en suite toilet and well equipped wheel-in shower with a fold-down seat.** The rooms have either 3 or 4 double bunk beds. In each room one of the lower beds is double size. To get to the other floors there is a lift (D80 W95 L140), which goes to all the floors. In the basement there is a large self catering kitchen area, where a section has lowered counter tops etc for chair users. Part of the room has a split level which is +5.

51. London Thameside Youth Hostel £ (almost NAT)

20 Salter Road, SE16 5PR *Tel:* 0845 371-9756

website: www.yha.org.uk

e-mail: thameside@yha.org.uk

The hostel has a brilliant location near the river, just over 2km downstream from Tower Bridge. It has an accessible riverside pub/restaurant the *Old Salt Quay* about 100m away. It's about 750m from Canada Water underground station (which is accessible). You can get there using the 381 or C10 bus (getting off at Smith Close) or you can go along the canal. No on-site CP but plenty of parking on the roads nearby.

Flat to reception, restaurant and lounge/bar and a low-level pay-phone, although the main door has a security system with an intercom and buzzer to ensure that only hostel users can get in.

There is step-free access throughout via two lifts (D80 W105 L150), and the one slight hassle is that the breakfast room/restaurant has a split level, accessed as a mezzanine from the lift. **Six accessible bedrooms,** two on each floor, which have two normal beds and one bunk-bed. Bathroom and toilet are en suite, with a sliding door. Flat access shower with hand rails and ST80+ to the padded seat with an adjustable back. Toilet with ST70+.

There is an **adapted toilet (D85 ST65)** on the GF, to the left as you enter.

The hostel has a policy of keeping the accessible rooms available for disabled visitors for as long as possible. However, since the facilities are such good value they are liable to get booked up, especially at peak times. The advice is therefore to book as early as is possible, and make your needs clear in relation to the accessible rooms so that they can be securely booked for you. We have stayed there in the past and been well looked after. It used to be known as the Rotherhithe YH, but has been renamed.

Lee Valley - Cheshunt £ (PFCU and NAT)

Windmill Lane, Cheshunt, Hertfordshire, EN8 9AJ

Tel: 01992 628-392 *Central bookings:* 0845 371-9057

website: www.yha.org.uk *e-mail:* leevalley@yha.org.uk

Although just outside the M25, unlike all the other accommodation described, the hostel has unique features of interest. It is about 400m from Cheshunt station, which has ramped access to both platforms and there's a level crossing just outside providing a step-free link. The trains go into Liverpool Street, but note that the station is not staffed in the evenings. The hostel is reasonably well signed from the A10, and at the end you go across the level crossing, over a small bridge, and turn sharp left. The main village with a big collection of shops, is about 1km away, and en route you will go past three pubs (which we didn't visit !).

There are 2 BB spaces in the CP.

The hostel has a main building plus six lodges, each with a group of rooms on two floors. The main building is step-free to reception, the dining room and a small TV lounge. There is also a GF wheelchair toilet.

Each lodge has a **wheelchair toilet** on the GF and a small lounge/kitchenette area. In lodges 4 and 5, one of the GF bedrooms which has 3/4 beds, has a fully en-suite bathroom with toilet and wheel-in shower. We saw one, and thought that it was very well set up.

Paths around the site are pretty hard gravel which is packed down into a steel mesh base, and the site is nearly flat.

It is part of the Lee Valley Park which has a whole variety of facilities, written up elsewhere.

Backpackers hostel

52. The Generator £ (VC)

Compton Place, 37 Tavistock Place, WC1H 9SE *Tel:* 020 7388-7666
website: www.generatorhostels.com/en/london
e-mail: london@generatorhostels.com

The Generator is a large back-packers hostel with more than 800 beds, good facilities and a lively atmosphere.

Located in a building behind the houses in Tavistock Place, between Hunter Street and Marchmont Street. Compton Place is reached under a blue archway in the terrace, and there are 40m of quite rough cobbles which cannot be avoided, down a gentle slope.

At the entrance there are +15 steps up to reception which is on the 1st floor. There's an alternative step-free entrance on the LGF to the accommodation designed for disabled visitors. Just past the steps, there's a blue door with a canopy over it. To the left of the door an intercom links to reception, who will open the door for you. Inside, −3 steps can be bypassed by using a platform stairlift, and the passageway leads to three rooms, one with twin beds, one with four beds and one with eight. Very close by, there is a **wheelchair toilet (D70 ST70)** and an excellent **wheel-in shower** with a fold-down seat, a shower curtain and plenty of space.

A lift (D75 W140 L90) goes to the 1st floor where there's the reception, bar, restaurant and breakfast room. There's also a lounge and internet room. The lift can be very busy at times, as it serves the whole hostel.

The cost of staying depends on which room you are in, but the hostel offers excellent value and all the facilities and atmosphere you would expect in a back-packers hostel.

A comment from the *Access in London* surveyor who visited The Generator was that it is in an excellent location about 500m from St Pancras station and just 200m from The Brunswick shopping centre with a bunch of restaurants with flat access and a wheelchair toilet. It's about 700m to the British Museum and there are other nearby sights including the British Library. It isn't a five star hotel, but if you want a lively place to stay and can manage the cobbles and one or two minor challenges, you should find it to be a great place to stay.

Staying in a "no-frills" hotel

The original "almost no-frills" hotels were the Formule One and ETAP chains of the Accor group, and most of these are on continental Europe, particularly in France. There are just a tiny number in the UK. In London we found a small number of Formule One and ETAP hotels, and have included the ETAPs at London City Airport and in Hounslow, near Heathrow.

The main "no-frills" providers with accessible rooms are easyHotels, and the Malaysian group, Tune hotels.

easyHotel is a member of the Stelios 'family' of enterprises. It sets out to provide the traveller with very low cost accommodation, in small, often windowless rooms, with no catering or other facilities. This is not a place to stay if you intend to spend a lot of time in your hotel room, as they are absolutely tiny - but if you want a clean room in a good location at a cheap price then this is for you. Rooms are effectively a bed, shower and a toilet. For details see *www.easyHotel.com*.

When you arrive at the hotel, the doors will probably be locked. Use the intercom system to gain entry, and a member of the team will answer and let you in. Once you have registered, you will be issued with a room key and this will activate the lock on the front door for the duration of your stay. Check in time is 15.00 and check out is 10.00.

Please note that the stairlift which provides special needs access to some of the hotels cannot accommodate electric wheelchairs. Please contact the hotel directly via e-mail if you have a specific question regarding building access or the room facilities. All of them have at least one accessible room, and some hotels have several.

We visited two easyHotels, and in 2011 there are three others at Heathrow, Paddington and Victoria. Both the ones we visited were within reach of Earls Court station, which is 'accessible'.

53. easyHotel Earls Court (NAT)

44-48 West Cromwell Road, SW5 9QL *Tel:* 020 7373-7457
e-mail: enquiries@earlscourt.easyHotel.com

The hotel is in a Georgian style terrace on the north side of the road and about half-way between the Earls Court Road and Cromwell Crescent.

There are +2+7 steps at the entrance, and the intercom is at the top of the steps. If you cannot reach this you are advised to ring the phone number above to get attention. There is a portable ramp for the +2 and a platform stairlift to bypass the +7.

The hotel has **six accessible rooms** 2 without a window, and 4 with a window. The room seen had a double bed with access from only one side, a wall mounted TV, and a well fitted bathroom with a wheel-in shower. All the rooms have a double bed and a wheel-in shower.

54. easyHotel South Kensington
14 Lexham Gardens, W8 5JE *Tel:* 07951 440-134
e-mail: enquiries@southken.easyHotel.com
The hotel is in a Georgian-style terrace with +6 steps at the entrance. There's a
platform stairlift to bypass these. On the GF there are **two accessible bedrooms**,
one single (G1) and one double (G2). Both have a wheel-in shower. En route to
the double there's a dog-leg in the corridor with W73. For breakfast you could
cheekily go across the West Cromwell Road to the Marriott (which is opposite
Sainsbury's), although that may cost a bit !

Tune have four hotels in London, and we visited two of them, at Westminster
and Liverpool Street. They provide minimal facilities, but the beds looked very
comfortable and the bathrooms in the accessible rooms were well designed and
equipped. They do not have a restaurant, bar or lounge. The Westminster Tune
had only one lift, but at Liverpool Street all the accessible rooms were on the
GF, and there's an extensive garden area,
One issue which might be a problem for some, was that the standard bed height
is 70cm, which is some 15cm higher than the 'average' wheelchair seat. The
Tune representatives we met said that they would look into the options.
The room costs are low, and there's an extensive list of 'extra's' which you may
choose to include in your booking. To make a reservation you have to put in
your proposed dates, select a hotel, and then when you do 'Next' the possibility
of choosing an accessible room appears.

55. Tune Hotel Westminster £/££ (almost VC)
118-120 Westminster Bridge Road, SE1 7RW *Tel:* 020 7633-9317
e-mail: manager@westminster.tunehotels.com
Located on the corner with Baylis Road, and just by Lambeth North tube station
(where there are steps). Step-free to reception and to the smallish lift (D80 L100
W115). **Four accessible rooms** all with a double bed. Two seen, both with good
bathroom design, ST80+ and a wheel-in shower with well designed fold-down
shower seat (H55) and plenty of fold-away supports. The shower had low level
folding doors. There was a Costa Coffee shop next door.

56. Tune Hotel Liverpool Street £/££
13-15 Folgate Street, E1 6BX *Tel:* 020 7456-0400
e-mail: manager@liverpoolstreet.tunehotels.com
Located by the junction with Blossom Street. Folgate Street is cobbled, but the
pavements are OK. +4 steps at the entrance, but there's a step-free way in from
Blossom Street, opposite the Water Poet pub where a platform stairlift bypasses
+3. Intercom outside. There are **thirteen accessible rooms**, all on the GF, ten
with double beds, and three with twins. In the room we saw the bathroom was

well equipped, with ST 70+, and had a flexible shower curtain to go round the area with the fold-down seat (H55). The hotel has a large and quite attractive garden area, where you can sit outside and enjoy a coffee.

57. Tune Hotel Kings Cross £/££ (NAT)

324 Gray's Inn Road, WC1X 8BU *Tel:* Not available at the time of writing.
e-mail: manager@kingscross.tunehotels.com
Located less than 500m from the 'accessible' Kings Cross/St Pancras tube station. Entrance with +3 steps, bypassed by a platform stairlift to reach reception. There are 4 lifts, two of which are described as wheelchair accessible.
Six accessible rooms, all with double beds.

58. Tune Hotel Paddington £/££

37-55 Praed Street, W2 1NR *Tel:* Not available at the time of writing.
e-mail: manager@paddington.tunehotels.com
Located near the junction with Sale Place and some 200m from Edgeware Road tube station (where there are steps).
Step-free entrance to reception. 2 lifts both described as suitable for wheelchairs.
Seven accessible rooms, five with a double bed, two with twins.

Camping & caravan sites

Perhaps a tent is not the most obvious accommodation for someone visiting London. However, many disabled people go camping, and the relatively low cost can make it an attractive proposition. People may also hire a motor home, or a fixed chalet. At peak times it is obviously sensible to book well in advance. In our view the London campsites are reasonably well equipped in terms of disabled access. Note that the sites we visited have provision for only one wheelchair toilet and\or bathroom, which could be a problem if your visit coincided with that of several other chair users or other disabled people.

Approximate opening times are given here but they may vary from year to year. Most of the sites cost less than £15 per person per night.

Crystal Palace Camping and Caravan Site

Crystal Palace Parade, SE19 1UF *Tel:* 020 8778-7155
website: www.caravanclub.co.uk
Near the Crystal Palace National Sports Centre. Terraced site with sloped tarmac paths and gravel chip/grass pitches. Ramped office. **Wheelchair toilet and shower** with fold down seat. Site open most of the year.

Lee Valley Camping and Caravan Park (Sewardstone)

Sewardstone Road, Chingford, E4 7RA *Tel:* 020 8529-5689
website: www.leevalleypark.org.uk *e-mail:* scs@leevalleypark.org.uk
On the A112 between Chingford and Waltham Abbey about 4km south of
junction 26 on the M25. The site has a barrier across the entrance with a parking
lay-by, but it might be sensible to get the entry code before coming as there isn't
an intercom.
Gently sloping site with tarmac paths and grass pitches. Reception and shop,
ramped. Spacious combined **wheelchair toilet/shower (D75 ST160)** with
ramped access, grab bars and a fold-down chair. This is part of the main toilet/
shower block about 200m from reception. It's kept locked, and disabled guests
on-site are given a key. The site is open most of the year.

Chertsey Camping and Caravanning Club Site

Bridge Road, Chertsey, Surrey KT16 8JX *Tel:* 01932 562-405
website: www.ukcampsite.co.uk
Located just inside the M25, alongside the Thames. Step-free access to reception
and a small shop close to the entrance to the site. The grounds are gently sloping
with tarmac paths. A spacious accessible toilet and shower with BCF is located
next to the reception building, though it is not 'protected' by a lock, and can
therefore be used by anyone. The site is open all the year.

Bookings via the internet to get lowest cost rooms

There are a large number of sites, including www.london-hotel-bookings.co.uk;
www.YourStay.com; www.hotel-assist.com; www.totalstay.com and
www.DiscountCityHotels.com.
You can get an updated list by using Google, and searching London Hotels. One
of the sites (hotel-assist) had a live chat facility which we used. Out of a huge
portfolio of hotels, they could only offer one with accessible rooms for a disabled
guest. When we looked through their list we immediately found half a dozen
others that had accessible rooms which the website operator had no knowledge
of. When we challenged our chat 'partner' he very honestly told us that *"In many
cases the web write-ups are delegated by hotel managements to a junior staff
member who doesn't understand the implications of what they are including or
excluding"*. This certainly makes it much more difficult for disabled people to
take advantage of discounts - but if you do a web search in conjunction with
the information in this guide it may at the very least give you a bargaining lever
which might help you negotiate a competitive rate.

Comparisons with the data presented by *Visit Britain, Tourism for All* and *Inclusive London*

A source that we thought would be well researched, accurate and reasonably balanced and comprehensive, is that from Enjoy England (the England Tourist Board ETB) whose information is used by *Tourism for All*.

The ETB introduced a series of classifications relating to accessibility, but their information about London accommodation seems to be almost non-existent, and some is seriously misleading.

A website search showed just three hotels within a 10 mile radius of London, only one of which is said to be "suitable for independent wheelchair users". It also inexplicably lists the London Thameside YH as being "Suitable for guests who can climb a flight of stairs with the aid of banisters or grip handles". Compare that with our write-up (based on our experiences of staying there several times) which says that there is step-free access almost everywhere, and six 4-bed rooms with an en-suite wheel-in shower and toilet.

They have adopted the approach of charging a fee to carry out an assessment and of having 'standards' (and thus a series of tick boxes to fill, rather than of providing a simple description highlighting any barriers.

We will explore these issues further on our website page entitled *Methodology* because we think that *Visit Britain* and *Tourism for All* are perpetuating a seriously flawed method of collecting and presenting 'accessibility' data, and we have similar problems with *Inclusive London*.

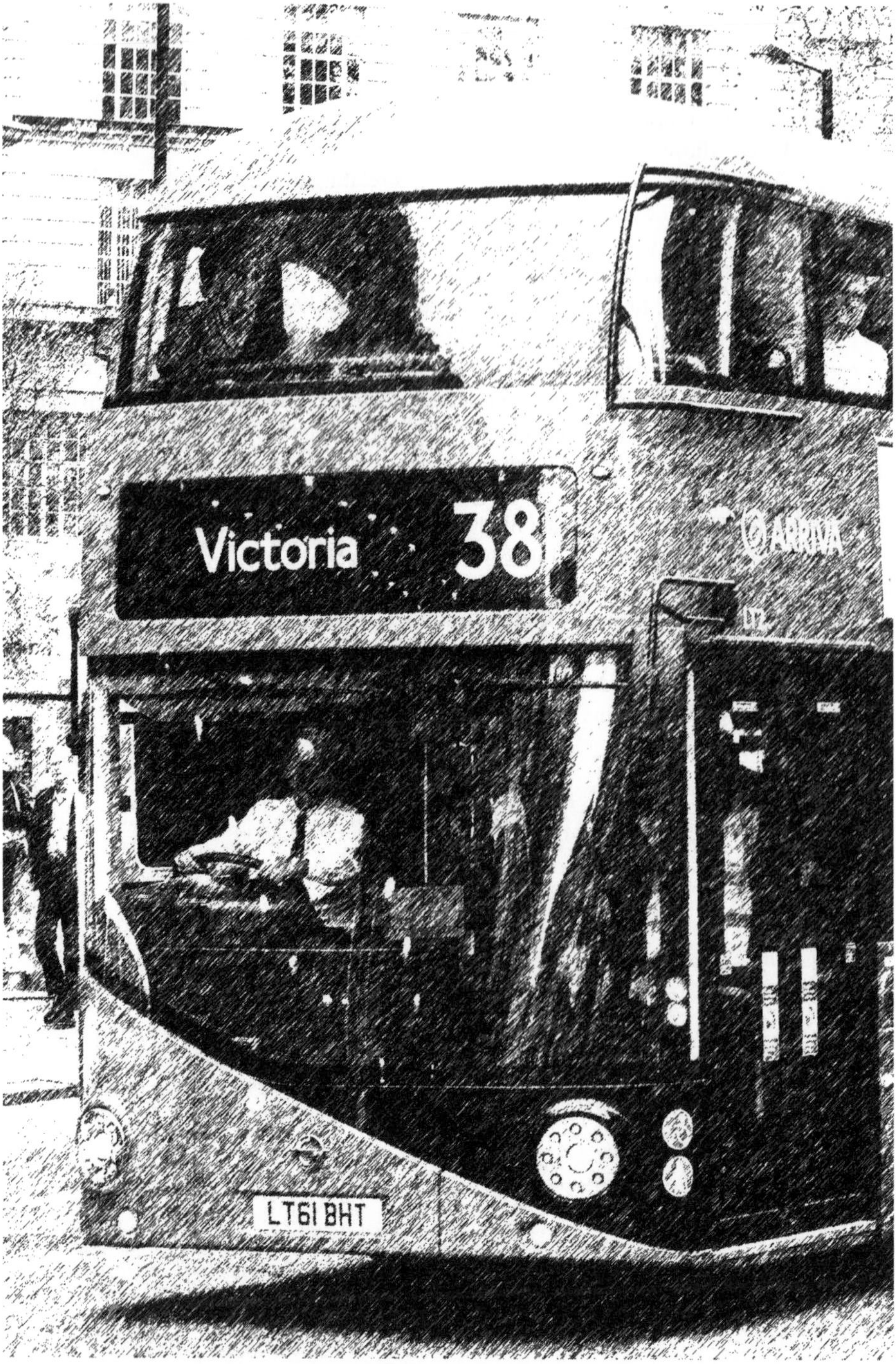
Victoria 38
ARRIVA
LT61 BHT

Getting around

This chapter is written from the point of view of someone coming to London, possibly for the first time. It presents information and practical advice about getting around, based on our experience and research.

It can, of course, be of value to residents who may want to use any of the transport methods described, and may be particularly useful to Londoners who have a disabled visitor.

You will almost certainly benefit from having good maps - discussed in the *General information* chapter.

There is no question that since the last edition of the guide in 2003 things have improved, but there is still a long way to go before the transport system can be described as accessible. Several specialist information and advice agencies have disappeared - like *Tripscope* (an independent and experienced resource) and the *Disability Unit at London Transport*. Information is now provided by well meaning people at the *Transport for London* (TfL) call centre, who have no specialist knowledge other than what they can read on the screen in front of them. There is an active *Equality & Inclusion* department, who reflect the current trend towards 'mainstreaming' accessibility issues, about which we have mixed feelings. We did, however, have extensive and helpful discussions with them when drafting this chapter.

In our view, some of the claims made about accessibility by TfL both in their literature, and on their website, are somewhat optimistic - and you need to *expect* that not everything will go entirely smoothly. It is therefore essential to allow extra time when travelling, especially if you are unfamiliar with particular parts of the system.

The campaigning group *Transport for All* (TfA) provide information based on their experience. They present an excellent overview of what is available to disabled Londoners, in a booklet titled *Get Moving*, which they will send you on request.

We would like to draw people's attention to a recent RADAR report, ***Doing transport differently*** available from *www.disabilityrightsuk.org* and it's on our website as well.

Transport for All
336 Brixton Road, SW9 7AA, *Tel:* 020 7737-2339,
website: www.transportforall.org.uk *e-mail:* contactus@transportforall.org.uk
The TfA website says "London's public transport system has become much more accessible in recent years, but it is far from being fully accessible. TfA believes that the key to using the system is to plan ahead and know as much as you can, to allow time for glitches, and be aware of your rights - so you don't get stranded if something unexpected happens during your journey."
Hopefully the information that both TfL and TfA can provide, together with help from TfL staff, will give you enough to make the transport system work for you. If you would like to talk about planning a journey, please call TfA's information line on 020 7737-2339 or e-mail them.

In this chapter there's an introductory section, setting the scene, and then one's covering:
• Transport for London (TfL)
• getting around using a car or adapted vehicle, or using taxis or minicabs
• using buses, the Underground (tube), the DLR, the *Overground*, and Tramlink
• using the riverbuses and other boats
• services for London residents, Dial-a-Ride, Taxicard and the Freedom Pass
• arriving in London from elsewhere by:
    • National Rail (NR), coach, *Eurostar*, or by air
We have included information about station improvements on both the Underground and *Overground* which are scheduled to become operational up to 2020, and on *Crossrail* which will have opened by then. There is also some discussion about the New London Bus.

What does accessible mean in relation to the transport provisions ?
Throughout the guide we use the descriptors 'accessible', and accessible.
What 'accessible' means is *accessible in principle*, and it applies to most tube and train stations where accessible (as described by the provider) means usually only from pavement to platform, and it is not necessarily step-free into the train itself. Getting on and off some tube trains, the *Overground* and all NR trains, involves a big step. Thus a chair user, and some walkers, would need help in overcoming the barrier.
'Accessible' (in our view) also applies to buses and to black cabs. The statement from TfL is that *"all are accessible"*, when in practice the traveller can run into significant barriers. These are discussed in the guide text, and by TfA - based on disabled peoples experience.
If we say that somewhere is accessible we mean that it is step-free, and thus suitable for an unaccompanied electric wheelchair user, possibly using lifts and/or permanent ramps. There are, of course, issues to do with distance and

slopes, and the roughness of slopes which affect accessibility, but in this chapter we are particularly concerned with questions to do with getting on and off buses, taxis and trains.

Much has been done to make travel easier and safer for people who are visually impaired (like the tactile strips and bright yellow lines warning of the platform edge on tube stations) and for people who are hearing impaired (with more loops). Our focus is on accessibility for those with physical mobility issues, not because other people aren't important, but because that is what our experience is based on. The best people to report on facilities for the visually or hearing impaired are those WITH the relevant challenges.

Setting the scene

London is big, and much of its transport system was designed a century ago, in particular its railways, both surface and underground. There has been some investment in improving the facilities, in particular on the buses. Nearly 70 underground stations and 40 on the *Overground* are 'accessible', together with 40 accessible ones on the DLR. All the buses and black cabs are now, in principle, wheelchair accessible (but see the detailed text and comments, later in this chapter). As a result, it is worth the adventure of trying out both the tube and the buses - particularly the buses, as the network is so extensive.

Partly because of the country's recent economic difficulties, the programme for making more of the tube system 'accessible' has, regrettably, been cut back. However, by 2018, *Crossrail* should have been completed, bringing significant improvements, and there are other things in the pipeline. *Crossrail* will go east-west, and there is already a partly 'accessible' north-south rail line called *Thameslink*. Both are described later, and *Southwest Trains* and other lines also provide some useful 'accessible' NR links.

In spite of the progress, travelling around in London is probably the biggest challenge/problem for the disabled person who wants to be both independent and mobile, and to visit many of the sights.

Planning, determination and a sense of humour are all essential - and some patience !

The authority responsible for the provisions is Transport for London (TfL), together with the various borough/city councils like Camden, Lambeth and Westminster.

Transport for London (TfL)

Windsor House, 42-50 Victoria Street SW1W 0TL

Tel: travel information 0343 222-1234 (24 hours) *Textphone:* 020 7918-3015
website: www.tfl.gov.uk *e-mail:* enquire@tfl.gov.uk

TfL runs the buses, the tubes, the DLR and a number of other services. It is
responsible for managing 580km of main roads, for managing the Congestion
Charge and for making London's transport more accessible.

Its principal function is to provide a fast mass transport system which best
meets the needs of Londoners and visitors. It was created in 2000 by the Greater
London Authority, ending the 67 year use of the name London Transport. The
Underground was integrated into TfL in 2003. Bus services are operated under
contract to London Buses, largely by private sector companies.

It is only relatively recently that the needs of disabled passengers have been
seriously addressed. This has resulted from increased awareness of need, and
from legislation to reduce discrimination against disabled people.

Things have undoubtedly improved, but there is a long way to go before disabled
passengers can get around on an equal basis with their able-bodied counterparts.
A survey some years ago showed that over 400,000 Londoners could not use the
normal public transport system because of their disability. That number is not
likely to have changed very much, since although some services have improved
significantly, the population is both growing and ageing. There will additionally
be thousands of visitors who will also have problems, and probably many more
who will be deterred from coming altogether.

In *Understanding the travel needs of London's diverse communities* April
2012, TfL recognises that some 11% of Londoners say that they are disabled,
representing more than 800,000 residents.

TfL has an *Independent Disability Advisory Group (IDAG)*, who feed in various
ideas and concerns. They are not, however, directly involved in management,
nor with the many difficult decisions relating to priorities, practicalities, budgets
and costs. We understand these, and know that many practical decisions are
compromises, but it seems that with 'mainstreaming' they are largely be made
by well-meaning able-bodied people with only an 'intellectual' feel for the
implications. The IDAG come up with some excellent thoughts and ideas, but
their stellar CVs (see the TfL website) suggest that they may sometimes be too
busy to reflect the experience of Mr Joe Public. The IDAG are not responsible for
either policy or management, but are a useful thinktank.

One problem with all the TfL information is that it seems to have been put
together by people with only a partial understanding of the needs of visitors
travelling around in a wheelchair or with other significant mobility challenges.
The perceptions and needs of regular travellers, and of 'locals', are often different
from those of a visitor.

We note that although this guide has been around since 1984, it is only in the last six months that we have been consulted about any aspect of transport in London !

Some good news is that all London's buses and taxis are now in principle 'accessible'. The use of the inverted commas is deliberate, as it implies that it is not necessarily a straightforward process (see the earlier discussion, and the later sections on the buses, and on taxi use). Many of the 'accessible' underground stations, together with the accessible DLR, are in east London, where there has been a lot of recent development. There are, however, some important 'accessible' tube stations in the west, and at several, staff can help chair users get on board using a portable ramp. Tramlink in the southern suburbs is an accessible system, and there are some 'accessible' stations on both the *Overground* and on NR. There is also the accessible Emirates cable car link across the Thames.

TfL have set up a detailed *Journey planner* on their website where you can input your proposed starting point and destination. This provides quite a lot of information, but we found that:

- it's quite clunky to use, and in relation to many enquiries provides too much information, which can confuse rather than clarify
- the text and structure had been input and designed (we would guess) by able-bodied people with computer/digital information backgrounds
- you can put in various mobility options, like not using escalators, and/or not using steps,
- it wasn't (in our experience) entirely clear or comprehensive, although some information is said to be updated to 'real time'
- it includes a lot of redundant information, making it difficult to identify what is relevant to your journey, particularly for a visitor
- it has the limitations of all computerised systems in that it cannot apply knowledgeable commonsense.

It is clearly easier to use if you're already familiar with London's geography and if you're familiar with using such computerised tools. It is also easier if you simply want to make one journey rather than consider plans and options (which is generally more common). If you're having a hassle, TfA may be able to help.

In the descriptions which follow, we describe the various transport system/s, and most of our comments about them are based on experience.

TfL Publications

TfL produces a range of maps and guides, all listed on their website - where it is also possible to place orders for delivery to a UK address. These can be found on the website under:

Getting around→Transport accessibility→Accessibility guides, and include an/a/ the:

- audio tube guide;
- large print tube map in either colour or black & white
- **Step Free Tube Guide** (SFTG) - an invaluable tool
- guide to River Thames boat services
- **Central London Bus Guide (large print)**
- **Getting Around London**, a guide to accessibility, and help with planning your journey using Tube, buses, DLR, taxis and private hire, trains, trams and riverboats
- **There is a specific page on the TfL website entitled** *Support for people with learning difficulties* which highlights the Travel support card - and there's a Travel support card User Guide. The card is to help communications with staff, and is mainly for London residents, but may be useful to a visitor who needs specific help in travelling
- **Assisted transport services** offer people who find it difficult to use public transport the freedom to travel around London. The travel support guide will help you decide whether you should apply to use assisted transport and which service suits your mobility and travel requirements, and
- **Getting around with Oyster**, which is the cheapest and generally easiest way to pay for journeys using TfL services

There are also some resources which are only downloadable, namely the:

- Avoiding Stairs Tube Guide, and the Tube Toilet map
- Making Rail Accessible: Helping Older and Disabled Passengers (available also in large print). This document includes station accessibility information for *Overground*, and shows how TfL is making rail accessible and working to improve the services provided

Also, of considerable value are the localised bus 'spider' maps, available at:

TfL→Getting around→Buses→Bus route maps→Select a borough→Select a location

There are 33 boroughs to choose between, but just looking in the centre, there are some 30 maps covering the City; >50 covering Lambeth and >70 for Westminster. Overall there are several hundred of these maps, all downloadable as pdfs.

We provide examples, and links, on our website to some of the key central ones, covering Parliament Square, Trafalgar Square, St Paul's, the Tower, and others.

Note that among the various downloadable resources, particularly the SFTG, when downloaded on a conventional desktop with an A4 printer, the output is too small to be useful. The printout is unreadable unless using a magnifying glass !

We suggested that a more user-friendly format is used, as is done for the Avoiding Stairs Tube Guide (which includes escalators)

When ordering these publications ourselves, we had a rather poor experience. Our first attempt at making an order was a complete failure, and none were delivered. We were told that they must have been 'lost in the post'. A couple of weeks later we tried again - and again nothing happened apart from the e-mail acknowledgement of an order, which included a telephone number for 'enquiries' which was a wrong number. We rang 'customer services' and eventually the various items were delivered, although they came in three separate packages on different days and from different places.

Rush hours
One thing that we have to warn people about, and that is that during the rush hour peaks, it's difficult enough for *anyone* to get on some of the central tube trains and/or the buses.
It depends on exactly where you are, but the rush hours last from roughly 07.30 to 09.30 and 16.30 to 18.30, with the deep sections of the tube being even more overcrowded than the sub-surface lines, which have bigger trains.
It's probably not practical for most disabled travellers to battle with the most overcrowded parts of the system. One has to recognise that it's not easy or even possible, to design facilities that can cope adequately with huge numbers of passengers, all wanting to travel at the same time. Some trains will be packed, with standing passengers filling every crevice.
Similar comments apply to getting to and from major events, and the advice has to be "*allow plenty of time, get there early - and just be patient when it comes to getting home*".

Using a car or adapted minibus
For many disabled people, getting around by car or in an adapted vehicle is the most practical way, since much of the public transport system is still difficult to use. Drivers have to face a fairly aggressive driving style and some congestion, especially during rush hours. Having said that, driving in London is certainly more disciplined than it is in other large European cities like Paris or Rome. Your reaction to driving in London will depend very much on your experience as well as on driving skills and temperament. Londoners tend to be positive (some would say aggressive) and to go quite fast. Major junctions are nearly all controlled by traffic lights. Most lanes are now clearly marked, and driving speeds have dropped over the years. This makes it easier for visiting drivers.

Problems include the one-way streets and no-right-turns (and sometimes no-left-turns), which seem to crop up unexpectedly. The secret is not to panic and just press on. Make sure that you've got a good map or Satnav. If you have a navigator, so much the better, and if you have a map you can at least stop and sort yourself out, working out another route if necessary, though it may be difficult to find somewhere to pull in (and you cannot stop anywhere on red routes).

There can be difficulties finding somewhere to park, especially for vehicles over 2m high which cannot use the majority of MSCPs and UGCPs. Parking regulations are slightly different in each of the central boroughs, and it's not always easy to find out just what they are. In the City, in Westminster and in some other areas the normal BB rules don't apply.

During 2003 the **Central London congestion charge** was introduced, in the area bounded by Park Lane in the west, the Euston Road and Pentonville Road in the north, Commercial Street and Tower Bridge in the east and the New Kent Road, Kennington Lane and Vauxhall Bridge in the south. It is administered by TfL. For details, contact:

Congestion Charging, P O Box 4782, Worthing, BN11 9PS
website: www.cclondon.com   *Tel:* 0845 900-1234   *Textphone:* 020 7649-9123
Vehicles used by disabled drivers which are exempt from Vehicle Excise Duty are not charged. BB holders need to register with TfL. This costs £10, and you can register up to two vehicles which you use regularly. The registration procedure takes several days, and the application form can be downloaded from the website. Exemption from the charge only applies if the BB holder is in the car. Once registered, the BB holder can ring to change the vehicle details, if travelling with friends in a different car for particular journeys.

If you're paying the charge, WATCH OUT for unofficial sites who will include extra fees when you pay - and make sure that you only pay through the TfL site. You have to register with them when you pay online, or you can simply ring and just pay for a single day.

It is not quite clear how it will work for a disabled visitor who uses a hire car, but doubtless the hire company will be able to advise. Note the time taken to register for exemption from the charge. For visitors from European countries, their BB should be valid, but the exemption does not apply to disabled visitors from other countries.

Parking for Blue Badge holders

The standard entitlements of the BB do not apply in the City of London, the City of Westminster, in Kensington and Chelsea and in parts of Camden. The BB normally entitles you to park on single yellow lines for up to three hours (providing you are not causing obstruction), and in pay and display, pay by phone or parking meter bays for free and without any time limit. In the areas of London mentioned, these entitlements do not apply. You cannot park on yellow lines during their period of application. You must pay to park in pay and display, pay by phone or parking meter bays and adhere to any maximum stay period.

There is detailed information on the TfL website:
TfL→Getting around→Transport accessibility, road users→Blue badge holders
where there is a downloadable guide for BB holders.

There's a comprehensive map entitled the *Blue Badge Parking Guide for London* showing the location of the BB spaces throughout central London. It doesn't, however, say how many spaces there are at each location. The map is available from:
PIE Enterprises Ltd *website:* www.thePIEguide.com *Tel:* 020 7952-0459
There is good practical advice in the Guide, and if you're planning to park in central London we recommend that you get a copy.
One of the ways to use BB spaces to best advantage is to park just after 14.00 in an area where the restrictions end at 18.00, and therefore you can stay for a good long time, if your BB gives you 4h of parking. A key practical issue is to find several BB spaces near each other, since if there is only one (or two) and they are occupied when you arrive, your chances of finding convenient parking are greatly reduced. We have made suggestions along these lines in the text in *Places of interest*.

Parking at or near your destination isn't always as difficult as people make out. If you can plan in advance, it is possible to reserve a BB space at some major sites and sights in London. Details are given elsewhere in the guide. Bear in mind that there are only a small number of such spaces.
Parking in the centre is much easier in the evening, and/or at weekends.

Note that BBs are issued throughout the EU, and are valid in the UK. **Disabled visitors from countries outside the EU will find that the entitlements and concessions do not legally apply.** This definitely makes it more difficult for the non-EU visitor who hires a car or who is a passenger in a friends car.
Disabled visitors from non-EU countries (without a BB) will, hopefully, be treated with understanding at some private CPs, but the legal position is that you cannot use public BB spaces unless you have the badge. The situation is made more difficult because of the level of abuse of the badges, and the need for enforcement. To justify concessions of all kinds, you may be asked for 'proof of disability', and carrying a copy of an appropriate doctors note or something similar, may help in some situations. It does not, however, alter the legal position over parking.

There are two kinds of penalty. Penalty Charge Notices are issued by councils while Fixed Penalty Notices are issued by the police. If your vehicle is missing when you return, call the TRACE service (*Tel:* 0845 206-8602, 24h) and someone will hopefully be able to tell you what has happened to it.

By taxi or minicab

If you cannot use the public transport system, and do not wish to drive around, taxis and/or minicabs are almost your only option.

Taxis

London taxis/cabs are of unique design, adapted from the hackney (horse-drawn) carriage of Victorian times. Black cabs are licenced by TfL. Taxi drivers all pass a challenging test called '*The Knowledge*' showing that they know central London's geography in great detail.

London taxis have a turning circle of just 8m (25ft), so that they can turn round in the narrow streets of the City. One story about this requirement is that it is based on the turning circle needed to get round the roundabout at the entrance to the (prestigious) Savoy hotel !

Taxis operate a meter on which the fare is recorded. Although cabs are relatively expensive as a way of getting around for individual travellers, they can offer great convenience, time saving, and reasonable accessibility. If the fare is shared between several people, the cost per person is proportionately reduced.

Taxis can be hailed (stopped) in the street, but while they are legally obliged to take a fare there are still a few drivers who seem to become temporarily 'blind', when they don't want to stop, possibly because they can't be bothered with the ramps etc. TfL provides Disability Equality training to all drivers of black cabs and the situation has certainly improved over the years.

All black taxicabs are wheelchair accessible in principle.

The newest cabs have the facility to fold back half the back seat, thus enabling a chair user to sit facing forwards. In practice, this is not something that has ever been offered to us when using a cab. The latest cabs have belts and restraints for a chair user. This, however can be a slightly mixed blessing, because it can take several minutes to fix all the necessary straps, and that may be time when the meter is ticking.

The design of the London cab is evolving, and is likely to change in the coming years, especially if some of the regulations are modified. New models may appear, offering more choice, although it will become even more of a lottery as to which cab drives past and/or is available.

The Mercedes Vito is a new larger cab with 6 rather than 5 seats. It has rear wheel steering to meet the turning circle requirement. The vehicle is 40cm longer and 22cm wider than the TX4, and so it's slightly easier to fit a wheelchair in and to face forwards. There's a specialist company providing these: **Mercedes London Taxis** *website:* www.merctaxi.com/Mercedes_London_Taxis/Home.html *Tel:* 020 7107-1646

We would simply comment here that the design has had a somewhat mixed reception within the black cab community.

The manufacturer of the conventional cab recently went into administration, but they have been taken over by a Chinese company, with the intention of continuing its manufacture and maintenance.

There are several rival designs, some of which provide better accommodation for disabled passengers. They are used in other English cities, but do not meet London's turning circle specification.

The conventional black cab can be particularly difficult for people with arthritis, as the main seat is some distance back, away from the door, and you have to bend down to get in. One American who wrote to us, said that it was undignified for an elderly gentleman to have to crawl on his knees to get to the seat, as he couldn't easily bend.

The newer vehicles have a fold-out seat on a hinge, which means that it can be unfolded, and will swing right outside the cab over the pavement. You can then sit down outside, and swing in while sitting on the seat. This may well help some, but cab drivers aren't necessarily quick to spot when you might need this facility. You also travel looking backwards, which doesn't suit everyone.

If you want to book a cab to go to the theatre, a museum or to the shops, there are three main companies. All offer the possibility of setting up an account for regular customers. They are:

Computer Cab

website: www.computercab.co.uk

Cash customers *Tel:* 020 7908-0207 Credit card customers *Tel:* 020 7432-1432
Taxicard holders *Tel:* 020 7763-5001

Dial-a-Cab

Owner Drivers Radio Taxi Service, Dial-a-Cab House, 39-47 East Road, N1 6AH
website: www.dialacab.co.uk *Tel:* 020 7251-0581
Cash customers *Tel:* 020 7253-5000 Credit card customers *Tel:* 020 7426-3420
With a fleet of over 2,500 taxis, Dial-a-Cab are the largest supplier of licensed taxis in Central London

Radio Taxicabs

website: www.radiotaxis.co.uk
 Cash or credit card customers *Tel:* 020 7272-0272

There are a few details to be aware of. If you order a cab by phone, there will be an initial charge to enable it to reach you.

If you're unlucky, the phone line to the cab company will be busy. One of us recently spent thirty minutes hanging on to the phone to a cab company being assured that 'we will answer as quickly as possible' (true) and that 'we'll be with you very soon' (a downright lie). The use of mobile phones can make all this easier, and if there are two or three people in the party, you can each phone a different company, and simply use the first call to get through. If it's raining, it'll be much much longer before you'll be able to get a cab, and you may have to be very patient and/or join the queue at a cab rank.

There's also a hassle, because even a 'booked' cab may not turn up. It is not guaranteed. One of our surveyors booked a ComCab to pick him up after a concert at the Barbican. None came and he was told that "no cab was available". As a result, he finished up pushing all the way to Waterloo.

As a casual user, there are limits to pre-booking. Houses, hotels and business premises are generally OK as a pick-up point, and restaurants are pretty much acceptable. When it comes to museums, theatres, cinemas and other places where you may need a cab, you will have to negotiate carefully. From the cab companies viewpoint, it is infuriating if you book a vehicle which isn't necessarily right outside the theatre door when you come out, and you take the nearest empty cab instead - ignoring the one you've booked. The different companies have slightly different approaches to all this. You are more likely to be able to pre-book if you pay by credit card, and you may well get through more quickly to an operator.

There's a useful service provided by **Black Taxi Tours of London**
website: www.blacktaxitours.co.uk *Tel:* 020 7935-9363
e-mail: info@blacktaxitours.co.uk who offer a two-hour tour for £130-140 (2012 prices). One great advantage of such a tour is that you can get into the squares, mews and back streets where no tour bus would be able to take you.

Minicabs

Minicabs are conventional cars or small people carriers, which are generally not wheelchair accessible (but see Addison Lee below). Because you can transfer sideways into a car seat, they will be easier for some people to use than a black taxi. They can only be booked at a minicab office, by phone or on the internet. You cannot stop or book one on the street. Minicabs have offered a variable level of service in the past. There is now a proper licensing system, making standards much more uniform. The TfL website has a searchable database of licensed minicab operators.

You need to check that the driver knows your destination before getting in, and that there is an agreed fare. People should normally sit in the back, and it's sensible to carry a mobile phone.

There are, unfortunately, unlicensed drivers around, operating illegally. Some may hang around outside stations or nightclubs. You are strongly advised NOT to use unlicensed minicabs, and ONLY to book through a licensed operator.

Addison Lee

35 William Road, NW1 3ER *Tel:* 020 7387-8888
website: www.addisonlee.com
Addison Lee is the largest minicab company in London, and you can book a cab either online or on the phone. At the time of writing, they don't mention on their website that they have **four accessible vehicles**, and are shortly to add to that number. Both Parcels and Private jets are mentioned, but not their wheelchair

accessible minicabs ! You can book one by ringing up, and may find that it is cheaper than using a conventional taxi for some journeys. It may also be more comfortable, as access is via a ramp at the back, rather than from the side.

Buses

A very constructive change in recent times, is that all London's buses, except for a tiny number on two heritage routes, are now in principle wheelchair accessible. They also 'kneel down' to make the step smaller when getting on and off, which is a very helpful feature for elderly people and/or disabled walkers. All buses have an extending ramp to facilitate a wheelchair user getting on board and all have a designated wheelchair space.

This reflects enormous progress.

A new bus design has been introduced which provides for an open platform at the back where people can jump on and off, and has a conductor on board, as well as being wheelchair 'accessible' like the others, see: *TfL→Corporate→Projects and schemes→New Bus for London*

All buses now have automatic voice announcements and visual information displays, telling you where the bus is eventually going, and the name of the next stop. The display is only visible from some seats.

Having said that, there's still some way to go before the system is really user-friendly, and we need to point out that:

- visitors to a city rarely use buses to get around, because the routeing is difficult to work out (see the picture/diagram for route 46, which is not untypical). The Underground lines are generally much easier to understand, and even Londoners who have lived in the city for decades, often do not know where the buses go, whereas they readily understand the tube
- for a wheelchair user, the number of different designs and layouts used inside the bus makes getting on and reversing against the vertical panel/support quite challenging
- the bus stop names are often of limited help to a visitor
- only relatively few mobility scooters have been approved for travelling on buses, see: *www.tfl.gov.uk/assets/downloads/tfl-guide-to-approved-mobility-scooters.pdf*
- buses can and do, accelerate quickly, brake and swerve (for example around mini-roundabouts and sharp corners), and this can be a challenge for both chair users and disabled walkers
- drivers often do not allow enough time for (generally older) disabled walkers to sit down before the bus pulls away
- in spite of improved driver training, not all drivers are equally helpful or knowledgeable. It is difficult for them sometimes, as they are on their own in a protected, boxed-in, somewhat isolated area, and are out of real contact with the human interactions among the passengers.

The first point we make in this list is very poorly understood. Our own experience of travelling widely is that in a 'strange'/new city, we would rarely try to use buses to get around. We would nearly always use the metro system (if there is one) or taxis - or even walk or wheel.

Bus route No 46

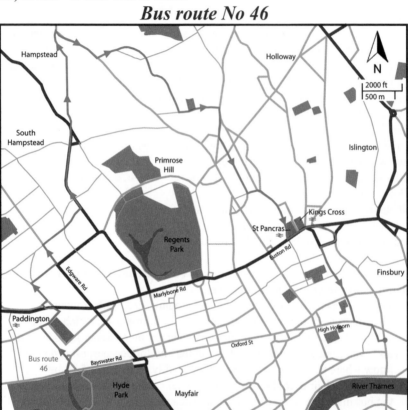

Bus No 46 does NOT go via a remotely direct route to get from Lancaster Gate on the Bayswater Road to Holborn and Farringdon Street, which would take it along Oxford Street and High Holborn. Instead it goes miles to the north via Hampstead ! Many of London's bus routes twist and turn in similar and (to the visitor) unforeseeable ways, and while there are good reasons for this, it doesn't make them easy to use.

There's a useful map of key central routes at:

www.londonmet.ac.uk/fms/MRSite/acad/lgri/summer-school/central_bus_map.pdf

We will mention again the bus 'spider' maps referred to under TfL publications. If they were more widely used, they would provide invaluable information. You will find a selection on our website.

Our experience some ten years ago was that only around 50% of the bus journeys attempted by our chair users on 'accessible' buses were actually successful. In 2011 this proportion had increased to some 65-70%, based on about fifty fairly random journeys by a chair user with an able-bodied friend. The journeys were mainly in central London, and the percentage would almost certainly be a bit lower for a solo wheelchair user.

The reasons why we didn't get on the bus were several. They included when:
- the bus couldn't get in the right position alongside the pavement;
- the ramp didn't work;
- the driver 'couldn't be bothered'; and,
- the space was already occupied by baby buggies, some loaded with shopping underneath - where it would have been very difficult (not to say slightly 'inhuman') to insist on priority for a chair user, thus effectively forcing one or more mums and babies off the bus.

Visitors do use the special sightseeing buses where the routes used are more easily understood. They are particularly attractive if you can climb up to the open deck on top. The view available to the passengers on the lower deck is much more restricted, and someone using the wheelchair space is on that deck and is facing backwards.

Some are circular hop-on hop-off routes:
- **The Big Bus Company** offers two main routes, with a pick-up link to St Pancras, see *www.bigbustours.com/eng/london*
- **The Original London Sightseeing Tour** highlights the accessibility of its hop-on hop-off tour options. They offer three routes, each lasting less than 2 hours from The Original London Visitor Centre, 17-19 Cockspur Street, Trafalgar Square SW1Y 5BL *Tel:* 020 7389-5040

  website: www.theoriginaltour.com *e-mail:* info@theoriginaltour.com

Note that there's an excellent itinerary on the website *London for free* under *www.londonforfree.net/outdoors/bustour/bustour.shtml* which sets out an interesting route which you can follow using conventional buses, and you will only need to get a TfL Oyster card. A full day's travelling by bus currently costs less than £5.

The underground (tube)

Because the system is old, and with deep tunnels in many places, there are steps and escalators at the majority of stations.

The London Underground has come a long way since the original proposal in 1845 of 'putting trains in drains' to reduce road congestion. This was extraordinary, as the first passenger steam service had only started in 1830, and it seems that pollution in the form of dirt and noise wasn't considered to be much of a barrier in those far off days !

The first railways were just sub-surface (as are some lines now). Later in the early 1900s, tunnelling techniques improved, and together with the possibility of using electric traction, the deeper lines became possible.

The current system consists of ten tube lines, six of which have deep sections in central London, and four of which run sub-surface, going through or around the centre. The deep tubes use smaller carriages than the sub-surface lines.

The lines are based on the routes followed by a range of privately owned companies dating from Victorian times. Some of the companies combined with others, or sold the infrastructure to someone else.

This complex history results in some routes where the station platforms are shared between the smaller deep tube trains and the larger, higher sub-surface carriages.

Thus (for example) at Acton Town and Hammersmith, there is a step down into the Piccadilly line trains and a large step up into the District line carriages from the shared platform.

Developments have included extensions to the Central line, the opening of the Victoria line and, for the Millennium, the building of the **Jubilee line extension (JLE).**

The JLE is of particular importance, since it is the only truly accessible part of the Underground, running between Westminster and Stratford. There are lifts at each station, and the gap from the platform to the train is less than 8.5cm and the step is less than 5cm. Thus most electric chair users could/would be able to cope with getting on and off.

Recently, some stations have had 'humps' installed, while others have portable ramps available, to facilitate people in chairs getting on and off.

General information

If you need help, ask one of the staff. All TfL staff have regular training on how to assist disabled passengers. If necessary, they will help you find a seat. They will then, hopefully, call ahead to your destination or interchange stations, and arrange for a member of staff to meet and assist you there too.

There are now more than 250 wide-aisle automatic ticket gates at the stations, so you don't have to try to squeeze through the standard barriers if that's a problem.

NOTE THAT if you arrive at a step-free station, and a lift is broken, talk to the staff about how best to get to your destination. If there is a single accessible bus journey from the next step-free station, then you will be advised to take that route. If there is not, TfL are obliged to order you a taxi, at their expense. This also applies to certain other service interruptions.

All trains have clearly marked priority seating for older or disabled passengers next to doors.

Pregnant women can wear a 'Baby on board' badge to let other passengers know they may need a seat. Badges are available from TfL Customer Service *Tel:* 0343 222-1234 or *e-mail:* babyonboard@tfl.gov.uk.

Most trains have automatic voice announcements and visual information displays, telling you where the train is going, and the name of the next stop.

Note that Assistance Dogs which have been specifically trained in how to use escalators (and carry the appropriate identification) are now able to use escalators.

Most stations have a vertical step into the train which may be as high as 12 inches (300mm). There may also be a gap between the train and the platform, and at a few stations the platform is curved, resulting in a variable size gap between the train doors and the platform edge.

Underground stations with step-free access from pavement to platform
The best information source will be the latest edition of the TfL *Step Free Tube Guide* (SFTG), which is a comprehensive map and description of both the 'accessible' and accessible stations. The description is, of necessity, highly abbreviated, and the alphabetical listing makes it quite difficult to use when trying to work out the best way to go, because the map and descriptions are on the opposite sides of a huge sheet of folded paper measuring 40x130cm.
If you're going to use the SFTG, we suggest that you order at least two copies, as the printed information is on both sides. With two of them (and a big flat surface to lay them out on) it's easier to get to the information you need.
It is such an important presentation of data that it would be helpful if it were available in more than one form, for example:
* with an 'along the line' listing rather than it just being alphabetical; and,
* in booklet form for the station descriptions rather than on the back of the map in twelve double-folded segments.

In addition, there are some interchange stations where long distances up to 500m are involved in changing trains, and at some the routes to be taken are not well signed. We include a brief list of some those with the biggest distances.
Note that TfL will only post copies to a UK address.

The original step-free map was published in the 1996 edition of *Access in London*. In 2002, SCOPE enhanced its presentation for London Transport, and it is now part of the standard information available from TfL. It is continually being edited, but (in our view) the latest version has become over-complicated, particularly for a first-time visitor.
The one used during the Olympics incorporated the *Overground* lines (which has very few links to 'accessible' tube stations) and it showed the places where ramps can be provided.
The editors seem to have forgotten that one of the beauties of Harry Beck's iconic Underground map developed in the 1930s, was/is its essential simplicity.
We have included a map showing the 'accessible' stations in the centre, including information about whether the 'accessibility' is dependent on a portable ramp, or a platform hump. They are all step-free from pavement to platform.

It is in this context that we hope that our parallel presentation of the 2012/13 data on a line-by-line basis, with some commentary, may help people use both the iconic Underground map and the SFTG version more easily.
We have not attempted here to present one vital piece of information about the 'accessible' stations, and that is "How do you get from street to platform ?". You

may be dependent on a single lift, or possibly on as many as three sequential lifts, as at Kings Cross/St Pancras, where all three have to be working. You may be dependent on a platform stairlift, and therefore on staff assistance. There may be ramped access to the platform, but you may depend on staff help to get an access gate opened.

We intend to put the basic information (as it is here) on our website, and to enhance it with a description of how to get from street to platform for all the 'accessible' stations. We will also include updated information during 2014 /15, and as we have said elsewhere, if you want a printed copy of this, please let us know.

We are including only the 'accessible' stations where there is access in both directions, and are using the same descriptive notation that TfL uses for defining how big the step is for getting on or off the train, and for how big the horizontal gap is.

The size of the step up/down to the train car is:

The horizontal gap to get in/out of the train car is:

(green circle)   0-5cm (0-2in)
(amber circle)   5-12cm (2-4.7in)
(red circle)   Over 12cm (4.7in)

A   0-8.5cm (0-3.3in)
B   8.5-18cm (3.3-7in)
C   Over 18cm (7in)

Thus the ideal requirement for disabled travellers, and particularly for chair users and for mums with buggies, is for stations with (**green** A).

Note that as this book is being written, a new category of step-free transfer from platform to train and vice versa is being introduced. This involves the provision of platform 'humps' which raise the platform height by a few cm along the length of a single car/carriage, making the transfer (**green** A) to and from that car.
We are using a different colour in the text to distinguish the information about humps where it is integrated into the line-by-line commentary, as it is quite complicated.

Humps are a very neat and relatively inexpensive solution to the problem caused by the difference of height between the platform and the train carriage is the provision of raised section along part of the platform length with a ramp at each end. It only works where there is a step up from the platform into the train.

It is essential to have a consistent and well explained policy relating to where these humps are provided, and about which section of the platform length is used. What has happened so far (by 2012/13) is a bit of a mixture !

The (**green** A) criteria are ONLY to be found at the DLR stations (described separately), and on the **JLE**.

The (**green** A) classification awarded on the current TfL map to the four Victoria line stations, and elsewhere on the maps in the trains themselves, because there are platform humps. We regret this 'award', and think that in spite of any complexity, there should be a clear distinction between where there is a platform hump and where the whole platform is (green A).

There are only a tiny number of 'accessible' stations in and near the centre. From the Bank and Tower Gateway, the DLR lines go to Canary Wharf, Greenwich, Lewisham, Beckton, Woolwich Arsenal, Beckton and Stratford. ALL the DLR stations are classified as (**green** A).

The JLE which is also classified as (green A) runs from Stratford and West Ham in the east, past the O2/Dome at North Greenwich, through Canary Wharf and via London Bridge and Waterloo, to Westminster. The Jubilee line then goes to Green Park and Kings Cross/St Pancras. Blackfrairs is 'accessible'. **These central stations do provide immensely useful opportunities for visitors,** particularly if used in conjunction with buses to go short distances from (for example) Westminster, Green Park, or Waterloo.

Accessible stations in central London 2012

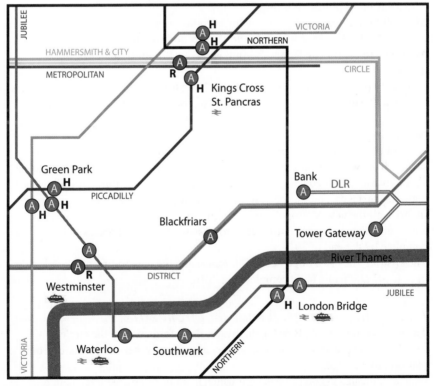

≋ Connection with National Rail	**H** Platform hump covering only 1 or 2 cars
🚢 Connection with River boats	**R** A portable ramp is available to facilitate transfer

While in general the bus route system is challenging for most people (both visitors and suburban residents) it is often possible to use just one route with relative ease.

Because the linkages and caveats are so complex, we suggest that you concentrate on the JLE stations, on the links with the DLR, and just a few other west London links like those on the Piccadilly line. If you can manage the big steps, the District line in from Richmond and Wimbledon in the west, and from Upminster in the east can be particularly useful, especially, now, with the provision of ramps at a good number of the outer stations. The only central one with ramps is Westminster.

One thing we discovered when looking into this and when visiting stations, is that the trains on different lines have different numbers of cars/carriages. On the Piccadilly and Northern lines there are 6, on the Bakerloo and Jubilee there are 7, while on the Central, Victoria and Metropolitan lines there are 8. The new trains on the H&C, Circle and District lines will have 7 cars.

This affects where it is sensible to put a hump, and how long it needs to be.

The location of platform humps:

Metropolitan (8 cars, with the new lower trains) - **cars 4 and 5, but the humps cover only the 3rd door of car 4, and the 1st door of car 5**

Northern (6 cars) - **car 5 northbound, car 2 southbound, for both pairs of doors**

Piccadilly (6 cars) - **car 5 eastbound, car 2 westbound, for both pairs of doors**

Victoria (8 cars) - **cars 4 and 5 in each case, for both pairs of centre doors.**

New trains

A major change that is underway is the introduction of new trains on the sub-surface lines which makes the step into the cars much smaller, although there's a slightly variable horizontal gap. The new trains also include through walkways between carriages, and for the first time on the tube, air conditioning.

In 2013, all the new Metropolitan line trains are in service. Those on the H&C and Circle lines are being introduced progressively, and the process will be complete by the end of 2014.

The District line has a large fleet of 80 trains, and the new rolling stock will be introduced gradually, to be completed in 2016.

Line by line listings. A snapshot from 2012/13

The notation (**colour** A, B or C), duplicates the information in the circles on the SFTG, so (**green** A) is the best, and means virtually step-free transfer from platform to carriage.

[Name] indicates the other lines with which there is a step-free interchange.

Humps are listed, which provide (**green** A) transfer from train car to platform only from a particular car/cars. Stations where portable ramps are available are shown by **R**.

Bakerloo

The line was opened in 1906 and runs from central London northwards. It has 25 stations, 15 of which are deep underground. The trains have 7 cars.
It has only three 'accessible' stations, all of which link with the *Overground*.
'Accessible' stations
Harrow & Wealdstone (red A) [NR] [*Overground*]
Wembley Central (red B) [*Overground*]
Willesden Junction (red B) [*Overground*]
There are useful step-free platform to platform transfers possible at Baker Street (to and from the Jubilee line) and at Oxford Circus (to and from the Victoria line).
With *Crossrail*, Paddington will become 'accessible'.

Central

The Central line has been extended in both directions. Its original route in the late 1890s was from Shepherds Bush to Liverpool Street, and the line was among the first to use electric locomotives. Of the 49 stations, 20 are deep underground. The trains have 8 cars.

There are only 5 'accessible' stations, four of them way out in the northeast suburbs (towards Epping). The fifth is the Stratford interchange.
'Accessible' stations
Epping (green C) **R** with 450m to get from platform to platform. See the SFTG.
Woodford (amber B)
Roding Valley (red C) with 520m to get from platform to platform. See the SFTG.
Hainault (amber C) **R**
Stratford (red C) **R** [DLR] [JLE][NR] A very large interchange station.
Four more stations in the Epping/Woodford area are 'accessible' in one direction only.
At Mile End (with **R**) and Ealing Broadway, useful line to line interchange is possible.
There will be additional 'accessible' stations when *Crossrail* opens in 2018, including Tottenham Court Road, Bond Street and Ealing Broadway.
Greenford station is due to have an inclined lift by 2015.

Circle

This sub-surface line is now a loop running from Edgware Road round the 'old' Circle, and past Edgware Road to Hammersmith. There are 36 stations. Most of the route, and all of the stations, are shared by the District, H&C and/ or Metropolitan lines.

There are just 4 stations which are 'accessible', but these provide key central links.

ALL the stations have really big steps to get up into the train carriage. This will change with the introduction of new 7 car trains in 2013-14.

'Accessible' stations

Westminster (red C) R [JLE]

Blackfriars (red A) [NR]

Kings Cross/St Pancras R (red A) [Northern] [Piccadilly] [Victoria] [NR] Some interchanges involve >500m.

Hammersmith (red A) R [District] [Piccadilly] It is 520m between the two stations. See the SFTG.

Liverpool Street **(red A)** and Euston Square **(red A)** are 'accessible' in one direction only.

District

This sub-surface line runs through the central area in shallow cut-and-cover tunnels. It has branches to Ealing, Richmond and Wimbledon in the south and west, and then a line going a long way east, to Upminster. It has some 60 stations.

It provides some key 'accessible' linkages, and several stations with portable ramps.

There are important interchanges at Richmond, Wimbledon, Earls Court, Westminster, Blackfrairs and West Ham.

It has 18 'accessible' stations, but ALL have a big step to get up into the train carriage. This will change as new lower trains are introduced in 2014-16.

'Accessible' stations

Acton Town (red B) [Piccadilly]

Richmond (red A) R [*Overground*] [NR]

Kew Gardens (red A) R and note the need to find the correct station entrance

Hammersmith [red A] [Circle] [H&C] [Piccadilly] with a bus station immediately above, but some 500m to the H&C station.

Wimbledon (red A) **R** [NR] [Tramlink]
Southfields (red A) **R**
Fulham Broadway (red A) **R**
Kensington Olympia (red A) [*Overground*] open part time only.
Earls Court (red B) **R** [Piccadilly]
Westminster (red C) **R** [JLE] [river boats]
Blackfriars (red A) [NR]
West Ham (red A) **R** [DLR] [JLE]
East Ham (red A) **R**
Barking (red A) [NR]
Upney (red A) **R**
Dagenham Heathway (red A)
Elm Park (red A)
Upminster (red A) [NR]

Ealing Broadway [line interchange with the Central and NR] will hopefully become an 'accessible' station after the opening of *Crossrail* in 2018.

Hammersmith & City (H&C)
A sub-surface line which includes the oldest part of the Underground system, dating back to the 1860s when the trains had steam locomotives.
ALL the stations have a big step to get up into the train carriage. This will change as new lower 7 car trains are introduced in 2013-14.
'Accessible' stations
Hammersmith (red A) **R** [District] [Piccadilly] with 520m and a road crossing between the stations.
Kings Cross/St Pancras (red A) **R** [Northern] [Piccadilly] [Victoria] is a big station.
West Ham (red A) **R** [DLR]
East Ham (red A) **R**
Barking (red A) [*Overground*] [NR]

Liverpool Street (red A) and Euston Square (red A) are 'accessible' in one direction only.

Jubilee (including the JLE)
From 1979 until 1999 the line ran from Stanmore to Charing Cross. Then the Jubilee Line Extension (JLE) was opened for the Millennium. **This is the only section of the tube providing step-free gap-free access from platform to car along the whole of the train.** It runs from Stratford to Westminster providing an enormous boost to accessibility. The line has 27 stations, 16 of which are listed below. Each train has 7 cars.

Accessible and 'accessible' stations
ALL the stations from Stratford to Westminster are accessible (**green A**), and they are:
Stratford [Central] [DLR] [JLE/Jubilee] [NR]
West Ham [District] [DLR]
Canning Town
North Greenwich (for the O2/Dome),
Canary Wharf [DLR 300m]
Canada Water [*Overground*]
Bermondsey
London Bridge [Northern with a 500m long interchange at street level] [NR]
Southwark
Waterloo [NR]
Westminster [Circle] [District]
Green Park [Piccadilly] [Victoria] **towards Stanmore, there's a hump covering only half of the 5th and 6th cars, ie one set of double doors in each car. Towards Stratford, the hump covers the 2nd car and the front half of the 3rd**
Kilburn (red A) and the step is up to get off the train.
Wembley Park for Wembley Stadium (**green B**) [Metropolitan]. The track and platform aren't exactly parallel, so the size of the step up varies, depending on which car you are in. Towards Stanmore the step is minimal (and <5cm) from the rear car, while towards Stratford you take the front car for the same reason
Kingsbury (green A)
Stanmore (red B) and there's a long ramp up to the CP and street.

Note that both Baker Street and Finchley Road have step-free interchanges between platforms for trains in the same direction and **humps are planned at Baker Street.**

Metropolitan
The line is sub-surface in the centre, and goes a long way out in the northwest.
It currently runs from Aldgate to Amersham, with branches to Uxbridge,
Watford and Chesham. It has 34 stations, 9 of which are 'accessible'.
It includes the route of the old Metropolitan Railway between Paddington and
Farringdon which was the first underground railway in the world, opened in
1863.
It is now operated with new lower trains with 8 cars and 'through' carriages
with the additional advantage of air conditioning.
**All the 'accessible' stations used to have a big step to get up into the train
carriage, but this has been substantially reduced with the new trains.**
'Accessible' stations
Chesham (green C)
Chalfont & Latimer (green A) [NR]
Chorleywood (green A) [NR]
Pinner (green A)
Uxbridge (red A) [Piccadilly]
Hillingdon (red B) [Piccadilly]
Wembley Park (green A) [Jubilee]
Kings Cross/St Pancras (green A) [Circle] [H&C] [Northern] [Piccadilly]
[Victoria]
Farringdon (green C) [NR including *Thameslink*]

Amersham (green A) and Rickmansworth (green C) are 'accessible' in one
direction only, as are Ruislip (red B) [Piccadilly], Euston Square (green A)
and Liverpool Street (green A). Farringdon will become a big interchange
when *Crossrail* is opened.

Northern

The line has quite a complicated history, and the current arrangement with two northern branches, two central branches and the southern 'tail', reflects its development from three separate companies that were combined in the 1920s and 30s. The trains have 7 cars.

There are 50 stations on the line, 36 of them are deep underground. 10 are 'accessible'.

The branch through the West End, including Leicester Square has no 'accessible' stations, while the City branch has only London Bridge and Kings Cross/St Pancras.

'Accessible' stations

Morden (red A) **R**

London Bridge has humps for the 2nd car southbound and the 5th car northbound [JLE] [NR]

Kings Cross/St Pancras has humps for the 2nd car southbound and the 5th car northbound [Circle] [Piccadilly] [Victoria] [NR] [*Eurostar*]

Golders Green (red B) **and humps are planned**

Hendon Central has humps for the 2nd car southbound and the 5th car northbound

Edgware all (red A) has humps for the 2nd car southbound and the 5th car on arrival BUT on two of the platforms they are slightly misplaced covering only one pair of double doors in the car

Finchley Central (red A) **R**

West Finchley (green B)

Woodside Park (red B) **and humps are planned**

High Barnet (red A) **and humps are planned**

Both Stockwell and Euston have no links to the surface but useful step-free links with the Victoria line, going in the same direction. **Euston has humps for the 2nd car southbound and the 5th car northbound. Humps are planned for both Stockwell and Kennington.**

Elephant & Castle and Borough, on the City branch, are 'accessible' in one direction only.

Piccadilly

The line dates back to the early 1900s, but its main developments, westwards to Hounslow and northwards to Cockfosters, took place in the 1930s. It has 53 stations, of which 25 are deep underground. The trains have 6 cars.

There are two branches in the west, including one to Heathrow Airport. It passes eastwards through the centre and then turns north. It has 11 'accessible' stations, and some key interchanges at Hammersmith, Earls Court, Green Park and Kings Cross/St Pancras.

'Accessible' stations

Heathrow Terminal 5 (green B) along the whole length of the platform
Heathrow Terminals 1/2/3 and 4 have humps for the 2nd and 5th cars.
The 2nd for getting off the train, and the 5th for getting on. We are told that these will shortly be properly signed.

Hounslow West has a hump for the 2nd car (just) westwards and for the 5th car east. To reach the road level above, there's a staff operated platform stairlift.

Hounslow East (amber A)

Uxbridge (red B)

Hillingdon (red B)

Sudbury Town (red B)

Acton Town (red C) [District] and the car is below the platform level

Hammersmith (red B) [Circle] [District] [H&C] and the car is below the platform level. There's a bus station immediately above. It's 520m to the H&C station.

Earls Court Hump for the 2nd car westwards and the 5th car east [District]

Green Park Hump for the 2nd car west, and the 5th car east [Jubilee] [Victoria]

Kings Cross/St Pancras Hump for the 2nd car west and for the 5th car east/north

Caledonian Road (red A) **R and a hump is planned**

Oakwood Hump for the 2nd car west and for the 5th car north

At Finsbury Park there is a step-free interchange with the Victoria line for trains in the same direction with **a hump for the 2nd car west and the 5th car north.**

Victoria

The line opened towards the end of the 1960s to make links between NR stations.

Several existing underground stations were rearranged to allow for cross-platform interchange with the new line. Particularly significant is the direct same-level interchange with the Bakerloo line at Oxford Circus.

There are 16 stations, only 4 of which are 'accessible', although the one at Victoria is due to become 'accessible' in 2018. The trains have 8 cars.

Platform humps have been installed on all the stations except Pimlico, ALL covering the two middle cars (the 4th and 5th) making it the same in each direction.

'Accessible' stations

Brixton has a platform hump covering the 4th and 5th cars

Green Park has a platform hump covering the 4th and 5th cars

Kings Cross/St Pancras has a platform hump covering the 4th and 5th cars

Tottenham Hale has a platform hump covering the 4th and 5th cars

At Stockwell there is an interchange with Northern line trains going in the same direction
and at Euston (with the City branch).

There are also useful step-free platform to platform interchanges at Oxford Circus, Euston Square and Finsbury Park.

Big interchange stations

A number of interchange stations are very large, often involving transfer distances of more than 500m and routes that are not necessarily well signed. These include:

*   virtually all the links with main line train stations, and at the Heathrow terminals
*   Canary Wharf (DLR/JLE)
*   Green Park (Jubilee/Piccadilly)
*   Kings Cross/St Pancras (with links between six underground lines)
*   Hammersmith (Distict and Piccadilly/Circle and H&C)
*   London Bridge (JLE/Northern)
*   Stratford

When *Crossrail* has been completed, it is anticipated that this list will be added:

*   Bond Street
*   Farringdon/Barbican
*   Liverpool Street/Moorgate
*   Tottenham Court Road
*   Whitechapel

Central tube stations due to be made 'accessible'

Date	Station	Further information
2016	Vauxhall [Victoria]	With lift access to the NR station above
	Whitechapel [**District & Metropolitan**] [*Overground*]	a *Crossrail* station
	Tower Hill [Circle & **District**]	
2017	Bond Street [**Central & Jubilee**]	a *Crossrail* station
	Tottenham Court Road [**Central & Northern**]	a *Crossrail* station
2018/9	Victoria [Victoria]	
	Paddington [**Bakerloo**]	part of *Crossrail*
	Barbican [**District, H&C & Metropolitan**]	part of *Crossrail* via Farringdon station

Other tube and *Overground* stations that are due to become 'accessible'

2013	Denmark Hill	*Overground* (completed)
2014	Brockley and Honor Oak Park	*Overground*
2015	Blackhorse Road and Hampstead Heath Kensal Rise and New Cross Gate Queens Road, Peckham South Tottenham and West Hampstead	*Overground*
	Greenford [**Central**]	Using an inclined lift alongside the escalators
2016	Finsbury Park [**Piccadilly &** Victoria]	
	Bromley-by-Bow [**District & Metropolitan**]	
2017	Watford Junction and associated stations	via the Croxley Rail Link
2019	Ealing Broadway [**Central & District**]	a *Crossrail* station
2020/21	Nine Elms and Battersea	a proposed Northern line extension

Information taken from *Your accessible transport network*   TfL December 2012

Looking into the future

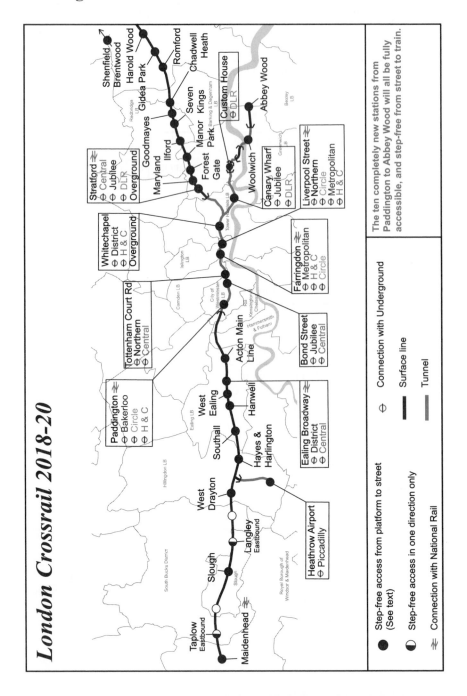

London Crossrail 2018-20

Crossrail

London's biggest infrastructure project is the development of *Crossrail*. This will
link west and east London and make several more central stations 'accessible'
with new links to and from various underground lines.

In particular it will have a link to Heathrow, and improve access into the centre
from both Acton and Ealing in the west. In the east there will be two lines, both
coming in to Whitechapel. One goes to Canary Wharf and Woolwich, and the
other to Stratford, Ilford, Romford and Shenfield.

Various key stations will be completely rebuilt, such as those at Bond Street
and Tottenham Court Road, and all the interchange lines there will become
'accessible'.

One major limitation is that at all the stations from Maidenhead to Acton, and
for those from Stratford to Harold Wood and Shenfield are only 'accessible',
since to get from platform to train a ramp is needed to bypass the substantial step
involved. We have it on good authority that it isn't possible to re-engineer the
platforms, or even to provide platform humps (as on the tube), because of the
mixed railway rolling stock using the lines including freight trains, which have
different shapes, sizes and specifications.

**The ten new stations, most of them in the tunnels, from Paddington through
to Whitechapel and then on to Abbey Wood, as well as the station at
Heathrow, will all be fully accessible from pavement to train.** Ramps should
not be needed for getting on and off, as the platform will be at the same height as
the train carriage. No other railway rolling stock will use these stations.

The tube stations which are linked, will nearly all have 'accessible' step-free
routes to and from *Crossrail* and to the Underground platforms, as shown,
including Ealing Broadway, Paddington (but excluding the District line), Bond
Street, Tottenham Court Road, Farringdon, Liverpool Street (but excluding the
Central line), Whitechapel, Stratford, Canary Wharf and Custom House. At some
of these stations, long distances of >500m may be involved in making transfers.
Some Underground platforms may have humps to facilitate transfer to and from
the train carriage.

The TfL programme for making more tube and *Overground* stations 'accessible'
is summarised in the Table on an earlier page.

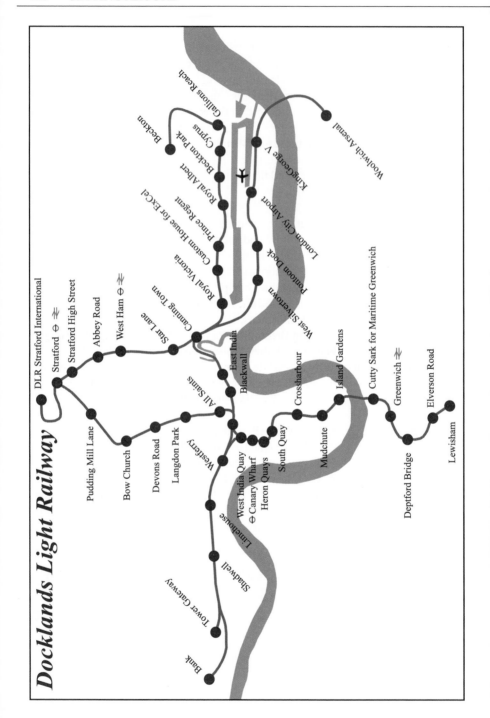

Docklands Light Railway

Docklands Light Railway (DLR)

website: www.dlr.co.uk or use the TfL site

The DLR and Tramlink are London's only fully accessible transport systems. The DLR links Lewisham and Greenwich, to Stratford, Tower Gateway or to the Bank. An extension goes on the north side of the docks past the ExCel Centre to Beckton, which is some 10km east from the centre. Another branch goes on the south side of the docks via London City Airport and then across the river to Woolwich Arsenal. The extent of the DLR is shown on the map, and it includes some important destinations. Links to other parts of the TfL system are quite limited and the key ones are shown on the map.

All the stations have step-free access with a lift or ramp from street to platform AND there is only a tiny step into the carriage. The cars have special spaces for a chair user, and most electric chair users would be able to manage getting on and off.

The railway has been built with some quite tight curves, and with some steepish gradients. As a result, the ride can be a bit rough on certain sections. Our advice is simply to 'hang on tight' and you'll be OK, but it's best to be prepared for a few jerks and turns !

NOTE THAT many of the DLR stations are unstaffed, and the trains have no driver. They do, however have a 'train captain' who can provide advice and assistance. After pressing the 'Help' button on the platform, you may have to wait a bit for any assistance.

During the early years of operation, there were some problems with the serviceability of the lifts, but the situation seems to have improved considerably. As the line runs at a high level over much of its length, the lifts are essential as you might otherwise have to manage anything up to 60 or 80 steps.

If you want to make enquiries about the serviceability of lifts at DLR stations you want to use on a particular day, ring 020 7363-9700 which is DLR customer service. Use option 4 to speak to a person. They can check with the control room about whether the lifts are working at particular stations. Out of office hours, the number to ring is 0843 222-1234.

If you are unlucky enough to encounter a non-operational lift, from most DLR stations the trick is to go on to the next station, and use the lifts there to come back to the station where you want to get off, using the 'other' lift from the opposite platform. Unfortunately this doesn't work where there is a central island platform, and only the one (non-functional) lift !

The Overground

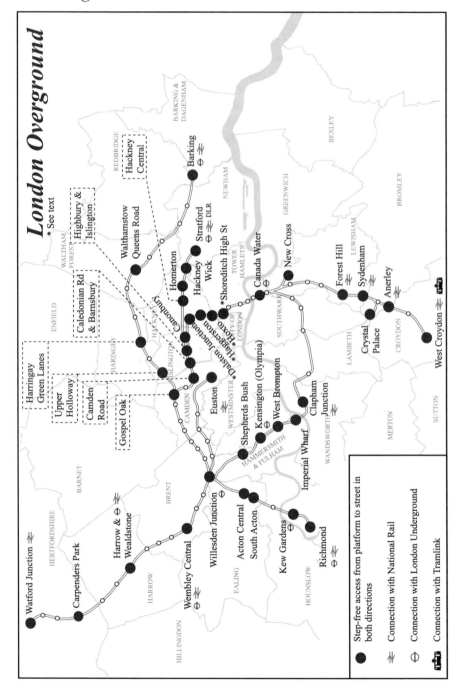

The *Overground* is a new network of suburban rail services, managed by TfL. It is based mainly on old/pre-existing railway lines together with some extensions. **The routes and the 'accessible' stations are shown on the map.**
The *Overground* goes to/from Euston, Stratford and Watford, and in the south to Clapham Junction, Richmond and to West Croydon. In the east it goes to Barking. There are a number of links to NR services, and just a few to the Underground. At Canada Water it links with the JLE.
All the trains have a large step to get into the carriage from the platform, and our map highlights the stations which are step-free from the street to the platform. A chair user is then likely to need a ramp (and staff help) to get on and off the train. To ensure assistance is available, you are asked to contact the Help Line *Tel:* 0845 601-4867 (open 09:00 to 17:00 on weekdays) at least 24 hours before you travel. TfL is trying to move to a 'turn up and go' service, and as all the stations are staffed, you should be able to do this.
The network is generally much less crowded than the tube, and than some NR services, and if it runs near where you want to go, it can be really useful.

Using the river

Taking a river trip is one of the best and most relaxed ways of seeing central London. You can go from Westminster, the London Eye or Embankment piers via the Tower to Greenwich and the basic route would take in many of London's more interesting sights. It is highly recommended. You can use the river to get to the O2/Dome.
London River Services, Tower Pier, Lower Thames Street, EC3N 4DT
Tel: 020 7941-2400 *e-mail:* enquiries@tfl-river.co.uk
As with other parts of London's transport system, the accessibility of the various boats which provide both scheduled riverbus services and river trips for tourists, has improved considerably in recent years.
All the piers are wheelchair accessible, but note that the slope down from the river embankment is dependent on the state of the tide and at low tide it can be quite steep. Not all of the boats are accessible, though many/most are. You need to check. Chair users may have only a very limited space on the boat in which they can 'park', but the view/s should be good.

TfL riverbuses go regularly from the Embankment pier (across the Jubilee pedestrian bridges from the Festival Hall and the South Bank) via the Tower and Greenwich to Woolwich Arsenal. These services are operated by *Thames Clippers* all of whose boats are wheelchair accessible and have an **accessible toilet**.
Most of the *City Cruise* tourist boats operating from Westminster Pier, and going via the Tower to Greenwich are wheelchair accessible, but you need to check at the ticket office.
There are also services from the Festival Pier on the South Bank, and from Embankment Pier.

The boats which operate services to Putney, to Richmond and to Hampton Court are older, and have access barriers - which we have not specifically checked out by visit. We don't think that they are readily wheelchair accessible..

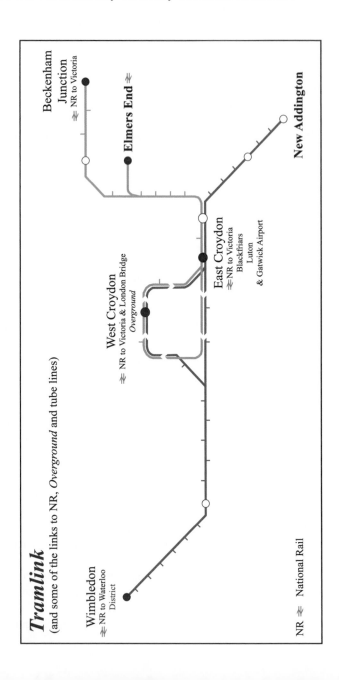

Tramlink

website: www.tfl.gov.uk at the bottom of the Home page see *Getting around London/Trams*

unofficial website: www.tramlink.co.uk

This is an extensive system in south London, using modern and fully accessible trams.

There's a central loop around Croydon (see the map), and then branches going both east and west through London's southern suburbs. These go eastwards to New Addington, Elmers End or Beckenham, or westwards to Wimbledon via Mitcham.

The trams provide step-free access, equivalent to (green A) on the underground, and are much easier for a wheelchair user or disabled walker to get on and off than a bus.

There is a reasonably generous wheelchair space in each car, which can also be used by people travelling with young children in buggies, although chair users have priority. The trams tend to accelerate and brake more smoothly than buses which makes for a more comfortable ride.

Since ALL the stations on the 28km length of the tramway are accessible, we have only included the names of the key junctions. Detailed maps are readily available.

Much of the route goes through suburban south London, making it of considerable value to local residents. Croydon has extensive shopping facilities, and the Fairfield Halls and the Clocktower arts centre. Both East Croydon NR station, and Wimbledon NR and tube stations are fully 'accessible', providing a quick way of getting to and from central London.

For information about Tramlink, ring the central TfL call centre *Tel:* 0843 222-1234 *Textphone:* 020 7918-3015 *website:* www.tfl.gov.uk. There are maps on the website which can be downloaded. Ring TfL and they'll send you a map and details, and the route is shown in the NR map *London connections.*

Services which are primarily for London residents

The principal additional improvements in the transport system for disabled residents in London have been the provision of **Dial-a-Ride** services, the use of the **Taxicard** and the availability of the **Freedom Pass**. All have gone through changes, some due to cuts in funding, and threatened cuts. In recent years, the provisions have varied from borough to
borough, and from year to year. **Some schemes have tight limitations on the number of journeys any individual can make, although the Freedom Pass is unlimited**. Dial-a-Ride is administered by TfL and operated by a single company. The Taxicard and Freedom Passes are issued by the different London Boroughs. If you have a hassle, and want advice about any of these services, the best place to go is TfA.

Dial-a-Ride (DAR)

DAR is a membership scheme run by TfL. It provides a bookable door-to-door service for disabled and older London residents who have difficulties using public transport. It can also be used by visitors who are visiting London as long as they can show they are a member of a similar door to door service where they live. The service uses accessible minibuses or other appropriate vehicles (depending on the needs of the user), and is free of charge.

You can get more information from:

Dial-a-Ride, Progress House, 5 Mandela Way, SE1 5SS

Tel: 0845 999-1999 or 020 7309-8900 if you don't want to use the 0845 number

e-mail: DAR@tfl.gov.uk   (or you can contact TfA)

The idea is excellent. You can ring up and they will organise a driver to take you shopping, to visit friends or to go to church, either alone or with companions. DAR can be used by people living in sheltered housing, where several people may want to go to the same destination, either on a regular basis or for one-off outings. The concept is fine, although it requires a little organisation to make use of the service. It inevitably has limited capacity, and may get more requests than it can fulfill. The timing of both pick-up and arrival at your destination cannot be precise. For pick-up, for example, DAR allow a 15 minute period on either side of the booked time, so you need to be ready to leave early. En route to your destination your vehicle may pick-up other passengers.

In some places, parts of the day will be busier than others, and you may have to be flexible about when you travel.

The Call Centre is open Monday to Friday, 9am – 4pm and, particularly in the mornings, it can be difficult to get through, so prepare to be both patient and persistent.

You are entitled to take a carer or someone to help you if there is space in the vehicle. Let DAR know that you want to bring someone when you book your trip.

According to TfL, DAR should be able to take you within a five mile radius of your home. However TfA reports that in practice this does not often happen – and it is only requests for very local trips that are generally being accepted.

If you want to travel further, then you may be able to get DAR to drop you at an accessible station or bus stop to continue your journey.

Please feel free to contact TfA for more advice or information.

Taxicard
London Councils TEC Taxicard
59½ Southwark Street, SE1 0AL *Tel:* 020 7934-9791
website: www.londoncouncils.gov.uk → services → taxicard
e-mail: taxicard@londoncouncils.gov.uk

The Taxicard Scheme is funded by the 32 London boroughs and by the Mayor of London. It aims to provide door-to-door transport for disabled and older people who have mobility impairments and have difficulty in using public transport.

The service is administered by individual London Councils, and is operated by Computer Cab. You can request an application form by phone, e-mail or post. Details of what your borough supplies can be found on the website, or you can ring the number above.

A Taxicard allows you to make a set number of subsidised journeys in licensed London taxis (or minicabs, by negotiation). The number of trips you are allocated differs depending on which borough you live in.

You can book with Computer Cab on *Tel:* 020 7763-5001, or it can be done online. There's a useful page on their website *www.computercab.co.uk/website/ taxicard.aspx*

The card provides a reduced price taxi ride but, like all schemes, it has its limitations.

Because of the current constraints, many boroughs are tightening up the assessment process. You will need to list exactly what your impairments are, how you are disabled by inaccessible transport services, and what effect this has on your daily life.

Talk to TfA if you are having difficulties with the process.

The Taxicard Call Centre is based in Scotland, and unfortunately it can be difficult to get through. Try to book your journey in good time to avoid disappointment. You will be asked for your Taxicard number, to confirm your name, the departure and arrival addresses. Always ask for a quote for longer journeys as it may be cheaper to book a local minicab rather than using your Taxicard.

There is a fifteen minute 'window' either side of your booking time, so make sure you are ready a quarter of an hour early, as the meter will be ticking. If you are ready on time, there should be no more than £3.40 on the meter. This is the maximum 'run in charge'.

If you find it easier to get in or out of a minicab, rather than a black cab, or vice versa, you may request that a note is put on your account so you are always sent the right type of vehicle. There is a service called **Capital Call** operating in some boroughs where black cabs are relatively scarce, which uses minicabs as 'first choice'. To register for this service *Tel:* 020 7275-2446.

Freedom Pass(es) for Disabled and Older Persons and the 60+ Oyster Card

The Freedom Pass is provided by local borough councils to give older and disabled Londoners free travel on almost all public transport in London. There are two passes with different eligibility criteria, one for disabled people, and the other for older people.

It includes some people who cannot drive, and some with learning difficulties.

The eligibility criteria are set out on the London councils website, or you can contact:

The **Freedom Pass Helpline** *Tel:* 0845 275-7054 (Mon-Sat 8am-6pm)
website: www.londoncouncils.gov.uk → services → freedompass
e-mail: info@freedompass.org

The TfA helpline will also provide advice about eligibility if you need it.

There is also free travel for Londoners on TfL services, using the 60+ Oyster Card. This bridges the gap created by increases in the age of eligibility for the London Councils Freedom Pass (which provides free bus travel all over the country as well as free travel in London on most services).

Arriving in London

You may arrive in London by train or coach from inside the UK, or by *Eurostar* or by air from abroad.

By rail

As there are so few journeys 'inside' London that it is possible to make by NR without major access problems, we are describing the network in detail in this section under *Arriving*.

National Rail (NR) services

There is a huge network of rail lines through the London suburbs. It is more dense south of the river, where there are fewer tube lines. In addition the lines end at about ten different stations, most of which are some distance from the central area/s (see the rail links map). The reason for this is that a Royal Commission in 1846, declared that central London was a no-go area for railway line construction.

Virtually all the central main line stations, being termini, have step-free access nearly everywhere. Most have taxi pick-up points just outside, or inside the station, and these will all be 'accessible' black cabs.

Kings Cross/St Pancras, London Bridge and Waterloo link to 'accessible' underground stations. Charing Cross is very central and within 500m of Trafalgar Square, while Blackfriars is actually in the City. Nearly all of them have accessible toilets, usually with a NKS lock.

You can pick up an excellent overall map of the system called *London Connections* from a number of information points, or from **National Rail Enquiries** *Tel:* 0845 7484-950 *Textphone:* 0845 6050-600 *website:* www.nationalrail.co.uk.

Note that chair users wanting to travel by a NR train, can reasonably easily travel with/near able-bodied companions, but if two or more chair users travel they will be located in different compartments on many/most trains.

The principal access issue connected with using trains, even at an 'accessible' station, is the substantial step that remains for getting into the carriage. At an increasing number of stations there are portable ramps available to facilitate boarding but use of the ramps is dependent on there being staff help available.

This is usually OK at big busy stations, but not always possible at smaller stations which may only be staffed part-time, or may even not be staffed at all. When using such stations it is almost certainly necessary to make arrangements in advance with the rail companies *Assisted travel* **service, unless you are travelling with strong and resourceful friends.**

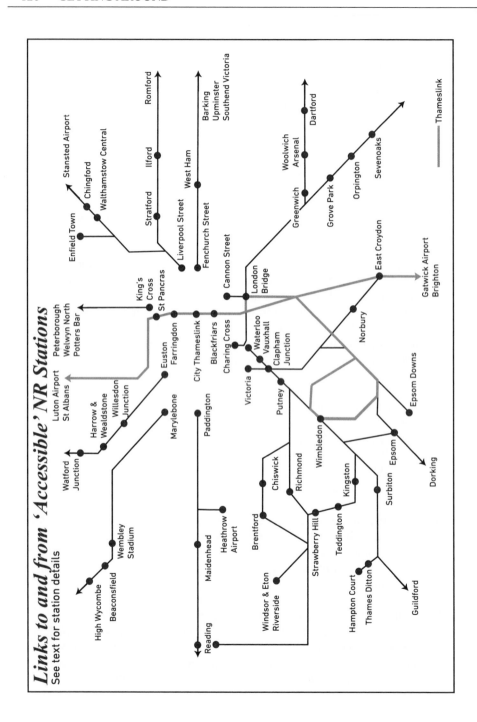

Links to and from 'Accessible' NR Stations
See text for station details

Thameslink

The ramps can be a solid piece of engineering, and may quite heavy to handle. Staff need training in their use. There are some newer and lighter ramps made of aluminium coming into use. These are slightly narrower, making it easier to fit into the doors. There are even some fibreglass ramps available which can fold up like a suitcase, and these are currently being used on First Great Western. Hopefully, good practice over the provision and use of ramps will be shared around among the different operators.

If you are using a smaller station, possibly one that isn't always staffed, most operators ask for at least 24 hours notice of your travelling plans, so that they can provide any assistance which is needed. If you are travelling with friends, so that assistance isn't needed, make sure that you don't depend on a staff operated lift at a place with no staff !

A booklet called *Rail Travel for Disabled Passengers* is available. This includes practical advice and contact phone numbers. It also contains details of concessionary fares, and of the **Disabled Persons Railcard**. This offers reduced fares for you and an adult companion. It is valid for a year, and at the time of writing cost £20.

Cards are available from **The Disabled Persons Railcard Office**, PO Box 11631. Laurencekirk, AB30 9AA
Tel: 0845 605-0525 *Textphone:* 0845 601-0132 *e-mail:* disability@atoc.org
The booklet and other leaflets are available at main stations and it can be downloaded from *www.nationalrail.co.uk*.

Access in London is not a guide about rail travel in the UK, and we are only looking at how to get to London easily from towns in the counties which border Greater London. There are, however, a few 'accessible' stations and potentially useful journeys within the M25.

We've made a map showing the principal lines into London's main stations, together with some of the useful links from various suburban stations. *London Overground* has a separate and more detailed map. The links south of the river are generally of greater interest/importance, since the rail network is more extensive there. North of the river the Underground and *Overground* are dominant. *Thameslink* runs generally north-south and passes through the newly 'accessible' Blackfriars station. It provides some useful links, and from 2018, Crossrail will provide additional east-west links.

One major thing that has changed is that there are now helpful phone contacts available - once you've found your way through several multiple choice menus - and the people who answer will generally try to get correct information, and to facilitate a smooth journey for you. The phone numbers in are in the Table on the next page.

Contact details for arranging Assisted Travel using the different train operators (as indicated on their websites in 2012/13, and checked when we wrote the book)

Operating company	Contact phone number	Textphone/ Typetalk	From (main line station/s)
c2c#	01702 357-640	18001+ 01702 357-640	Fenchurch Street
Chiltern Railways	08456 005-165 (selecting option 3 then option 3 again)	08457 078-051	Marylebone
East Coast	08457 225-225	18001+ 08457 225-225	Kings Cross
East Midlands Trains#	08457 125 678 option 3	08457 078-051	St Pancras
First Capital Connect (Thameslink & Great Northern)	0800 058-2844*	0800 975-1052*	St Pancras, Kings Cross, London Bridge, Blackfriars
First Great Western	0800 1971-329*	18001+ 0800 1971-329	Paddington
London Midland	0800 092-4260*	0844 811-0134	Euston
Greater Anglia	0800 028-2878*	18001+ 0800 028-2878	Liverpool Street
South West Trains#	0800 528-2100*	0800 692-0792*	Waterloo
Southeastern#	0800 783-4524* or 01732 77 00 99	0800 783 4548*	Victoria, Charing Cross, London Bridge
Southern#	0800 138-1016*	0800 138-1018*	Victoria, Charing Cross, Cannon Street, London Bridge
Virgin Trains	08457 443-366	08457 443-367	Euston

* Note that the 0800 numbers are FREE when you call from a landline
# There is a map on their website showing the 'accessible' stations.
Note that if you need help, you should check on whether staff will be available.

If you are not sure what train company you are travelling with, contact National Rail Enquiries *Tel:* 08457 484 950 *Textphone:* 0845 605-0600

In researching this section, we found that access information for disabled travellers is fragmented, and presented in a different way on each of the various company websites. Various menus eventually led to an *Assisted travel* page. Some sites had a map showing accessible stations, some had a Freephone number for making enquiries, but only after visiting several websites did we find this vital statement:

- *"We participate in the national 'Assisted Passenger Reservation System' (APRS) used by all train operators. We can book assistance for your whole trip, including on trains and stations run by other operators. We will enter your trip details into APRS which automatically tells other operators if assistance is required at one of their stations. We will contact other operators directly if this is necessary to ensure your booked assistance is delivered"*

The official policy of most station/train operators is that passengers requiring assistance should give 24-hours notice of their intention to travel. This is certainly necessary if you are making a journey which needs a train company organised taxi to complete it. However, if you are simply travelling between well staffed stations, giving notice isn't usually needed.

If you need help it is obviously sensible to arrive in good time, and to negotiate with the staff who are on duty. If you're making a journey for the first time it might be a good idea to ring first to check as to whether there are likely to be problems, and if you need help to get on or off the train you need to make sure that the station is adequately staffed when you want to travel.

There are useful links to/from 'accessible' step-free stations like Reading, Maidenhead, Guildford, Watford, Sevenoaks, Romford, St Albans and Watford. There are also useful 'internal' links (inside the M25) from places like East Croydon, Wimbledon, Chiswick, Stratford, Willesden Junction, and many more.

National Rail (NR) has moderately good information about their stations, most of which can be found at: *www.nationalrail.co.uk/stations_destinations/* The information includes a bar entitled *Accessibility and Mobility Access* in which there are details about which platforms can be reached step-free. It also provides a station map with a clever system of symbols so that when you 'hover' over them there are photos of each facility (which show seats, help point and steps). The written description doesn't always accord with the station map.

As is common with this kind of data, it is input according to a fixed pattern which doesn't deal well with different circumstances and station layouts.

The format was almost certainly both designed and input by able-bodied people, who don't necessarily understand what the disabled traveller needs to know, but are ensuring compliance with the 'standard format'.

It is not clear when the information was provided/updated, and we were told several times that updating is irregular, and may take a long time.

For many of the fairly straightforward stations like (say) Charing Cross or Wimbledon, the description and the diagram are reasonably adequate. For slightly more complicated stations like, for example, Willesden Junction or Stratford, more explanation is needed. We found some instances where the information was incorrect, incomplete and in some instances seriously misleading, like that about Twickenham where access to all the platforms is via steps. Even though we reported the mistake/s, nothing changed on the NR Stations website for months. **Where there are NR and TfL services operating from the same station, the station 'map' may only show the area regarded as belonging to NR, while common sense would suggest that the whole of the station should be shown. The outcomes are sometimes seriously confusing, as parts of what to the passenger is simply 'the station' aren't shown.**

Stations in and around London with step-free access, some via service lifts

NOTE that a * indicates that there is some reservation, either about the whole of the station having step-free access, or about the hours of operation, or that the station is not staffed at all. If the station is listed without comment, there should be step-free access throughout the day and staff assistance to get on board.

This section is best used in conjunction with the *London connections* map.

c2c

website: www.c2c-online.co.uk

Fenchurch Street

on two levels. The lower concourse at ground level is approached from Fenchurch Place. There's a **wheelchair toilet (NKS),** and lift (D125 W150 L190) up to the 4 platforms, both to the left of the entrance

West Ham

* with step-free connections to the District and H&C line platforms, and to the JLE and DLR via three service lifts. The station is listed as not being staffed, and there are only ticket machines, and no ticket office

Barking

* all eight platforms can be reached using a service lift (D180 W180 L200) off the concourse down to platform 1. Then there are steepish ramps down to a subway, and then up to the other platforms, and longish distances are involved. There is an **accessible toilet (NKS)** with BCF off the upper walkway. It is inside the ticket barriers. There is step-free interchange with the District line platforms

Upminster

> * level access to platform 1 via a new ticket office by the Station Approach CP. Service lift (D200 W200 L200) to platforms 2, 3, 4 and 5 so that interchange between Fenchurch Street trains and the District line is possible. **Wheelchair toilet** on platform 1

Southend Central

> * there is ramped access to both platforms, but (looking at Google maps) the only step-free route from one side to the other is via the bridge on the High Street, involving a distance of around 750m. There's an **accessible toilet (NKS)** with BCF on the concourse by platforms 3/4.

Chiltern Railways
website: www.chilternrailways.co.uk

Marylebone

> off the main concourse, shops and ticket office area there are two **wheelchair toilets (D100 ST85 NKS)**. They are just inside the door to both the womens and the mens toilets. Both have BCF

Wembley Stadium

> * lifts from each platform to overhead bridge. The station is not generally staffed

Beaconsfield

> * ramped access from both sides, but it's about 800m via the Station Road bridge to get from one side to the other. The station is not always staffed, particularly in the evenings

High Wycombe

> * flat access to platforms 1 and 2. Platform 3, for trains to Marylebone, is reached via a ramped underpass from platform 2.

East Coast (plus First Capital Connect FCC)
website: www.eastcoast.co.uk

Kings Cross

> recently redeveloped with step-free access to all platforms. The **accessible toilets** are past the ticket barriers for platforms 9-11, where there's a *Changing places* facility, or on the 1st floor in the new shops/cafés development with lift access. 30p charge at the entrance. There's a good **accessible toilet** in *The Parcel Yard* pub near platform 9 and with lift access. The toilet is discreetly located at the left end of the long corridor reached by going to your right as you come into the pub

Potters Bar (via FCC services)

> * there are steepish ramps up to the platforms

Welwyn Garden City (via FCC services)

> there is ramped access from both sides of the station, and lifts down to the platforms.

Peterborough
> step-free to platform 1 where there is an **accessible toilet (NKS)** with BCF. At the north end of the station there's a bridge with steepish ramps to and from all the platforms. In addition there's an electric golf-type buggy to take a chair user and/or disabled walkers plus their luggage over the bridge to platforms 3/4/5.

East Midlands trains and *Eurostar*
websites: www.eastmidlandstrains.co.uk & www.eurostar.com
St Pancras International (has its own website: *www.stpancras.com*)
> the main station concourse is below the platforms, all of which have lift access. There are two **accessible toilets** and BCF. One is on the side of the Arcade by the Eurostar Ticket Office. The other is to the right from the main entrance in Pancras Road and reached via the Circle. They are by the cash dispensing machines

Luton Airport
> step-free via lifts to all platforms

Bedford
> lift access via the bridge to all platforms. **Accessible toilet (NKS)** on platform 1

First Capital Connect (*Thameslink*)
website: www.firstcapitalconnect.co.uk
Blackfriars
> there is lift access to all 4 elevated platforms from both ends of the bridge. On the south bank there is a ticket office before the lifts, with the same provision on the north (City) side. Two platforms handle the through trains, including those on *Thameslink*. There are toilets on the north side at ground level, to the left past the ticket office. These include an **accessible toilet** with a separate BCF, but when visited (in October 2012) turnstiles had been installed and a gate, and it looked as though it might all become a 'pay' area.

East Croydon
> steepish ramps lead to and from all platforms. **Wheelchair toilet (D95 ST90 NKS)** on platforms 3/4. Tramlink stops nearby.

Gatwick Airport
> Step-free via lifts to all platforms

Brighton
> two **accessible toilets (NKS)** near the WHSmith bookstore.

First Great Western

website: www.firstgreatwestern.co.uk

Paddington

step-free throughout with lifts up to the mezzanine at the back of the station. Access to platforms 13 and 14 for suburban services is via a ramp which is half way along platform 12. Most of the trains that go to and from Reading start on the main line platforms. **Two wheelchair toilets (D80 ST75),** one with BCF, inside the first aid room signed Station Reception, near the start of platform 1. There's another 24-hour **accessible toilet (NKS and *Changing Places*)** with BCF by the end of platform 12 on the other side of the station

Heathrow Airport

via the Heathrow Express (*www.heathrowexpress.com*) and Heathrow Connect

Maidenhead

* step-free access via lifts from a subway to all platforms, and **accessible toilet (NKS)** with BCF on platforms 4/5

Reading

step-free access via lifts to and from the bridge. Step-free link between First Great Western and South West Trains. **Accessible toilet (NKS)** with BCF off the main concourse and ticket office area. The 'accessible' toilet off the Waiting Room on platforms 8/9 has very restricted ST space.

London Midland & Virgin Trains

websites: www.londonmidland.com & www.virgintrains.co.uk

Euston

both side entrances to the station have steps (+4 from Melton Street, +14 from Eversholt Street). Ramped entrances from the Euston Road and the bus station. **Two wheelchair toilets (D75 ST80 NKS)** off the concourse near the end of platform 1. The BCF a little further along are said to be inaccessible to a chair user

Harrow & Wealdstone

lifts to all platforms, and interchange with the Bakerloo line. **Accessible toilet** off main concourse, but you may have to ask staff to unlock it

Watford Junction

* lifts to all platforms. **Wheelchair toilet (D95 ST75 NKS)** by the ticket office.

Greater Anglia

website: www.greateranglia.co.uk

Liverpool Street

on two levels, with lift (D90 W145 L210) access near the huge overhead departures board. **Wheelchair toilet (D85 ST75 NKS)** some 50m off the main concourse between platforms 10 and 11

Stratford

large interchange station with step-free access everywhere using lifts

Romford

* steepish ramp to the left of the main station bypasses +11+12 steps. All the platforms have ramped access

Southend Victoria

terminus station with step-free access. **Accessible toilet** at the end of platform 1

Enfield Town

* ramped access to the platforms. **Accessible toilet (NKS)** with BCF off the main concourse but just inside the ticket barriers

Walthamstow Central

* ramped access from either side, but it's some 500m via the Hoe Street bridge to get to the other side

Chingford

* step-free terminus station. **Accessible toilet (NKS)** with BCF off platforms 1/2

Stansted Airport

South West Trains

website: www.southwesttrains.co.uk

Waterloo

there are 19 platforms in this elevated station. The Eurostar platforms are out of use as the services have transferred to St Pancras. Step-free access everywhere, including Waterloo East via lift and ramps. **Wheelchair toilet (D70+ ST70+ NKS)** in the foyer by the womens, off the main concourse in line with platform 19. The BCF here involve steps. There's another **wheelchair toilet (NKS)** on Station Approach Road just outside, where the 211 buses pull in. Step-free station exit through the arch by the big central clock, and through to the taxi rank (and the toilet is just to the left of the arch/exit). Note the accessible link to the JLE via the lift in line with platforms 5/6, which also gets you down to the Waterloo Road level

Vauxhall

work is in hand to provide lift access to all the NR platforms, and in 2016 there will be lift access to the tube station as well

Clapham Junction

a large and very busy station where there's a split in the lines going south and west. It's an important junction with the *Overground*. The 17 platforms are linked by either an underground tunnel or an overhead footbridge. **There is now a lift to and from every platform from the footbridge reached step-free via the St Johns Hill entrance from Brighton Yard**. Accessible toilet (NKS) with separate BCF just inside the ticket barriers.

Also note that the station has a path for blind or partially-sighted passengers, making it easier to use the footbridge. This is the first time a UK station has been equipped with a guided path. There are also tactile and Braille signs at the top of each stairwell leading to the platforms

Putney

work is in hand to provide lift access to all the platforms

Chiswick

* flat/ramped access to both sides, and there are portable ramps on both platforms. Not always staffed, and it's nearly a km to go over the road bridge to get from one side to the other

Brentford

* there's a lift at either end of the footbridge over the line, with step-free access on either side. A road bridge also links the two platforms, but it's about 750m to go from one to the other. The angle of the track means that the step getting on and off trains is particularly big on both sides. **Accessible toilet (NKS)** with BCF off the ticket hall on platform 2

Richmond

* a key station on the District line tube, South West Trains, and at the end of an *Overground* line. The platforms are reached via −22 steps, but there are staff operated lifts (D160 W190 L290) to all platforms. There is alternative step-free access from the CP alongside the station. **Wheelchair toilet (D90 ST200 NKS)** with BCF at platform level near the end of platform 6

Wimbledon

lift access to all platforms, and link between NR trains, the District line and Tramlink. The **accessible toilet (NKS)** on the lower level was temporarily closed when we surveyed

Kingston

step-free to all platforms via lifts to and from the subway. **Accessible toilet (NKS)** with BCF on platforms1/2, by the waiting room

Surbiton

lift access to all platforms from the bridge. **Accessible toilet (NKS)** with BCF on both platform islands

Woking

> lift access via a bridge to all platforms. **Accessible toilet (NKS)** with BCF on platform 5/6

Guildford

> step-free access to all platforms from the main entrance in Walnut Tree Close. via steepish ramps from a subway with no handrails. **Accessible toilet (NKS)** with BCF on platform 2.

Windsor & Eton Riverside

> * step-free until 20.00 after which there are +3 steps and assistance may be needed

Hampton Court

> * has +2 steps at the entrance kerb which can be bypassed by a ramp at the side, towards the back of the station, otherwise step-free with **accessible toilet (NKS)** on concourse.

Southeastern

website: www.southeasternrailway.co.uk

Victoria

> big terminus station with 19 platforms, and a bus station outside. There will be a step-free tube link in 2018. **Wheelchair toilet (D70+ ST70+ NKS)** by the main toilets on the right side of the station, looking towards the platforms (in line with platform 17)

Charing Cross

> small terminus station with 6 platforms. Close to the Strand, Trafalgar Square and Covent Garden. **Wheelchair toilet (D70+ST80+ NKS)** with BCF off the central corridor linking the concourse to the street

Cannon Street

> To the left of the steps, there's a lift up to all 7 platforms. Two accessible toilets (NKS) with BCF, near the ticket office

London Bridge

> has lift access up to the main concourse with 13 platforms, including some for through trains (such as those of *Thameslink*). At the time of writing, the station was being completely redeveloped, with a programme which will not be complete until 2018. A new toilet block has been built at ground level, off Joiner Street (which is an underground passage linking Tooley Street and St Thomas Street). About half-way along Joiner Street there's a side passage (called The Vaults), lined by small shops and stalls. This leads to escalators and a lift, taking people up to the station concourse. The toilets (with an entry charge) are to the right of the escalators, and include an **accessible toilet** and separate BCF. There's a second **accessible toilet** on platform 5. Lifts go to both the JLE and Northern lines, but the stations are separate, and are nearly 500m apart.

Greenwich
> * step-free links using a lift and underpass are not shown on the NR station map - and when we queried this we were told that this route was a TfL responsibility ! Note the link to the DLR

Woolwich Arsenal
> * ramped access to both sides of the station through gates which can be opened using an intercom. **Adapted toilets (ST60 NKS)** on platform 1. Link to the DLR

Dartford
> * platforms accessible via lifts to and from the bridge. **Wheelchair toilet (D140 ST95 NKS)** just inside the womens entrance

Lewisham
> * lift access to and from both subways under the lines. **Accessible toilet (NKS)** on platform 2 but with inward opening door

Orpington
> * lift access to all platforms via the bridge. **Accessible toilet (NKS)** on platforms 3/4

Sevenoaks
> * lift access to all platforms via the bridge. **Wheelchair toilet (ST70 NKS)** just past the ticket barriers

Southern
website: www.southernrailway.com
Victoria, *London Bridge* and *Clapham Junction* have already been described
Norbury
> step-free access to platforms via steepish ramps

West Croydon
> * there's a step-free entrance on either side of the station, quite a distance from the bridge over the railway where the ticket office is. On one side there's a CP with a gate and intercom while on the other the gate (for platform 4) is by the Tramlink stop on Station Road. It is an *Overground* terminus

East Croydon
> steepish ramp access to all platforms. **Accessible toilet (NKS)** on platforms 3/4. Tramlink stop outside.

Gatwick Airport
Brighton
> terminus station with step-free access to all 8 platforms. Two **accessible toilets (NKS)** off the main concourse

Sutton
> * lift access to all platforms via a bridge. **Accessible cubicles** in both the mens and womens toilets on platforms 1 and on 2/3

Epsom Downs
> * terminus station with ramped access

Epsom
> * ramp down to subway under the platforms with lift access described as 'staff-operated'

By coach

Coach travel not only offers good value, but there are some routes where it will be even easier to make the coach journey than to use trains. These may include some which go to some of the airports, particularly Heathrow where there is an extensive hub.

Department of Transport regulations require that all vehicles seating more than 22 people must comply with accessibility requirements by 2020, and *National Express*, the biggest coach provider in England, plan to have made their entire fleet accessible by the end of 2013. However, what this will mean in practice, and in practical terms is not entirely clear - and coach travel won't appeal to everyone.

National Express
Tel: 0871 781-8178 *website:* www.nationalexpress.com/coach
There's a list of currently accessible coach routes on the website.
An 'accessible' coach has a wheelchair lift at the front entrance to bypass the steps. A chair can be locked firmly in place, with access to a three-point seatbelt. Each coach has only one such space. A disabled walker can ask to use the lift which provides access to a step-free upper level.
It is essential to book use of the lift at least 36 hours in advance via the Assisted Travel Helpline *Tel:* 0871 781-8179 (option 3 then option 2)
or you can *e-mail:* DPTH@nationalexpress.com
Note that the on-board toilets in coaches, where provided, are tiny, and for all practical purposes should be regarded as 'inaccessible'.
Megabus is another big company providing inter-city services to and from London.
Tel: 0871 2663333 (general enquiries); 0900 1600-900 (bookings)
website: http://uk.megabus.com/ *e-mail:* enquiries@megabus.com
If you use a wheelchair and need to remain in it, or have other access needs, don't purchase your ticket online, but *Tel:* 0141 332-9841.

London's central coach station and the arrival and departure point for most coach services to places all over Britain and the continent is at Victoria. It comes under the TfL umbrella, and you can find information and a plan on the TfL website *www.tfl.gov.uk* under *Coaches*.
Victoria Coach Station (VCS) 164 Buckingham Palace Road, SW1W 9TP
Tel: 020 7222-5600 (the TfL number) *DisEnq:* 020 7027-2520 (Mobility lounge at VCS)
It is some 500m from the Victoria train (and underground) station.

The main entrance is on the corner of Elizabeth Street. There are two separate sections to the station on either side of Elizabeth Street, the smaller one for arrivals, and the larger one with numbered bays, for departures. There is step-free access throughout, with good signage.

If you need assistance, there is a Mobility Lounge, near the Ticket Hall on the Buckingham Palace Road side and near Gate 21.

There are **four accessible toilets (NKS)**, one in Arrivals, two adjacent to the National Express office and one inside the Mobility Lounge opposite Gate 21 in Departures. BCF are located next to the toilets in Arrivals, and next to the toilets by gates 2 and 12 in Departures.

Arriving at St Pancras International

St Pancras is a large station built on two levels. The platforms are the upper level with lift access down to the main concourse with its shops and cafés.

The underground station is 'accessible' with lifts, linking the two surface rail stations (St P and Kings Cross) with six tube lines, three deep underground (Northern, Piccadilly and Victoria) and three near the surface (Circle, H&C and Metropolitan). It's a good hub if all the lifts are working. Quite long distances are involved, up to 1km from Kings Cross platforms.

The station is on the inner ring road A501 Euston Road, just north of Bloomsbury, and there are a variety of buses going into central London.

By air

If you fly into London, you will have needed to find out from your airline about access problems en route, and their policies regarding disabled passengers. Unfortunately, all the airlines seem to have slightly different rules and approaches.

It is essential for you to tell your airline of your needs, since they (and not the airport) are responsible for your various transfers getting on and off the plane and through the airport system.

Note that assistance dogs can only travel if they are registered with The Pet Travel Scheme (PETS), and if allowed by the airline.

We include information about meet and greet valet parking which may be of use to UK travellers going abroad from the big London airports.

There are five relevant airports, the two largest being Heathrow and Gatwick (to the west and south). In addition there are Stansted and Luton, both to the north, and London City, very near the centre.

Airports were among the first places to provide facilities for disabled passengers, and on a relative basis, they are quite good from an access point of view. Note that:

- if you use the biggest airports, there should be step-free access through the terminal to the aircraft door, but occasionally this may not be so, either because of a breakdown, or possibly for security reasons. Chair users quite often have to transfer to an alternative 'loading' chair in order to get to a seat on the plane;

- at both Heathrow and Gatwick, very long distances are involved although both have little buggies to take elderly and/or disabled walkers through the terminal to their departure lounge;
- at certain times, airports can become extremely congested. For example, it is wise to avoid Friday evenings and bank holiday weekends if you possibly can;
- a big problem for most travellers tends to be handling their luggage, getting to the airline desk, and simply finding out where that is for a start ! Most terminals now have a Help Desk near where you first come in;
- for passengers arriving, luggage handling on to whatever transport is used to reach the hotel or other accommodation is a potential hassle;
- at smaller airports (like London City), access to the aircraft will be via a flight of steps.

There's a useful guide available at *www.parkat.co.uk/disabled-travel-guide.pdf* with advice and information for a wide range of disabled travellers.

If you make prior arrangements it is normally possible to ease your passage through the system, including the security and passport checks. This must be done directly with your airline when you book, and if you can, we recommend that you get some kind of proper acknowledgement (a note or e-mail) confirming the arrangements. If you have difficulty in walking long distances then it is almost certainly a good idea to organise appropriate assistance, and possibly the use of a wheelchair to facilitate transfers inside the airport.

Virtually all airports have accessible toilets on both sides of the security desks. However, there are only a limited number. If you want to use a toilet you would almost certainly be wise to do so before the departure gate. Don't let 'the system' whisk you through too quickly without giving you the chance of going to the loo, as the ones on the plane will be quite small, and will be inaccessible to some. There are usually accessible toilets in the arrival areas where you are waiting for luggage, and off the corridors leading to passport control, but they're not always well signed, and you may have to ask.

Transport links to and from the airports

There are 'accessible' transport links to and from the five airports we've mentioned.

What is practical for you depends on:

- where you are going (you will probably want to go first to where you are staying);
- the comparative costs of different routes; and,

- the various practicalities, including how much luggage you have. Handling it on and off trains and buses can be a considerable hassle.

The ideal way of arriving, of course, is to be met by a relative or friend who has appropriate transport and/or who knows the local system. Many people, however, have to make their own arrangements, and much depends on whether you are in a group (including, perhaps, some resourceful able-bodied people) or are on your own.

As London is such a big city, you may have a long way to go, and cost becomes an issue, particularly if you are using a taxi or minicab. Pre-booked minicabs are generally (but not necessarily) cheaper than using a taxi, but apart from London City, the airports are a long way out.

All the airports have 'accessible' rail links into central London, and taking the train and then using a taxi for the final bit of your journey may be the best way overall. Heathrow also has an 'accessible' tube link on the Piccadilly line (see the detailed write-up about using the Underground).

The *Heathrow Express* train goes to London Paddington, the *Gatwick Express* to London Victoria, and the *Stansted Express* to London Liverpool Street.

Note that while some airports have 'accessible' black taxis which you can take from outside (again, see the detailed write-up about taxis), at both Gatwick and Stansted, the taxi contract has been given to a company who use conventional cars. If you need an 'accessible' vehicle it would be wise to pre-organise this.

Gatwick airport, Gatwick, West Sussex, RH6 0NP
Tel: 0844 892-0322 (and passengers with special needs should select option 2)
Parking: 0844 811-8311 or *e-mail:* gatwick.customerservice.apcoa.com
Meet and greet valet parking: www.firstchoiceparking.co.uk
website: www.gatwickairport.com
There are two terminals with a short train link between them which has step-free access. Overall, the site is large, so be prepared for long distances, and at busy times for congestion and crowds of people. If you have walking difficulties, make sure that your airline knows about it, and use the buggies provided to make things easier.
Travel-care offer advice and information to anyone who has a problem connected with special needs. They may be able to ease your passage, and can be particularly useful if you are travelling alone.
Contact details *Tel:* 01293-504283 *Fax:* 01293-503317
e-mail: travel.care@btconnect.com

There are numerous parking options which are advertised on the net, but you will need to check on the accessibility of the transport used to get to and from the CP. Some are quite difficult to find. The meet and greet service we mention above, avoids those potential hassles.

One feature at Gatwick is that the taxis in use are conventional cars, and not the 'accessible' black cab (see the section on *Taxis and minicabs*). Thus if you want an accessible vehicle, it would be wise to book it in advance through:

Airport Cars Gatwick *Tel:* 01293 550-000
website: www.airportcars-uk.com/airports/gatwick-airport-taxis
e-mail: enquiries@airportcars-gatwick.com
They are associated with Road Runners Ltd which has at least 25 wheelchair accessible vehicles locally.

Heathrow airport, The Compass Centre, Nelson Road, Hounslow, Middlesex, TW6 2GW
Tel: 0844 335-1801 *Textphone:* 0844 571 7410 (for enquiries related to check-in, lost baggage, flight delays and cancellations, please contact your airline)
website: www.baa.com (look at the pages on 'special needs' under Heathrow airport guide)
Meet and greet valet parking providers include:
* www.fastparkheathrow.co.uk,
* www.mbwparking.co.uk, and,
* www.prontoparking.co.uk.
There are three terminal areas, three (1, 2 & 3) of which are linked by underground passages with step-free access, although there are several hundred metres between them. Terminals 4 and 5 are on quite separate sites, some distance away. They can be reached by the underground with only single steps involved (getting on and off the trains). In one direction you have to go via Hatton Cross and change trains. You can also use the Heathrow Express train/s which link the different terminal areas.
Note that at the time of writing, Terminal 2 is closed for rebuilding. It is due to reopen in 2014.
Travel-care *Tel:* 020 8745-7495 *e-mail:* heathrow_travel_care@baa.com can provide information and assistance for passengers with special needs although they say that many of their past functions in smoothing people's journeys, have been taken over by the airlines themselves.

London City airport, Royal Docks, E16 2PB
Tel: 020 7646-0088 *website:* www.londoncityairport.com
The Terminal entrance is located on Hartmann Road, E16 2PX.
London City is a small airport, so boarding the aircraft involves steps. Assistance with boarding can be arranged, and you can be 'transferred' up the steps in a narrow, powered, ambulance-type chair. They use a chair called S-Max aviation (see *www.aat-online.de*). Although aircraft boarding is slightly more of a hassle than at the other London airports, the terminal itself is small, and is just 200m from the accessible DLR station. There are nearby hotels (see the *Accommodation* chapter).

Luton airport, Navigation House, Airport Way, Luton, Bedfordshire, LU2 9LY
Tel: 01582 405-100 *website:* www.london-luton.co.uk
e-mail: disabledfacilities@ltn.aero
Luton has a small terminal, and passengers who cannot manage the steps up into the aircraft can be 'loaded' via an Ambulift (a pod using hydraulics which can lift a chair user up level with the 'plane door). Make arrangements for assistance with your airline before travelling.
The rail station is nearly 1km away, with an 'accessible' shuttle bus to facilitate transfer to and from the terminal.

Stansted airport, Enterprise House, Bassingbourn Road, Essex, CM24 1QW
Tel: 0844 335-1803 *Textphone:* 0741 571-7410
website: www.stanstedairport.com
There are Long Stay and Mid Stay CPs run by the airport, with 'accessible' buses linking to the terminal.
Meet and greet valet parking providers include:
• www.ukparkandfly.co.uk
• www.looking4parking.com
• http://stanstedvaletmeetandgreet.co.uk
Stansted has a relatively small terminal. The rail station is directly underneath, and the platforms are reached via ramps or lifts.
There are some 'air bridges' to facilitate step-free transfer into the aircraft, but not all flights use these, so sometimes there are steps involved. If necessary you can be transferred up or down to get on/off the aircraft by Ambulift or using a powered stairclimber. As well as informing the airline, you can contact ISS, the special assistance provider at Stansted, *e-mail:* stn.prm@uk.issworld.com. There's a page on the website headed 'Request special assistance' with a list of airline phone numbers, and the instruction to book such help 48h in advance.

Train access for wheelchair users is via a portable ramp, and assistance will be provided by National Express staff. Assistance should be pre-booked if possible by calling the National Express helpline on 0845 600 7245.
The company **24x7** operate a 24hour taxi service with their main desk in the International Arrivals concourse and a courtesy phone in the Domestic Baggage Reclaim area.
Tel: 01279 661-111 *website:* www.24x7stansted.com
e-mail: stansted@24x7Ltd.co.uk
A taxi journey into London for one to four people costs about £100, depending on the exact destination. Most of the vehicles are conventional cars, but wheelchair-accessible vehicles are available on request. They also operate an interesting 'shared taxi' scheme to help people minimise the cost.
Stansted was one of several places where we found it very difficult to get the information we required, and it took several months and a lot of persistence !

Places of interest

This chapter covers many of London's historical buildings and attractions. Museums, galleries and places of worship, are nearly all cross-referenced to other chapters, as we were anxious that the write-ups don't get too 'chunky'. **Entries are split into geographical areas and are then, generally, listed alphabetically.**
There's an extensive *Index*.

The grouping of nearby sites/sights is taken further under *Recommended itineraries* which we will put in much fuller detail on the website. The *itineraries* aim to include places of contrasting nature, outlining smallish areas where a visitor might spend a whole day with relatively short distances to travel.
There will also be suggestions about places to go if it's raining.
There are enough ideas in our write-ups to keep you busy for several weeks if you take advantage of all the opportunities.

We will add new places and *Updated information* to our website, which is also where we have put some sites/sights which are outside the north/south circular roads.
If you want print-outs of any of the website material, please let us know.

An increasing number of the sights are accessible without much hassle, and a great variety of things can now be seen with minimal difficulty. In addition, staff attitudes and understanding have improved, although the best person to understand your particular limitations and needs is yourself. Sometimes, clearly and patiently (!), you may have to explain.

There are, some inevitable challenges. These are usually because the buildings are old with inbuilt barriers, because there are long distances involved and, of course, because disability awareness is by no means universal or uniform.
Many people do not understand the importance of distance when describing accessibility. Signage is often poor, and certainly not put there by people who understand access. The 'accessible toilet' may have been installed many years ago to a rather poor specification.
In addition there are serious problems/challenges associated with the transport system, and with parking. Hence the importance of the chapter on Getting around.

Note that the information about access on the websites in our listings is highly variable - some is really good, while some is just awful. Sometimes there's so much of it, that the key relevant bits become difficult to identify.

Many places offer special facilities and visits/tours for both visually and hearing impaired visitors, and sometimes for visitors with learning difficulties.
BSL tours and Touch tours may be provided.

These are nearly all available on an occasional/intermittent basis, and we feel that it is best for people to get this information by making direct enquiries to the venue concerned, since this will be necessary anyway. In addition, information for those with other disabilities is best researched by those with the appropriate skills.
See our website page/s on *Methodology*.

We don't set out to duplicate information about opening times and entry fees which can easily be obtained elsewhere, and which change more often than does the physical accessibility of the building. Generally we will only indicate if a facility has restricted or unusual opening times, and we will say if there was an admission charge when we made our visit.

Most major museums and galleries are open every day, and currently offer free entry. There may be a charge for special exhibitions. They offer a wide range of different things to see and do. At some smaller galleries and at some major sights, there is an entry charge, and if it is more than about £10/person we describe it as a 'significant charge'.

A number of major sights, including those operated by Merlin Entertainments, a couple of London's big churches and most of the Royal Palaces, do make a 'significant charge'. Note that if you get a ticket to several attractions run by Merlin, or to several of the Royal Palaces, there's a discount - as there is for family groups - but check first on the practicalities of travelling before buying a multiple-site ticket.

If the cost is more than £20/person, we describe it as a 'very significant charge'.

What you can see from the pavement
There are plenty of opportunities for seeing famous buildings and getting a feel for important aspects of London's life and history without actually going inside the buildings. You can wander around the City, for example, and have lunch in a pub there - and get a sense of its busyness. If you go near the Royal Courts of Justice and the Inner and Middle Temple Gardens, you will get a flavour of the legal world.

Some major sights do not have an 'inside' which you can visit, such as Admiralty Arch, the Albert Memorial, Big Ben, Cleopatra's Needle, Marble Arch, and

Trafalgar Square. In each case some sense of the history comes from the architecture, the facade and the location.

Taking in history from the statues and monuments

There are statues and monuments all over the place, most of which, by their very nature, can easily be seen. They are generally overlooked and undervalued. Some are described on *www.londondrum.com/cityguide/monuments-and-statues.php*. There are more extensive descriptions in books, and you can pick up an enormous amount of interesting information about London and its history from a study of the statues and monuments. You discover, for example, that Marble Arch was originally a gateway into Buckingham Palace but was moved to its present location in 1851 when the Palace was extended.

There are particularly good descriptions by Rupert Hill in *Walking London's statues and monuments* published by New Holland in 2010. This sets out thirteen fact-filled walks with maps and distances, and while individual walks may be too long for some people, it's easy to pick out the best bits which might suit both your interests and capabilities.

A much bigger book published by Merrell is *The statues of London*, by Bullus, Asprey & Gilbert. This contains some brilliant photos of eighty of London's major monuments. It is certainly not something that you would want to carry around with you (because of its size and weight), but having a look at both the pictures and descriptive history would add an extra and enriching dimension to your visit.

Getting good overviews of London

There are now a number of places where you can get good views of and over London, and they include the Shard by London Bridge station, the London Eye, Tower Bridge Walkway and from the Orbit in the Olympic Park, which is due to reopen late in 2013. In addition, there are good (free) views from Waterloo Bridge; the OXO Tower; the Royal Festival Hall level 5, and the upper levels at Tate Modern. Good vantage points are also to be found further out from Hampstead Heath, Primrose Hill, Greenwich Park (by the Observatory), and Alexandra Palace. All of these can be reached step-free.

A completely different approach is to take a trip on the DLR, or on the *Overground*, as there are places where you'll get a rooftop view of different parts of London, even if this is slightly fleeting. You will see all kinds of different things reflecting London's diversity.

Remember that our write-ups are descriptive, and a listing does not mean, and is not intended to mean, that a site is fully accessible. In all cases we describe the barriers, if any, and in some instances we are describing serious challenges !

Inner London
City area

This comprises the City itself, together with the area just to the north and east. It includes the Tower, which is not strictly in the City, Tower Bridge and the St Katharine Dock. The write-up covers two areas in the Eyewitness guide; the City and Smithfield/Spitalfields.

The so-called Square Mile is an area with a high concentration of commercial buildings where millions of pounds change hands every hour. The pavements in the City are often a bit narrow, and can be crowded during the week. However, it's a fascinating area and there are many old and famous buildings. Remember that many of the pubs and restaurants will be shut on both Saturdays and Sundays, although this depends on exactly where they are.

If you need specific information, for example about opening times, then visit the **City Information Centre** just south of St Paul's Cathedral, and across the road (St Pauls Churchyard, EC4M 8BX, *Tel:* 020 7332-1456 *website:* www. visitthecity.co.uk). The staff were helpful, but we found that they knew relatively little about access or the practical issues involved, and we left them a copy of the PHSP guide !

The **City Access Group** publish a booklet which is updated every couple of years giving details about access to various buildings, parking and the location of accessible toilets. It is available on *www.cityoflondon.gov.uk* - go to A (in A-Z menu) and then Accessibility and then Access to city buildings, or via:
Access Team, Department of Community Services,
Corporation of London, PO Box 270, Guildhall, EC2P 2EJ
Tel: 020 7332-1995 *Textphone:* 18001 020 7332-1995.

Accessible rail and tube links are very limited, although the DLR goes to both Bank and Tower Gateway. For many the best way to come will be by road (bus, car or taxi) or from 'accessible' tube stations on the JLE south of the river. Blackfriars and City Thameslink NR stations are 'accessible', as are those at Liverpool Street and Fenchurch Street. Blackfriars also has an 'accessible' tube station on the District line.

Parking in and around the City

Parking is inevitably difficult, and the normal BB rules do not apply, see *Getting around*. There are more than 200 roadside BB spaces, which can be used by Red Badge holders (who work in the area) with no time limit, as well as by BB holders with a prescribed time limit.

Groups of BB spaces (with, of course, no height restriction) can be found at/in:
Aldermanbury Street - with 4 separate BB spaces along the length of the road. 4hr max.

Bartholomew Close - with 16 BB spaces in small groups along the road. Because of one way systems, these can be approached from either Edward Street or Cloth Street. 6hr max, and,
West Smithfield - where there are 13 BB spaces outside St. Bartholomews Hospital around the circus, with a **wheelchair toilet (D85 ST70 NKS)** nearby on the inner ring.
There are CPs at Minories, West Smithfield, White's Row (Spitalfields) and the Barbican, and there's a good CP near the Tower in Lower Thames Street (SatNav EC3R 6DT). All have BB spaces, although holders pay the standard charges. Most have low costs/charges at weekends. For more details see *www.cityoflondon. gov.uk/Corporation* → Services → Transport and streets → Parking → Car parks - council.
The Minories CP (SatNav E1 8LP) is of particular interest, as the GF has a height restriction of 4.26m and so it can be used by taller vehicles.

All-Hallows-by-the-Tower (for brass rubbing) see chapter on *Places of worship*.
Bank of England Museum see chapter on *Museums & galleries*.

The **Barbican** is a sizeable area which has been redeveloped on two levels. It is bounded by London Wall, Moorgate and Aldersgate Street. There are historic sites, high-rise blocks of flats, offices, pubs and shops, both at ground level and on the high-level walkway called the Podium, which covers much of the development. The most interesting places are the Barbican Centre (see the section on *Entertainment*), St Giles Cripplegate church, restored after extensive bomb damage, and the Museum of London (see chapter on *Museums & galleries*). Signage around the area has been improved, but having a good map helps you find your way around.

Broadgate is a massive complex, built near Liverpool Street station. It consists mainly of office blocks, but there are shops, bars and restaurants. Broadgate Arena is a skating rink in winter and an entertainment venue in the summer. When we visited, there were some radio controlled car races taking place. Access is pretty good with ramped/lift routes to most places, although a lack of signposting makes it confusing to a stranger, and there is only stepped access to the arena. There's a **wheelchair toilet** in Liverpool Street station by platform 10, and several others around the development.

Guildhall
Guildhall Yard (PO Box 270), EC2P 2EJ *Tel:* 020 7606-3030
website: www.guildhall.cityoflondon.gov.uk
e-mail: guildhall.events@cityoflondon.gov.uk
This has been the administrative centre of the City of London for nearly 900 years. The current building dates from the 15thC. Guildhall Yard outside has

been pedestrianised, with some slightly bumpy surfaces. Around the Yard you will find the Guildhall Art Gallery; the Guildhall itself; a modern building with a large crown/porch jutting out, and the St Lawrence Jewry church. There are 4 BB spaces in Aldermanbury.

In the Guildhall, you can visit the famous Great Hall, unless there's a council meeting or other event. The entrance and security check are located to the left of the modern building (opposite the Art Gallery). It is all flat, and the +3 steps into the Hall can be bypassed by a ramped route. It is less than 100m from the Yard, and there's a **wheelchair toilet (D80 ST70)** just past the security/bag search point.

There are other halls in the building, used for special events. The main access to these is from 71 Basinghall Street. In the basement that are two crypts and the Livery Hall, while the Old Library is on the first floor. There's a lift quite close to the Basinghall Street entrance linking all three floors. In the basement there's a **wheelchair toilet (D80 ST80)** between the Livery Hall and the Crypt. An alternative access can be provided to the basement via a platform lift (D90 L130) near the entrance to the Guildhall Great Hall, and the two crypts are linked by another platform lift bypassing −4.

Just around the corner in Aldermanbury is the **City Business Library** (CBL), **Guildhall Library**, **Clock Museum** and a bookshop. All are reached via +3 steps with a platform lift (D80 L110) bypass. Inside, the CBL has flat access while the Guildhall Library is reached via a platform lift (D80 L130) bypassing +12 steps. The Clock Museum is flat from the CBL, to the left of the entrance.

There's a **wheelchair toilet (D80 ST80)** on the 2nd floor in the admin area, reached via a separate staff operated lift.

Guildhall Art Gallery and Roman Amphitheatre see chapter on *Museums and galleries*.

Leadenhall Market

Gracechurch Street, EC3V 1LR *website:* www.leadenhallmarket.co.uk
A small but attractive Victorian market located near the Lloyds building and another entrance from Leadenhall Place. It has a variety of clothes and food shops. It's generally flat and compact but the main roadway is cobbled and there are kerbs. The nearest accessible toilets are in the Royal Exchange or in Fenchurch Street station.

Lloyds of London

1 Lime Street, EC3M 7HA *website:* www.lloyds.com
This is an interesting modern 'inside out' building with the piping, ducting and the lifts built on the outside. Lloyd's is the centre of the world's insurance market. The public gallery was closed some years ago although the building is open on one of the Open House weekend days. A virtual tour of the building is available online from the website.

Mansion House

Walbrook, EC4N 8BH   *Tel:* 020 7626-2500   *website:* www.cityoflondon.gov.uk
Located between Walbrook and Lombard Street, almost opposite the Bank of
England. It is the residence and office of the Lord Mayor of the City of London. It
is therefore very much a working building.
There are tours once a week on Tuesdays at 14.00, when you just come along
and join the queue. The tour lasts about an hour, and you will go only about
200m. Admission charge.
Entrance +2 small steps, but there's a step-free alternative about 10m away which
can be made available. You enter the Walbrook Hall, coming in the same way that
all visitors come, including the Queen. There's a security/bag check. Then during
the introductory talk, there are chairs to sit on.
Much of the visit is to the rooms on the 1st floor, via +23 steps, with a lift (D70
W100 L160) to bypass these on request. During the tour there are two other
rooms with seats which can be used. The Egyptian Hall is very grand (and
interesting). **Wheelchair toilet (D90 ST80)** on the GF, to the right of the guests
cloakroom, and the corridor leading to the mens and womens toilets.

Monument

Monument Street EC3 8AH   *Tel:* 020 7626-2717
website: www.themonument.info
A giant Doric column commemorating the Great Fire of London. It is 62m high
and lies the same distance from the supposed site of the outbreak of the fire in
Pudding Lane. There are +311 spiralled steps, so it can hardly be described as
accessible !
The recent development plan included arrangements for live views to be relayed
from the gallery to visitors on the ground, especially useful to those for whom
311 steps is a problem.

Museum of London see chapter on *Museums & galleries.*

Old Bailey (Central Criminal Court)

Old Bailey Road, EC4M 7EH   *Tel:* 020 7248-3277
website: www.cityoflondon.gov.uk (reached via *City of London* → *Services* →
Advice and benefits → *Legal advice* → *Central Criminal Court*)
On the corner with Newgate Street, this is the central court complex where many
famous criminal cases have been tried. It was located next to Newgate Prison.
It is, of course, an old building which was opened in 1907, and whose design does
not lend itself to modifications which would improve access. All the courts have a
public gallery, but these have fixed seating and small gangways.
Although virtually all of the public part of the building is not accessible, we
were told that, on the 'other side' of the facility, for the court officials, lawyers,
witnesses and those charged, changes are being made to make some of the courts
accessible.

Courts 1-4 are entered from Newgate Street, with +60 or so steps. Court 18 is a further +17. From the entrance in Warwick Passage, Courts 13-16 are +30; Courts 5-8 +30+40, and Courts 9-12 are +30+40+40.

One courtroom where a visit might be possible for a chair user or disabled walker, is court 17. A specific visit would be an entirely chancy business, as the lists of which cases go where are only prepared the day before. If you are very keen to see/hear a case, we suggest that you turn up on the day at the main entrance, ask for Customer Services - and just see what is possible.

Old Spitalfields Market

16 Horner Square, Spitalfields, E1 6AA *Tel:* 020 7247-8556
websites: www.oldspitalfieldsmarket.com *and* www.visitspitalfields.com
e-mail: info@oldspitalfieldsmarket.com

A modern market development on the site of Spitalfields, some 500m east of Liverpool Street station. It is in an area known for its spirit and strong sense of community at the heart of the East End. It has been a place of almost constant change, and over the years has been a magnet to numerous waves of immigrants. The market lies between Brushfield Street and Lamb Street, and stretches for some 120m by 50m with a big office block in the centre. Much of it is covered. The surfaces are smooth, and it is mainly step-free, apart from ±2 steps which run along much of Brushfield Street. Some of the shops in the old buildings have a step or threshold at the entrance.

There's a **wheelchair toilet (D75 ST80 NKS)** in a corner near Lamb Street, by the Wollstonecraft Gate.

The **Royal Exchange** is on the corner of Threadneedle Street and Cornhill, opposite the Bank of England. It was opened in 1844 to replace an earlier trading centre. In 2002 the central courtyard was reopened and contains a restaurant and bar, surrounded by some high class shops. There are +8 to10 steps at entrances on three sides, but there's step-free access from the back, opposite the statue of Reuter. The ramps bypassing the small steps are slightly rough. The facades in and around the courtyard are magnificent, even if you can't afford to go shopping! There's a lift (D80 W100 L110) in the far right corner (from the step-free entrance). This goes to a further and much enlarged bar and restaurant gallery on the 1st floor, and there's a **wheelchair toilet (D70+ ST70+)** in the basement, to the left from the lift.

St Katharine Docks

50 St Katharine's Way, E1W 1LA *Tel:* 020 7264 5318
website: www.skdocks.co.uk

A busy and attractive area by Tower Bridge, forming one of the earlier stages of the Docklands Development. The dock consists of three separate basins protected from the river tides by a lock. Various bridges can be opened to let the yachts in and out.

It is located alongside Tower Bridge between St Katharine's Way, East Smithfield and Thomas More Street. It can be accessed by several different step-free routes, including the riverside walk by the Tower of London. The area is generally flat but there are some cobbled and bumpy sections. There are expensive boats (to view !), shops, restaurants, cafés, bars and offices. The website includes a good map showing what is where.

There are 4 BB spaces in Mews Street, behind the *Dickens Inn* which are protected by a security barrier with an intercom button. You can approach the spaces from St Katharine's Way. If you come from Thomas More Street they are on your right when you get to the No Entry sign into St Katharine's Way. We were told that any BB holders could park there, and did so ourselves. It is potentially a very useful location, from which people could visit the Bridge or Tower and come back for a drink or a meal afterwards at the Inn (which has a **wheelchair toilet**, accessed by a lift, see *Recommended itineraries* on the website, where other restaurants are also listed).

St Bartholomew the Great see chapter on *Places of worship*.
St Paul's Cathedral see chapter on *Places of worship*.

Tower Bridge (Walkway & Exhibition)
SE1 2UP *Tel*: 020 7403-3761
website: www.towerbridge.org.uk *e-mail:* enquiries@towerbridge.org.uk
One of London's major landmarks, completed in 1894. It houses a museum with an imaginative presentation of the history of the bridge, and there are potentially superb views from the walkways joining the towers. Unfortunately, some ramped platforms on the walkways to enable both chair users and young children to see properly, have been removed. These were put in more than ten years ago at our suggestion, and were enormously helpful to many. We understand that they have been removed so as to facilitate the use of the space for corporate events - to which we say Hmmmm....... So far we have failed to get them put back. Admission charge.
Entrance in the north-west tower, nearest the Tower of London. To avoid steps from the riverside, approach it along the main (elevated) Tower Bridge Road. Step-free access throughout the five floors via lifts (D120 W350 L150) at each end. These bypass some 200 steps. Visiting the engine room which houses the mechanism for raising the roadway to allow big ships to pass, is now much easier. There is a glass lift from the side of the bridge to get to the lower towpath level. Thus the distance involved is more like 100m, compared with the previous step-free route southwards of around 400m. It involved going along the bridge to its end, and doubling back along Horselydown Lane (which is what you would need to do if the lift isn't working).
Adapted toilet (D90 ST65) on the 2nd floor of the SE tower, by the lift, and a **wheelchair toilet (D90 ST75)** in the engine room (see above).

Tower of London

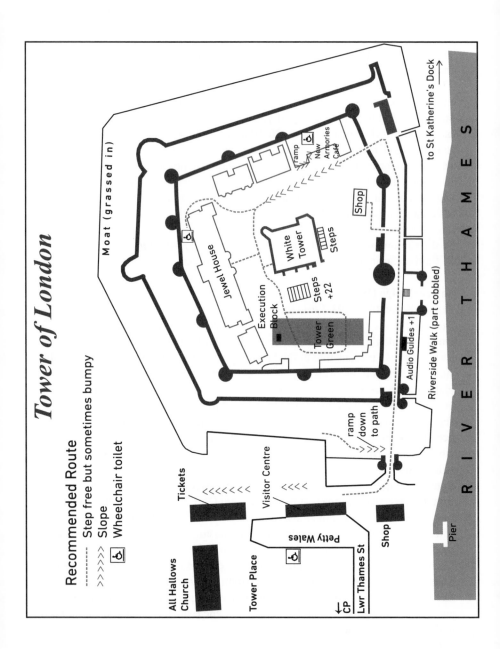

Recommended Route

------- Step free but sometimes bumpy
>>>>> Slope
♿ Wheelchair toilet

All Hallows Church

Tower Place

Petty Wales

Lwr Thames St

↓CP

Tickets

Visitor Centre

Shop

♿

ramp down to path

Moat (grassed in)

Jewel House

Execution Block

Tower Green

White Tower

Steps

Steps +22

ramp

New Armouries Café

Shop

Audio Guides +1

Riverside Walk (part cobbled)

to St Katherine's Dock →

Pier

R I V E R   T H A M E S

Tower of London
Tower Hill EC3N 4AB
Tel: 0844 482-7777 (the HRP switchboard) *DisEnq:* 020 3166-6266
Textphone: 18001 0844 482-7777
website: www.hrp.org.uk/toweroflondon *e-mail:* visitorservices.TOL@hrp.org.uk
One of London's prime tourist attractions. The Tower is both a fortress and a
royal palace, and its history goes back some 900 years. Significant admission
charge.
There's a CP at the end of Lower Thames Street with BB spaces a height
restriction of 1.98m, and lift access (D80 W130 L130) to get in and out. Tower
Gateway DLR station has step-free access.
There is smooth sloped access down Tower Hill from Byward Street and from
Tower Place. A new *Ticket Office and Welcome Centre* are alongside Tower
Hill on the right. There are also some new toilets off Petty Wales, including a
wheelchair toilet (D80 ST80). There's a charge for the general toilets, but the
accessible one uses the NKS and is free.
There may be long queues to get in on popular days such as bank holidays and
summer weekends. **Chair users and other disabled visitors should make their
presence known at the Welcome Centre (on the right, coming down the hill
called Petty Wales)**. There is an excellent *Access Guide* which you can download
from the website. This is found under *Tower →Plan your visit→Visitor access*.
They would post you a copy if you don't have an internet connection. There's
also a good diagram (as a pdf file) on the Visit Planner page of the website, at the
bottom, simply labeled Tower of London.
You need to allow at least 2 to 3 hours for a relaxed visit. There are accessible
(ramped) catering facilities in the New Armouries Café. Audio-guides and
conducted tours are available.
The Tower consists of a group of buildings with two surrounding walls. The inner
area is roughly 250m square and many of the paths and courtyards are cobbled
and sloping. Since the buildings are several hundred years old, access to many of
them is a major challenge !
A complete visit to the various towers involves well over 200 steps, some of them
irregular, spiraled and steep. **However, it's possible to see a lot from outside
and chair users can get in to see the Crown Jewels, and go down to the
basement of the White Tower by lift.**

The flat/sloped route shown on the diagram, takes you through the Middle and
Byward Towers and along Water Lane parallel to the river. On the left is the
Gallery shop with step-free access. Turning left further on, go through the arch
and up the hill past the White Tower, turn left again at the top, and the entrance
to the Crown Jewels is on your right while that to the White Tower lift is on
your left. Ahead is Tower Green where executions used to take place, and you'll
probably see some of the famous ravens. You have to go back by the same route,

and the whole distance is about 700/800m, partly cobbled.

The **Jewel House**, where you can see the **Crown Jewels,** now has step-free access. Visitors pass through three halls, walking past large video presentations. You see the Jewels from a horizontal moving walkway. There are +3 steps to the viewing platform if you want to take a more leisurely look.

The **White Tower** has 11+12+13+5 steps from the entrance towards the river. **There is a lift (D75 W75 L130) which goes to the basement exhibition**, accessed from the upper level opposite the Jewel House (via what is normally the White Tower exit). You need to ask one of the Yeoman Warders to be able to use it. The basement is −15 from the north (upper) exit.

The wheelchair toilet outside the Tower off Petty Wales has been described above.

Inside the Tower there are only two **wheelchair toilets** for general use:
- one is behind the Jewel House (as shown on the diagram) where the attendant in either the womens or mens should have the key;
- the other is off the New Armouries Café, where there are also BCF, although to use it you'll need to ask one of the staff.

We were told that there are additional accessible toilets in the educational facilities for school groups.

The **Ceremony of the Keys** is the ritual of locking up the Tower, which takes place every evening between 21.30 and 22.05, and has done so in much the same way for some 700 years. Apparently, it was a little late one night in 1941 when a bomb blew the escort off their feet. Admission by ticket only from the Keys Clerk at the Tower. Although there are no steps, for getting into the Tower, disabled visitors should mention their disability when applying.

From the entry gate the total distance involved is <250m, and note that there's nowhere to sit down en route.

The conventional exit is through a small door (for pedestrians) which is part of the main gate which has just been ceremonially locked. The bottom of this door is about 60cm high, and it's quite narrow. Wheelchair users, and anyone else who might find this exit to be difficult will be escorted out using an alternative step-free route.

The advice on the website is that bookings must be at least two months in advance through the winter, and three months in the summer.

Wesley's House & Chapel

49 City Road, EC1Y 1AU *Tel:* 020 7253-2262
website: www.wesleyschapel.org.uk
e-mail: administration@wesleyschapel.org.uk
About 150m from Old Street tube station. A space in the small CP outside the chapel can be reserved. Via the back entrance to the House, there are −15 steps to

the basement, then +1−1, and +15 to the GF, +21 to the 1st floor and +21 to the 2nd. The front door gives flat access to the GF, which has two rooms. Audio guide available, describing the rest of the house.

Access to the Chapel is step-free, with lift (D80 W105 L140) access to the basement. This contains a Museum of Methodism, with uneven but step-free access, and a **wheelchair toilet (D85 ST75)**.

The South Bank & Southwark

The south bank of the river opposite Westminster and the City, has developed rapidly in recent years. There is a pleasant riverside walk along much of it, going from near Westminster Bridge by the old County Hall, right the way along to Tower Bridge. There is a longer description of the route in the chapter entitled *Recommended itineraries*. There are several accessible tube stations relatively near this part of the riverside, and the RV1 bus route from Covent Garden to Tower Gateway as well. There are **accessible toilets** in the Festival Hall, British Film Institute, National Theatre, OXO Tower, Tate Modern, Shakespeare's Globe, Southwark Cathedral, Hays Galleria (though you need to get a key from security staff for this one) and City Hall. There are also accessible toilets in several pubs en route, notably the *Founders Arms* and the *Anchor*.

Parking at the Festival Hall and National Theatre end is relatively good, in that there are three CPs along Belvedere Road, but fewer choices at the Tower Bridge end. There's a Q-Park at Butler's Wharf in Gainsford Street, although this doesn't appear to have any BB spaces, nor a lift.

Some of the sights are grouped around the Jubilee gardens, notably the London Eye, London Aquarium, London Dungeon, and the Festival Hall complex. Others are grouped near Tate Modern, with the Millennium Bridge linking across to St Paul's Cathedral. There's another group between Southwark and London Bridges, and then there's HMS Belfast and Tower Bridge.

Note the viewing gallery in the Shard by London Bridge station.

Anchor pub (Bankside), 34 Park Street, Bank End, SE1 9EF *Tel:* 020 7407-1577 On the riverside by Cannon Street railway bridge, at the junction with Bank End. Attached to the Premier Inn. The pub dates from the late 17thC, after the Southwark fire of 1676 and is full of split levels. There is, however, a step-free entrance on the corner as you come from the west and the Millennium Bridge. This leads to a GF bar where 30% is step-free. **Wheelchair toilet (D80 ST70 but somewhat congested)** with BCF on the GF, through the door marked 'toilets'. Just to the right is a platform lift (D100 L130) going to the 1st floor where there's another bar/eating area. There is a ±1 [10cm] threshold to get to the outside seating at this level.

The riverside terrace across the road has step-free access from Bankside and moveable chairs and tables. A very pleasant spot in the summer.

Bankside Gallery see chapter on *Museums & galleries*.
Belfast see *HMS Belfast* below.

Borough Market
website: www.boroughmarket.org.uk
Under railway arches this market is located between High Street and Southwark cathedral. There's an early morning fruit and vegetable market which closes around 09.00. There's a range of bars and eating places that would be quite lively on weekends and lunchtimes. The **wheelchair toilet** off Jubilee market towards the cathedral end was locked when we visited.

Britain at War Experience
64 Tooley Street, SE1 2TF *Tel:* 020 7403-3171
website: www.britainatwar.co.uk
This small exhibition attempts to recreate the fury of the London blitz and to articulate people's other experiences during WW2. You can sit in an Anderson shelter and hear the raids overhead.
Ramped entrance. There is a route without steps, but you need staff help. There's a door to bypass the +1−1 steps into the simulated lift (to the underground). The room where the film is shown about the history of the war has movable seats. The Anderson shelter is step-free with two side benches, and space in the middle for a wheelchair user. You can hear the sounds of war with both the air raid warning siren, and the all clear. The sinister wail of the air raid warning is the abiding memory of all who lived through the war.
The Rainbow Club room has +3, but you can see in. The Blitz Experience area is normally reached +3+9 −11, but can be accessed step-free if you ask a staff member. There is an **adapted toilet (D70 ST40)**.

Bubblecafé
Blossom Square, Potters Field Park, More London SE1 2AA *Tel:* 020 7407-9760
Located right by Tower Bridge but on the riverside level. A small café with both inside and outside eating and sitting areas. **Wheelchair toilet (D80 ST70)**.

City Hall
Queen's Walk, SE1 2AA *Tel:* 020 7983-4100 *Textphone:* 020 7983-4458
website: www.london.gov.uk/city-hall
City Hall is located on the south bank of the Thames, halfway between Tower Bridge and HMS Belfast, near one end of the Riverside Walk.
The newly constructed offices of the Mayor of the Greater London Authority is often described as a glass onion. Its design makes great use of glass, and the Council Chamber is surrounded by glass so that it's easy to look in and see what is happening. The architect has made extensive use of curved ramps in the building. There is public access to galleries in the Council Chamber.

The main entrance is through two revolving doors from the riverside, but there's an alternative entrance for chair users some 15m away through a conventional door. There is the usual bag search procedure as you come in. The building has ten floors, but the public only has access to the GF, LGF, and to floor 2 to see the council chamber, and attend meetings when the council is sitting.

The GF is a reception area. At the back of the GF are two public lifts (D100 W120 L180).

A curved ramp in the centre of the building leads down to the LGF which is entirely step-free. It houses ten public meeting rooms and a universal prayer room. There is also a café and an impressive scale model of central London, best viewed from the ramp.

Floors 1 and 2 house the Assembly Chamber where council meetings take place. You can get a good view, even when the council is not sitting. Next to the lift on floor 2, there are spaces for wheelchair users at the back of the large public gallery. There are also some spaces at the front, but access to these must be arranged in advance. You will be escorted to the 1st floor via separate lifts, which are identical and immediately next to the public lifts, but are behind a security barrier.

All the meeting rooms have an induction loop.

There are **wheelchair toilets**:

- on the GF opposite the entrance and near the lifts. This is a *Changing places* facility, with BCF. It is spacious, and with a hoist to facilitate transfer to a temporary chair which fits over the toilet (if needed);
- on the LGF between meeting rooms 5 and 6, where the wheelchair toilet (D90 ST100) also has BCF.

Clink Prison

1 Clink Street, SE1 9DG *Tel:* 020 7403-0900 *website:* www.clink.co.uk
Located under the railway arches leading to Cannon Street with a cobbled stretch outside. Admission charge. There are −10 steps down to the ticket office where there is a turnstile W50 to gain access. The prison is small and there are −2 and then +10 to get out via a separate exit (bypassing the turnstile).

Design Museum see chapter on *Museums & galleries.*

Gabriel's Wharf

website: www.coinstreet.org/developments/gabrielswharf
A small, flat pedestrianised area located on the South Bank between the National Theatre and the OXO tower, off Upper Ground. It has eateries and bars together with a number of shops which have step-free access. There's a slope down from the riverside walk. There are **two adapted toilets (D85 ST85 inward opening door NKS)** next to the Studio 6 bar/restaurant. Outdoor seating in the summer.

Garden Museum see chapter on *Museums and galleries.*

Hays Galleria

Tooley Street, SE1 2HD *website:* www.haysgalleria.co.uk

Situated just opposite Weston Street, this is an attractive development on the riverside on the site of an old tea wharf. The centrepiece is a covered courtyard with a remarkable working sculpture of a fantasy ship in the middle. There are good views of *HMS Belfast* and Tower Bridge from the river frontage, and several restaurants and shops, together with a pub. Most of the shops have flat access and there are some stalls. What is disappointing, is that the new *Horniman* pub and *Côte Brasserie* restaurant have split levels. The planning permission regulations don't seem to work somewhere along the line.

On the approach to the Galleria from Tooley Street, there are some cobbled roads, presumably left to retain some of the areas original character. Around the Galleria there are ramped bypasses to all the steps, though they're not always obvious. There are several eating places with flat access, including a large *Café Rouge*. During the summer most of them have outside tables which are easily accessible. The upper, rather cramped parts of the *Horniman* pub, are step-free. There are −5 steps to the bar, or −2 through a side entrance.

The situation over toilets would be laughable if it wasn't so infuriating. There are three wheelchair toilets on site, one inside, off the reception area of Counting House (near Tooley Street), one off the reception of Shackleton House (to the right of the four curved steps in the centre) and one ostensibly public one, with a green door, to the left of the four curved steps.

This is kept locked, and has a notice on it saying *"Accessible toilet. To gain access please contact security on 020 7403-3583."*

There is a key held at Shackleton House on the opposite side to the Galleria, or you can ask any of the staff at the various restaurants to call security for you. It is a **wheelchair toilet (D75+ ST75+)**. In our view, this isn't a very satisfactory arrangement, and we suggested that it should be fitted with a RADAR NKS lock.

HMS Belfast

Morgans Lane, Tooley Street SE1 2JH *Tel:* 020 7940-6300

website: www.iwm.org.uk/belfast

This cruiser saw service during WW2, and supported the Normandy landings. She was active until 1965 and served in Korea. She is now permanently moored on the riverside just upstream of Tower Bridge and run by the Imperial War Museum. Significant admission charge.

In the description below, we have used numbers from the *Audio points* on the Visitor Map/plan you will be given with your ticket.

To get on board from the riverside Queen's Walk, the distance, going via the ticket office/shop and along the gangway is nearly 150m. The shop area is quite congested. If you take the right-hand side of the gangway you can use the platform lift (D80 L130) at the end to bypass the −4 steps to the deck.

They have gone to considerable lengths to make parts of the ship accessible,

and chair users can get to most of the Quarter Deck (where you arrive) and of the Upper Deck.
Going up to see the bridge and wireless room, and down to the engine room, involves steep ladders and well over 100 steps, and is only possible for the relatively agile. In spite of this, there's enough to see in the accessible parts of the ship to make it a really interesting visit. While there are certainly some slightly uneven surfaces on the two accessible decks, and some ridges to get over, generally they have done a good job in easing/improving access for chair users. There's a platform lift (D80 L130) near the torpedo and between *4* and *6* on the plan, to get to the upper deck (and to avoid having to use the steep ramp). On the upper deck it's by *30*. It is shown on the plan, but you have to look very closely to see exactly where it is.
There's a **wheelchair toilet (D90 ST100+)** on the Quarterdeck level, which is about 40-50m along the left side of the ship from your arrival point via the lift. It is very spacious, and as a result was also being used as a storeroom for two spare chairs. For some reason it is not shown on the plan.
On the website we found an interesting *Virtual Tour* of the ship with some additions to the information generally available, including the following:
- "School classes and youth groups, from aged 8, can now sleepover in unique, stimulating and affordable accommodation on board. HMS Belfast's sleepover provides the opportunity to experience what it is like to live and sleep in 1950s renovated messdecks. Children sleep in original bunks, with authentic lockers. Modern shower facilities are available and separate cabins with en-suite for adults."

What one can do in 2012 ! It was never like that on warships when I grew up ....

London Aquarium (SeaLife)
County Hall, Riverside Building, Westminster Bridge Road, SE1 7PB
Tel: 0871 663-1678 (tickets)
websites: www.londonaquarium.co.uk and www.visitsealife.com/london/
e-mail: sllondon@merlinentertainments.biz
The aquarium is in the basement of the former Greater London Council headquarters, where three huge tanks have been installed together with several smaller tanks, all containing fish and sea creatures from different parts of the world.
Substantial admission charge (and note that this is another Merlin Entertainments site).
A wheelchair can be borrowed if you leave a deposit of £200 (Hmmmm......). This is completely out of line with what happens in other places.
The entrance is from the riverside close to the London Eye. From Westminster Bridge there are 40+ steps, but there is step-free access via Belvedere Road and Chicheley Street through the Jubilee Gardens. The route is some 600m from the top of the steps from the bridge.
Step-free entrance, and the aquarium is accessible throughout without steps using the lifts. The distance involved is roughly 750m. There are almost no seats

en route. Some passages have a low level of lighting.

The two lifts (D90 W140 L200) take you to level −2 and then the route leads upwards. It takes you through different regional zones where you can see the large Indian Ocean, Pacific Ocean and Atlantic Ocean tanks, along with freshwater fish. In between the big tanks, there is a series of small tanks with different groups of species which you can also view from the side. Most of these tanks can be viewed by young children and chair users, though in a few the window is quite high up and therefore more difficult to see from a low eyeline. The rays tank is accessed via a slight ramp and seeing them is not a problem. Most displays are easily seen by a chair user. The tanks are well lit, but the corridors are often quite dark.

There's a single lift at the other end, alongside an escalator to get up to level −1, where there are more exhibits including another view of the big tanks.

From here you can take a lift (D130 W150 L200) to the shark walk where you look down through a glass floor, bypassing a set of stairs. Then you take the same lift back to level −1. From here you can exit using another lift or there's an escalator further down the marked route. Before leaving there is a shop.

There are **wheelchair toilets** all of which included BCF:

* on the GF to the right of the lifts that take you down to level −2 (D80 ST80);
* on level −2 near the entrance to the Thames Walk (D90 ST80); and,
* on level −1 between the rivers/ponds section and the Pacific tank (D90 ST110).

London Bridge Experience & London Tombs

2 Tooley Street, London Bridge, SE1 2PF *Tel:* 0800 0434-666
website: www.thelondonbridgeexperience.com

Located directly under the Bridge, and on the Thameside Path, it can be approached either from London Bridge station along Tooley Street or from the Borough Street market past the Southwark Cathedral refectory.

There is a significant admission charge, but *The Experience* offers a unique interactive attraction with actors playing various roles. You can reduce the cost quite a lot by booking online.

You go through a succession of dark and dingy rooms with impressive displays and special effects, covering the entire history of the bridge. Then you descend into the Tombs where there are a whole range of scares and surprises. It is all very dark, and there are strobe lights, loud noises, and (the only bit a chair user would have to bypass) the Big Squeeze where the walls come in and try to squeeze the life out of you. It is NOT an attraction for the faint hearted, but our survey team were impressed. You go around in groups of about 12-15.

The site is quite compact, and most of the floor surfaces are reasonably smooth. There's only one slightly unexpected short slope and a small +1−1 over a short bridge in the Tombs. It IS dark, almost throughout. There's a platform lift (D90 W90 L120) to bypass the ±19 steps between the two levels. A chair user (with strong nerves !) can see and do almost everything, and there'll be a staff member on hand to guide you through any bypass when necessary (particularly for the Big Squeeze).

A visit takes about an hour, and you'll be able to sit down three times en route for various presentations and confrontations.

Café, shop and toilets at the end of the visit. The **adapted toilet (D70 ST30)** had a washbasin blocking the ST space and we suggested moving it to another wall when we visited.

London Dungeon

Riverside Building, County Hall, Westminster Bridge Road, SE1 7PB

Tel: 0871 423-2240 *website:* www.thedungeons.com/london/en

e-mail: londondungeon@merlinentertainments.biz

Situated between the Eye and the Aquarium, the Dungeon consists of a series of dark vaults with gruesome actor-led tableaux. The stories represent some of the darker and grimmer aspects of British history. You will find ghosts, the Plague and the Great Fire of London.

It moved to this site from Tooley Street, where it had been for many years,.

There's a surprisingly good description about Accessibility on the website.

Substantial admission charge and you may be asked for 'proof of disability' to justify free entry by a carer/companion. Entry is based on time slots and queues outside.

There are +6 steps at the entrance, but they have a Stairclimber to facilitate (manual) wheelchair users to get in. Electric chair users need to contact the Dungeon in advance, and will need to come in via the London Eye booking hall (see the London Eye write-up). This is the normal exit route from the Dungeon. The number of chair users in the venue is limited to 1 per tour group, and a total of 3 in the building at any one time.

The floor surfaces are quite rough in places and it's dark inside, with eerie sound effects and some strobe lighting. The tour is spread over two levels, so there are some steps. Staff members will show you step-free routes if you ask, and there's a platform lift. There are two places where the floor 'shakes' briefly from side to side, and disabled walkers need to be aware of this. The first is during the initial '*Descent*' and the other is in the Guy Fawkes section.

The site is quite small, and a visit takes about 90 minutes. You go around with a group of about 25 into a series of quite small caverns. In order to see, those with a low eyeline need to position themselves towards the front. Hopefully the 'cast' will facilitate this, but don't rely on them as this didn't happen when we visited. There are few opportunities for sitting down.

Care is needed because of low lighting levels and uneven floor surfaces. You can expect to be startled by loud noises, and members of the cast may jump out at you in the dark.

You'll need to take your own view about participating in the two rides. The first is a boat trip where you will get wet and the other (at the end) is a sudden drop to replicate the drop when people have been executed by hanging. Both involve transferring to a seat at a different height from a wheelchair, and will need you to have some body strength in being able to sit vertically. The warnings from the owners are written (as is quite common these days) more to protect themselves from litigation than to provide practical advice. With appropriate help, people may be able to cope, though both rides can be bypassed, and if you need to do this, just ask.

There's a **wheelchair toilet (D80 ST85)** just past the entrance foyer (marked Knights). The mens and womens toilets are adjacent (labelled Kings and Queens). There are other wheelchair accessible toilets at the end of the tour in the London Eye reception area.

The exit is through the shop which leads into the 4D Experience and London Eye reception area which is ramped at the end of the building.

London Eye
Riverside Building, County Hall, Westminster Bridge Road, SE17PB
Tel: bookings 0871 781-3000 *DisEnq/bookings:* 0871 222-0188
Textphone: use the prefix 18001 *Customer services:* 0870 990-8883
website: www.londoneye.com
e-mail: accessiblebooking@londoneye.com

The London Eye is a huge observation wheel on the riverside near Westminster Bridge and by a corner of Jubilee Gardens. Erected to mark the Millennium, it is some 135m high and dominates the London skyline. The pods (or capsules) are mounted on the outside of the rim of the wheel, and electric motors independently rotate each pod to keep it upright.

The area around, and alongside the river is flat.

Significant admission charge. It is part of the Merlin Entertainments group.

The Eye closes for part of January for essential maintenance.

There are BB spaces some 300 to 600m away on Belvedere Road, under the Hayward Gallery and under the National Theatre. The accessible JLE tube stations at Waterloo and Westminster are both about 800m away. From Westminster, go over Westminster bridge.

The London Eye ticket office is in the corner of County Hall, with a rather badly signed ramp on the side of the building past the *Zen café/kiosk* to bypass the +6 steps at the principal entrance opposite the Eye. You have to go back towards Chicheley Street. At busy times, most people pre-book a timed slot for their 'flight'. This can be done either by phone or on-line. It is also possible to just turn up and go, though at busy times you may have to wait a while. The 'flight' lasts for about half an hour.

Wheelchairs are available on loan from the customer service desk inside the ticket office foyer, but a deposit of £350 is required, using a credit card (!). We did query this (as it seems to be a quite extraordinary requirement), but were told that this is correct. It's now included on the website, but is totally out of line with practice elsewhere at London's attractions.

There's an information page for disabled guests on the website. Only two chair users are allowed in each capsule, with a maximum of eight using the wheel at any one time.

From the riverside walk, the approach to the Eye itself is up a ramp about 40m long. For chair users the staff will stop the wheel and slot in a little cover plate to make getting in and out easier. Each capsule or pod takes up to thirty people. There's a central seat, but most people stand up and move around during the flight to see the views on different sides. There's adequate room for a chair user. There are two **wheelchair toilets (D80 ST90)** both with BCF, off the ticket office foyer. You have to go 100m from the start of the outside ramp all the way through the foyer (turning first right, and then left) to reach the loos. The foyer is commonly congested and busy, as it's where people buy or collect tickets.

London Fire Brigade Museum
94a Southwark Bridge Road, SE1 0EG *Tel:* 020 8555-1200 ext: 39894
website: www.london-fire.gov.uk
For prearranged group tours only, just over 120m from the junction with Marshalsea road. Admission charge. The museum holds exhibits depicting the history of firefighting in the capital from the Great Fire of London in 1666, up to and including the present day. The half of the museum with the larger exhibit is accessible step-free. The other half containing smaller artifacts can only be reached by flights of curved stairs but specific items can be brought out to the main room on request. The **wheelchair toilet (D80 ST90+)** with BCF is on the far side of the exhibition hall on the GF.

Old St Thomas's Operating Theatre
9A St Thomas' Street, SE1 9RY *Tel:* 020 7188-2679
website: www.thegarret.org.uk *e-mail:* curator@thegarret.org.uk
West of Guy's hospital and about 60m from Borough High Street. The museum is in the barn-like roof space in a church tower, and used in the 19thC as an operating theatre before the days of anasthetics. Admission charge.

Access is difficult even for the fit and able. It involves +1+2 steps, and then +34 up a narrow spiral staircase with only a vertical rope handrail to hang on to. This leads to the ticket desk. Then there are +17, through a walkway W53cm, then −2. Access to the operating theatre where doctors demonstrated their techniques to colleagues and students, is via +1−2, or +1+10−6 via the balcony where the audience sat. The staff are willing to organise an educational tour/event in nearby premises for groups who would find the physical access to the museum to be too challenging, describing the development of medical techniques over the centuries.

Oxo Tower
OXO Tower Wharf, Barge House Street, South Bank, SE1 9PH
Tel: 020 7803-3888
website: www.harveynichols.com/oxo-tower-london
e-mail: oxo.reservations@harveynichols.com
The tower was built in 1928 to advertise a meat extract. It now houses some
shops and restaurants at riverside level, and a bar and restaurant on the eighth
floor together with the public viewing gallery from which you can get superb
views. The Riverside Walk entrance is flat and there are two large lifts at the back.
On the riverside level there are two eateries and there's a **wheelchair toilet (D90
ST90+)** on the same level in the U-shaped loop that goes past the lifts. The loo is
on the Gabriel's Wharf side.
On the 8th floor is the Oxo Tower bar, brasserie and restaurant which is step-free
with good views. **Part of the balcony/viewing area is in fact a 'public' area,
reached via a public right of way,** so even though it looks as though it's part of
a privately owned bar, you don't have to buy an expensive drink!
Adapted cubicle (D70 ST65) with BCF in the mens toilets on the 8th floor, and
we assume that the womens is the same.

Shakespeare's Globe Museum see chapter on *Museums & galleries.*
Southwark Cathedral see chapter on *Places of worship.*
St George's RC Cathedral see chapter on *Places of worship.*
Tate Modern see chapter on *Museums & galleries*

The Shard
Joiner Street, SE1 9SP
Tel: 0844 499-7111 (for bookings) *website:* www.the-shard.com
see: http://www.theviewfromtheshard.com/#plan-your-visit/visitor-information
e-mail: enquiries@theviewfromtheshard.com
The Shard is a dramatic addition to the London skyline. At 310m (1,016ft), it is
the tallest building in Western Europe housing hotels and offices, as well as two
viewing platforms which have step-free access.
*The view over all the Thames-side sights is superb, and you look down on the
diminutive Tower of London. Seeing the extent of the railway network, with
its toy-size trains moving from station to station is remarkable. You may also
see maintenance teams going past outside in well secured cradles, keeping the
windows clean !*
It is located between London Bridge station and Guy's Hospital. The station is
built on a massive viaduct, above ground, and is currently being redeveloped.
The View is approached from ground level on Joiner Street.
If you come to London Bridge on the Jubilee line and use the lift, you go through
the ticket barriers, and turn right, using the only step-free exit which leads into
Joiner Street. You turn right again into an underground passageway underneath

the NR station. After about 100m, you come out into the open air, and just before that is the entrance to *The View* on your left.

If you approach it from St Thomas Street, go to the junction between Joiner Street and Great Maze Pond, where Guy's Hospital is. The entrance to *The View* is about 50m up Joiner Street on the right, just past the escalators. It is surprisingly unobtrusive, with just a couple of staff members standing outside a small door. Signage in the area to help you find it is poor.

A lift from the Joiner Street entrance bypasses the steps up to the 1st floor booking hall.

Very significant admission charge, with discounts for disabled visitors and their carers/companions. Entrance is in a series of half-hour time slots, though you are then free to spend as long as you like on the two viewing platforms. If you're not familiar with London's buildings, buying the Guidebook before going up is potentially a good investment.

Because of the cost, and the possible effect (on the view) of low cloud and rain, there's a fine balance between saving money by booking on-line in advance, and waiting until you're sure of good visibility.

The only toilets are in the 1st floor booking hall area, and when we visited the provision was seriously inadequate, as there are just six unisex cubicles off a narrow corridor, where people were queueing. One cubicle is a **wheelchair cubicle (D90 ST150)** with BCF. The management said that there are plans to provide more toilets, but this may mean that the provisions aren't unisex any more. Note that there's a unisex **wheelchair toilet** at GF level off Joiner Street as part of London Bridge station.

The 1st floor hall with its queues, ticket desk, shop and security check, is quite congested.

As with the viewing platforms, there is nowhere to sit down, although the management say that there are now some seats in the booking hall, and that some 'seating on request' can be provided on the viewing platforms. Talk to the staff. Disabled visitors are taken by a staff member, bypassing the queue, to the security check - which is operated airport style. A lift then takes you to floor 33, and another one goes to floor 68. *The View* is on floors 69 and 72, and you can either take the stairs, or use an 'internal' lift which links the three levels 68, 69 and 72. Floor 69 is an enclosed viewing area, with glass windows right down to floor level, so the view is superb. Floor 72 is a similar area, but is open in the corners, and so can get quite blowy. It is 240m (800ft) high, and can be, literally, up in the clouds.

Floor 69 has some interactive telescopes which will help identify some of the nearby buildings. These are around 1 to 1.1m high, and although the mount will swivel around, they won't suit everybody.

We noted that on Floor 72 there are some horizontal handrails by the windows, useful to some disabled walkers, but there are no handrails on Floor 69.

On Floor 72 you get to the lift by going through a door marked 'No exit'.

Vinopolis
1 Bank End, SE1 9BU   *Tel:* 020 7940-8322
website: www.vinopolis.co.uk *e-mail:* events@vinopolis.co.uk
Situated at the junction with Clink Street, right by the Anchor pub and under the railway arches. Vinopolis offers wine tastings and a self-guided interactive tour covering 'the world of wine'.
Very significant charges for various tastings. A full tour will take you some 400m, and might last a couple of hours if you linger over your wine tasting. The venue is sometimes hired out for events.
The step-free entrance is through the Cantina and Bar Blue on the corner, though when we visited, two signs on the door pointed to the 'main' entrance some 20m along Bank End where there are +3 steps. If it's easier, go in through the bar !
It is step-free throughout, though a few of the surfaces are slightly rough.
Adapted toilet (D75 ST60 - the side wall is angled) with BCF, near the main entrance/exit, and some 15m to the left past the ticket desk. On the way round you will go past the *Wine Wharf* restaurant where a platform lift (W80 L110) bypasses +3 steps, and there's a **wheelchair toilet (D70 ST70)**.

Docklands

An extensive area to the east of London where there has been massive redevelopment, mainly of business and commercial premises. It is served by the only fully step-free access transport system in London, the DLR. This runs mostly at a high level from the Bank or Tower Gateway to Lewisham, Beckton and/or Stratford. It goes to Greenwich, and a trip is recommended in itself, as it provides good views of the redeveloped area. The main part of docklands is north of the river and stretches for nearly 10km eastwards. The area starts at Tower Bridge. St Katharine Dock is described in the City section. A leaflet called *Discover London's real history* is available on the DLR website (*www.dlrlondon.co.uk/history.aspx*). It provides a well written and interesting account of what you can see in the area.

The dominating landmark is the Canary Wharf office development which was the tallest building in Britain until the Shard was built near London Bridge station. There's the O2 Arena on the south side of the river, the Museum in Docklands and an interesting little farm on the Isle of Dogs. together with the City Airport further east. There are an increasing number of budget priced hotels with accessible rooms. Near the airport is the ExCel exhibition centre. During quiet times when there are no big exhibitions or major meetings, some of these hotels can be quite cheap to stay in, and near DLR (accessible) stations.

Canary Wharf shops
Under the Canary Wharf office block is a substantial underground centre with
both shops and restaurants, see *www.mycanarywharf.com*. There are a number of
interlinked malls at/under Cabot Place, Jubilee Place, Churchill Place and Canada
Place. Maps/plans are available showing all the malls, but these are not always
easy to follow. Signage showing the links is not particularly good, but there are
usually security staff around who can tell you how to get from one mall to the
next step-free. All have **accessible toilets**.

ExCel London
One Western Gateway, Royal Victoria Dock, E16 1XL   *Tel:* 020 7069-5000
website: www.excel-london.co.uk *e-mail:* info@excel-london.co.uk
ExCeL is a massive international exhibition and convention centre. It hosts a huge
variety of events in a cavernous but rather soulless building measuring nearly
500m by 200m. It is located some 10km east of central London, and is almost
level with the Thames Flood Barrier. There are numerous BB spaces in a CP for
more than 3500 cars. Custom House DLR station is some 200m from the west
end while Prince Regent station is just over 300m from the east end.
Access is step-free throughout using various lifts. There are numerous bars and
catering outlets, and adequate (though not generous) provision of **accessible
toilets**. From some meeting rooms you may have to go to a different floor to find
one. *Changing places* facility at the east end on the GF.

Mudchute Park and Farm
Pier Street, Isle of Dogs, E14 3HP   *Tel:* 020 7515-5901
website: www.mudchute.org *e-mail:* info@mudchute.org
The mudchute was formed from silt out of the Millwall docks together with
waste clinker from local industries. The area is now wonderfully quiet, and
there's a delightful (and totally unexpected) urban farm with sheep, cattle, pigs,
goats, chickens, rabbits and riding stables. There's even a llama. Local groups
organise riding for disabled people. The farm occupies an area of something over
150x150m. The DLR stations at Crossharbour and Mudchute are both some 400-
500m from the main farm buildings - which are on the other side of the farm.
There's a small CP just inside the gate at the end of Pier Street about 100m from
the main buildings. You might alternatively use the adjacent ASDA CP which has
30+ BB spaces and there's an entrance in the far right corner. BB holders may
also be able to park just outside the entrance to the courtyard. Ring first to reserve
a space. The yard is in the middle of a building measuring about 50m by 20m
with a step-free shop, café and **wheelchair toilet (D85 ST80)**. There are BCF
in the womens toilets. You can feed and touch many of the animals in the pens
behind the building. There are rough slightly hilly paths around parts of the farm
and there's a largely paved perimeter path W65-70 in places which is about 700m
long. When it's been raining, some paths and routes can become quite muddy.

Museum in Docklands see chapter on *Museums and galleries*.

O2 Arena
Peninsula Square, SE10 0DX
Tel: 020 8463 2000 *DisEnq:* 020 8463 3359 (for both bookings and BB parking)
Textphone: 18001 020 8463 3359 *website:* www.theo2.co.uk
e-mail: customerservices@theo2.co.uk access@theo2.co.uk
Under the iconic Dome roof, there is the huge Arena, a live music club (indigO2),
an 11 screen multiplex cinema, an exhibition centre (the O2 bubble), and an
entire street of bars, restaurants and leisure attractions (Entertainment Avenue).
The Arena has a capacity of around 20,000, and has adequate provision for
wheelchair spaces, seats with step-free access, and of accessible toilets. The
lower, generally more expensive seats have the easiest access. The upper levels
are considerably steeper, although there are handrails which make climbing the
steps both easier and safer.
There are more than 2000 parking places with three different areas of BB spaces
all about 400m from the venue. For big events booking is strongly advised. The
accessible North Greenwich station is on the JLE, and is only about 200m away.
Thames Clippers have an 'accessible' pier if you are coming by boat.
There's a good Sitemap on the website.
There are a number of exhibition spaces, one of which was occupied by **Britain's
Museum of Popular Music** see *www.britishmusicexperience.com*. This is on the
1st floor, and can be accessed by lift.
Around Entertainment Avenue, all the main bars and restaurants have an
accessible toilet, and we checked eight of them. Some of the toilets were located
upstairs, but are accessed by an internal platform lift. Check before you order if
you're likely to want to use it.
Basically, as a modern venue, everywhere is wheelchair accessible (either
at ground level, or by lift), but quite significant distances may be involved,
especially if you don't know your way around.
North Greenwich tube station has an **adapted toilet**. There's a **wheelchair toilet**
part way along Entertainment Avenue. Others are near wheelchair spaces. There's
a *Changing places* facility on Level 1, Block 106.

Holborn, Bloomsbury and the Strand
This comprises four areas in the Eyewitness guide, with important sites and sights
like the British Library, British Museum and the Royal Opera House. It includes
Bloomsbury, Covent Garden and Trafalgar Square and extends as far north as the
Euston Road.

British Library see chapter on *Museums & galleries*.

British Museum see chapter on *Museums & galleries.*

Building Centre
Store Street, WC1E 7BT *Tel:* 020 7692-4000
website: www.buildingcentre.co.uk *e-mail:* reception@buildingcentre.co.uk
Houses interesting architectural and design exhibitions, and is an independent
forum providing information to all sectors involved in building.
Located on a corner of South Crescent, almost opposite Alfred Place.
The entrance is step-free with a revolving door, but there is a conventional door
W80 to bypass this. There are three floors, linked by a lift (D80 W160 L105).
Most of the centre is step-free, and the +4 steps on the GF can be bypassed using
a platform stairlift. The +2 in the basement can be bypassed using a ramped route.
Some seating, and small GF café.
There are **wheelchair toilets**:
* in the basement (D90 ST90 NKS) but with a button flush that is virtually
  unusable
* on the GF just 10m before the +4 steps, to the right down a little corridor, and
  then it's on your left (D80 ST90) with a much easier flush mechanism.
Note that for specialist information about architecture and accessibility the
Centre for Accessible Environments (*www.cae.org.uk*) is the relevant agency
complementing the work of the Building Centre.

Brunswick Square, by the Foundling Museum (WC1N 1AZ), provides a quiet
leafy spot ideal for a rest or a picnic.

Chinatown is centred around Gerrard Street just north of Leicester Square. It has
brightly coloured Chinese gates at each end, and is pedestrianised with smooth
surfaces throughout. Most restaurants have at least one step at the entrance, but a
few are step-free or have only a tiny lip. A really good place to go for the Chinese
New Year celebrations.

Corams Fields
93 Guilford Street, WC1N 1DN *Tel:* 020 7837-6138
website: www.coramsfields.org *e-mail:* info@coramsfields.org.uk
An open playground now occupies the site of the original Foundling Hospital
established in 1739. It was opened under its new name "Coram's Fields" in 1936.
To visit, any adult has to be accompanied by a child !
It has a wide variety of facilities including lawns for free play (suitable for family
picnics), artificial turf sports pitches, a paddling pool, sandpits, slides, a pets
corner (with sheep, goats, ducks, and hens), a vegetarian café, a nursery and drop-
ins for under 5's as well lots of organised activities.
The organisers aim to make all of the play areas are suitable for use by children
with disabilities, including a new sensory play area. There are children's toilets

including some accessible to disabled children. The main unisex **accessible toilet/ changing area** has a hoist and showering facilities that would be large enough for an adult to use **(D105 ST105)**.

Covent Garden is the area around the Royal Opera House and just north of the Strand. It is a development on the site of the old Covent Garden fruit and vegetable market.

It's a lively place and is often crowded, especially in the evening. There are plenty of small shops and stalls and **there is frequently open-air entertainment from buskers, small music groups and Punch & Judy shows**.

Note that parts of the Opera House are open during the day.

Parking can be quite a challenge, but there's an NCP at Parker Street, Parker Mews WC2B 5NT with 2 BB spaces. In the evenings the single yellow lines rule for BB holders is valid after 18.00.

Access by underground from the Piccadilly line involves less hassle than at most stations. Getting off the train there are +19 steps, and then a lift. The nearest 'accessible' station is Westminster.

Little thought has been given to the needs of disabled visitors except in the provision of toilets, and even these aren't brilliant. Surfaces are commonly a bit bumpy, and consist mainly of cobbles or rough paving. There's an unavoidable step at the far end of the Apple Market.

The shops are mostly small, and with +1 or +2 steps. However, there are a good number of market stalls, restaurants and cafés with step-free access. It's therefore easy just to stop for a coffee or a glass of wine. Much of the area is under cover, so it's a good place if the weather is uncertain. There's an open-air crafts market (that is, open at the ends but roofed over) on the south side.

Wheelchair cubicles (D85 ST85 NKS) with BCF in both the mens and womens public toilets on Tavistock Court. They were described by our surveyor as being 'somewhat congested' and are located on the south side, between the Jubilee Hall Sports Centre and the London Transport Museum.

The *Punch & Judy* is the main central pub, and must rate as (probably) having the most inaccessible bars in London, involving either +30 or −30 steps. This didn't deter one of our more intrepid survey teams, who made it up to the balcony overlooking the entertainments area so that our chair user could get a good view !

Nearby restaurants which have step-free access and a **wheelchair toilet** (and BCF) include:

Masala Zone (Indian), 48 Floral Street, WC2E 9DA, *Tel:* 020 7379-0101, and

Pizza Express, 9 Bow Street, WC2E 7AH, *Tel:* 020 7240-3443 (there's a step-free way in to bypass the +2 at the entrance. Just ring the bell).

Both are near the main Opera House entrance from Bow Street.

There's an extended list of accessible pubs and restaurants in the area which we include on the website under *Recommended itineraries*.

Dickens House see chapter on *Museums and galleries*.

Fitzroy Tavern
16 Charlotte Street W1P 1HJ *Tel:* 020 7580-3714
On the junction with Windmill Street. A traditional pub which was a meeting
place for artists and writers between the wars, who gave the area the name
Fitzrovia. Two entrances have flat access.

Freemasons Hall
60 Great Queen Street, WC2B 5AZ *Tel:* 020 7831-9811
website: www.ugle.org.uk/freemasons-hall
Located just off Kingsway, towards Covent Garden.
Freemasons' Hall is the headquarters of the United Grand Lodge of England, and
the principal meeting place for Masonic Lodges in London. The present building
was built as a memorial to the Freemasons who died in the First World War. Free
tours are available several times a day.
There are +2 steps at the entrance for which a ramp can be put in place.
Visitors go via a security check and get a temporary pass. Photographic ID such
as passport or driving licence may be required.
The tour takes place on the 1st floor, and there are 20+ steps to get up there,
bypassed (on request) by using the lift (D70 W90 L100). It starts in the Library/
Museum, and includes the Grand Temple and ceremonial areas.
The tour lasts about 35-40 minutes and there are a couple of opportunities to sit
down en route. It covers about 200m. There's an **accessible toilet** (not seen) on
the 1st floor.
Gift shop on the GF on the opposite side of the building from the entrance.

Hunterian Museum see chapter on *Museums and galleries*.

Leicester Square is now in quite a big pedestrianised area. The square is well
paved, with a good number of seats around. Buskers and portrait sketchers can
often be found in the NW corner. When we visited, the central Shakespeare
statue and its associated fountain, were being restored. The square is surrounded
by several major cinemas, and the new Warner West End a short distance away
has flat/lift access throughout. There's a **wheelchair toilet (D90 ST80)** in the
Moon under Water pub (entrance +2 steps, but a portable ramp is available).
There's also one in *McDonalds* **(D80 ST120)** at the junction of Swiss Court and
Whitcomb Street. Those in the National Gallery are not far away.

London Silver Vaults
53-64 Chancery Lane, WC2A 1QS (by the corner of Southampton Buildings)
Tel: 020 7242-3844 *website:* www.thesilvervaults.com
The Vaults, in the heart of London's legal district, are home to the world's largest
retail collection of fine antique silver. They are located about 100m from High

Holborn. The entrance is from Southampton Buildings, and is ramped. There is a lift (D80 W105 L110) by the security desk which goes down to floor −2. There are more than fifty strong rooms to explore, where the sellers will welcome you, particularly if you have a fat wallet with you.

London Transport Museum see chapter on *Museums & galleries*

Royal Courts of Justice (RCJ)
Strand, WC2A 2LL *Tel:* 020 7947-6000 (*switchboard*)
website: www.hmcourts-service.gov.uk/infoabout/rcj/rcj.htm
The Royal Courts cover the most serious civil trials, and include the Court of Appeal, the High Court and the Administrative Court. Criminal cases go to the Old Bailey. They are housed in an imposing Victorian Gothic building opened in 1882 and are said to contain a thousand rooms and about 5km of corridors.
The RCJ are situated at the junction between the Strand and Aldwych, just outside the City.
Helpful and knowledgeable staff will provide information.
Photography is forbidden throughout the buildings, and you can be imprisoned for up to two years for breaking the rules !
It is a difficult group of buildings to get around, but there's a seven page booklet detailing the *Accessible routes* (almost exactly as we published them in our 1996 edition, but the new version is in colour, and is updated). The booklet is available online from the website above using the menu on the right side, where it is listed as *RCJ Accessible routes*, when you look at 'Information about' and you get the FAQs. There is also useful information in the ten page document entitled *Facilities and Services for Disabled Visitors*. If you cannot download these you can ask for them to be sent by post.
If you find stairs difficult or impossible, but want/need to get into a particular court, we are told that this is possible, and you will have to negotiate through the Personal Support Unit (*Tel:* 020 7947-7701/3). This is staffed by volunteers and exists primarily to help those involved directly in court proceedings.
Very limited parking facilities are available on site for BB holders with court business. Contact the Superintendent's Office on 020 7947-6506 at least 24 hours in advance to request a space.
There is a Courts Service Disability Helpline on 0121 681-3475 (a freephone number available from 09.00-17.00).

The principal entrance to the Main building from The Strand has +3+4 steps. This leads straight through via a security check, to the Great Hall which is the main place of interest to the casual visitor. Security personnel can be alerted by pressing the intercom button, located to the left of the main gates. An alternative route provides step-free access to the Main building, and to Thomas More, Queen's and West Green. It starts 50m west of the principal (stepped) way in at the West Green entrance with an alternative security check. *We are using this in the write-up as a point of reference.*

The large complex of courts is spread over five buildings. These are the Main, West Green, Queen's, East Wing and Thomas More buildings. The accessible entrances to the RCJ are from West Green (as already described) and from Bell Yard (north) into the East building.

For people who want to see the Main Hall, the accessible route is as follows: taking the West Green checkpoint as your start, enter the main building via a steepish ramp, which bypasses −6 steps. There are two platform stairlifts (bypassing −5 and +16 respectively) giving access to the Main Hall, which is large and impressive.

There are organised tours twice a month booked via *Tel:* 020 7947-7684 (only a voicemail number) or by e-mail from the website. It is possible to arrange a wheelchair accessible route if you negotiate well in advance. The 'normal' route involves ±31, together with steps into the court visited, and a few other steps while wandering around.

For people coming on court business or those listening to a case, the following description outlines access to all the courts. We describe the situation in 2011, but there will be ongoing changes, and the accommodation office will be able to advise.

From the security checkpoint, courts 52-62 and 77-79 in the Thomas More building can be reached via the route shown on the diagram. There is a ramp bypassing the steps at the entrance and from here two sets of lifts (D90 W135+ L110+) give access to all floors. Court 51 can only be reached up a flight of steps from the GF. **Two wheelchair toilets (D85 ST70)** with a choice of low or high pedestals are located by the second set of lifts around the corner from the entrance.

The Queen's building, which houses courts 39-50, can be approached step-free from the Thomas More building. Three lifts inside give step-free access to all the courts. Two are by the main entrance (D100 W200 L110) and one by a side entrance (D85 W120 L150).

Access to the West Green building from the security checkpoint is shown on the diagram. Going up the ramp into the Main Building gives access to courts 37 (GF) and 33-35 via the lift (D75 W125 L100) to the left of the entrance. The West Green building also houses the interim and preliminary application sections. The 2nd floor of the West Green building links to the first floor of the Main building. This is important as it is the only step-free link to the courts in the main building. Courts 1-19 are on the first floor of the Main building. There are **wheelchair toilets (D70+ ST70+)** on the right side of the corridor towards the end.

Courts 63-76 in the East Block (north) are reached from the other site of the site on Bell Yard. A lift (D90 W155 L140) give access to the courts. There are **two wheelchair toilets (D70+ ST70+)** on the 3rd floor. East Block (south) is reached from a separate entrance off the Strand into the Main building, shown on the diagram. Just inside is a lift (D85 W125 L110) which takes you to the first floor from which there is a step-free route into the other building.

Two wheelchair toilets (D70+ ST70+) are at the southern end of the East Block; access depends on the use of platform stairlifts, which were not operational when we visited.

The Royal Opera House is described under Entertainment on our website. From 10.00 to 15.00 you can access the Paul Hamlyn (glass roofed) Hall and the Amphitheatre bars, unless there's a matinee performance. From the box office area, the Paul Hamlyn Hall is reached using the first set of lifts. The Amphitheatre bar with the glass panel overlooking the glass roofed hall, and the outside terrace, are accessed step-free using the second set of lifts at the far end of the foyer (and just past the main entrance from Bow Street). From the Covent Garden piazza, the distance to the terrace is about 300m.

There are **two wheelchair toilets (D70+ ST70+)** with BCF off the Amphitheatre bar at the very far end, to the left (you pass them when coming along the corridor from the lifts).

St Paul's Church, Covent Garden see chapter on *Places of worship.*
Sir John Soane's Museum see chapter on *Museums and galleries.*

Somerset House
Strand, WC2R 1LA *Tel:* 020 7845-4600 (use option 9 to speak to a person)
website: www.somersethouse.org.uk *e-mail:* info@somersethouse.org.uk
Somerset House is a spectacular 18thC neo-classical building in the heart of London, sitting between the Strand and the river. Until quite recently, the main occupants were government departments, including that keeping records of Births, Marriages and Deaths.

The grand building alongside Waterloo Bridge now houses varied exhibition spaces, including the Courtauld Gallery. The central courtyard has a magnificent fountain in the centre which becomes a playground for children when the weather is warm. In the winter there's an ice rink. It has a lovely terrace overlooking the river.

Somerset House hosts open-air concerts and films, contemporary art and design exhibitions, family workshops, and there are free guided tours of spaces usually hidden to visitors.

There is an isometric diagram of the layout on the website, under *Plan your visit,* although this does not show certain access aspects very clearly. The bi-monthly *What's On* leaflet currently only includes a very crude plan showing the four wings at the upper level.

The site is huge and measures about 130m by 160m. There are several accessible refreshment facilities including *Tom's Kitchen*, *Tom's Café* and the *Courtauld Gallery Café*. The *Terrace Café* is only open during the summer months (and best accessed from Waterloo Bridge).

The major access glitch on the site is the ±8 steps between the Seamen's Hall in the Riverside building, and the Riverside Terrace.

They can offer some BB parking, bookable in advance via the phone number above. You get in through the main archway on Aldwych, which is a one way east-west road at that point.

There are three pedestrian entrances, from different levels:

- **from the Strand**, you come immediately to the **Courtauld Galleries** in and over the archway. To avoid +2 steps, you have to come in via the central arch, where there are cobbles at the end. Access into the Courtauld Galleries is described below. Going about 100m directly across the courtyard, which is slightly rough in places, there are two ramped entrances to the upper level of the main **riverside building**;

- **off the Embankment**, under the big arch, about 80m from Waterloo Bridge. There are −2 steps, bypassed by a ramp to the left. This is the riverside building, and leads into the lower riverside level. To get into the building (at the level of the Embankment Galleries) there are +2, bypassed by a platform lift (D90 L130). This has slightly temperamental controls, and you may need to summon staff help to get it to work. Just what that mini-lift is doing there is difficult to imagine, as a ramp would have been simpler, cheaper and better;

- **from Waterloo Bridge** there's a ramp down on to the Riverside Terrace which is a nice spot in the summer, but there's no step-free access into the building. To get into the building from here you have to go about 400m (turning left under the second arch, and then left and left again) to bypass the +8 steps up to the Seamen's Hall in the centre of the building. Alternatively you can go via Lancaster Place (at the end of the bridge) and turn right into the Strand.

Our description generally assumes that you enter from the Strand.

There are effectively seven different parts of the buildings, namely:

- the archway building/s off the Strand (where the Courtauld Gallery is);
- the open courtyard with, at different times, its fountains, its ice rink and other structures, and with tables and chairs in the summer near the catering facilities;
- the East wing, with a café and shop;
- the West wing with exhibition space;
- the riverside building at Strand/courtyard level;
- the riverside terrace, which is separated from the riverside buildings by ±8 steps; and,

- the (lower) Embankment level facilities in the riverside building.

The numbers used in the text below (in brackets) are those used in the website floor plan.

Note that Tours take place on Thursdays and Saturdays, lasting a little over an hour. They can take you up to about 400m, and involve going over some roughish surfaces. The exact route is somewhat weather dependent, but during the tour you'll be told about various links with London's history. There is nowhere to sit down en route.

The Courtauld Gallery (1)

Tel: 020 7848-2526 (*24-hour information line*)

website: www.courtauld.ac.uk/gallery *e-mail*: galleryinfo@courtauld.ac.uk

Housed in the rooms over the main entrance archway off the Strand. The paintings include some by famous Impressionist and Post-Impressionist artists. Access from the Strand is via +2 steps on the right side of the arch, or along the partly cobbled roadway. There is a rather steep ramped kerb on to the pavement. At the main entrance (on your right) there are +2 to the ticket office, then +5 to the lift. There's an intercom to the right of the door to attract attention and facilitate the use of an alternative entrance. There's a steepish ramp en route, on which most chair users would require assistance. This gives step-free access to the lift (D150 W250 L150) which goes to all three floors.

The lift has quite an awkward ridge by the door when getting out, and the chairs available to be borrowed have small wheels. We saw an inexperienced user having quite a lot of trouble getting over it as the front wheels got stuck and the occupants' ankles were jabbed by the footplates. Using the lift bypasses +59+34 spiralled steps to the upper galleries, or −24+2 to the basement. On the top floor, room 12 has +1, but a temporary ramp is available.

The café and the **wheelchair toilet (D80 ST80+, but with a high pedestal)** are in the basement. BCF are incorporated. The shop (3) is on the other side of the arch has +2 at the entrance, but again, a portable ramp is available.

Off the courtyard, there is the East wing to the left, with a ramped entrance into the corner of the first building, closest to the arch. The ramp leads to a slightly congested café and then to a shop. There is a **wheelchair toilet** with BCF off the corridor outside, and this is a quieter area than the one near the restaurant in the Riverside building.

To the right is the West wing, with more gallery space. Step-free access for chair users is via the ramped entrance on the right side, then you go right (you are near *Tom's Deli*) and go through the doors next to the Nelson Stair.

Going across the courtyard past the fountains, there are ramps leading into the **Riverside building** from both corners of the courtyard, each bypassing +4 at the central entrance. In the middle of the building, with an information desk and an open area with seats, is the Seamen's Hall.

The ramp on the right side of the building leads into *Tom's Deli* (6) and *Tom's*

Kitchen (8), and to a **wheelchair toilet (D80 ST80)** with BCF. Although it came within our 'definition' of a wheelchair toilet, when we visited, the BC table was down and with the large bins in the ST space would be quite a hassle for a chair user to sort out. The restaurant *Tom's Kitchen* is a more wheelchair-friendly place as the Deli has a high counter and the seating is a bit cramped and inflexible. The restaurant is also significantly more expensive !

The ramped entrance into the **Terrace Rooms** (13) is towards the left-hand corner under the sign saying Stamp Office (10). Inside the Terrace Rooms exhibition area there's an **adapted toilet (D80 ST60)**.

Inside the Riverside building, a lift (D80 W100 L130) links the courtyard level G with the Embankment level L2/LG, and the alternative entrance/exit. There is a **wheelchair toilet (D80 ST75),** and although the door opens in, the cubicle is deep enough for most chair users. There is a separate BCF. To find the toilet from the Embankment entrance, come into the lobby and turn left.

Admission to the Embankment Galleries is from this level (L2). They are step-free throughout, using a second lift (D80 W100 L130). Using the Embankment Galleries lift, you can go down to L1 which is the King's Barge House under the shop.

There is a confusion in/between the labelling of the floor levels in the two lifts. They were probably installed at different times and floor labels were changed in the meantime.

The **Riverside Terrace** has seats overlooking the river and during the summer there's a café with tables and chairs, and a ramp at one end of the wooden plinth. The easiest access to this is via the ramp from Waterloo Bridge. Near the ramps and under the first arch by the war memorial, there's a **wheelchair toilet (D80 ST80)**. The outer door is split, and when we visited, both the (heavy) doors were propped open, as they need to be.

Trocadero
7-14 Coventry Street, W1D 7DH *Tel:* 020 7439-1719
website: www.londontrocadero.com *e-mail*: info@londontrocadero.com
A cavernous shopping and entertainment complex undergoing seemingly constant refurbishment, encompassing buildings between Piccadilly Circus, Shaftesbury Avenue and Rupert Street. The main entrance gives flat access from Coventry Street to some step-free shops. The entrance from Shaftesbury Avenue is at a different, slightly higher, level.

The main way of getting from floor to floor is using the numerous escalators. Alternatively, there are now a number of platform lifts bypassing steps and split levels, but they're not always working, and the layout is quite complicated. A chair user is advised to ask a staff member if he/she wants to go to other floors and there are two staff-operated lifts which link all the floors. In the basement (LGF) there's a **wheelchair toilet (D95 ST100).**

A platform lift (D75 W100 L130) to the right of main escalators bypasses +9 steps to the upper GF where there are more shops and access to the staff lift (D80 W100 L140) operated by security guards. This goes to all other floors, including the basement. Various mezzanines can be reached by three user-operated platform lifts. The most accessible entrance (by lift) to the UGC cinema is from Great Windmill Street.

Westminster and St James's

This is covered in two sections of the *Eyewitness* guide. The area includes some of London's most important sights, in particular the Houses of Parliament (with Big Ben), Westminster Abbey and Buckingham Palace. Behind the Whitehall government offices is St James's Park, a quiet and attractive area with a lake, fountains and a bandstand.

Parking is generally difficult, but note that close to Parliament Square is the:
Abingdon Street (Q-Park), SW1P 3RX *Tel*: 020 7222-8621
183 spaces, UG, 230cm clearance, Mon-Sun 6:00-24:00. Off Great College Street by the junction with Abingdon Street. Parking is on levels −1 and −2, with 4 BB spaces to the right of ticket barrier on level −1. Past the office there is a **wheelchair toilet (D90 ST90 NKS)** with BCF. People get in and out of the CP using pavement alongside the car ramp.

Banqueting House
Whitehall, SW1A 2ER   *Tel:* 020 7930-4179
website: www.hrp.org.uk/banquetinghouse
The house is the only remaining publicly accessible part of the Palace of Whitehall. Charles I was beheaded just outside in 1649. It contains the Banqueting Hall on the 1st floor, with magnificent Rubens paintings on the ceiling.

It is located opposite Horseguards Parade with quite an inconspicuous door, by the corner with Horesguards Avenue. Admission charge.

There is +1 step at the entrance, leading to the ticket desk and small shop. An area called the undercroft is −3 from the entrance, but there is a ramped bypass behind the door to the left of the steps. Visitors are shown a video there about the building and its history. **Wheelchair toilet (D80 ST80+)** at the bottom of the ramp, which could be accessed even if you are not visiting the Hall upstairs. From the ticket desk there are then +17+6 to get up to the Hall. There are seats around the walls and mirrors for looking at the ceiling.

A route to bypass the steps through an adjacent office building (the Royal United Services Institute) can be made available for chair users and disabled walkers. The lift is small, with (D75 W100 L85). Only a small chair can get in, and you may need to take the footplates off. The lift is normally available Mon-Fri if requested 24 hours in advance. Check on *Tel:* 020 3166-6155/6152 - especially if you plan to visit on a Saturday or are attending a private function.

Buckingham Palace
Buckingham Palace Road, SW1A 1AA
website (for visits): www.royalcollection.org.uk/visit/buckinghampalace
The Palace is an imposing building at the end of the Mall. It is the Queen's
London home and lived in by members of the royal family, and their staff. When
the Queen is in residence, the Royal Standard is flown. The website for the British
Monarchy is: *www.royal.gov.uk*
The State Rooms in the Palace are currently open to the public for about two
months each summer. During the visit to the State Rooms, Terrace and Gardens
you can learn about the workings of the monarchy, see where state banquets
and investitures are held, and see the magnificent interiors decorated by many
impressive works of art. You are 'escorted' by an audio-guide, and although we
had a few problems with the sequencing of the descriptions, nearby staff were
always able to sort it out. There's a special audio-guide setting that follows the
access-friendly route.
Significant admission charge, and a typical visit takes between 2 and 2.5 hours.
To book tickets: *Tel:* 020 7766-7300 or book online at *www.royalcollection.org.uk*
e-mail: bookinginfo@royalcollection.org.uk
Wheelchair users and disabled walkers are asked to phone 020 7766-7324.
BB holders may be able to arrange for parking inside the palace grounds, which
can be an enormous advantage compared with coming by public transport.
Chair users are only admitted by prior arrangement, and need to fit into a pre-
booked time slot. People with limited mobility should look at our description of
the tour to assess whether they would be wise to request the use of a wheelchair
to make their visit easier and/or to use the access-friendly route. Note that
visitors are welcome to bring and use walking sticks or folding stools with seat
attachments, provided they have rubber stoppers.
While some 4500 people visit every day, only about 25 chair users are allowed,
because of perceived problems of evacuation.
In view of the transport challenges and parking difficulties in central London, you
might like to consider visiting all the sights around the Palace in one day. These
include the State Rooms already mentioned, together with the Queen's Gallery
and the Royal Mews. The 'Royal Day Out' ticket/visit including all these would
take something like four, possibly even five or six, hours to complete, including a
break in the *Garden Café*.

Tickets for 'general' entry are picked up or purchased from the Ticket
Office at the Visitor Entrance on Buckingham Palace Road if they
haven't been sent to you in the post, but if you're using the 'access-
friendly' route you'll almost certainly have booked this well in advance.
There are two routes for the Palace tour:
* **an 'access-friendly' route which is step-free. You may have the
opportunity of parking in the forecourt inside the gates. All vehicles are
thoroughly security checked. If you're coming by taxi, then you need**

to be dropped off at the North Centre Gate in front of the Palace. Both disabled walkers and wheelchair users can use the access-friendly route. It involves a minimum distance of about 350-400m, and going around slowly takes about an hour and a half to two hours. Nearly all the internal floors are covered in thick carpet. If you go out into the gardens, the distance you go can increase to anything between 500 and 700m, and the path there is quite rough;

- the main 'line of route' involves around 120 steps, and a distance of more than 1km. It takes you out through the gardens and up to Grosvenor Place. There may also be a longish queue to get in, going to where you have your bags checked.

Seating en route is very limited. You can find a seat in the Ballroom, and there are benches in the garden outside.

If you are using the pre-booked 'access-friendly' route, you can park in the forecourt, and be taken by a 'wheelchair accessible' golf buggy into the inner Quadrangle. The surfaces in the CP area and in the Quadrangle are of quite difficult gravel. There are friendly staff members around to help throughout your visit, and we were particularly impressed by the ease with which assistance was given.

We visited in 2010, and from the Quadrangle, there was a slightly temperamental platform lift (D80+ L150+) to take chair users up and down to/from the main GF level bypassing +14 steps. This is installed/used only during the period of opening of the State Rooms to the public. There's an alternative step-free route if needed, involving +1+2 steps which are well ramped, followed by a platform stairlift (D80 L110).

There is a lift (D80 W95 L160) to the main rooms on the 1st floor (bypassing about ±50). Because of your starting point, you follow a slightly different line of route to everyone else, as you have to go to and from the lift.

Note that the only inside **wheelchair toilet (D115 ST115)** is off the corridor on the GF near the lift.

At the end of the tour inside, you can go out on the Terrace via a slightly bumpy ramp, where there's the *Garden Café* with movable chairs and tables and a hard (though gravelled) surface. To get down to the Gardens there are −10 steps, but wheelchair users can go back through the palace GF to the Quadrangle where the wheelchair accessible golf buggy will take you round to the garden, in front of the Terrace. The path here consists of quite difficult gravel which provides access to the gift shop in a large marquee.

If you simply leave the palace at the end of the tour, or after taking refreshments in the café, there's a shop for buying souvenirs on the GF as you leave. If necessary, the golf buggy will take you back to near your car.

On special occasions and for distinguished foreign visitors, there are processions going to the palace. **The Changing of the Guard** both at Buckingham Palace and at Horse Guards Parade, Whitehall, is a regular attraction for visitors. Mounted Life Guards pass the palace regularly at *10.50 and return at about 11.35, except on Sunday when they're an hour earlier.* Check the details in a conventional guidebook, or contact the HRP enquiry line.

If you want to go and see **Trooping the Colour** for the Queen's birthday, or other major parades that take place on Horse Guards Parade, the tickets are allocated by ballot in Jan/Feb each year. There are some wheelchair spaces for spectators, otherwise most of the seats are up steps in the temporary stands which are erected for each event.
Apply to: The Brigade Major, Headquarters Household Division, Horse Guards, Whitehall, SW1A 2AX

Churchill War Rooms see chapter on *Museums and galleries*.

Clarence House
St James's Palace, SW1 1BA *Tel:* 020 7766-7300 (for tickets)
website: www.royalcollection.org.uk
e-mail: bookinginfo@royalcollection.org.uk
The official residence of the Prince of Wales and The Duchess of Cornwall is normally open for a month each summer. Visitors are taken on a 45-minute guided tour of the five GF rooms.
Accessibility is well described on the website, and we are taking the unusual step of including the description, even though at the time of writing we haven't made a visit.
Some nearby BB spaces can be pre-booked.
Visitors entrance from the Mall. Entrance +3 steps, bypassed by a platform stairlift. There are benches at the entrance, but no seating inside. There are no toilets inside, but the public loos opposite the House in St James's Park have an **accessible toilet**.

Houses of Parliament & Westminster Hall
St Margaret Street, SW1A 0AA *Tel:* 020 7219-3000 *Textphone:* 0800 959-598
House of Commons information *Tel:* 020 7219-4272 (for *Textphone* dial 18001 first) *e-mail:* hcinfo@parliament.uk
House of Lords information *Tel:* 020 7219-3107 *e-mail:* hlinfo@parliament.uk
If you need to borrow a wheelchair *Tel:* 020 7219-3003.
website: www.parliament.uk

The Palace of Westminster

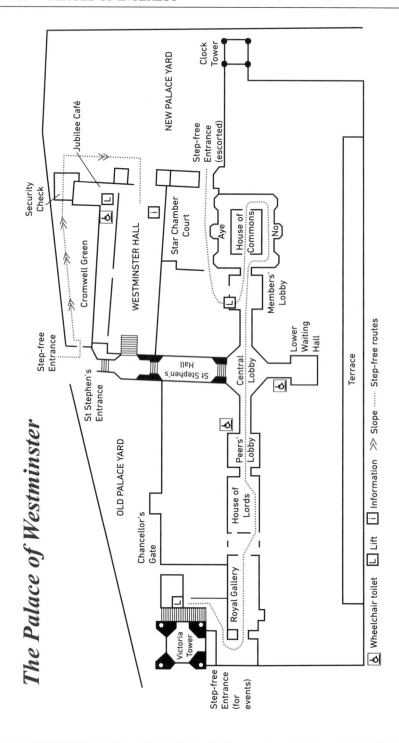

The Palace of Westminster has been the home to the two Houses of Parliament since the 16thC. The present mock Gothic building was built in Victorian times, although Westminster Hall dates back to the 11thC. For obvious reasons, there is tight security, with airport-style searches on anyone entering the buildings. When the Commons is sitting, you can get into the public gallery via a step-free route. For the Lords you will have to view proceedings from alongside the chamber and it is necessary to book first via Black Rods office. Most of the various committee rooms are accessible, and you will be escorted from the information desk in Westminster Hall using a step-free route.

Tours are possible at the invitation of a Member of Parliament.
Alternatively, a tour can be booked on a Saturday or during the summer recess, through *Ticketmaster*. Except for one stop (of 15), the tour is wheelchair accessible. There are only limited opportunities for sitting down during the tour which lasts about 75 minutes.
Tickets can be booked in advance via *Tel:* 0844 847-1672 or at:
http://www.ticketmaster.co.uk/Houses-of-Parliament-tickets/artist/107973
The on-site ticket office address is: 6/7 Old Palace Yard, Abingdon Street, SW1P 3JY (by the Jewel Tower, and with step-free access).
There is a significant admission charge.
If you are tempted to try to join a tour up the clock tower to see Big Ben, be warned that there are 334 spiralled steps to go up (and down).

The normal entry route for members of the public is to go down the 40m slope in Cromwell Green, to the left of St Stephen's entrance. At the bottom there's a small building where they carry out an airport style security search. When you come out you turn right and go up the slope to the entrance to Westminster Hall. Just inside there's an information desk, and if you would find the 30+ steps up to the level of the Central Lobby to be a problem you can ask to be escorted via an alternative route using the lifts. The same applies if you are going to the Visitors Gallery or to a Committee Room.
There are alternative routes shown on the plan, and for more information, *Tel:* 020 7219-3070 for visiting the Commons or 020 7219-3100 for the House of Lords.
Parking for disabled visitors or dropping off in New Palace Yard can be arranged if you give sufficient notice, and there are a small number of BB spaces. The police or staff on duty will escort you everywhere because of security. There are two wheelchair spaces below the Bar in the House of Lords (so you are actually sitting in the chamber, rather than in the inaccessible Strangers Gallery - but we should make clear that the Bar in this instance, has nothing to do with the serving of drinks!).

In the Commons there are 4 chair spaces at the back of Strangers Gallery which can be reached step-free via lifts and ramps. The view from the Strangers Gallery is somewhat restricted, and our surveyor could only see about half of the chamber, but you can't see much more from the main seats.

If you go on a tour of the Commons and Lords, you will find that there is flat access throughout the main floor, and through the Commons lobbies (where they vote). The main "line of route" for members of the public visiting the building when the Houses are not sitting is shown on the plan, together with the location of the principal lifts. There are some fifteen lifts in different parts of the building, but only the two of relevance to visitors doing a tour, are shown on the plan. There are **wheelchair toilets (D70+ ST70+)** off the Peers' Lobby and off the Lower Waiting Hall, both on the main floor level of the lobbies. Towards the end of the tour, able-bodied visitors walk down the 5 steps to St Stephen's Hall and then the −36 into Westminster Hall. Those unable to do this can ask to get down to New Palace Yard via the lift, and from there, Westminster Hall is reached via several shallow ramps.

Off Westminster Hall, is the Jubilee café which is for visitors, and accessed by a lift bypassing −4 steps. There's a nearby wheelchair toilet (D70+ ST70+).

The Education Unit run a special visits programme for schools and would be pleased to discuss arrangements for disabled students (*Tel:* 020 7219-4750).

A *Changing places* toilet, including a changing bench and a hoist, can be found in Lower Waiting Hall, located just off Central Lobby.

There are **two accessible toilets** on the 1st floor of Portcullis House.

Jewel Tower

Abingdon Street, Westminster, SW1P 3JX *Tel:* 020 7222-2219
website: www.english-heritage.org.uk/daysout/properties/jewel-tower
One of the buildings from the medieval Palace of Westminster which survived the fire of 1834. It is just across the road from the Houses of Parliament. −6 −5 steps from the main road are bypassed by ramped access from the back of Old Palace Yard and to the left of Westminster Abbey. Admission charge.

There is about a 10cm threshold at the entrance to the GF vault with ornate ceiling carvings. To climb the tower there are +26 to the 1st floor and a further +20 to the 2nd. The spiral staircase is 90cm wide.

Parliament Square and Westminster Bridge

The square features statues of famous statesmen such as Disraeli and Churchill. It was Britain's first official roundabout (an oddity, given that it's square !), and has been the site where many demonstrations have taken place.

Wheelchair toilet (D80 ST80 NKS), just outside the QE II Conference Centre, and there are **accessible toilets** in the Supreme Court.

From the Bridge you can get fine views up and down the Thames. Westminster

Pier is a starting point for river trips to the Tower and Greenwich. The entrance
is cobbled at the junction of Broad Sanctuary and Storey's Gate and down to
the toilet door (at the top of some steps leading to some public toilets). There's
another **wheelchair toilet** by the pier for river trips. To reach the pier from
the bridge and bypass the steps, you need to go nearly 100m east along the
Embankment, and then come back towards the bridge. Alternatively you can get
there from the ticket hall of Westminster tube station (which can be accessed by
lift).

The **Parliamentary Bookshop** is on the corner of Parliament Street and
Bridge Street. Step-free access into the small shop which has some interesting
publications and reports produced by Parliament and its committees.

Some business is carried out in **Portcullis House**, just across the road from Big
Ben. This is a new building for various aspects of Parliamentary business which
has modern facilities including lifts and **accessible toilets**. Getting in involves
similar security checks to those carried out for the main Parliament building.

Royal Mews

Buckingham Palace Road, SW1A 1AA   *Tel:* 020 7766-7302
website: www.royalcollection.org.uk
The entrance is between Palace Street and Bressenden Place on the other side of
the road. The stables and coach houses were designed by Nash in 1825. You can
see all the royal coaches used on different occasions. Admission charge.

The ticket office, security check and the mews are all basically flat and the route
is step-free. You'll find a few cobbles. The whole tour is about 400m. **Adapted
toilet (D80 ST65)** in the corner of the courtyard, just past the state coach display,
about 150m from the entrance. BCF in womens toilets in the same location.

Queen's Gallery see chapter on *Museums and galleries.*
Photographers Gallery see chapter on *Museums and galleries.*

St James's Park and Green Park

Park Office, The Store Yard, Horse Guards Approach, St James's Park SW1A 2BJ
Tel: 020 7930-1793   *website:* www.royalparks.gov.uk
The two parks are attractive, well shaded and centrally located around
Buckingham Palace. They are flat or gently sloping and have tarmac paths
throughout. Both have good maps at key entry points. There are refreshment
facilities in St James's Park towards Horseguards Parade at the end of the lake.
There's also a bandstand with occasional performances. From the nearby bridge
over the lake in St James's there's a unique view of the Whitehall offices, and
by taking a judiciously framed photograph, you can persuade your friends that
you've been to Istanbul. **Wheelchair cubicles (D80 ST80 NKS)** inside both the
mens and womens toilets, on the north side of the St James's Park at the junction
with Marlborough Road.

Spencer House

27 St James's Place, SW1A 1NR *Tel:* 020 7514-1964 *RecM:* 020 7499-8620
website: www.spencerhouse.co.uk
The 18thC townhouse of the Spencer family, restored and refurbished at great
expense by Lord Rothschild. It contains a fine collection of paintings and
furniture.
Admission charge. It is only open on Sundays, and tickets cannot be prebooked.
The house is situated just to the east of Green Park, in a cul de sac off St James's
Street. It is at the end on the left opposite no15 with no sign outside indicating its
presence. Parking is difficult, with three metered spaces, but no BB spaces by the
house.
Portable ramps can bypass the +2+1 steps at the entrance. From here the GF
is step-free, including the ticket office, cloakroom and **wheelchair toilet (D80
ST90+)**. You may have to ask the cloakroom attendant to move his table to let
you past. The tour starts with a video, and then lasts an hour, with very limited
seating en route.
A lift (D75 W115 L85) bypasses +36 to take you to the 1st floor, which is step-
free. The garden is open on specific days during the summer, via +2 from the GF,
bypassed by a portable ramp.

Supreme Court

Parliament Square, SW1P 3BD *Tel:* 020 7960-1500/1900
website: www.supremecourt.gov.uk
Housed in the old Middlesex Guildhall which has been completely refurbished
inside, the Supreme Court sat for the first time in 2009. There are three courts,
and an exhibition space and café on the LGF.
Entrance +3 steps bypassed on either side by a platform lift (D80 L130). There's
a security/bag check. There is step-free access throughout the building using the
lifts (D75 W100 L130) which go to all four floors and there's a platform lift to
bypass +4 into court 3.
There are **wheelchair toilets** on all floors, one of which is near the café on the
LGF.

Wellington Arch

Hyde Park Corner, W1J 7JZ *Tel:* 020 7930-2726
website: www.english-heritage.org.uk
Situated in the centre of the Hyde Park Corner roundabout, the arch was built to
commemorate various victories in the Napoleonic wars. There is a series of shows
exploring various aspects of England's history. Admission charge.
There are step-free road crossings from most sides of the roundabout. Car drop-
off can be arranged, but there is no parking because of security considerations.
The entrance on the inside of the arch is flat to the ticket office and lift (D75
W110 L130). This goes to the other three floors, each with various exhibitions

and videos. All are step-free. From the 3rd floor, which is over the arch itself, there is an platform lift (D90 W100 L135) to two outside viewing galleries on opposite sides. There are +2 steps on one side, and a ramp on the other. There is a solid stone parapet of height 100cm in each case, but there are some fine views if you can see over the top.

There's an **accessible toilet** in the basement, accessed by the lift with staff assistance, so you have to ask.

Whitehall

Whitehall is one of the most famous streets in London, lined with government buildings at the Westminster end, particularly the Treasury and the Defence Department. It leads from Parliament Square to Trafalgar Square.

In the centre of the road there is the national War Memorial, the Cenotaph, commemorating in particular, the dead from both the World Wars. A recent addition is the black memorial a little further up to the Women of WW2. On the sides of the road there are numerous statues, including ones of Monty, Allenbrook and of Field Marshall Slim. There are also the entrances to Downing Street (where the Prime Minister lives) and to Horse Guards Parade.

There are details of the accessible pubs in Whitehall in the *Recommended itineraries* section on the website. Starting from Parliament Square, they are *St Stephens Tavern*, the *Clarernce*, the *Silver Cross* and the *Old Shades*.

Kensington and Chelsea

Chelsea Physic Garden

66 Royal Hospital Road, Chelsea SW3 4HS *Tel:* 020 7352-5646
website: www.chelseaphysicgarden.co.uk
e-mail: enquiries@chelseaphysicgarden.co.uk

Located in the triangle formed by Royal Hospital Road, Chelsea Embankment and Swan Walk. It was established in 1673 by the Society of Apothecaries to study plants used for medicinal purposes.

The area has provision mainly for residents parking but with some coin operated meters (at £1 for 20 minutes). There's a single BB space immediately outside the step-free entrance at 66 Royal Hospital Road (almost opposite Christchurch Road). Parking was not restricted on Sundays or on Saturdays after 13.30 when we made our survey. It would be possible to park in Battersea Park and come across the river using the Albert Bridge.

At the door at Number 66, there's both a bell and an intercom to attract someone's attention.

Admission charge. At the door at the main public entrance is in Swan Walk but this has −3 steps.

The garden is flat, with gravel paths throughout. There's the occasional ridge or bump to overcome. Its shape is roughly triangular, with the longest side being about 150m. The facilities such as the shop, café and toilets are near the step-free entrance. Guided tours start from the Swan Walk entrance, and audio tour headsets are available.

There are two quite spacious **wheelchair toilets**:

- one **(D90 ST90)** is by the shop, and has an adaptation to raise the seat height to SH53
- the other **(D75 ST80)** with SH48 and which includes BCF, is by the café.

Hyde Park and Kensington Gardens W2 & W8
Rangers Lodge, Hyde Park, W2 2UH
The Magazine Storeyard, Magazine Gate, Kensington Gardens, W2 2UH
Tel: 0300 061-2000 *website:* www.royalparks.gov.uk
e-mails: hyde@royalparks.gsi.gov.uk and kensington@royalparks.gsi.gov.uk
This vast stretch of parkland which covers over 240 ha (600 acres), was a hunting ground for Henry VIII. It measures some 2km by 0.75km and includes a large artificial lake. The whole area is fairly flat, and there are tarmac paths throughout. Where there are slopes they are fairly gentle, such as those going up to the bridges, towards South Carriage Drive, and at the east end of the lake from Rotten Row up to the Serpentine Road.
The West Carriage Drive, going broadly north-south, and including the Serpentine Bridge, separates the Park and Gardens. There are numerous entrances, and there's a perimeter road running on both the north and south sides of the Park. Major landmarks include Hyde Park Corner in the SE, Marble Arch in the NE and Kensington Palace in the far west. The Serpentine and Long Water lakes are important features, and there are numerous memorials and special areas.
There are good downloadable maps on the website.
There is BB parking:
- by the Serpentine Gallery (with 4 spaces);
- in the CP at the south end of the Serpentine Bridge (with 6 spaces);
- in the Triangle CP at the north end of the Bridge (with 6 spaces);
- by the Lower Dog Gate into Kensington Gardens (with 2 spaces);
- by Alexandra Lodge, on the South Carriage Drive (2 spaces); and,
- it is possible for BB holders to park in 'public' parking spaces in the Park, without charge
- in addition, there is a large UGCP with entrances off Park Lane and North Carriage Drive run by Q-Park, but note that there's a longish walk of approaching 500m to get out. It is huge, and all on one floor, with space for nearly 1000 cars. Height restriction 2.08m. Finding where the 8 BB spaces (which are near the Marble Arch exit) is a challenge, as is finding the pay station when you want to get out. There is a ramped route out at both car entrances/exits, but these too are a challenge to find ! Signage is non-existent.

Note that on sunny summer bank holidays and weekends there is enormous demand for parking spaces in and around the parks, and you may have to be both patient and persistent.

Liberty Drives www.royalparks.org.uk/parks/hyde_park/disabled_access.cfm,
Tel: 07767 498-096, provide free five seater electric carts which take disabled
people around the park. When we visited they were available five days a week
during the summer. They are operated by volunteer drivers with pick up points
at most of the main gates, and at the Triangle CP north of the Serpentine Bridge.
You can arrange to be dropped off anywhere in the park, and be picked up
later. The carts are primarily designed for disabled walkers, but they can now
accommodate a wheelchair user. It's a brilliant initiative, and seems to be well
used.

These parks are a lovely place to come and sit outside on the grass in the
summertime - where it's easy to forget that you're in the middle of a big city.
You can take a long 'green' route through central London by going from
somewhere like the Serpentine Gallery, through Hyde Park, Green Park and then
St James' Park - possibly ending in Trafalgar Square, or Parliament Square. You
could even start at Kensington Palace.

Some of the Parks' principal features, starting in the east from Hyde Park
Corner, are:
- **the 7/7 Memorial**, near the Curzon Gate;
- **Speaker's Corner**, near Marble Arch which has good access and you can
  listen to people talking about anything and everything- particularly on a
  Sunday afternoon;
- the substantial **Rose Garden** as you go towards the lake from Hyde Park
  Corner;
- the **Holocaust Memorial**, near the eastern end of the Serpentine;
- the *Serpentine Bar and Kitchen* at the east end of the lake;
- the boathouses for the hire of small boats in the summer, on the north side of
  the lake;
- the **Lido** swimming area on the south side, and the *Lido Bar and Café*;
- the **Princess Diana Memorial Fountain** which is built of Cornish granite
  and was designed to express Diana's spirit and her love of children;
- the **Serpentine Gallery**, now in two parts;
- the **Albert Memorial**;
- the **Round Pond** for model boats, ducks and swimming dogs is towards
  Kensington on high ground, approached by a broad tarmac path;
- **Kensington Palace**;
- an open-air market mainly for paintings on Sundays just outside the park
  railings, right down the Bayswater Road as far as Queensway;

Serpentine Gallery
Kensington Gardens, W2 3XA *Tel:* 020 7402 6075
website: www.serpentinegallery.org *e-mail:* information@serpentinegallery.org
The **Serpentine Gallery** is a major facility, now having two separate spaces for
exhibitions. It presents modern and contemporary art. The original gallery has
a new cloud-like installation outside it, including a step-free route through the
middle. In the grounds, there's a work dedicated to Diana, Princess of Wales,
comprising eight benches, a tree-plaque, and a carved stone circle at the Gallery's
entrance.
The gallery is step-free, and you go in past the bookshop on your left and into a
small hallway. There's a **wheelchair toilet (D90 ST80)** through a door on the left
also leading to the womens toilets. There are separate BCF through a door on the
right leading to the mens.
The gallery lies beyond the hallway.
A new space, the **Serpentine Sackler Gallery** opening in 2013 is housed a little
over 300m away in The Magazine (which used to be used for storing munitions)
with an adjoining extension used as a café/restaurant.
It will almost certainly have **accessible toilets** and BCF.

There are benches scattered around the parks, but in the summer it is possible to
hire deck chairs from the north side of the Serpentine, or from the Round Pond in
Kensington Gardens. There are tracks for both cycling and horse riding, and in
some places you need to keep your eyes open, so that you can avoid the cyclists
whizzing by.

*Because the Parks are so big, we will restrict our description to specific areas
near the main CPs; to the approach from Hyde Park Corner, and to the Princess
Diana Memorial Playground, in Kensington Gardens.*
From the CP on the south side of the Serpentine Bridge, the Serpentine
Gallery is just on the other side of the road. Going east, and slightly downhill,
there's the **Princess Diana Memorial Fountain**, and the **Lido Café** and **Lido
swimming area**.
The Memorial is an oval stream of cascading water about 50 by 80m made from
Cornish granite, surrounded by a grassy field. The granite bed is quite shallow
and is laid out on a gently sloping portion of the park, so that water pumped to
the top of the oval flows down either side. One side descends fairly smoothly
while the other side has a variety of steps, rills, and curves so the water flow is
much more disturbed. It is intended to show two sides of Diana's life: the happy
times, and the turmoil.
A little further along is the *Lido Bar and Café*, with tables both inside and out.
The +2+1 steps in front can be bypassed using the ramp at the eastern end which
is by the **wheelchair toilet (D80 ST75)** in an adjacent building.
Just past the café is **The Lido** *Tel:* 020 7706-3422 *www.serpentinelido.com*. This

includes changing rooms and access to a part of the Serpentine which is cordoned off for swimming (maxdepth 2m). There's a **wheelchair toilet (D85 ST100)** and changing space behind the stairs on the GF. Step-free access to the pool is from the GF opposite the entrance, where a gate may need unlocking. There's a ramp leading down into the water with handrails on both sides, but a slightly rough surface if you want to slide down on your bottom !

The Lido also has a lovely children's playground and paddling pool, grass and deckchairs for sunbathing - all up on the roof. A platform lift (D75 W105 L130) goes up from the GF. On the top, there is a raised section with +2 steps where there are some pub benches. The playground is −3−4−3 steps but these can easily be bypassed by going down on the grass slope. The main route for swimmers is to go across the bridge over the public footpath and via −8−12.

From the Triangle CP on the north side of the Serpentine Bridge, there's the new Serpentine Sackler Gallery just across the road. In the other direction, along the lakeside, are the boatouses. There's a solar powered boat, which is said to be wheelchair accessible, and provides a half hour trip around the Serpentine. It is run by **Bluebird Boats**, The Boathouse, Serpentine Road, Hyde Park W2 2UH, *Tel:* 020 7262-1330.

Staff members will also help transfer people into rowing boats if necessary and practical.

From Hyde Park Corner, it's amazing how as you get further into the park, the noise from the traffic almost disappears. Going west, you can go through the extensive Rose Garden, towards the Holocaust Memorial and/or the east end of the lake.

The Princess Diana Memorial Playground is near the NW corner of the Gardens. It has a huge wooden pirate ship as its centrepiece. The design has created an area where less able and able-bodied children can play together and seeks to provide for their physical, creative, social and educational development. Inspired by the stories of Peter Pan, the playground encourages children to explore and follow their imaginations, learning whilst they play. It is a fitting tribute for a Princess who loved the innocence of childhood. We are told that there are toilets, including an **accessible** one, and BCF.

For food and drink, see some of the descriptions above. The principal places are:

* in Kensington Palace;
* at the Serpentine Sackler Gallery;
* the *Lido Bar and Café*;
* the *Serpentine Bar and Kitchen*;
* several kiosks near Marble Arch and by the Black Lion Gate, Queensway.

There are **accessible toilets**, some needing a RADAR key, scattered around the park. We haven't visited all of them, and you'll see which ones we have by the measurements. There is a mixture of unisex and of cubicles in the mens and womens areas. Several were installed quite a number of years ago, so the provisions are a bit variable. There are new ones in the Serpentine Gallery, Kensington Palace, the Serpentine Bar and the Lido Café.

We start in the east from Hyde Park Corner:

- opposite the Bandstand, near Nannies Lawn, where there are **accessible cubicles NKS** in the mens and womens toilets, which have been recently refurbished;

- at the Serpentine Bar and Kitchen café at the east end of the lake. The toilets are in a block attached to the café, reached from the lakeside corner by going around the outside seating area. **Wheelchair toilet (D80 ST70)** with BCF, but a slightly constrained space;

- by the Reservoir;

- at the Lido Café on the south side of the lake (see details above);

- in the new Serpentine Sackler Gallery (in the Magazine building), which was still under construction at the time of writing;

- by the Marlborough Gate, on the north side near Lancaster Gate tube station. The **wheelchair toilet (D90 ST100 NKS)** with BCF is right by the entrance to the womens toilets;

- in the Serpentine Gallery, where you go in past the bookshop on your left and into a small hallway. There's a **wheelchair toilet (D90 ST80)** through a door on the left also leading to the womens toilets. There are separate BCF through a door on the right leading to the mens;

- just to the south of the Gallery, near the Mount Gate, there are **adapted cubicles (D75 ST50 NKS)**. Their design is quite old;

- by the Palace Gate, on Kensington Road on the south side;

- in Kensington Palace. From the Round Pond, there's a gentle slope down to the Palace entrance. **The café and shop which are open to all, are located to the right**. The loos off the café area have a **wheelchair toilet (D80 ST100)** whose door opens in either direction (ie it can open either outwards or inwards) and there are separate BCF.

Kensington Palace

Kensington Palace Gardens, *Tel:* 0844 482-7777 (24-hour information line)
website: www.hrp.org.uk/KensingtonPalace

Built on the west side of Kensington Gardens the original house was Jacobean, which was upgraded and extended by Wren around 1700. It has been a royal palace ever since, and Victoria grew up there. The house has recently been extensively redeveloped, and its gardens relandscaped. It reopened in 2012 with greatly improved access, including the provision of a lift.

The Palace is about 300m from Kensington High Street (from the Royal Garden Hotel) and 500m from the Bayswater Road. There are 6 BB spaces by the Orangery, approached from the Orme Square Gate off the Bayswater Road (where there's a coach park). Spaces need to be booked at least 24-hours in advance with details of the car being used, since there's a Security gate to be opened to let you past. From the BB spaces it's about 100m to the Palace entrance down a sloping route.

Significant admission charge for the Palace.

From the Round Pond, there's a gentle slope down to the Palace entrance. **The café and shop which are open to all, are located to the right**. The loos off the café area have a **wheelchair toilet (D80 ST100)** whose door opens in either direction (ie it can open either outwards or inwards) and there are separate BCF. In the shop there are ±2 steps, which can be bypassed, using a platform lift (D90 L130) which blends into the flooring.

As you enter the main doors to the Palace, there's a ticket desk. Everything is step–free if you use the lift (D80 W150 L150) to the 1st and 2nd floors. There is a room on the GF with some dresses worn by Princess Diana, and on the upper floors, there are rooms associated with Queen Victoria and with other royal occupants. Although you will follow a slightly different route using the lift, you can see and visit everything.

One interesting feature of the exhibitions is that instead of providing an audio-guide, visitors are encouraged to interact with the staff and volunteers on duty, who will be only too pleased to explain the background to the various places and artefacts. There are some activities specifically for children.

There are a few places where lighting levels are quite low, and if needed, please don't hesitate to request guidance through these areas.

There are a number of seats around, and some lightweight fold-up stools can be borrowed. A full visit inside the Palace would involve less than 250m, but could still take you 1 to 2 hours if you want to explore it properly.

Wheelchair toilet (D80 ST70) on the GF in the ticketed area where, again, the door opens in both directions.

National Army Museum see chapter on *Museums and galleries*.

Royal Hospital Chelsea
Royal Hospital Road, SW3 4SR *Tel:* 020 7881-5200 (switchboard) or 020 7881-5516 (friends)
website: www.chelsea-pensioners.co.uk
A unique retirement home for soldiers; there are always Chelsea Pensioners around in their distinctive uniforms who are happy to chat. It is possible to visit the gardens and some of the Wren buildings, including the Great Hall and the Chapel. Three BB spaces by the Chelsea gate. From either gate the grounds are flat, and it's about 150m to the main courtyard and hall. There are +10 steps to the chapel, and the same number to the Great Hall, with platform stairlifts to bypass the. The Museum entrance is ramped bypassing +2 steps. There's an **adapted toilet (D90 ST100+ with inward opening door)** between London Gate and the entrance to the Great Hall and Chapel.

The Roof Gardens
99, Kensington High Street, W8 5SA *Tel:* 020 7937-7994
website: www.roofgardens.com
Overlooking Kensington from the back of the old Derry's department store is one
and a half acres of spectacular garden, with trees, ponds, tropical plants and even
flamingoes ! The gardens on the 6th floor are open to the public throughout the
day. They are available as a setting for 'corporate events', so if you want to be
sure they're open, ring first to check. On the 7th floor is the *Babylon* restaurant,
Tel: 020 7368-3993 *e-mail:* babylon@roofgardens.virgin.com.
**Access to the gardens is from a totally unmarked entrance under the canopy
some 60m down Derry Street on the right.**
Inside the doors is a reception desk, and the +3 steps at the front can by bypassed
by a platform lift (D85 L100). An outside button will open the door automatically.
From the foyer, the lifts (D110 W160 L180) on the right go to floors six and
seven, but only the left-hand lift goes to the 7th floor restaurant.

On floor six, turn left to get out into the gardens, and once outside, go right. There
is then a step-free though slightly bumpy path which goes round about 80% of the
gardens which cover about 100m by 40m.
The Babylon restaurant has an **adapted toilet (D85 ST60)** with BCF, and it is
step-free both to the balcony where there are tables and you can enjoy a drink,
and to most of the tables inside.

Regent's Park area
Described in one section of the Eyewitness guide as Regent's Park and
Marylebone. The area includes the north end of Baker Street, the Marylebone
Road, the Regent's Canal, Little Venice and Camden. Pay and display parking
is possible round the Inner Circle, and on Chester Road. There are a substantial
number of BB spaces on the Inner Circle (not marked in the *Blue Badge User
Guide with map of Central London*). There is also pay and display parking around
long stretches of the outer circle.
Note the wheelchair toilets in Regent's Park and the one opposite Madame
Tussauds.

Camden is just north-west of Regent's Park, and the canal passes through. With
its locks and canalside developments it has its own unique character. There are
hundreds of small shops and stalls (many as part of open markets). They stretch
for more than a km along Camden High Street and Chalk Farm Road, with
particular market areas near Camden Town station, at Inverness Street, and at
Camden Lock. Further up the Chalk Farm Road is the Stables Market.

Camden Road, on the *Overground* is less than a km away, and is 'accessible'. The
nearest 'accessible' tube station is Kings Cross/St Pancras some 2.5km away.
Parking is difficult, although one possibility would be to use the Zoo CP off the

Outer Circle, about 1km away.
Buses include the 168 from Waterloo; the 24 and C2 from Victoria (the C2 also passes Green Park); and the 214 from Kings Cross/St Pancras.

Our description starts from (the inaccessible) Camden Town tube station. Camden Market is opposite Inverness Street and is flat. Much of it is covered. It can be congested, with narrow gaps between stalls. Camden Lock Market, across the canal, has three courts: east, middle and west. There are two levels, but both have (steep) ramped access from Chalk Farm Road. A lift from Camden Lock Place goes to the upper level. The surfaces are rough in places, and it's often crowded. There is an **adapted toilet (D85 ST60)** on the 1st floor of West Court, accessed via the road or the lift. The key is available from the nearest shop. *Weatherspoons* pub is located across the canal from Camden Lock Market, on the towpath (there is a step-free bridge over the canal, although it is cobbled and very steep), which has a **wheelchair toilet (D80 ST85 NKS)**.

Little Venice
The Regent's Canal was opened in 1820, joining the Grand Union Canal and the busy port at Paddington Basin to the river Thames at Limehouse. A hundred years ago it was busy with horse-drawn barges. Now it is a quiet waterway taking people on a scenic route through parts of London not otherwise seen.
It lies just west of the centre, north of the Westway and of the rail lines coming into Paddington. There's a triangular basin or lake which breaks the line of the canals at either end.
Little Venice itself provides a quiet retreat from the general 'rush' in London. Near the junction of Blomfield Road and Warwick Avenue are the Rembrandt Gardens with ramped access to a rose garden and **wheelchair toilet (D80 ST75 NKS)** with BCF.
Jason's Canal Trip goes from opposite 42 Blomfield Road, W9 2PD
website: www.jasons.co.uk
The company no longer has a phone contact, but trips are bookable on-line. Not a trend that we like.
When we went, getting on and off the boat involved going through a gap 60cm wide and ±3 steps. Staff there are used to helping disabled walkers getting on and off.

There are two restaurants nearby with accessible toilets:
* *The Summerhouse* opposite 60 Bloomfield Road near the junction with Clifton Villas and nearly 200m from the Westbourne Terrace bridge. There's a **wheelchair toilet (D80 ST80)** with BCF, but note that there's a high kerb outside;
* *Bridge House* pub and café, on Westbourne Terrace Road right by the bridge. Step-free with adapted toilet (D65 ST70) which was being renovated when we visited.

Additionally there is the *Café Laville* nearly 700m along Regent's canal past Warwick Avenue. It is on a bridge over the canal and while this has +2 steps at the entrance that provides a brilliant view.

London Canal Museum see chapter on *Museums and galleries*.
London Central Mosque see chapter on *Places of worship*.

London Zoo
Outer Circle, Regent's Park, NW1 4RY *Tel:* 020 7722-3333
Enquiries: 0844 225-1826
Booking motorised scooters and electric wheelchairs: 020 7449-6576
website: www.zsl.org *e-mail:* info@zsl.org
The Zoological Gardens was the first institution in the world dedicated to the study and display of animals. It has recently evolved and diversified, and a principal focus now, is in the field of conservation.
The zoo is in the northern part of Regent's Park, and the Regent's Canal passes alongside. It is triangular in shape with sides approximately 500m/500m/800m. The main entrance is, oddly, inside the triangle, because the road (the Outer Circle) passes through the zoo, and the various houses and terraces on the far side are reached via one or other of two ramped tunnels.

A full visit could well involve more than 2km, although it is possible to see a lot and only walk/wheel less than 1km from the entrance. There are a number of slopes, as the site is slightly hilly. The two tunnels to get to and from the enclosures on the other side of the Outer Circle road, have a steepish 30m long slope at each end.
Most surfaces are tarmac or paving.
There's quite a good plan/map on the website, and you can get a bigger version in the Visitors Guide when you go in.

Parking facilities for disabled visitors are not brilliant, considering the size and importance of the zoo. For BB holders there is a single space on the road outside, plus five BB spaces in the CP opposite the main entrance (with no time limit). BB holders can park free for up to 4 hours on the road, but if you want to stay longer, someone will have to go out and put some money in the meter! The main zoo CP with more free BB spaces is nearly 400m away. If you get there early, you're more likely to be able to get a BB space opposite the entrance.
There are usually taxis available outside when you leave.
There is a significant admission charge, though as is now relatively normal, there is no charge for a carer. Both power and manual chairs are available to be borrowed, but if you need one of these, book it in advance.
Guide dogs are not allowed on site, but your dog can be looked after while you visit, and (given notice) the zoo can provide an escort to enable you to get around.

Visitors are now required to enter through a queueing system off the Outer Circle, and to leave through the Gate into the park, past the *Oasis Café* and Zoo shop.

A considerable amount has been done to improve the facilities for disabled visitors, although some minor problems and challenges remain. As already mentioned, there are some slopes - and the ramped route in the big cats area isn't very obvious or well signed, especially if you want to go up. There are a few enclosures where hedges or walls may obstruct your view if you use a chair, but you generally only have to move around a bit in order to be able to see. If the animals or birds happen to be on the ground when you are going past, they may be difficult to see from a chair-user's eyeline. Fortunately, of course, many of them will be in branches or high up in their cages.

There are a good number of seats for when you want to take a break. There's a great variety of things to do with demonstrations and feeding times to go to. Some things happen in the Amphitheatre near the *Oasis Café* where there is fixed bench seating (backless), and space enough for a chair or two at ground level behind these. As you come in through the main entrance, which can be quite congested on busy days, there's an Information Kiosk immediately to your right. If distance is an issue, then you need to plan a manageable route. This might take you along the central path past the gorillas, to the big cats and/or to Animal Adventure. Coming back via Meet the Monkeys, Bugs, Butterfly Paradise and Penguin Beach, you could finish at the Oasis Café. There are many variations on this. **Some major enclosures are on the other side of the Outer Circle road**, including many African animals, the Snowdon Aviary and Rainforest Life.

Several of the houses allow the animals to mix with the visitors. This does mean that there are several sets of doors and/or plastic strips or linked chains that must be pushed through. The places where you can do this include:
- Butterfly Paradise;
- Meet the Monkeys (outside); and,
- Rainforest Life.

There is also interaction of a different kind, with a number of animals in the children's area now called Animal Adventure. There's a ramped entrance to the Aquarium to bypass the +5 steps at the entrance. Below the Rainforest life is the nightlife area. There is a lift to bypass the −17 steps. In both the nightlife area and the aquarium there is subdued lighting. Penguin Beach is a much improved facility compared with the old Penguin Pool which cannot be changed in any way as it is an iconic listed building.

During school holidays, and at weekends and bank holidays, the zoo can be very busy, with a lot of families with young children.

The provision of accessible toilets is limited, and they tend to be used a lot by parents with young children. They are located:

- near the entrance, at the bottom of a slope, there's a **wheelchair toilet (D80 ST100)** and although there are BCF in the adjacent mens and womens loos, it is heavily used by parents with children. The BCF in the mens is on a shelf at the end of the cubicles, and is not very obvious;
- near the Aquarium there is a **wheelchair cubicle** in the mens toilets;
- near the Animal Adventure, and through the shop. Wheelchair toilet with BCF. There are additional BCF in the mens and womens toilets;
- by Bugs, **wheelchair toilet (D80 ST100, and although the door opens inwards, the cubicle is large)**. There are BCF in both the mens and womens loos;
- at the Oasis Café to the left of the main entrance. **Adapted toilet**, as the door opens inwards, with BCF. Very busy toilet, mainly used by mums with buggies. The mens and womens toilets also have BCF.

Note the +2 steps in front of the Oasis Café are bypassed by a ramp to the right.

Madame Tussaud's

Marylebone Road, NW1 5LR *Tel:* 0871 894-3000
website: www.madame-tussauds.com
e-mail: guest.experience@madame-tussauds.com

Madame Tussaud's is one of London's most popular attractions, with waxworks including sports stars, entertainers, royalty and politicians, both past and current. Admission charge.

It is situated some 50m left from main exit from Baker Street tube, and by the junction with Allsop Place. The tube station is 'inaccessible', and the nearest 'accessible' one is Kings Cross/St Pancras.

There's a taxi/car/coach drop-off zone outside the main entrance. Parking can be quite problematic, although there are meters around and a few BB spaces (see the Pie parking guide). There are no nearby multi-storey CPs. There are, however, a good number (20+) of BB spaces in the Inner Circle in Regent's Park, about 500-700m away. The slight doubts about parking can be a hassle in terms of fitting in with the timed ticket entry system.

The displays offer many opportunities for the visitor to be photographed with their favourite public figures, and you can have your picture taken with the Queen if you wish.

Madame Tussaud's was built long before 'access' was considered, and while the management have made considerable efforts to provide for wheelchair access, it is still quite challenging.

Disabled walkers need to look at our description of the conventional route for getting around and decide whether or not they might be wise to use a chair during

the visit.
There are very few places where you can sit down, and also few toilets.

The venue gets extremely busy, and is strict about only allowing three chair
users to visit at any one time. It is therefore necessary to telephone and book in
advance to ensure entry, which will be on a 'timed ticket' basis. You can borrow
a wheelchair for use in the venue, but, again, pre-booking is essential. Children's
buggies are not allowed, and you need to leave your buggy near the entrance and
collect it at the end.
There is a *Disabled Guide* on the website, but it's quite difficult to relate its brief
description to what actually happens during a visit.

A chair users experience.
There is step-free access for wheelchair users using a service lift (D80 W110
L185) behind reception, which goes to all floors. The tour begins on the 3rd floor
and continues down the floors to the GF. The Chamber of Horrors and Scream
interactive experience is in the basement.
Chair users and disabled walkers can use the lift, in order to get to the next level,
although this means taking a slightly different route from everyone else, and
sometimes you are going against the general flow of people. There is step-free
access throughout except for +3 steps to a mezzanine including an information
desk on the 2nd floor (in the Grand Hall). On the GF, the Spirit of London
ride is +9, although there's a slightly easier route going up only +4 through an
unmarked door on the right, just before the +9. The ride has to be boarded while
it is moving, and that might be a problem for some. It also takes you down some
steepish slopes, and the mini-cab seats you're in are quite slippery. It is regarded
by the management as 'inaccessible', although if someone can be lifted on an off
easily the staff are quite accommodating (and we saw this happen when visiting).

The Chamber of Horrors and Scream interactive exhibits are in the basement in
an area that is very poorly lit (to heighten the element of scariness), and has rough
flooring in places.
From the area where people collect their photographs, and where there are some
toilets, most of the time guests using a wheelchair are taken round outside the
building to visit the shop and the Entertainment Venue.
Alternatively there's a platform stair lift to bring a chair user up to the shop
(bypassing +15) and there are two platform stairlifts (bypassing −4 and −5 steps
en route in the shop) which is quite congested. There is a single (well marked)
step at the entrance/exit from the shop to the pavement, and a ramp is available if
needed.

To get to the Entertainment Venue (in what used to be the Planetarium), chair
users go a short distance outside the building and come back inside at entrance 5,
where there's a lift up to the Showdome.
The building tends to be very crowded and the layout somewhat confusing; as a

204 PLACES OF INTEREST

result, the staff may have a few problems coordinating their guidance in getting you from floor to floor.

Wheelchair toilets (D85 ST85) are located:

- on the GF at street level as you come in, and another in the main queueing (admissions) area which has BCF;
- on the 2nd floor (Grand Hall/World Stage) with BCF;
- on the GF just past the end of the Spirit of London ride in the Game Zone, also with BCF; and,
- on the 1st floor by the exit from the Entertainment Venue (Showdome).

The 'conventional' walkers route around

Taking the standard route from the entrance hall there are +16 steps to the three lifts (D110 W125 L180) which take visitors to the 3rd floor from where they continue steadily downwards through the various exhibition halls, on the designated route using the stairs. In total, there are more than 250 steps (including going down into the Chamber of Horrors, up again to the Showdome and then back to street level). There are steps between each floor.

The whole visit takes about an hour and a half to two hours, depending on how many photo-stops you make. If you find the steps are a problem you can ask the staff to use the designated lift linking the various floors. There are at least half a dozen level changes.

Primrose Hill rises gently up from Prince Albert Road, and you can get fine views over London on a good day. Two **adapted toilets (D85 ST60 NKS)** by the entrance to the womens toilets by the Children's Playground at the bottom of the hill, about 100m from the park entrance. See the write-up on Hampstead Heath later on.

The Regent's Park

Manager's Office, The Storeyard, Inner Circle, Regent's Park NW1 4NR
Tel: 0300 061-2300 *website:* www.royalparks.gov.uk (and then select the park)
e-mail: regents@royalparks.gsi.gov.uk
A large and attractive area of parkland just north of Marylebone.

The park was enclosed in 1812, and Nash developed a grand design consisting of a garden suburb including a palace for the Prince Regent. Only eight villas were ever built. There is now a mixture of formal gardens and of open parkland.
The area is fairly flat, until you get to Primose Hill to the north. Most of the paths are tarmac. It measures about 1.5km N/S and about the same E/W. There's a largish lake with facilities for boating, and in the NE corner is London Zoo. The ring road round the outside is nearly 8km long.

There are BB spaces along Chester Road, and a good number around the Inner Circle. Off the Inner Circle, there's a small open-air theatre with step-free access - an attractive spot during warm summer evenings. Queen Mary's Garden has an attractive rose garden where there are +2 steps to get to the fountain, but these can be bypassed by taking any other path.

We found four places selling refreshments: a cafeteria on the Broadwalk (near Chester Road); a restaurant on the Inner Circle in Queen Mary's Garden, near the theatre; another cafeteria by the tennis courts towards York Gate; and another restaurant by Hanover Gate. All have step-free access, and both outdoor and indoor seating. There are also several refreshment stands scattered around the park during the summer.

The Hub is a two storey multisports facility which offers a wide range of sporting activities, exercise classes and children's activities for the local community. It includes a café on the 2nd floor that offers a 360 degree view of the park, accessible by ramps to the left of the main entrance or a lift (D85 W95 L140) in the centre of the building.

There are several **accessible toilets**:

- just off Chester Road where it is crossed by Broad Walk, and behind the *Cow and Coffee Bean* café. **Wheelchair cubicles (D80 ST80 NKS)** in both mens and womens toilets;
- in the *Garden Café* on the Inner Circle to the left of the food counter and you can bypass +5 steps from the road by taking the path to the main entrance. **Wheelchair toilet (D75 ST100)** with BCF;
- by the boating lake just north of Hanover Bridges, **wheelchair cubicles (D80 ST120 NKS)** in both mens and womens areas;
- at the Hub, the entrance to the lower floor is along the paved path. The toilets are directly inside with **wheelchair cubicles (D100 ST80)** and BCF, in both the mens and womens toilets.

There are **adapted toilets/cubicles**:

- in Queen Mary's Garden near the end of Chester Road, **cubicles (D80 ST45 NKS)** in both mens and womens;
- by Gloucester Gate with an accessible toilet inside the children's play area, to the left of the main children's toilets. This was not seen this time because adults are only able to go in when accompanied by a child. When previously visited, it was measured as **(D75 ST60 NKS)**;
- in the Pavilion Café near the Jubilee Gates, and to the right of the food and tennis desks. **Unisex (D85 ST45 because when visited the ST was blocked by a storage locker)**. There are BCF in both the mens and womens toilets.

Outer London
Barnes and Chiswick
Chiswick House and Gardens
Burlington Lane, Chiswick, W4 2RP
Tel: 020 8995-0508 *website:* www.chgt.org.uk
The house is a magnificent Palladian villa built around a central octagonal

room with several interesting 18thC portraits. There are also extensive grounds measuring some 500m by 500m.

To get there by car, take the A4 some 500m past the Hogarth roundabout. It is on the left as you are going towards Heathrow. Well signed. However, disabled visitors should use the main gate which is about 30m BEFORE the well signed entrance for the CP. *It's very easy to overshoot the main entrance gates, and a long way round to get back to them - so approach with some care.* When you go through the main gates, you can follow the drive all the way round to the forecourt of the house where BB holders can park. You would do best to ring first and get 'authorised'.

From the official CP there's a 600m walk over a roughish path, and including a step.

Pedestrians can enter through any of the gates: from Great Chertsey Road, Burlington Lane, or Staveley Road.

To enter the house from the forecourt there is +1 step, then +1, bypassed by a portable ramp. The rest of GF is step-free but has a narrow passage of 70cm connecting the main building to some statue exhibits and the toilet; both of which can be reached through a side door opened by staff. There is a cellar on the lower floor reached by −12.

The 1st floor holds the main interest. There are +16 spiral stairs or you might use the grand staircase outside (+7+6+6) if you ask staff to remove the 'No Entry' sign. If you ring in advance they can charge up a stairclimber to bypass these steps, but it cannot be used in wet weather. Using the stairclimber involves transferring into its seat from your chair. **Adapted toilet (D85 ST65)** with BCF off to the right of the modern annexe, opened on request. Alternatively there is a **wheelchair toilet (D80 ST130)** on left side of a step-free café 50m from house. Some paths around the house and through the gardens are gravelled.

Wetland Centre
Queen Elizabeth Walk, Barnes, SW13 9WT *Tel:* 020 8409-4400
website: www.wwt.org.uk *e-mail:* info.london@wwt.org.uk
A unique reserve for wild birds created on decommissioned reservoirs. As well as facilities that allow keen birdwatchers to look out for periodic visitors, there are a number of rare and endangered species kept there for breeding. The entrance is about 200m down Queen Elizabeth Walk from the junction with Castelnau by the Red Lion pub. The 283 bus, runs to the Centre from Hammersmith bus station, where the stations are 'accessible'.

The CP is about 100m from the entrance, just beyond the bus stop, and has 12 BB spaces. From the CP the route leads over a small wooden hump-backed bridge. Step-free to the ticket office. This leads into a courtyard. To the left of the door you have come through is the entrance to the shop, which is step-free. To the right of the door from the ticket office is the entrance to the Discovery Centre. This includes the *Secrets of the Wetlands* exhibit and entrance to the GF section of this is step-free. The *Wetlab* section of the exhibition with interactive displays, is +19 steps, but there's a lift (D80 W100 L140) to bypass these. A further door from the courtyard leads to the Observatory, a large glass-fronted room with views over the Wetlands. Step-free entrance, with a ramp bypassing −4 to the front of the room. Gallery level +20. Between the Observatory and the Discovery Centre is the Tower, where the lift provides step-free access to the *Wetlab* and via high-level open-air walkways, to the gallery in the Observatory and the binocular shop *In Focus* (which is above the souvenir shop). The second floor of the tower, also accessible by the lift, contains a children's area. **Wheelchair toilets (D75 ST75)** with BCF on both the GF and 1st floor, ahead and to the right when coming out of the lift.

The theatre is opposite the main building and has step-free access. It shows a short film about wetlands. Chair users can either sit in front of the front row of seats (which possibly restricts their view of the edge of the screen), or transfer to the front row, which is step-free from the entrance.

The café can be entered from the GF of the Tower or from outside, towards the *Waterlife* walk, and has step-free access with movable tables and chairs.

The *Waterlife* walk is reached from beyond the café, and consists of a number of areas with examples of wetland life and flora, as well as a number of hides (for bird watching) with views over the main lagoons. It is approximately 500m to the far end of the walk, by the most direct route, but rather longer if you wish to divert off the main path to the hides or exhibits. The main paths are tarmac, but a few outlying paths have loose compacted surfaces. These, however, are generally flat and should not pose problems to most chair users. All the hides and the *Wetland Living* hut have step-free access and low level viewing holes at 100 to 115cm from the ground. The Wader Scrape hide has +3, bypassed by a ramp, to the viewing area. The Peacock Tower, at the far end of the route contains a lift (D80 W110 L140) to the viewing levels. **Wheelchair toilet (D85 ST75)** with BCF, in a block about two-thirds of the way around the route, by the entrance to the Explore Adventure Area.

The *World Wetlands* and *Wildside* walk is reached from behind the theatre, and consists of a series of gated areas which try to create different international habitats, in which several endangered species of birds are being bred in captivity. Distances and the state of the paths are similar to the Waterlife walk, and a large (though not particularly heavy) gate separates the Wetlands and the Wildside areas. The Wildside Hide at the far end of the walk has +16 steps to the upper viewing level and no lift. There are no low-level viewing windows on that level (although there are on the GF level, which has step-free access). The Headley hide has step-free access and low-level viewing holes.

Signage is reasonably good throughout the centre. The map provided is useful for getting around and clarifies where you can go. Our (non-twitcher) surveyors enjoyed their visit there, and would recommend the centre to birdwatchers and interested non-birdwatchers alike. There is another **accessible toilet** by the CP but it was locked when we visited.

The **National Archives** (previously called the Public Record Office), Ruskin Avenue, Kew, although strictly just inside the South Circular road, are included on the website in the write-ups titled *Kew* (and under *Sights outside the N/S Circular*) as otherwise they are isolated from other sites.

Greenwich

Greenwich is on the south bank of the river, and about 8km downstream from Tower Bridge.
It was the birthplace of Henry VIII, and of his two daughters, Mary and Elizabeth. Many of the buildings were designed by Sir Christopher Wren, including the Naval College and the Observatory, (hence the several domes). The Queen's House was designed by Inigo Jones.
Charles 11 supported scientific research in Greenwich; commissioned the Observatory; and appointed the first Astronomer Royal, John Flamsteed. Britain's ships all over the world needed accurate time and astronomical measurements to facilitate safe navigation. In 1884, Greenwich Mean Time became the global basis of time measurement.

Maritime Greenwich has been declared a World Heritage Site (WHS) see www.greenwichwhs.org.uk and it became a Royal Borough in 2012.
It has a unique collection of sights and places of interest in quite a small area, and we therefore describe them together in this section.
The WHS comprises the town centre and Park, together with buildings associated with:
- the Naval College and the Cutty Sark, AND the foot tunnel under the Thames;
- the Maritime Museum and the Queen's House; and,
- the Old Observatory and the Astronomy Centre.

It has some spectacular classical buildings, together with the famous Meridian Line. Its history is tied up with the Tudors, with things naval, and in particular with the study of navigation.
Note that there's a steep hill between the Maritime Museum and the Observatory.

Greenwich can either be just a place to visit, or it could be somewhere to stay, from which you can get to other parts of central London. A number of local hotels are listed in the *Accommodation* chapter.
It has good transport links, with 'accessible' riverboats to and from central

London. Greenwich NR station is 'accessible' and trains go to London Bridge, and Cannon Street. There is also the DLR which links to Tower Gateway and Bank, with an interchange at Canary Wharf for the JLE.

This means that someone staying in Greenwich can reach a large number of central London sights in less than an hour, using 'accessible' transport. Note, of course, that there is a sizeable step up into the trains, but portable ramps are available. Greenwich station is currently staffed from about 06.00 to 21.30. For a chair user the river can provide a relatively easy way to get to the Tower, to the Embankment, and/or the South Bank, or to Westminster.

Parking is free for BB holders in the Council CPs, but note that the one in the Park is run by the Parks Authority. There are CPs:

- off Welland Street, by the Cutty Sark. A small CP with no marked BB spaces and a height limit of 2m. The only step-free way in and out is via the slope the cars use. It is very centrally located
- off Burney Street behind the Ibis hotel with 3 BB spaces. Height restriction 2m.
- by the junction between Romney Road and Park Row with 2 BB spaces, and no height restriction; together with
- a weekend overflow CP at the other end of Park Row right by the Maritime Museum, which BB holders can use (with prior permission) during the week if visiting the Museum or Queens House, again with no height restriction
- in Greenwich Park itself, in Blackheath Avenue, near the Royal Observatory and by the Pavilion Tea House. There are 5 BB spaces by the Observatory and no height restriction. BB holders should be able to park without charge, but there's a 4 hour time limit.

For more information, see: *www.en.parkopedia.co.uk/parking/greenwich* (but this does not show the parking in Blackheath Avenue).

If you're using a vehicle then one good way of organising a visit is to use the Park Row facilities for visiting the riverside sites, and then driving up the hill and parking in Blackheath Avenue to visit the Observatory.

Greenwich Tourist Information Centre ⑨
Pepys House, 2 Cutty Sark Gardens, SE10 9LW *Tel:* 0870 608-2000
website: www.visitgreenwich.org.uk/tourist-information-centre
e-mail: tic@greenwich.gov.uk
Located near the Cutty Sark and by the pier, in a pedestrianised area.

The Centre provides an excellent *Visitors Map* which you might do well to get hold of before visiting. It can be downloaded from the website.

There is a *Discover Greenwich* exhibition; a café; shop, and an **accessible toilet** with BCF. Although the door opens inwards, it is quite a big cubicle. It is all step-free.

On our map, we have used the same numbering system as that on the *Visitors Map*.

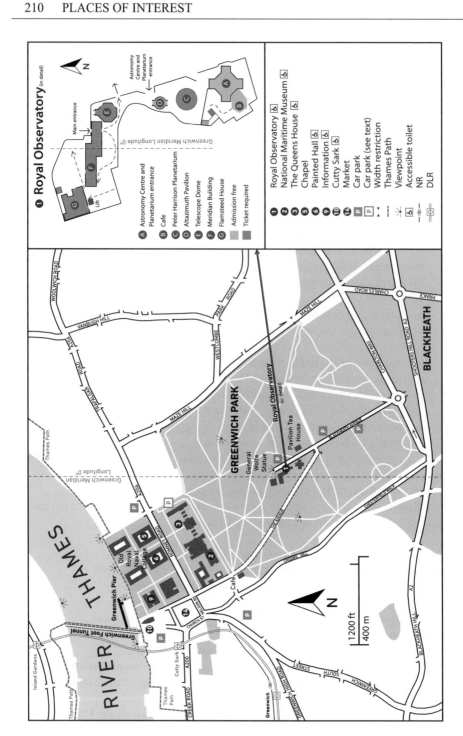

Royal Observatory (in detail)

Main entrance

Astronomy Centre and Planetarium entrance

Greenwich Meridian Longitude 0°

Lift

A Astronomy Centre and Planetarium entrance
B Cafe
C Peter Harrison Planetarium
D Altazimuth Pavilion
E Telescope Dome
F Meridian Building
G Flamsteed House

Admission free
Ticket required

1 Royal Observatory
2 National Maritime Museum
3 The Queens House
4 Chapel
5 Painted Hall
6 Information
11 Cutty Sark
14 Market
Car park
Car park (see text)
Width restriction
Thames Path
Viewpoint
Accessible toilet
NR
DLR

WOOLWICH ROAD
VANBRUGH HILL
PARK ROAD
WESTCOMBE
MAZE HILL
CHARLTON WAY
CHARLES ROAD
PRINCE
A2
SHOOTERS HILL ROAD A2
BLACKHEATH

A206
TRAFALGAR ROAD
MAZE HILL

GREENWICH PARK

Royal Observatory
(in detail)

Pavilion Tea House

General Wolfe Statue

BLACKHEATH AVENUE

CHESTERFIELD WALK

THE AVENUE

CROOMS HILL

THAMES
RIVER

Island Gardens
Thames Path

Greenwich Foot Tunnel
Greenwich Pier

Old Royal Naval College

Greenwich Meridian Longitude 0°

ROMNEY ROAD

Cafe

CHURCH ST

Cutty Sark
A200
CREEK ROAD
Thames Path

Greenwich
GREENWICH HIGH ROAD
SOUTH STREET
GREENWICH SOUTH
BLACKHEATH HILL
A2

N

1200 ft
400 m

From the riverside, there's the **Old Royal Naval College (ORNC)** which includes some remarkable sights. The College buildings are another Wren masterpiece. *Tel:* 020 8269-4799
website: www.ornc.org *e-mail:* info@ornc.org
The website highlights the top ten must-see details in the College. For parts of the College, access is a bit of a challenge, but there's a lift to the Painted Hall, and a Stairmate to facilitate getting up to the Chapel. The Information Centre is in part of the ORNC.

The **Royal Museums Greenwich** include the Cutty Sark, Maritime Museum, Queen's House, and the Old Observatory. They have just one telephone enquiry number and website.
Tel: 020 8858-4422 (from which you are directed to the appropriate site).
website: www.rmg.co.uk
There are admission charges to the Cutty Sark, Meridian Courtyard and Flamsteed House, and to the Planetarium. Some are significant. You can get tickets for various combined visits at reduced overall cost. Entrance to the Maritime Museum, Queen's House, and to the Astronomy Centre at the Observatory is free.

Much of **the ORNC** is taken up by the University of Greenwich, but some parts are open to the public, including:
The Painted Hall ❻ in College Way
This has a platform lift (D100 W200 L150) in the corner of the building, which goes to floors 1 (for the Hall) and −1 for the restaurant. To call and to use/operate the lift, you have to hold the button down continuously. It is then ALL automatic (so trying to open the door manually may cause a malfunction).
The Painted Hall has a magnificent ceiling, but the mirrors for looking at them are 96cm high which is slightly too high for many chair users. There are +6 steps to an upper level.
In the basement (level −1) there's a nice quiet restaurant and bar, in the King William Undercroft. There are toilets just across the corridor. Follow the sign for ladies and disabled toilets. There are **two wheelchair toilets (D70+ ST70+)**, one of which has BCF.

To get to the **Chapel ❺** from the Painted Hall, there are −15. Then you can go across the gap to the next building, where there are −1+1 (very small) and then +3+13 up to the Chapel.
For a chair user, or walker who has a problem with steps, there is a way to get to the Chapel from the Painted Hall. At the far end, they have a vehicle with small tank tracks which can go down and up steps called a Stairmate. This can be used, to carry wheelchair users from the Hall to the Chapel. The maximum weight the Stairmate can take is 200 kg. The maximum chair width is 69.5cm (27"). Most

electric chairs will, of course, exceed this weight. If you are able to transfer, a manual wheelchair can be provided to make the Chapel visit possible. It is worth ringing the Information Centre in advance to make sure that there's someone on duty who is qualified to operate the Stairmate, and that it is charged up.

The **town centre** is compact, and therefore quite crowded and congested through the summer and at weekends. The pavements can be quite bumpy, and are a bit narrow in places. The *Visitors Map* shows the layout of the ORNC, close to the river, and we describe the access into buildings 4 and 5. We also describe access to buildings 1, 2, and 3, as well as to 14 (the Greenwich Market).

There's a wide range of pubs and restaurants, and several places of entertainment including the Greenwich Theatre, and the Picturehouse. There's also the Fan Museum, and St Alfege's church.

The area around the Pier and the Cutty Sark has been pedestrianised, though watch out for some long angled steps which are quite difficult to spot when it's overcast because of a lack of colour contrast. There is wheelchair access almost everywhere. Near the pier there are three new restaurants which will almost certainly have accessible toilets.

Greenwich Market ⓮ is covered, and is quite small, so that it can be congested at busy times. Some of the surfaces inside are rough and quite bumpy.

Cutty Sark ⓾
King William Walk, SE10 9HT (by Greenwich Pier)
Tel: 020 8858 4422 *website:* www.rmg.co.uk/cuttysark
A famous tea clipper that sailed both the Atlantic and the Pacific in the 19thC. Its principal cargoes were tea and then wool. After a disastrous fire in 2007, the ship was raised about 3m, and is now suspended on struts. A glass skirt has been put around the ship and dock, making it an all-weather attraction.

Significant admission charge. Closed some Mondays. The number of wheelchair users who can visit is limited to three per hour.

A new and separate glass tower contains two lifts giving access to and from the Main Weather Deck and the Sammy Ofer Gallery around the ship's keel.

The standard visitor route takes you from street level through a gap in the glass surround into a rather congested shop and ticket area. This is on the Lower Hold level where there is a video presentation and a computer game trying to get the ship to use the fastest winds from Australia to England. The route through this deck is via narrow walkways and you can see the cramped crew quarters. A chair user or disabled walker has to double back against the flow, in order to take the internal platform lift (D90 L150) up to the 'Tween Deck, and then to the Main Deck. Be careful when exiting the lift, because the 'Tween Deck is sloping. From the Main Deck the view is very limited, as the sides are about 1.5m high. There are raised areas with ladder steps and rope handrails at both the bow and stern ends.

From here you take one of the lifts in the tower alongside down to the keel level, where there's a café and gallery. From here, there's a platform lift at the prow end to take you up to a viewing gallery, described by one of our visitors as 'strangely dull'. To get back to ground level, there's another platform lift (D90 L150) from the Sammy Ofer Gallery to the shop, near the ships stern.

There are **wheelchair toilets** at both the top (Main Deck level) and bottom (Keel level), of the tower containing the lifts. The Keel level one includes BCF.

The Greenwich Foot Tunnel
This pedestrian route under the Thames was built more than a hundred years ago, and is nearly 400m long. There are large lifts at each end, and the tunnel is an unusual example of Victorian/Edwardian engineering. The dome over the lift shaft is fairly obvious from the Cutty Sark.

National Maritime Museum and Queen's House ❷ and ❸
Romney Road, Greenwich, SE10 9NF
Tel: 020 8858-4422 (bookings 020 8312-6608) *RecM:* 020 8312-6565
website: www.nmm.ac.uk *e-mail:* bookings@nmm.ac.uk
An extensive museum whose exhibits illustrate the key role that seafaring has played in British history. Built in the 19thC as a school for sailors' children, it was completely renovated in 1998 when some of the outside walkways were enclosed under a large glass canopy. It combines several buildings. Three of them surround the covered courtyard behind the entrance portico, and there's a largely new central building in what was the (open) courtyard.

There is limited parking for BB holders on the east side of the site, approached from the end of Park Row (off the A206 Romney Road). Spaces are bookable 24 hours in advance. The CP gates say "Parking on weekends and bank holidays only" but if you have pre-booked a space, you will be allowed in. It's some 200m from the CP to the main museum entrance, where you can drop off a passenger if that's necessary.

The immediate area around the museum is flat, but there's a steep hill in Greenwich Park up to the Observatory, which is at least 700m away.

There are two step-free entrances, on opposite sides of the museum. One is from the Romney Road side, towards the river, and you go in through an old and rather grand portico. The other is from the Park side, and is a very modern glass construction, entering what is called the Sammy Ofer Wing.

A diagrammatic Floor Plan is in the *Visitor maps*, available at the information desk just inside both entrances. As a first time visitor, we found this quite difficult to follow, and in particular to sort out which lift was which. Signage is quite poor, and there aren't many seats around. However, you can borrow a folding stool.

The whole building is about 100m deep and a little over 150m wide in places. The exhibitions are on several floors. The newest parts are the large covered atrium, designed in a similar way to the one in the British Museum, and the Sammy Ofer

Wing, which has a basement gallery for special exhibitions.

A two-level central area is linked by walkways to older wings which contain most of the exhibits and form a horseshoe around the atrium. Nearly all the exhibits can be reached step-free.

There are five lifts in the areas which were open when we visited. All were >D75 W100 L100, and most are much bigger than that:

- one is found from the Romney Road entrance by going left and left again, and then you can see the glass shaft, but have to go down a narrow corridor to your left to get to the lift doors. This goes from the GF to floors 1 and 2. It is close to room 4;
- two other lifts go from different corners of the building, by room 8 and to the right of room 9 (the shop). Both go to floors 1 and 2, while the one by room 9 also stops at a mezzanine where there are toilets;
- in the Sammy Ofer Wing, there's a glass lift from the GF to the basement. There's another one past the toilets, which isn't signed, and is out of sight (it's to your right at the end of the corridor), which goes up to the Brasserie on floor 2.

The staff are friendly and well-informed.

There are six **accessible toilets**:

- one is on the GF near the Romney Road entrance is an **adapted toilet (D85 ST60)** with BCF, and the ST is restricted because of the BC table;
- one is past room 21, on a mezzanine level (accessed by lift), and is a **wheelchair toilet (D80 ST80)** with BCF;
- one is shown on floor 1 in room 23 (the Caird Library) but we didn't see this;
- one is on the GF of the Sammy Ofer Wing, a **wheelchair toilet (D80 ST80)** with separate BCF;
- one is in the basement of the Sammy Ofer Wing, a **wheelchair toilet (D80 ST80)** with separate BCF;
- and there is one by the Brasserie restaurant.

Adjacent to the Maritime Museum back towards the CP is **the Queen's House**. This was designed by Inigo Jones for Anne of Denmark who was James I's queen. The other buildings towards the river were carefully sited so that the queen had an unobstructed view of the river. It has been restored and houses a series of exhibits which reflect its history, and that of Greenwich, and of things maritime. Step-free entrance from the Romney Road side, and through a door under the stairways. This leads to the ticket office. To the right is a lift (D100 W205 L100) that goes up to floors 1 and 2. On the GF −3−1 steps from the Great Hall will take you into a roadway and then +1+3 take you to the Orangery, with a lovely view of Greenwich Park. Ramps are available if you make arrangements in advance, but they're quite steep. **Wheelchair toilet (D85 ST70)** with BCF on the GF, to the left of the entrance.

The **Fan Museum**, 12 Crooms Hill, SE10 8ER, *Tel:* 020 8305-1441, is said to have lift access and an accessible toilet, but we haven't visited. When we phoned we were told that most of the steps could be bypassed using either a ramp or internal lift. It is closed on Mondays. **St Alfege's Church**, where General Wolfe is buried (he is famous because he led the forces who captured Quebec from the French in 1760), is said to have a steepish ramp to facilitate access via the south entrance. Probably a portable, temporary ramp. The church is in Greenwich Church Street, SE10 9BJ, *Tel:* 020 8853-0687 *website:* www.st-alfege.org.

Greenwich Park (a Royal Park, *Tel:* 0300 061-2380)

The park extends some 1km north/south and 600m east/west with a substantial hill between the Maritime Museum and the Observatory. It covers around 180 acres (74ha) stretching up the hill from Greenwich and linking with Blackheath. The park was originally the grounds of the royal palace, while Blackheath was common land, and was often a meeting point for groups entering London from the east. These included Wat Tyler's group of rebels at the time of the Peasants' Revolt.

In parts of the park the squirrels are so tame that they will eat out of your hand, but be careful, some may bite ! There is a bandstand, with occasional performances and several other features, including a Deer Park. There's car access from Blackheath along Blackheath Avenue.

There's a magnificent view over London from the General Wolfe statue at the end of Blackheath Avenue. The general is buried in St Alfege's church.

The park includes the Old Royal Observatory and a new Astronomy Centre at the top of the hill (see the inset in the Greenwich map). Rangers House is in the SE corner.

The shortest route to the top from the Maritime Museum, involves a very steep path with 10 single steps. There is a gentler, step-free route using the gate at the end of King William Walk, following The Avenue up to the CP at the top. In total this is >750m long, but from March to October an 'accessible' shuttle bus runs up and down every half-hour.

Just past the park entrance from Blackheath there are **mens and womens toilets with adapted cubicles (D80 ST75 but inward opening doors)**. They're about 50m from the entrance and just to the left. There are parking spaces on the left of the road.

The Astronomy Centre is located in the Royal Observatory South building, and its galleries are free.

In its courtyard there's a big dark grey construction that looks a bit like a ship's funnel and is the dome of the Planetarium.

The main building has three levels with lift access. The GF has three galleries. The 1st floor is an education centre while the lower level has a Café, shop and toilets including a **wheelchair toilet**. The Café has an open balcony for eating out during the summer. The **Planetarium**, for which there is an admission charge, is also approached from the lower level and has 3 wheelchair spaces.

There is one other small gallery in a separate building at ground level which is step-free from one entrance but +2 from the other.

The Old Royal Observatory, Meridian Building, and Flamsteed House

This group of buildings is approached from just past the statue, and visiting this area involves an admission charge.

The observatory is administered from the National Maritime Museum at the bottom of the hill, and the number for enquiries is *Tel:* 020 8858-4422 *website:* www.rmg.co.uk

The Meridian Building and Telescope Gallery are both step-free on the GF, and most of the exhibits can be seen. The route around leads to the Astronomers Garden, which is partially cobbled.

There's a **wheelchair toilet (D70 ST80)** which is between two buildings and is signed from the courtyard. It is down a small dead-end passage off the garden.

Also in the garden there's an external platform lift to bypass most of the stairs in **Flamsteed House**. You may have to use the bell to attract attention. The lift goes to both the upper and lower levels. The conventional route involves +4, and then +17 to the 1st floor. Then stairs −3−7−7, followed by −20+16 (via the basement) to the gardens.

Finally, you can go and cross (or straddle) the famous Meridian Line in the Meridian Courtyard. This is also partially cobbled. The exit route takes you through the shop.

Pavilion Tea House

The Tea House has a ramped entrance and is step-free throughout. In the summer there's a lovely outside eating area. **Wheelchair toilet (D90 ST110)** with BCF, located to the right of the service desk.

Ranger's House

Chesterfield Walk, Blackheath, SE10 8QX

Tel: 020 8294-2548 *website:* www.english-heritage.org.uk

This is located in the SE corner of the Park. It is administered by English Heritage. The website describes access as follows. No parking. There are +9 steps both at the front and back of the house. At the back, a platform lift bypasses the steps to the GF. Inside there are four flights of stairs, with nearly 70 steps in total. These have a chair stairlift (with a chair into which you can transfer).

The Greenwich good loo guide

The disabled persons' toilets in Greenwich are of slightly variable design (and therefore accessibility). A few have an inward opening door. Several pubs and restaurants have an 'accessible' toilet, but these too vary in ease of use.

There are **accessible toilets**:

- near the Cutty Sark (a Tardis loo, 24h **NKS**) located by the entrance to the Welland Street CP, and opposite the *Gipsy Moth* pub
- in the Tourist Information Centre (at the junction of King William Walk and College Way)
- in the basement of the Painted Hall building   , accessed by lift
- in the Maritime Museum (several - see description above)
- in the Ibis hotel, Stockwell Street off the foyer to the left
- in the Royal Observatory complex (see description above)
- in the Astronomy Centre on level −1.

In addition, there are **accessible toilets** in the following eating places and bars

- The *Gipsy Moth* pub, 60 Greenwich Church Street, next to the Cutty Sark. Flat side entrance into the garden, leading to a ramped entrance to the inside. **Wheelchair toilet (D85 ST80 NKS)** with BCF, but it was not in a good condition when we visited;
- *McDonalds*, 2 Crescent Arcade, next to the Cutty Sark DLR station. Flat entrance and an **adapted toilet (D85 ST55 NKS)** with BCF just left of the service desk;
- *Gate Clock Bar*, 210 Creek Road, near the Cutty Sark DLR station. Flat entrance, and lift (D85 W100 L130) to 1st floor where there is a **wheelchair toilet (D80 ST90 NKS)**;
- *Gourmet Burger Kitchen*, 45 Greenwich Church Street. Flat entrance, and **wheelchair toilet (D90 ST85)**;
- *Pizza Express*, 4 Church Street. Flat entrance and **wheelchair toilet (D90 ST75)**.

There will, of course, be more, but we were only looking for enough to make some adequate suggestions. The new eating places by the pier will almost certainly have accessible toilets.

Woolwich

The **Royal Arsenal**, in Woolwich is a famous location whose history dates back to the 1600s. The Ordnance Factories closed in 1967 and large parts of the site have become a massive (and slightly confusing) housing development.

The Arsenal gave rise to the name of a well known football team in the late 1800s, and it carried out large scale armaments manufacture and explosives research for the British Army for several centuries.

The Royal Arsenal Woolwich Historical Society website is:

http://www.qq22.net/raw

It is located off the A206 Plumstead Road, near the Woolwich Ferry.

The Woolwich Arsenal main line and DLR stations are about 250m away. The DLR station is accessible, and NR say that all the platforms on the main line station are also accessible step-free.

Two interesting centres for visitors are located near the 'old' main entrance down No1 Street. These are the Royal Artillery Museum and the Greenwich Heritage Centre, both described below.

The simplest place to park is in the Town Centre CP just past the main site entrance and reached through a width limit of 2.1m (7ft), but without any height restriction. The CP can be reached without a width limit (eg for a minibus) if you approach via the Duke of Wellington Avenue. It's about 200m from the CP to the two centres, via some gentle slopes, and on No 1 Street there's a smooth path for wheelchairs to bypass a really rough cobbled area which is probably part of the site 'heritage'.

Both centres have BB parking, but these are VERY difficult to locate if you're visiting for the first time. There's quite a good map on the Greenwich Heritage Centre website showing the BB spaces. The route is entirely unmarked/unsigned, and what you need to do is to turn left off Plumstead Road (going east), through the width barrier, and past the entrance to the Town Centre CP. Go about 100m past the new flats to the Duke of Wellington Avenue, where you turn left. Go a further 150m where you turn right (at a crossroads which is some 50m short of where you can see a red and white barrier across the road). About 40m in front of you is another barrier, which when we visited was completely unsigned in relation to access to the BB spaces. There was a large 5 sign (indicating the speed limit) and a No Entry sign on a tall pole ! There's a short square post on your right some 10m before this barrier, with an intercom. You can press the button and request entry to the BB spaces which are less than 50m from each centre. Drive around Cartridge Place, and you'll find them if you keep veering left. There are different BB spaces for Firepower and for Greenwich Heritage, but once you've parked for one, they're so close together that it's not worth re-parking.

Both buildings are quite compact, and are readily 'accessible'.

Firepower, The Royal Artillery Museum
Royal Arsenal, Woolwich, SE18 6ST *Tel:* 020 8855-7755
website: www.firepower.org.uk *e-mail:* info@firepower.org.uk
This has a fascinating collection of military hardware and among other things tells the story of the development of the artillery.

Step-free entrance to the ticket desk and shop area, and there's a ramp up to the exhibition area. Lift (D85 W120 L100) to the first floor. This bypasses ±25 steps between the floors. To get into the GF exhibition area a chair user would have to go through the doors marked No Entry. These open towards you, and a staff member would facilitate this if you ask.

There are toilets on both the GF and 1st floors, near the lift. On the GF it's an **adapted toilet (D90 ST65)** with BCF, and two big bins in it. On the 1st floor it's a **wheelchair toilet (D90 ST90)** again with BCF and bins, but there's considerably more space.

Greenwich Heritage Centre
Artillery Square, Royal Arsenal, Woolwich, SE18 4DX (SE18 6ST for *SatNav*)
Tel: 020 8854-2452
website: www.greenwichheritage.org *e-mail:* info@greenwichheritage.org
The Heritage Centre is a small modern building with a series of temporary
exhibitions relating to the history of Greenwich, particularly reflecting it maritime
associations. There is also a history of the Arsenal and of the Woolwich Dockyard
covering over 400 years. It has research facilities.
Access is step-free throughout, and on the GF there's a particularly well designed
and spacious **wheelchair toilet (D80 ST90)** with BCF.

Hampstead

Hampstead Heath
Superintendent's Office, Heathfield House, 432 Archway Road, N6 4JH (for
correspondence)
Tel: 020 7332-3322 for general enquiries, 020 7332-3773 for sports enquiries
websites: www.cityoflondon.gov.uk/hampsteadheath, is the official management
site and has an enormous amount of information, while www.hampsteadheath.
org.uk/info.htm has some good historical stuff.
The website leads to a section via *Visitor information* → *Access for everyone*
e-mail: hampstead.heath@cityoflondon.gov.uk

The Heath is a huge area of grassland, woodland and ponds, covering more than
320ha (nearly 800 acres), just 7 km from the centre of London and managed by
the City of London Corporation. It includes the Kenwood estate managed by
English Heritage.
It is very hilly in parts, and the approach through Hampstead village is up a steep
hill. From the top of the hill there are superb views over London on a clear day.

The Corporation of London, publish an excellent diary/guide (available at several
places in the park) which lists various events.
These include performances in the bandstands, children's activities and fairs. In
the middle of the guide is a map showing the principal facilities.
You can also find it via the *official website* → *News* → *Hampstead Heath diary*

There are also 'Enabled maps' which include what they describe as graded and
easy to read maps, with step-free routes around Hampstead Heath. The 'Maps'
are a series of photographs of the route, and seem to be presented in a format that
would appeal to (and possibly be useful to) someone using a smart phone. See:
http://enabledmaps.com/col/using_enabled_maps.html
We aren't quite sure who these would be useful to, although finding routes
with distances well described is a good thing. They look slightly like an idea
that appeared to be good to able-bodied sponsors wanting to promote more
inclusiveness, but who were not able to assess their practical application.

There is an the Education Centre, off Gordon House Road near Gospel Oak
NR station. The entrance is 10m away to the right of the Lido. A ramp bypasses
+2 steps. CP with three BB spaces shared with the Lido. An electric buggy is
available which can be booked a week in advance, and they hope to have more
soon, *Tel:* 020 7485-5757 to book. The centre can also provide a good map
showing the paths over most of the Heath with an indication of the steepness of
the slopes and the roughness of the terrain.

The Heath can be approached from many different directions including its lower
reaches near Parliament Hill. There is a CP in East Heath Road at the South
End Green end, from where it is possible to enjoy a pleasant wander without
encountering severe slopes. Another recommended access point is at the end of
Parliament Hill which is a Mecca for kite-flying enthusiasts. If you can climb up,
you can get an excellent view over London; or, if you feel less athletic, you can
take the path to the left and enjoy a less exacting amble towards Highgate Ponds.

Hampstead Heath has about 30 beautiful and much-loved lakes, referred to as 'the
ponds'. Although they look natural, most are formed by dams, some of which are
nearly 300 years old.
The open-air swimming facilities are internationally famous, with the Ladies'
Pond, the Men's Pond, the Mixed Pond and the Parliament Hill Lido. The Ladies'
and Men's Ponds are unique in the United Kingdom in being the only life-
guarded open-water swimming facilities open to the public every day of the year.
The Lido is a 60x27m uncovered, unheated swimming pool at Parliament Hill.
The Ladies' Pond and Lido are described as being fully accessible, and there are
hoists to facilitate transfer into the water. This is not the case at the Men's and
Mixed Ponds (although there are plans to provide hoists in the future). There are
always staff on hand who will be willing to help. Some pond users with limited
mobility are happy to make use of these informal arrangements.
For details of opening hours and prices telephone the Swimming on Hampstead
Heath Information Service on 020 7485 3873. BUT it's an entirely automated
service, and you can't speak to a person! Hmmmmmm. To do so, you will have to
try the general enquiries number.

Fishing is allowed in a number of the ponds, but anglers must have a current
Environment Agency licence, and a Hampstead Heath fishing permit, *Tel:* 020
7332-3773 for details.

There are two cafés:
- Parliament Hill café *Tel:* 020 7485-6606, located off Highgate Road,
  Parliament Hill, between the tennis courts/bowling green and the bandstand;
  and,
- Golders Hill Park café *Tel:* 020 8455-8010, located close to the North End
  Way entrance to Golders Hill Park.

Seven **accessible toilets** are shown on the Corporation of London listing/map mentioned above, and we have visited most of them. They are:

- in the heath 'extension' to the north. It is in the red tile complex next to the sports pitches, some 400m from Wildwood Road and 600m from Hampstead Way **(D80 ST130 NKS)**. The paths were rough and are muddy when wet;
- 100m from the entrance on North End Road (on the West Heath) **(D85 ST90 NKS)**; there is nearby parking for BB holders;
- by the animal enclosures near West Heath Road there are two unisex toilets with BCF out of order at time of visit;
- on what is called East Heath, almost due south from Spaniards Inn. Gravelly paths, and in a hilly area. The toilet **(D75 ST85 NKS)** is in a mock Tudor complex hidden amongst some trees;
- about 200m from the Nassington Road entrance, to the south of the Heath. It is between the athletics track and the playground. About 800m from Gospel Oak station. **(D90 ST150+ NKS)** with BCF;
- those shown next to Highgate Road on the east side by the tennis courts **(D80 ST120 NKS)**;
- by Highgate Ponds by Millfield Lane. Down a steepish ramp **(D75 ST115 NKS)**.

Highgate Cemetery

Swain's Lane, N6 6PJ *Tel:* 020 8340-1834 *website:* www.highgate-cemetery.org
Full of graves and tombs that reflect high Victorian taste, and best known for being the burial place of Karl Marx. Admission charge. It is divided into two sections, west and east. The western part is only open to prearranged groups. Parking in the area is restricted from 10.00 to 12.00 (at the time of writing). There is a flat entrance to the east side and the main path is smooth. Long distances of over 500m may be involved, depending on what you want to see. The west section is on a steepish hill, and there are few paths. Most chair users would need assistance in the western part, but there's plenty of interest. The cemetery is always closed during funerals, so call beforehand.

Kenwood House (The Iveagh Bequest)

Hampstead Lane, NW3 7JR *Tel:* 020 8348-1286
website: www.english-heritage.org.uk/daysout/properties/kenwood-house
Kenwood House is on the northernmost edge of the Heath. It is a handsome period house with a fine picture collection given to the nation in 1927, and currently run by English Heritage. Open-air concerts are held in the grounds, and it is hired out from time to time for weddings and corporate events.
The house is closed for most of 2012/2013 for renovations, and our visit was made early in 2012.
Parking is provided in the West Lodge CP (pay and display). BB holders may park free in any space and there are seven designated BB spaces. There is a

mobility vehicle for those with difficulty walking from the CP. This is a minibus with 2 big steps get in, and an extendable ramp for a chair user. It can be requested by using the intercom (H85) just to the left of the two pillars by the CP entrance marking the main path to the house which is about 400m away. Disabled passengers may be dropped off in front of the main house, accessed via the East Lodge entrance where again, there's an intercom for requesting entry. All vehicles have to be parked outside, either in the free parking on Hampstead Lane or in the West Lodge CP.

The house itself has step-free access to the GF, where there are some spectacular rooms including various paintings and antiques, as well as a shop. The first floor is reached via +3+18 steps.

The café/restaurant area is on the other side of the house at a lower level and can be reached step-free by going around the left side. Large parts of this are step-free, including the small Information Centre. There is a 3cm ledge getting into the restaurant and −1 going out to a step-free area on the patio.

There's a **wheelchair toilet (D80 ST80)** and separate BCF in a large cubicle off the collonade by the chairs and tables out in the open.

The audience area for concerts is about 450m from the house reached by gently sloping gravel paths.

Spaniards Inn
Spaniards Road, Hampstead, NW3 7JJ
Tel: 020 8731-8406 *website:* www.thespaniardshampstead.co.uk
Where the road joins Hampstead Lane and with an awkward pinch point in the road outside. Famous 16thC pub that Dick Turpin is said to have frequented, and which numbers famous poets amongst its previous patrons. On-site CP, and then there's a flat way in through the door on the corner by the road. 50% is step-free from this entrance. +13 steps to the Turpin bar. Outside there's a large garden area with split levels although parts have step-free access from the CP. Unfortunately accessible toilets weren't a design feature in the 16thC !

Lee Valley

A remarkable series of developments were started in 1967. These have resulted in the regeneration of largely derelict areas along the river Lee, into a huge Park. This provides a 'green chain' stretching from London's East End, through Walthamstow and Tottenham right up past the M25 to Broxborne and Ware. Most recently the Olympic Park has been established at the southern end of the valley near Stratford.

We would like to acknowledge and to express our thanks for the help of Naomi Chant, and various members of the Park Information Service, in collecting and collating much of the data included in this section.

Lee Valley

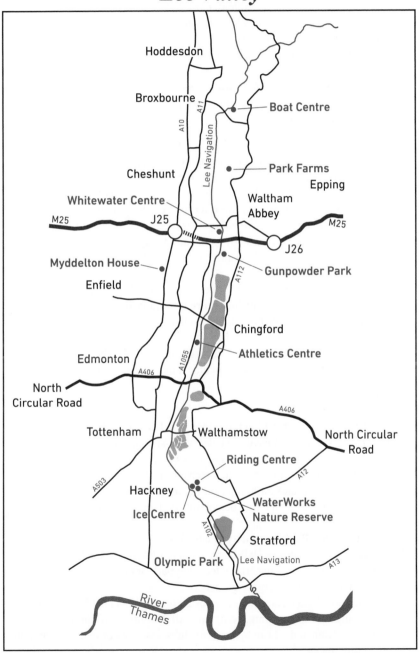

For information about the park, contact:
Lee Valley Regional Park Information Service
Myddelton House, Bulls Cross, Enfield, EN2 9HG
Tel: 0845 6770-600 *e-mail:* info@leevalleypark.org.uk
There are complementary websites:
* one of which, *www.visitleevalley.org.uk* is the practical one about the activities available,
* while the other, *www.leevalleypark.org.uk,* is about the Regional Park Authority who have the responsibility for planning. This website includes some excellent maps.

The extent of Lee Valley, and some of the key facilities, are shown on the map. There are nature reserves, sports and entertainment facilities, an excellent choice of places for fishing, a boating centre and camp sites.
The river along which the Park has been developed is variously called the Lea or Lee. For the sake of consistency, we refer to everything here as Lee. *Because many facilities have the prefix 'Lee Valley' it is not always clear, initially, which part of the valley they are in.* Some of them sound very similar, and yet are 15km apart, and we have tried to use descriptive names to clarify their location.

The sites of interest inside the North Circular Road are described here, in the *Places of interest* chapter. **In addition, there are many interesting facilities further out, which are described on our website.**
We start at the southern end of the Valley (nearest central London) and describe the various places going northwards. Our first entry is about the fisheries, which are located throughout the valley, and include a number of sites for disabled anglers.

Lee Valley Fisheries
There are opportunities for fishing throughout the Lee Valley Regional Park area. The fishery department have a special multi-site permit for anglers with disabilities and details of the venues, specific swims and accessibility is included on the fisheries section of the Lee Valley website. There are also details of concessionary reduced rates on full permit purchase at specific venues. The 36 page booklet *Get hooked* can either be downloaded, or you can get a printed copy from:
Lee Valley Regional Park Authority (Fisheries)
Holyfield Hall Farm, Stubbins Hall Lane, Waltham Abbey, Essex EN9 2EG
Tel: 01992 892-291 *e-mail:* fisheries@leevalleypark.org.uk
website: www.visitleevalley.org.uk/go/fisheries
Lee Valley Regional Park currently operates 29 gravel pits and 17 stretches of river that facilitate coarse angling, comprising of 25 venues, 12 directly managed by the Fisheries team and 12 run by angling clubs, societies or consortia and one which is jointly managed.

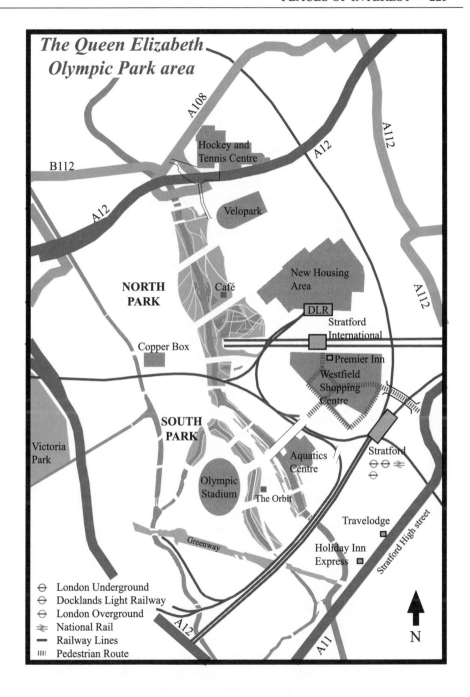

The Queen Elizabeth Olympic Park area

A108

A12

A112

B112

A12

Hockey and Tennis Centre

Velopark

NORTH PARK

Café

New Housing Area

A112

DLR

Stratford International

Copper Box

Premier Inn

Westfield Shopping Centre

SOUTH PARK

Victoria Park

Aquatics Centre

Stratford

Olympic Stadium

The Orbit

Travelodge

Stratford High street

Greenway

Holiday Inn Express

⊖ London Underground
⊖ Docklands Light Railway
⊖ London Overground
⇌ National Rail
▬ Railway Lines
‖‖ Pedestrian Route

A12

A11

N

The special permit which allows use of the specifically designed facilities for disabled anglers at eight of the fisheries must be obtained by post from the address given above. If you want further details, use the contacts given for Holyfield Hall.

The south end of Lee Valley, around Stratford, Leyton and Hackney

The Queen Elizabeth Olympic Park

In 2012 the Park area provided the central venues for the Olympic Games.
The 200ha (500 acre) site will be progressively developed to provide a mix of facilities. These will be both for local people, and for visitors - and will provide an important part of the Olympic Legacy. The extent of the Park is shown on the map, although this was put together before some of the details had been finalised. There will be large areas which include waterways and wetlands, and even larger stretches of parkland. As it is all built around rivers and canals, the whole area is fairly flat, although there will be some slopes in places - mainly fairly gentle ones. Many of the paths will be tarmacked, although some will have a rougher surface.

The North Park will reopen in mid 2013, with a community hub building set amongst an extensive area of parkland and footpaths between the River Lee waterways. It will include the Copper Box indoor entertainment venue.
In the north there will be the Velopark for cycling, and the centres for both tennis and hockey, all providing world class facilities.

The South Park is planned to reopen in 2014 including the ArcelorMittal Orbit 115m high 'sculpture' (see below), and the Aquatics Centre.
The south area includes the Olympic Stadium itself, which is due to reopen for both football and athletics in 2016, although there are several planned events which will take place well before this.
There will be up to 11,000 new homes provided in five distinct neighbourhood areas, with appropriate infrastructure.
To follow progress with the developments, see:
* *www.stratfordlondon.info* or
* *www.londonlegacy.co.uk.*

The Orbit

website: www.arcelormittalorbit.com *e-mail*: orbit@bbworkplace.com
At the time of writing, visits are being organised via:
www.noordinarypark.co.uk/events
Located close to the Olympic Stadium, this iconic steel ArcelorMittal 'sculpture' has two elevated viewing platforms 80m and 76m high. These provide brilliant views over the Olympic Park, down into the Stadium itself and (on a clear day) over much of London.

It is not going to be fully open until April 2014.

Admission charge. Your visit starts under a huge black steel dome, giving an impression of darkness. There are two large lifts, to the upper platform. Varying special exhibitions, relating to the 2012 Olympics and to the development of the Park are being hosted. There are outside walkways, quite blowy when it's windy, but with excellent views all around. The walkways include some ramped/elevated sections to help chair users see over the outside railing.

You can then go to the lower viewing platform either via −24 steps, or using one of the lifts, where there is further exhibition space. On this level there are **two wheelchair toilets (D90 ST150+)** each with BCF, located just outside the mens and womens toilet areas.

There are again some outside walkways. To get back to ground level you can go via −431 steps circling around outside, or use a lift.

When we visited, the area around was a building site, but as development proceeds, there will be pedestrian access from all around the Park.

Ice Centre
Lea Bridge Road, Leyton, E10 7QL
Tel: 020 8533-3154 *e-mail*: icecentre@leevalleypark.org.uk
Situated just east of the River Lee Navigation on the A104, almost next to the Riding Centre.

Large, on-site CP with four BB spaces.

Step-free access throughout the Centre to the changing area and to the edge of the rink.

Access to the rink is via single step. Limited space for chair users at the corners of the rink with relatively poor view due to surrounding wall. Fixed tiered seating with steps.

Ramped access into the café area providing an elevated view of the rink.

Wheelchair toilet (D70 ST140) by the café. Key available from reception.

Riding Centre
Lea Bridge Road, Leyton, E10 7QL
Tel: 020 8556-2629 *e-mail*: ridingcentre@leevalleypark.org.uk
Situated east of the River Lee Navigation on the A104 next to the Ice Centre.

CP with two BB spaces. Step-free access throughout the site, although it may get a bit muddy when wet !

The centre works in partnership with *Riding for the Disabled* providing lessons for both adults and children with disabilities. A ramp is available to assist riders with limited mobility to mount their horse.

Fixed tiered seating with steps overlooking indoor school. Ramped access to the café.

Wheelchair cubicles (D90 ST80) in both the mens and womens toilets opposite reception.

WaterWorks Nature Reserve
Lammas Road, off Lea Bridge Road, Leyton, E10 7NU
Tel: 020 8988-7566 *e-mail:* thewaterworks@leevalleypark.org.uk
Located opposite the Riding Centre on the A104. On-site CP with three BB spaces.
The Nature Reserve is on the former site of the Essex Filter Beds. It hosts more than 500 species of plants and animals and has one of the largest bird hides in London, with low level viewing flaps. Surfaced pathways (some uneven and cobbled) and boardwalks provide access routes throughout the site. Interpretation panels provide natural and industrial history information.
Step-free access throughout the visitor centre and café area.
Adapted toilet (D90 ST60) located behind reception.

Museums and galleries

London has one of the greatest collections of museums and galleries in the world. The variety of subject, size, and interest, is vast.

Nearly all of them are places where anyone in the family can find things of interest to see and do, and the facilities for children have been greatly improved. **Most of the big museums and galleries in London are free.** You only have to pay when there are special exhibitions. Some smaller ones charge for entry, generally fairly modestly.

Much effort and thought has been put into providing improved access for disabled visitors. Staff members are usually helpful. Many museums and galleries now provide facilities for visitors who are partially sighted to touch and feel some exhibits. In addition, many have BSL tours.

Many of these facilities are available on an occasional basis or by special arrangement, so it's worth phoning in advance, and/or looking it up on the website. We haven't tried to cover these in our descriptions, as we haven't tried them out, and our reporting is based almost entirely on experience. Similarly, many museums and galleries have large print descriptions relating to the exhibits, which you can take around with you, and you can ask about this facility.

Patience is occasionally required to get special step-free access routes opened up. Art collections and historical artefacts are valuable, and security is important, so it is not always possible to leave particular doors open. It may also take a little time to find the right person to operate platform stair lifts to bypass steps.

Some major museums and galleries are very large. You would do well to look at the map/plan, either by writing in first to get a copy, or using the plans in a standard guidebook (such as the Eyewitness guide, which we recommend because of its cutaways and maps). Then you can choose some of the things of greatest interest and go and see those, while walking/wheeling the minimum necessary distance.

In several of the big museums and galleries, there are guided tours which cover a particular topic, and these can be an excellent way of (slightly randomly) choosing what you see and learn about. Some places provide audio-guides.

The presentation of many exhibits has been improved, and facilities, such as catering and the provision of toilets, have been upgraded. Many places now provide portable folding stools, which can be an enormous help for those who find standing for long periods is a challenge. A few have electric buggies which can be borrowed, though you may have to say whether you have had previous experience in using these vehicles. Some need charging before use. It is therefore sensible to ring first, and make your own enquiries.

There are many guidebooks around. *London Museums and Galleries* published by Insight Guides, and the *Museums and Galleries of London* by Abigail Willis from Metro Publications, are two which stand out. They are both well presented and informative.

One particular location needs a separate comment, and that is **Exhibition Road** in Kensington. This runs from near South Kensington station in the south, to Hyde Park in the north. It is home to some of the most important museums in the country. These are the Victoria and Albert (V&A), Natural History and Science Museums. Most date back in part to the Great Exhibition of 1851. Very nearby is the Royal Albert Hall, the Albert Memorial, and Imperial College London.
During 2011, Exhibition Road was radically changed, into a step-free 'streetscape' where there are no kerbs to separate cars from pedestrians. It is therefore easy for chair and electric buggy users, and for those with pushchairs, to move around. Traffic is subject to a 20mph speed limit. It is one of the biggest tests in the UK of the step-free 'streetscape' concept.
There are two parking areas for BB holders, each taking up to 6 cars, outside the Science Museum and outside the Natural History Museum, opposite the V&A. The best approach to the road is via Queen's Gate and Prince Consort Road. You can also enter it easily if you come from Hyde Park. Some of the more obvious turns into Exhibition Road are banned. There's a detailed road plan at *www.rbkc.gov.uk/ subsites/exhibitionroad.aspx* with an explanation of the whole concept. A cultural guide to what is on in the area is available at *www.exhibitionroad.com*.

In addition there's a group of a dozen important and varied museums lying between the Euston Road (Kings Cross), and the Thames, in an area called *The Museum Mile* which is described at: *www.museum-mile.org.uk*.

Apsley House see Wellington Museum.

Bank of England Museum
Threadneedle Street, EC2R 8AH *Tel:* 020 7601-5545
website: www.bankofengland.co.uk *e-mail:* museum@bankofengland.co.uk
Historical and financial displays, including some real gold bars! The nearby Bank station has step-free access from the DLR.
The entrance is in Barthomolew Lane with +4+3 steps. There's an intercom button

to the right of the steps to attract attention, and ramps can be brought out to facilitate entry. Inside there are ±3 to see all the exhibits, but all the steps can be bypassed by portable ramps. If you let them know in advance, some of these can be put in place before you get there. The museum is quite compact, measuring only some 20m by 80m, and there are plenty of seats. **Wheelchair toilet (D90 ST85)** at the rear of the museum. The cinema, used by groups, has chair spaces and an induction loop. The *Museum Guide* has a good plan showing where the steps are, and this can also be printed off from the website. Audioguides are available. The nearby *Phoenix* pub is accessible, as is the upmarket café/ restaurant in the *Royal Exchange*.

Bankside Gallery
48 Hopton Street, Bankside, SE1 9JH   *Tel:* 020 7928-7521
website: www.banksidegallery.com *e-mail:* info@banksidegallery.com
Situated on the South Bank, to the east of Blackfriars Bridge and just before Tate Modern. From the Riverside Walk, a ramp near the pub bypasses the −7 steps outside. The small gallery is on one floor. Ramps bypass +2 steps at the entrance, and there is flat or ramped access throughout.
There's a **wheelchair toilet** in the *Founder's Arms* pub less than 100m away, and there are several in Tate Modern.

British Library
96 Euston Road, NW1 2DB
Tel: 020 7412-7332 or 0843 2081-144   *Textphone:* 01937 546-434
website: www.bl.uk *e-mail:* customer-services@bl.uk or disability-officer@bl.uk
The library houses the national collection of books, manuscripts and maps, as well as the National Sound Archive. Its books are available to *Registered Readers* who are doing bona fide research, and who cannot get their material through other public libraries. It contains the *John Ritblat galleries* where the Magna Carta, the Lindisfarne Gospels and Shakespeare's First Folio can be seen.
It is located on the north side of Euston Road, between Midland Road and Ossulston Street and about 400m from King's Cross station. The tube station there is 'accessible'. The roads on either side have BB spaces while Euston Road is a busy red route allowing no stopping.
From the Euston Road there are +4 steps, followed by a large stepped courtyard. Just around the corner in Ossulston Street there's a ramped way in, with a step-free route running for about 100m around the edge of the courtyard. There's also a ramped way in from Midland Road.
The building measures about 100m by 200m, including a huge area for book storage. Its layout is quite confusing, partly because of the split-level GF, and because some lifts only go to two or three of the floors.

The main entrance is flat, with an information desk almost straight ahead in the foyer. **There are step-free routes throughout the building** and the steps to the UGF can be bypassed.
Working upwards the flooring system is labelled, LG (lower ground), G+UG (ground and upper ground), 1st, 2nd and 3rd floors. A plan/map of the library is available both from the information desk and the website, but it has various symbols plonked down all over it and is, in our view, quite difficult to interpret in detail. In addition it does not define which floors the various lifts go to, and doesn't make clear that in the main block of six lifts (shown in red on the library plan) only one stops on the GF.
On the map the public galleries are coloured yellow and are spread across the LGF, GF and UGF including the *Ritblat galleries* which measure roughly 40m by 40m on the UGF. There is also the *PACCAR gallery* and the Conservation display.
From the foyer,

- *to the left* is the shop, and just to the right of the shop is the entry to the main public galleries. Through that door you'll find lift 10 which goes to the LG/G/UG floors;
- *to the right* is a ramp down to the LG level where there's a cloakroom, and access to lifts 1/2/3 and 4/5 (D105 W150 L130) which lead to the library sections on the upper floors and to all the floors except the ground G. The ramp can be bypassed using lift 6 which goes to the LG/G/UG floors.

The building is step-free throughout. On the upper floors there's a route around the 'well' which contains the Kings Library. Many of the doors can be opened by buttons on the side. The UG level has a large café at the back, and there's a restaurant on the 1st floor. Both are near the public galleries. Lift 9 goes to the restaurant.
Reader Registration takes place on the UG level.
The **wheelchair toilets (D70+ ST70+)** are nearly all on the left side of the building where the *John Ritblat gallery* is, and on floors LG/UG/1/2/3. In the toilets near the two blocks of lifts numbered 1/2/3/4/5, there are **wheelchair cubicles** inside the mens and womens areas on floors UG/1/2/3.
There are BCF in the wheelchair cubicles in the mens and womens toilets on floor 1 near lift 9 (linking G/UG/1) by the restaurant, and in the open area part of the toilets in the mens and womens areas in the toilets on the LG.

British Museum
Great Russell Street, WC1B 3DG
Tel: 020 7323-8000 *Info:* 020 7323-8299
website: www.britishmuseum.org *e-mail:* information@britishmuseum.org
It is one of the largest museums in the world, and houses the national collection of archaeological remains covering two million years of history. A central architectural feature is the Great Court, which now has a glass roof, and incorporates the old British Library Reading Room.

In 2013/14 a new World Conservation and Exhibitions Centre is planned in the NW corner of the museum, see *www.britishmuseum.org/pdf/wcec_exhibition_panels.pdf.*

The museum is approximately 200m square, with two main floors, but with exhibits and activities on as many as five other levels:
- the north end has gallery rooms on seven levels from −1 to 5;
- the main part of the museum has galleries on just two floors; and,
- at the south end of the building there two lower floors with facilities for school parties, for meetings and for lectures.

The museum has gone to considerable lengths to make sure that almost everywhere can be reached step-free, but some of the lifts which make this possible are well hidden (for example the one to the Gallery Café, and the one between rooms 21 and 22).

The provision of accessible toilets is somewhat scattered, and slightly eccentric. When we visited early in 2011, half of them were closed.

Parking for up to four BB holders can be arranged in advance (*Tel:* 020 7323-8299). The spaces are in the museum forecourt off Great Russell Street with no height restriction. This is a valuable provision, although you'll often get to a voicemail (ansaphone) on option 4 when you ring, and have to leave a message to get them to ring you back. We found that one way round this was to ring earlyish in the morning, before the staff are busy with visitors.

> **The museum is absolutely huge and you will get more out of a visit if you are selective in what you try to see, join an organised group and/ or if you use an audio tour.**

The website has useful information, and the floor plans are quite good, although they are currently very 'busy' because they are showing the locations of exhibits highlighted in an excellent series called *A history of the world in 100 objects*. The use of plans rather than an isometric is highly commended. Plans are much easier to relate to. As always, however, the information is almost certainly put together by an able-bodied person who does not think in terms of providing clear accessibility information.

You can print the floor plans from the website via Visiting/Floor plans.

> **The main museum entrance from Great Russell Street has +12 steps, bypassed by slightly hidden platform lifts (W115 L200) on either side of the steps.** If neither lift is operational, staff can take you to another way in about 40m away, giving access to an inside lift on the basement level.

> **The alternative entrance from Montague Place is at level −1** . You can take the North lift to get to the main part of the museum on level 0, bypassing +12. You pass through room 24 which provides easy step-free access to the Great Court.

Coming in from Great Russell Street, the first hall is quite gloomy. You go past the South lifts, and then you reach the dazzlingly white Great Court with its four classical porticos. In the centre is the Reading Room, which is currently used for special exhibitions.

There are nearly 100 galleries, and potentially some 4km of walking/wheeling to see all the exhibits. Almost all the museum now has step-free access via various lifts, and **where there seems to be a problem, ask one of the staff,** who are generally helpful.

> To the right, as you come in, is the **information desk**, and to the left is a sales point for museum plans and itineraries, and a little further on is the desk for the audio guides. There are plans of the different floors in the museum available from the information desk, and an *Access guide* for disabled visitors. This has almost no detailed information for the mobility impaired visitor.

To make the best use of a visit, you would do well to get hold of the plan before coming, and choose which parts of the museum to have a look at. Alternatively or additionally, join one of the excellent guided tours that take place regularly, or take an audio tour. **There are displays on either side of the Great Court atrium showing the various tours and talks available on each day.**

There are five main lifts. All have D75+ W95+ and L120+. Note that you sometimes come in through one door and go out from another.

As you come in from the main entrance, you pass the **two South lifts** just before you get to the Great Court. These go to levels −2, −1, 0 and 3, and are particularly important for getting to the two lower floors.

Three-quarters of the way around either side of the oval shaped central construction in Great Court are the **East and West lifts**. These link to room 25 on level −2, to accessible toilets on level 1, and they go up to level 3.

The **North lift** at the Montague Place end of the building goes to levels −1, 0, 1, 2, 3, 4 and 5.

There are several platform lifts around the building to facilitate getting around split levels, but these aren't always very obvious.

Places where steps may appear to be a problem include:

- room 22 where there are +8 from room 23, but there's an alternative route via room 21, with a platform lift (D90 L110) to bypass the steps;
- there are now platform lifts at each end of gallery 18 to bypass the +3 steps;
- at the end of room 66 on level 3, there are +3+14 steps to level 4, but these can be bypassed by using the North lift;
- between galleries 33 and 33b on level 1 at the north end of the building, there's a platform lift to bypass +3, but at the end of the gallery there would be −17 on the east stairs to get down to the toilets. This is not clearly shown on the map;
- there's a lift to link rooms 33a (on level 1) and 95 (on level 2);
- from the Montague Place entrance the −4 in both directions (to room 34 and to the Anthropology Centre) are bypassed by platform lifts.

The **Court Restaurant** is on level 3, at the Reading Room roof level, and reached by the East or West lifts, or from the North lift.

There are **cafés** on the GF of the Great Court (level 0), and the Gallery Café by Room 12 (in the SW corner). This as reached via +12. There is a staff operated lift (D90 W130 L130) to bypass these, but no sign saying that it is possible. To use it you need to grab/ask a passing staff member ! Only about 25% of the Gallery Café is step-free as much of it is on a raised level +4, however there are movable tables and chairs in the step-free part.

At certain times, the cafés and restaurant get very crowded.

The various **wheelchair toilets (all D70+ ST70+)** are not particularly well signed or marked, although they are shown on the floor plans. When we visited, it was disappointing to find that nearly half of the accessible toilets were closed/locked. Four were said to be under long-term repair and refurbishment.

There are:

- **two** on the GF of Great Court (level 0) on either side of the oval structure, just before you get to the shops (coming from the main entrance). Unfortunately, these are located at the top of a flight of stairs which go down to the conventional toilets, so there's a strong temptation for non-disabled people to use them. On the east side there's a separate BCF;
- **one** off the bookshop on level 0, just before room 11. This is a unisex wheelchair toilet with BCF, but it is marked up as being for general use as well;
- **one** by/under the East stairs on level 0, between rooms 1 and 27. This is a unisex wheelchair toilet with BCF. There are other toilets alongside;
- **two** at level 1, one on either side of the oval structure and accessed only by using the East and West lifts. You might use these if you were using the restaurant on level 3;
- **one** by the North lift on level 3, where there are BCF in the womens toilets; and,
- **two** in the Clore Education Centre on level −2, reached easily from the south lifts, and with one in each direction, about 15m from the lift;
- there are also two in the Ford Centre for Young Visitors on level −1, where there are also BCF.

There are BCF on level 1 from the North lift.

The museum is huge and has limited seating, but is a fascinating place to visit.

The recent provision of portable stools is immensely valuable.

Churchill War Rooms

Clive Steps, King Charles Street, SW1A 2AQ

Tel: 020 7930-6961   *Textphone:* 020 7839-4906

website: www.iwm.org.uk/churchill *e-mail:* cwr@iwm.org.uk

In the late 1930s, there was an awareness of the potential damage that bombing might cause in the event of war. Concern that the public might think their leaders

were deserting them persuaded the planners to provide a secure 'Central War Room'. Many vital Cabinet meetings were held in these rooms, and there is an extensive Churchill museum.
The museum entrance is tucked in alongside the −15 steps from King Charles Street.
There is step-free access from St George Street and Horse Guards Road.
Significant admission charge. This includes an audio-guide, and an excellent plan/map is available.
A lift (D80 W110 L150) can bypass the −15 steps down to the rooms.
The rooms are all on one level, and although there are some narrowish gaps, the minimum width is W76 so most chair users can get through. Lighting levels are quite low in places. The rooms are about 100m long, and with side visits into the museum, you would go some 300m altogether. Folding stools can be borrowed.
A thorough visit would take a minimum of an hour and a half. People may well want to stay longer, and there is a café at the far end. Visitors should note that there are few seats.
All three **accessible toilets** are near the entrance (so there isn't one near the café). Two are shown on the plan:
• opposite the lift **wheelchair toilet (D90 ST70)**; and,
• just past the Cabinet War Room, to your left **wheelchair toilet (D80 ST80)**.
The third one is just off the shop, and is huge. When we visited there were renovations taking place.

Cutty Sark see the chapter on *Places of interest* under Greenwich

Design Museum
28 Shad Thames, SE1 2YD *Tel:* 020 7403-6933 *RecM:* 020 7940-8790
website: www.designmuseum.org *e-mail:* info@designmuseum.org
The museum highlights classic design from the past 100 years, and state-of-the-art innovations from around the globe. It has changing exhibitions.
Shad Thames is a continuation of the riverside walk which passes under Tower Bridge Road, and has been partly pedestrianised. To get to the museum from the Bridge it is necessary to go via Queen Elizabeth Street. From City Hall the distance is about 500m and from the southern bridge Tower it is about 1km.
There are 2 unreservable BB spaces behind the museum. Alternatively there's a Q Park MS/UGCP with a lift, on the corner of Gainsford Street and Curlew Street. Height restriction 2m. 9 BB spaces, 3 of which are on the GF.
Significant admission charge. Folding stools available.
Entrance +5 steps with a ramped bypass. Displays on the 1st and 2nd floors, reached via a lift (D75 W110 L150). Ask staff. Coffee shop on the GF. There are **two wheelchair toilets (D80 ST70)** just outside the main mens and womens toilet areas.

Dickens House

48 Doughty Street, WC1N 2LX *Tel:* 020 7405-2127

website: www.dickensmuseum.com *e-mail:* info@dickensmuseum.com

Charles Dickens house is near Corams Fields, and Doughty Street is parallel to Grays Inn Road. Admission charge.

Entrance +1 step, then two rooms of memorabilia with flat access and −1 to shop. The rest of the house has steps, −14 to the basement and wine cellar, +19 to the first floor and a further +20 to the second floor. From the GF there are two small lips into the garden. A new wing to provide lift access to all the floors together with accessible toilets is planned for completion by the end of 2012. This should make the whole museum step-free.

Dulwich Picture Gallery

Gallery Road, Dulwich Village, SE21 7AD *Tel:* 020 8693-5254

website: www.dulwichpicturegallery.org.uk

This building, designed by Sir John Soane, provides a wonderful setting for an art gallery. It is located in south London, just over 3km from Brixton tube station, which is 'accessible'.

Closed on Mondays.

CP for BB holders by the main entrance from Gallery Road. It does not have marked spaces but can take four or five cars. Ring in advance to book a space. There's a smart new glass entry corridor called the Cloister. It runs past the toilets and café, with a step-free main entrance, and an alternative through the bookshop. The whole gallery is on one level, and step-free, apart from ±2 steps in the tiny mausoleum. It is quite compact. There are seats in the main part of the gallery, and folding stools are available.

The **adapted toilet (D80 ST70 but inward opening door)** with BCF is exceptionally badly designed in terms of its position. The architect has made absolutely minimal toilet provision, and the three entry doors (mens, womens and disabled/BCF) are very close together at the end of a narrow corridor with a 90degree turn. A chair user, or family with a buggy, who get to the toilet/BCF and find it occupied, will block the corridor and will probably have to back down its whole length in order to let the person in the toilet go past.

Foundling Museum

40 Brunswick Square, WC1N 1AZ *Tel:* 020 7841-3600

website: www.foundlingmuseum.org.uk

e-mail: enquiries@foundlingmuseum.org.uk

The Museum tells the story of the Foundling Hospital, the first purpose built home for abandoned children in Britain, established in 1739. It is also London's first ever public art gallery.

Closed on Mondays. Admission charge.

It is located at the end of a cul de sac on the north side of Brunswick Square.

There is metered parking opposite, but BB holders may be able to book a space in the staff CP about 50m away. The frontage is just over 30m long. There's a ramp to bypass the +5 steps at the entrance. Using the lift (D75 W95 L130), all four floors can be accessed step-free. There's a café on the GF, with tables outside during the summer.

Wheelchair toilet (D75 ST75) on the LGF. Watch out, because you're in danger of setting off the alarm, as the cord hangs down in the middle of the ST space !

Garden Museum

5 Lambeth Palace Road, SE1 7LB *Tel:* 020 7401-8865
website: www.gardenmuseum.org.uk
Located just south of Lambeth Bridge, and situated in an old church, this small museum is famous for having Bligh of the Bounty buried in its garden.
Admission charge. The entrance has a 3cm ridge. Inside there is a shop, then +3 steps with a ramped bypass, to the café and museum. Flat access to the small garden with a bumpy paved surface and some very narrow paths, so that chair users can only access about 70% of it. A platform lift (D100 L140) goes up inside the church to a separate part of the exhibition bypassing +22. **Wheelchair toilet (D80 ST80)** on the way to the garden.

Guildhall Art Gallery and Roman Amphitheatre

Guildhall Yard, EC2V 5AE *Tel:* 020 7332-3700
website: www.guildhallartgallery.cityoflondon.gov.uk
e-mail: guildhall.artgallery@cityoflondon.gov.uk
Built over a Roman amphitheatre, the gallery houses paintings and sculptures belonging to the Corporation of London. It is located 50m from the Guildhall, across Guildhall Yard.
Admission charge at some times of the day and it can be closed for an event. The entrance is step-free and two lifts (D90 W140 L160) to the left of the entrance connect the six levels. There are three floors of galleries, as well as the remains of a Roman Amphitheatre in the basement. One gallery floor and the balcony is above ground level, and other galleries are below ground.
Access is step-free throughout, though the thick carpet may hinder movement for some. It is quite compact and measures around 50m by 70m overall. There are **wheelchair toilets** by the mens **(D80 ST85)** and the womens **(D70 ST75)** on cloakroom level (level C in the lift). There's also a **wheelchair toilet (D80 ST85)** on level A2 opposite the lifts but marked 'private'. We were told that there was no objection to disabled visitors using this.

Hayward Gallery

Southbank Centre, Belvedere Road, SE1 8XX
Tel: 0844 875 0073 (for access information select option 2)
website: www.southbankcentre.co.uk/venues/hayward-gallery
e-mail: accesslist@southbankcentre.co.uk

A compact gallery which holds regular special and innovative exhibitions. Admission charge.

The main pedestrian entrance is from the upper walkway/terrace between the Festival Hall and the Queen Elizabeth Hall. This can be reached from the National Theatre, or from the Golden Jubilee Bridge walkway originating in Charing Cross station.

There's a CP immediately under the gallery off Belvedere Road with about 20 BB spaces. A lift (D75 W105 L125) will take you up to the main gallery entrance. There's an intercom by the lift in the CP for attracting someone's attention if necessary. The CP is also convenient for BB holders going to the Festival Hall.

The gallery is on two levels with a lift to bypass the ±40 steps between them. The main floor on the lower level is part ramped and there's a split level with −9 steps. These are bypassed by a platform lift (D100 L220) where you need to hold the button down all the time to operate it.

At the upper walkway level (by the ticket office) there is a café and shop. There is also a **wheelchair toilet (D70+ ST70+)** with BCF at this level. There are other toilets inside the gallery, but these can only be reached via steps.

Note that there's a platform lift to QEH rooftop events near the Hayward Gallery entrance.

Horniman Museum and Gardens
100 London Road, Forest Hill, SE23 3PQ *Tel:* 020 8699-1872
website: www.horniman.ac.uk
A museum about world arts, craft, religion and history which is very family friendly and surrounded by attractive gardens. It is situated in a really hilly area. Its main entrance is off the A205 South Circular Road with red lines outside indicating 'no stopping'. The entrance is 50m to the left of the main building and reached by a steep hill through the gardens.

Limited parking on site is available if requested/arranged in advance, and this can be reached from Westwood Park on the other side of the grounds from the main entrance. It can be reached from Honor Oak Road, or from Wood Vale. There are parking possibilities in the streets a little way away.

They have an exceptionally brief and well expressed 'access statement' which says *"The Museum and Gardens are both wheelchair and pushchair friendly with accessible toilets. A lift gives access to all the exhibition areas. Baby changing facilities are available in Gallery Square."* We can confirm that this is correct, although it doesn't mention that the area is hilly!

The museum is step-free. A plan/map is available at the front desk. A lift (D120 W130 L200+) goes to three of the floors. A separate lift (D110 W110 L240) links the Basement (where the Aquarium is) to the LGF - although the elevator will tell you that it's the GF.

There are **wheelchair toilets**:

- by the entrance on the GF **(D75 ST145)** with BCF. It has an unusual sliding/ folding door, which can be sticky to open and close;
- on the LGF **(D75 ST130)** reached from the main atrium, and in the Library (not seen). There is another wheelchair toilet (not seen) in the gardens near the museum, which was being refurbished when we visited. A café on the GF serves snacks and drinks.

Hunterian Museum

35-43 Lincoln's Inn Fields, WC2A 3PE

Tel: 020 7869-6560 for the *Textphone:* dial 18001 first

website: www.rcseng.ac.uk/museums *e-mail:* museums@rcseng.ac.uk

The museum is on the 1st and 2nd floors of the Royal College of Surgeons building. It contains the specimens of body parts (animal and human) collected by the surgeon-scientist John Hunter from the 18thC. It is on the south side of the square.

One BB space outside the Nuffield College entrance, and three more in the NE corner of Lincoln's Inn Fields.

The main entrance has a ramp to the left followed by +1 step, or there's a platform lift (D100 L120) at the Nuffield College entrance which is 20m further to the left.

From the main entrance, there's a lift (D75 W75 L120) to the 1st floor, past the stairs down the hallway in front of you, and about 20m on the left. Just past the staircase inside the museum there's a platform lift (D80 L120) to get to the 2nd floor. Both floors are step-free.

Wheelchair toilet (D90 ST75) on the GF reached by a somewhat tortuous route, but it's well-signed.

Imperial War Museum

Lambeth Road SE1 6HZ *Tel:* 020 7416-5000

website: www.iwm.org.uk *e-mail:* mail@iwm.org.uk

A fascinating collection of historical military equipment, with numerous changing exhibitions. It is housed in a building that, more than 150 years ago, was a lunatic asylum.

BB parking can be arranged (*Tel:* 020 7416-5320/1) with no height restriction. The main entrance is 50m from the road via a tarmac path through the Geraldine Mary Harmsworth Park, and has +9+1+3 steps leading to the GF. These are bypassed by using the West/Park entrance, reached by going to the right of the big guns, and then continuing nearly 100m down the right side of the building. This leads to the LGF/basement.

This way in can be quite busy and noisy if you happen to get there when a large school party is either arriving or leaving. It is also slightly disorientating to arrive in the basement, and if you want to get a better 'feel' for the place before visiting particular collections, go to the left, and take one of the lifts up to the GF where there's some open space and you can see the shape of the building.

The diagram on your ticket, which you get on entering, has an isometric, showing the main central lifts and the location of the **accessible toilets**. There is also a lift (D80 W90 L250) by the West/Park entrance which gives access to the picnic room, where there are two **wheelchair toilets (D70+ ST70+)**.

There is flat, ramped or lift access to the exhibits on all six floors except to the upper story of the 1940s house.

The two central lifts (D90 W160 L150) by the main staircase serve the LGF, GF and 1st floors. A separate lift (D80 W110 L150) must be used to reach the 2nd floor. This goes from the 1st floor - turn right from either of the main lifts until you reach the far wall, and go through the door marked 'disabled lift'. The self-service café and the shop are both step-free from the GF.

There are **wheelchair toilets (all D70+ ST70+)**, reasonably well marked on the plan, and signed. These are in the basement, and on the GF, 1st and 2nd floors as well as the 5th. The museum has gone to considerable lengths to make the building step-free via the new lifts.

London Canal Museum
13 New Wharf Road, N1 9RT *Tel:* 020 7713-0836
website: www.canalmuseum.org.uk
This unique waterways museum is housed in a former ice warehouse built in about 1862. It features both the history of the canals, and of the ice cream trade. Located about 0.5km from Kings Cross station alongside the canal, off All Saints Street. Entrance step-free but slightly cobbled outside. Admission charge.

This small but interesting museum is on two floors and the GF is divided into a street-level gallery and a mezzanine area. At the far end of the hall there is a platform lift (D80 L110) to access the mezzanine bypassing +9 steps. From here a separate platform lift (D100 L140) goes to the 1st floor bypassing +15. If these aren't operational there is a steep ramp to access the 1st floor. On the GF there is a cut away of a narrow boat, *Coronis Cabin*, with a door D50 and +1 en route. Alternatively there is a good virtual tour by the entrance.

There is a **wheelchair toilet (D85 ST80)** with BCF just opposite the reception desk by the entrance.

London Transport Museum
Covent Garden Piazza, WC2E 7BB *Tel:* 020 7379-6344 *RecM:* 020 7565-7299
Textphone: 020 7565-7310 *website:* www.ltmuseum.co.uk
The museum is housed in the old Victorian Flower Market. It covers the development of London's transport from the 1800s and Victorian times. This includes the building of the first ever underground railway (using steam engines!). By implication the exhibition reflects much of London's social history. There are

plenty of hands-on exhibits for children.

The website has limited information about access.

The museum is located in the SE corner of the Covent Garden piazza, backing on to Tavistock Street. It measures about 80m by 50m with exhibits and displays on three floors although the upper floors are relatively small. A visit could take anything from an hour and a half upwards, and in exploring around, you could walk/wheel anything from 300 to 500m.

Significant admission charge for adults, but children under 16 are free.

The museum is approached from the Piazza across a cobbled area. The entrance can be slightly confusing (or so we found !). At the ticket desk, you are given a museum plan, and children will be given a 'Stamper Trail' card. This has a diagram on the back.

You enter into a slightly anonymous corridor inside, and turn right. What you need to know (and is not properly explained) is that the exhibits are arranged chronologically. Just opposite the cloakroom is a longish grey-coloured ramp, near a well signed **accessible toilet**. What you need to do is to go up the ramp which leads to two lifts (D80 W100 L250). This takes you to level 2 where the 'trail/tour' begins. Unfortunately, the lifts are not clearly labelled to correspond with the plan/map where they are shown as lift 1. The map does, however, show the route you need to take.

You then take lift 3 (D80 W120 L130) to level 1, explore these displays and then use lift 3 again to get down to level 0 where the main exhibits are. Almost everything on level 0 is ramped (or flat). Getting inside some of the buses, where this is allowed, might be challenging.

If you need to go to the Mezzanine with the Outdoor Gallery, you can get there using lift 5.

On your way out, you mingle with people entering the museum from the ticket desk, in the 'slightly anonymous corridor'. You then go through the shop, and can visit the Upper Deck café/bar on level 1 which is accessed using lift 4 from the shop. Lift 4 is by the exit, on the left, and is slightly hidden. Both the shop and the café/bar are slightly congested.

Lift 4 (D70 W95 L125) also goes down to the Cubic Theatre where there are occasional talks and presentations. Wheelchair spaces can be provided.

There are three **wheelchair toilets**, marked on the plan/map:

* at the start and end of the tour **(D80 ST70)**, just past the bottom of the ramp to lift 1, and past the cloakroom;
* on level 0 on the opposite side of the museum from the ticket desk **(D90 ST75)**. This has an internal BCF, and there's a separate BCF as well;
* on level 1 by the Upper Deck café/bar **(D80 ST70)**.

Museum in Docklands
No1 Warehouse, Hertsmere Road, Docklands, E14 4AL *Tel:* 020 7001-9844
website: www.museumoflondon.org.uk/docklands

Housed in an old warehouse, the museum celebrates the impact of the port activity on the social and economic life of the area from Roman times to the present day. Part of the exhibition covers war-time experiences in docklands. Displays illustrate working methods and equipment in different eras, with interactive exhibits and a children's area. It all makes for a fascinating experience. The entrance is about 300m from the West India Quay DLR station. It is on the quayside, past the *Ledger Buildings* pub if you approach from Hertsmere Road. There are 4 BB spaces outside the main entrance between the trees. There is a MSCP a little over 500m away, on Hertsmere Road, just past the cinema.

Step-free entrance, with an information desk, café, a children's interactive exhibition area and a hall for special exhibitions on the GF. The museum layout is organised to take you through a series of exhibits in sequence, starting at the top of the building. **Everything can be reached step-free via lifts and ramps.** The two lifts (D80 W120 L240) take you to the 3rd floor at the top of the building. The route around the exhibition is about 100m long on each floor, with exhibitions on the 3rd, 2nd and 1st floors. Getting from the 3rd to the 2nd and from the 2nd to the 1st involves the use of one of two pairs of platform lifts (D90 W105 L120). To leave the building by a step-free route, you have to take the platform lift back to the 2nd floor and find the two main lifts in order to get back to the GF.

There is an induction loop and wheelchair spaces in the lecture theatre which is on the top/3rd floor. Folding seats are available as there are virtually no benches or seats in the museum.

There are three **wheelchair toilets**:

* on the GF in the exhibition hall **(D80 ST80)** where there is a separate BCF, and in the restaurant **(D80 ST90)**;
* on the 3rd floor **(D100 ST80)** with BCF.

Museum of London
150 London Wall, EC2Y 5HN *Tel:* 020 7001-9844 (to speak to a person use 0) 020 7814-5552 (to book BB spaces); 020 7814-5660 (to book a mobility scooter or a chair) *website:* www.museumoflondon.org.uk
e-mail: info@museumoflondon.org.uk or access@museumoflondon.org.uk
The museum includes some fascinating and well presented displays covering the history of London, dating from the very earliest times. It covers war-time London, and comes right up-to-date with recent developments and discoveries. It was extensively redeveloped during 2002/3, and virtually all the displays can be seen and appreciated easily by both chair users and others. The Lord Mayor's gilded coach is magnificent.

There are three BB spaces which should be booked in advance. They are reached by taking the first left turn off London Wall, going about 150m east from the roundabout. It is just past the MSCP, and the turning is marked Goods Inward. You drive in underneath the building. A staff member will need to come down and operate the lift to provide access to the building. Having a mobile phone could be useful, as the parking area is unstaffed.

The entrance is located on an upper level (the Podium level of the Barbican development) at the junction between London Wall and Aldersgate Street. There are three lifts nearby providing access to the upper (Entrance) level, and in each case they are almost underneath the overhead walkways going over the road, one in London Wall about 80m from the roundabout and opposite 140 London Wall, and the other two are on either side of Aldersgate Street near or on the roundabout. You can also approach the entrance across the Podium from the Barbican.

From the museum foyer/entrance everything is step-free, and there is an information desk, and a shop and café. In addition to wheelchairs to borrow, there are three mobility scooters available and plenty of fold-up portable seats.

There are two lifts just past the information desk providing access to most floors. There's another lift at the far side of the building, but it was out of service when we visited.

There are two main levels E and L2, each measuring something like 100m by 50m (though neither is an exact rectangle). On the lower level, L2 there's step-free access into the Garden Court area in the middle of the building.

There are there are 4 wheelchair spaces in the Weston theatre.

There are **wheelchair toilets (D70+ ST70+)** on:

- level E, near the main lifts, with separate BCF nearby;
- level L2, again with BCF, en route to the café;
- L1 en route to the Weston theatre; and,
- on U1, used for group activities.

National Army Museum
Royal Hospital Road, Chelsea, SW3 4HT *Tel:* 020 7730-0717
website: www.nam.ac.uk
Quiet museum with an excellent *Story of the Army* gallery. Located just past the Royal Hospital, between West Road and Tite Street.

There is some BB parking off Tite Street, but you should call ahead (*Tel:* 020 7730-0717 *Ext* 2250).

Entrance +3 steps with a ramped bypass.

There is step-free access to all of the museum, using two lifts, five platform stairlifts and a platform lift. You can get a key to facilitate use of all the platform stairlifts, from the information/welcome desk. Folding stools are available.

The first lift (D120 W200 L135) on the right after the entrance, serves the upper levels of each floor. The other lift (D80 W100 L140), reached by a steep ramp from the GF, serves the rest of the museum. There are +7 at the exit of the *Changing the World* gallery, which can be avoided by doubling back. The main lifts do not serve the small gallery and lecture theatre on the lower level, but a platform lift (W85 L130) can be used to bypass the −8.

The museum has a shop and café. The **adapted toilet (D90 ST110 but with an inward opening door)** and BCF is on the GF quite near the entrance, and well signed. There are more BCF in the toilets on the LGF.

National Portrait Gallery

2 St Martins Place, WC2H 0HE *Tel:* 020 7306-0055 *RecM:* 020 7312-2463
website: www.npg.org.uk
Situated to the north of Trafalgar Square towards Charing Cross Road and behind the National Gallery. It houses a remarkable collection of portraits of those who have shaped British history. The gallery has been extensively modernised and extended, with much improved access. There are 5 (unreservable) BB spaces on St Martin's Street opposite the Sainsbury Wing of the National Gallery. Portable stools are available.

The main entrance has +2 steps, but there are alternative step-free ways in either via the Gift Shop (25m to the left of the main doors) or using a ramped route from Orange Street. **Inside, all the galleries are accessible without steps**. The plan which you can get at either entrance shows clearly which floors the various lifts go to, and these can be previewed on the website. The only slight confusion is that the Gift Shop and in entrance hall are both referred to as level −1, while the 'upper' GF approached from Orange Street is referred to as level 0. There is a short flight of stairs between the two, bypassed by a lift.

There are six lifts:

*   from St Martins Lane, the lift (D80 W100 L150) in the Gift Shop goes to the main entrance (level −1, bypassing +4 steps) and the basement, level −3, which contains a café and bookshop;
*   from the main entrance (level −1) a second lift (D80 W160 L170), goes to the theatre on level −2, to the main GF (level 0) bypassing the flight of steps, and to floors 1 and 2;
*   from Orange Street, three lifts (D80 W100 L140), go to the upper floors (1, 2 and 3), including the top floor where there is a restaurant with superb views (*Tel:* 020 7312-2490 for bookings);
*   a single lift (D75 W90 L140), near the Orange Street entrance, links level 0 with the IT gallery.

There are four **wheelchair toilets**:

*   on level −3 through the bookshop and at the bottom of the stairs **(D80 ST100+)**;
*   on level −2 by the theatre **(D80 ST70)**;
*   on level 0 near the Orange Street entrance **(D90 ST75)**; and,
*   on the top floor by the restaurant **(D90 ST70)**.

Facilities include a touch tour of various sculptures, large print guides and sound guides, induction loop in Ondaatje theatre and wheelchairs on request, as well as a good access booklet and good signage.

National Gallery
Trafalgar Square, WC2N 5DN   *Tel:* 020 7747-2885
website: www.nationalgallery.org.uk   *e-mail:* information@ng-london.org.uk
The Gallery has interesting collections from various painting schools from the
13th to the early 20thC. It is big, with a frontage on Trafalgar Square almost
200m long and it's about 40m wide. Most of the collection is on one floor
(level 2).
Limited parking is available for BB holders and pre-arranged groups (*Tel:* 020
7747-2854).

**The north side of Trafalgar Square has been pedestrianised, and the whole
area has become much more wheelchair friendly.** The Portico entrance from
Trafalgar Square with the big columns has +35 steps. There are step-free ways in
either at the Getty entrance 40m to the right, or through the Sainsbury Wing some
80m to the left. There's also a step-free entrance from Orange Street.
**The Getty entrance leads up to a large foyer with, café and shop, toilets, and
to lifts going up to the main gallery level. There's a lift at this entrance to
bypass the +6 steps.**
The Sainsbury Wing has five floors, with the middle one at level 0. The top
floor (level 2) contains several galleries and the link across to the main building.
All floors are accessible via the lift. There's a theatre on level −1 with three
wheelchair spaces.

Just inside both the Getty and Sainsbury wing entrances there's an information
desk where good floor plans are available. **The main level with the majority
of the galleries is level 2**. **Almost all the building has step-free access via the
various lifts**, and where there seems to be a problem, ask one of the staff, who
are generally helpful. Audio guides offering a choice of 'tours' can be a useful
help to exploring the collection, and are recommended for the casual visitor.
In terms of getting to know 'where you are' as you're going round, you'll have
to get used to the very unobtrusive system of indicating the room numbers. This
is done on the white notices about a metre off the ground located by the doors
into the room where the origin and the dates of the paintings in the room are
described. Once you've discovered this, finding your way is much easier.
There are eight lifts (all D80 W105 L140 or larger):
* **two** are in the Sainsbury wing, going to every level (−2, −1, G/0, 1 and 2);
* there's **one** at the entrance from Trafalgar Square to get to level 0 at the
  Getty entrance;
* **two** separate lifts are accessed from the Getty entrance both of which go to
  level 2;
* **two** go from the Orange Street entrance to level 2 (and don't get confused
  by the relabelling of the buttons). The lifts clearly had a different system in
  the past, and now both labels are there. As far as we can see, ground level=1
  (level 0 on the new system) while level 2=M;

- **one** goes down from level 2 (near rooms 15 and 26) to room A, which is only open on Wednesday afternoons.

All are clearly shown on the plan, though a numbering system would help.

There are **wheelchair toilets (all D70+ ST70+)**:
- at the Getty entrance (level 0) and near the café. Also by the cloakroom on the same level;
- near the Orange Street entrance (with the female one on level 0 and the male one on level 2 near room 22;
- in the Sainsbury wing on level 1 near the restaurant, and on level −1 by the theatre.

BCF are located near the Getty entrance (level 0) both towards the café and by the cloakroom; in the Sainsbury wing at level 1, and in the level 0 womens toilets by the Orange Street entrance.

There are a number of good catering facilities, with the main restaurant on level 1 of the Sainsbury wing, and a café near the Getty entrance.

National Maritime Museum see chapter on *Places of interest* under Greenwich

Natural History Museum
Cromwell Road, Kensington SW7 5BD
Tel: 020 7942-5000 *Info:* 020 7942-5011 *Customer services:* 020 7942-5511
Textphone: via Typetalk prefix 18001 and then 020 7942-5000
website: www.nhm.ac.uk *e-mail* via the website

Massive museum full of models and remains, of all types of animals, plants, gems and minerals. The exhibits explain both the evolution of the planet, and how humans and other species evolved. Well presented.

Most famous for the dinosaur skeletons and the model of a blue whale.

The Romanesque frontage is hugely impressive, and the interior is cathedral-like, designed to show off the wonders of creation.

The museum is split into the Earth Galleries (the former Geological Museum) which tell the story of the geological development of the planet, and the Life Galleries covering both plants and animals. A new section at the Queen's Gate end is called the Darwin Centre, with 22 million zoological specimens, and opportunities for meeting museum scientists.

There are twelve BB spaces in Exhibition Road as described in the introductory paragraphs. When we visited, there were no time limits set on these spaces (a somewhat mixed blessing). Pre-booked BB parking can be arranged in the CP alongside the museum at the end of Museum Lane, off Queens Gate (*Tel:* 020 7942-6230). Set your *Satnav* to SW7 5HD which will bring you to the Dana building on the corner. This is a better option than taking a chance on there being a BB space outside. The spaces on Exhibition Road are commonly full for much of the time. One obvious tip for getting a space is to come really early, just before the museum opens at 10.00.

The website has useful information, and you can download an isometric diagram showing the museum layout via *Visit us→Floor plans*. A larger-scale version of this is available from the information desk as you come in.

When we visited some of the facilities were not very well marked and the representation of the Darwin Centre was particularly confusing.

Different parts of the collection are colour coded, and to find your way, you need to know what colour zone you are heading for. The zone colours provide the basis of the wayfinding/signage scheme, and from the Exhibition Road entrance the sequence is **Red** (the Earth/Geological galleries); **Green** (including birds, creepy-crawlies and the Vault, with some spectacular minerals); **Blue** (including dinosaurs and mammals) and **Orange** (with the Darwin Centre cocoon, the Attenborough Studio and the Wildlife Garden outside).

Nearly all of the galleries are flat or ramped, but the distances involved are considerable. To go through the museum from the Exhibition Road entrance and visit the Darwin Centre, you will walk/wheel something approaching 1km.

It is around 350m to the Mammals Gallery (in the Blue zone) - which is one of the places that most people want to go. The signage is just about adequate (when you get used to it), and you may need some help from the staff. The galleries are no longer numbered, which makes it more difficult to establish exactly where you are. The lifts are not particularly well signed. There are relatively few seats.

There are three ways in:
- **the entrance on Exhibition Road to the Earth Galleries provides step-free access;**
- if you use the Museum Lane CP, you will enter the LGF step-free, through the Picnic area, and there's a single lift near one exit which goes to the GF, while a pair of lifts from another corridor (go past the Investigate Centre) leads to all the other floors in the Green zone. NOTE that to get back to the CP, the exit is to the left of the small café and the accessible toilet, and through doors marked *Emergency exit only*;
- at the main entrance on Cromwell Road, there is a 40m long sloped approach, and then +10 steps.

At the Exhibition Road entrance you go in via a bag search desk. There's an information desk, and an **accessible toilet**. The entrance is on the LGF. The lift (D90 W100 L110) to take you up to the main GF level is on your left, bypassing the +15+3 steps in front of you. There's a second lift at the other end of the hall past the toilet which will also take you to the GF (one level up).

The step-free route through the museum on the GF to the Darwin Centre isn't obvious. You initially follow signs to the green, blue and orange zones, going to the left past the big escalator. At the end of the Earth Hall (red zone) there's a wide ramp to bypass ±3 steps. After the ramp, you turn left, and go about 30m past the exhibits of birds, where the corridor can be quite crowded and congested. Then you turn right, past the fossils of marine reptiles, and a restaurant. This corridor leads into the vast **Central Hall** with its dramatic Diplodocus fossil. Almost directly opposite is a corridor through the blue zone which leads to the Darwin Centre.

Unfortunately, coming this way, you lose something of the 'wow' factor, which you can experience coming in through the Cromwell Road entrance and seeing the massive dinosaur right in front of you.

If you want to see the upper Earth Galleries in the red zone, take the big lift which is shown in the far corner of the red area and right by the wide ramp. The galleries on the 1st and 2nd floors are step free. However the Earth Lab, tucked away in a corner under the 1st floor, can only be accessed via −17−4 steps. The Flett Events Theatre on the 1st floor has a platform lift to bypass +4 in order to get into the back of the auditorium.

The different levels of the green zone (the LGF, 1st and 2nd floors) are accessed using one of the two lifts just off the Central Hall. The lifts are slightly hidden on your left as you come from Exhibition Road, just before you reach the Central Hall (almost opposite the creepy crawlies). In this zone you can discover amazing facts about life, the planet, our environment and evolution. The exhibits include a cross-section from a 1300 year old sequoia tree, a variety of creepie crawlies, British fossils, and you can meet our ancestors, including Homo erectus, Neanderthals and Australopithecines. The LGF has the Investigate Centre, and a huge picnic area.

The blue zone is mainly on the GF, with an extensive dinosaur exhibition. You can find out about fishes, amphibians and reptiles, and about human biology. There's just one gallery on floor 1 accessed by a platform lift near the blue whale. The corridor off the Central Hall leads to the Darwin Centre lift, while the corridor from the separate smaller hall (where there's a café) leads via a zig-zag route to the Mammals room, and another part of the Darwin Centre.

In the orange zone, the isometric map/plan really doesn't work! At the very least it needs re-labeling, and in particular the 7th floor needs marking. As you approach via the corridor passing the dinosaurs, there are **two accessible toilets** to your right, a café in front of you, and two lifts at the far end. On the isometric, the word Entrance points to the middle of these lifts, though it refers to an outside way out/in on the LGF. The lifts go up to level 7, which is just below the title Darwin Centre. Quite extraordinarily, the GF is apparently floating above Floor 7, and the isometric does not describe the link at LGF level between the Cocoon and the Attenborough Studio and Zoology area.

The new building is an eight-storey high 'cocoon' for the specimens, with a tightly controlled environment. It is some 65m long and 12m wide. Access to the 'tour' route is in fact quite simple. Just past the café there are two lifts (D110 W135 L145). These are pre-programmed, and initially will take you from the GF to level 7, high up in the cocoon. The lifts go sequentially to the following levels GF, 7, 5, LGF, GF.

From the level 7 exit you proceed down a series of gentle ramps past a whole series of exhibits and videos. The distance totals about 300m with occasional seats en route. This brings you back to level 5, from where the lift takes you down to the LGF (for the courtyard outside and to go across to the zoology section) and then it goes back to the GF.

If you get out on the LGF there's a walkway across the whole width of the cocoon and a lift at the other end goes up to the GF right by the Attenborough Studio where there occasional talks and lectures. This is in the area on the isometric which is apparently floating above level 7, but labeled Ground Floor. The Studio has a number of wheelchair spaces on either side, otherwise the seats are steeply tiered.

If you have any access requirements, it is essential to pre-book Darwin Centre Spirit Collection Tour. *Tel:* 020 7942-6128 or book in person at one of the information desks.

The **Wild Life Garden** can only be accessed from the Darwin Centre LGF, and isn't open in the winter, nor when it's raining.

There are **restaurants/cafés** on the GF in the red zone, the green zone, and off the Central Hall, and in the orange zone, all with movable chairs and tables. There's a picnic area on the LGF in the green zone. The GF shops all have step-free access.

The provision of toilets is limited, considering the size of the museum.

There are **wheelchair toilets all (D70+ ST70+)**:

* in the hall at the Exhibition Road entrance (red zone LGF). There's a BCF alongside this loo, and another BCF in the red zone on a mezzanine;
* in the basement of the green zone off the picnic area there's both a loo and BCF, in the corner, to the left of the small café (by the exit to the accessible parking);
* on the side of the Central Hall on the GF where there's a loo and a large BCF;
* in the Darwin Centre (orange zone),
* just before the café on the GF, and to the right, there are 2 unisex toilets,

together with BCF in both the womens and mens toilet areas;
* there's a wheelchair toilet on level 7 opposite the lift exit;
* at GF level, at the entrance to the Zoology exhibition, behind the information desk;
* en route to the mammals on the GF of the blue zone, off the other corridor.

Photographers Gallery
16-18 Ramillies Street, W1F 7LW   *Tel:* 020 7087-9300
website: www.thephotographersgallery.org.uk *e-mail:* info@tpg.org.uk
On the corner with Ramillies Place, and just south of Oxford Street. Quite near the M&S at no 173 (the Pantheon branch).
The gallery moved from Great Newport Street in 2008. It is reopening during 2012 after extensive refurbishment which will improve access. It will be on several floors, linked by a new lift. Step-free to an information desk, and a GF café/bar. There will be **accessible toilets** on the 2nd and 5th floors.
The gallery presents some really interesting and unusual exhibitions.

Queen's Gallery
Buckingham Palace Road, SW1A 1AA   *Tel:* 020 7766-7301
website: www.royalcollection.org.uk
e-mail: bookinginfo@royalcollection.org.uk
Located just south of Buckingham Palace. Admission charge, and pre-booking is probably desirable. Gallery shop, and ticket counter are step-free on the GF as is the security check. The gallery is small, and has a policy to limit visitor numbers to avoid overcrowding.
To get to the lift, go between the two staircases (+17 steps) down the corridor. To the right of the cloakroom, the lift (D70 W125 L150) gives step-free access to the 1st floor which contains all the exhibits, which are from the Queen's extensive collection. **Wheelchair toilet (D90 ST80)** under the stairs on the GF. Separate BCF by the main toilets.

Pollock Toy Museum
1 Scala Street, W1T 2HL   *Tel:* 020 7636-3452
website: www.pollockstoymuseum.com
A small and fascinating museum, with entrance in Whifield Street. It occupies two small houses joined together, with small rooms connected by narrow winding staircases.
Admission charge. Entrance +1 step to two sections of the museum shop, linked by a narrow corridor (D65cm). The museum is on the 1st and 2nd floors. To visit the whole of the museum would involve ±44 steps.

Royal Academy Of Arts
Burlington House, Piccadilly, W1J 0BD   *Tel:* 020 7300-8000
website: www.royalacademy.org.uk
The oldest and most prestigious fine arts institution in Britain, known particularly for its summer exhibition. In addition, it has its own permanent collection, and hosts a variety of exhibitions through the year.
Significant admission charge for most exhibitions.
The entrance from Piccadilly is just 400m from the 'accessible' Green Park tube station. Two BB spaces in the large slightly sloping courtyard outside, which should be reserved in advance (*Tel:* 020 7300-8028). A ramp bypasses the +4 steps at the entrance, and central doors can be opened to bypass the revolving doors.
The main exhibition on the 1st floor can be reached by a glass lift (D80 W135 L280). Flat access to some of the 1st floor galleries may be organised by going through private rooms. Some seats are available throughout the 200m route around the main gallery. Folding stools can be borrowed. The lift also goes to the smaller 2nd floor galleries. Some exhibitions have audio guides.
Shop on 1st floor. Ramped access to the GF restaurant. There is a **wheelchair toilet (D80 ST80)** with BCF, by the mens, on the GF, just to the right of the staircase.
A massive development is under way to link Burlington House with the building behind it in Burlington Gardens, which previously housed the Museum of Mankind. This is to be undertaken during the next 4 or 5 years, and it is to be hoped that the facilities for disabled visitors will be improved.
The Burlington Gardens building currently has a wooden ramp which bypasses the 4+4 steps at the entrance.

Saatchi Gallery
Duke of York's HQ, King's Road, Chelsea, SW3 4RY   *Tel:* 020 7811-3085
website: www.saatchi-gallery.co.uk   *e-mail:* admin@saatchigallery.com
The Saatchi Gallery has a series of very tall, modern, light and airy exhibition spaces built behind the traditional facade of the Duke of York's HQ building. These provide an innovative forum for exhibitions of contemporary art.
The facade is more than 100m long, and the galleries go back about 40m.
It is located about 300m from Sloane Square and less than 100m from the Peter Jones department store. Two BB parking spaces can be booked in advance (*Tel:* 020 7811-3085). These are approached from Lower Sloane Street. You turn into Turk's Row (with the *Rose & Crown* pub on the corner). Then immediately right through the big gates labelled Cavalry Square. The security staff will show you where to park, and Gallery staff will lead you in step-free via the large goods lift at the back. If you're using Satnav SW3 4RY should bring you to this back entrance.
If you approach from the Kings Road the front/main entrance is just over 100m

away. Keep to the right of the curved wall on the edge of the square for step-free access. The gallery entrance is through a grand collonaded portico. The +4 steps can be bypassed using the portable ramp on the far side, but there is +1 [7cm] at the main door.

Inside, the galleries are step-free throughout with two lifts linking the various levels. One (on the left) is (D75 W90 L120) while the other is (D75 W120 L120). There are very few seats in the gallery, and no internal café. We mentioned the potential value of providing some fold-up seats for people to borrow. Until that happens, if you need a seat, bring your own (!), although wheelchairs are available on loan.

There are **wheelchair cubicles/toilets**:

* on the LGF in both the mens and womens areas **(D80 ST75)** each with BCF;
* on the Mezzanine between levels 1 and 2, **(D80 ST80)**, only reachable using the left hand lift.

The *Gallery Mess* winebar and restaurant is nearly 100m away, approached step-free by going back to the left of the curved wall, and then turning right. It has an **adapted toilet (D85 ST65)** with the ST reduced by the BC shelf provided. There are other restaurants in the immediate vicinity.

Science Museum
Exhibition Road, South Kensington, SW7 2DD
Tel: 020 7942-4000   *Textphone:* 020 7942-4445
website: www.sciencemuseum.org.uk   *e-mail:* info@sciencemuseum.ac.uk

The museum shows centuries of continuing scientific and technological development, and includes steam engines, the first mechanical computers, and spacecraft. The various exhibitions and displays are under continual development and there are ambitious plans for a roof-top expansion by 2015. It is one of the country's most popular museums, with some excellent 'hands on' galleries for children.

Access has been carefully thought about, and the management have an ongoing programme to make all areas fully accessible. The principal problem that we encountered was in wayfinding, as the map/plan available isn't very accurate or detailed, particularly of the GF, as it doesn't attempt to show the two different levels.

We have included a GF plan here, ascribing letters to the lifts to clarify where they are and where they go.

The Exhibition Road streetscape and the BB parking is described at the start of this chapter.

Prior arrangement can be made to use the museum's own CP, and this would ensure that you have a space. The nearest 'accessible' tube station is at Earls Court.

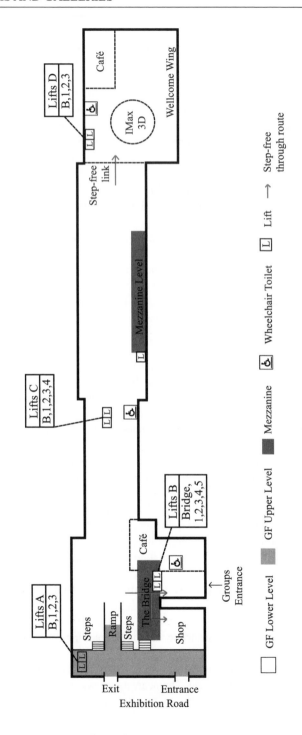

Science Museum ground floor plan
showing which floors the lifts go to

Flat entrance, where you turn left into a fairly long, seemingly quite empty, foyer. After the bag check there's an information desk on the left where you can pick up the museum map.

The entrance foyer is some 50m long. Past the +14 steps to the Bridge, there are lifts at the far end. To the right is a wide ramp leading down to the lower level and bypassing −8 steps. The (lower) GF areas include the Energy Hall with some spectacular old engines, Space Exploration and Making the Modern World as well as two cafés, the step-free entrance to the shop and the IMAX cinema.

There are not many seats, and those that are there are mostly quite low and without arms.

The museum is on six floors, with over fifty galleries, and covers a total area of some eight acres (3.2 ha). **The main hall (at right angle from the entrance foyer) is over 250m long**, and several of the floors above are nearly as long. **There are four pairs of lifts (all D100+ W150+ L150+) providing access throughout**, and you will find them:

- **at the end of the entrance foyer** (just past the exit door). These are the only ones going to the basement cloakroom, and they also go to floors 1,2,3 and 4. *Lift A on the plan*;
- **off the Energy Hall**, by the first café (on the right past the end of the long ramp) and these link to all the floors except the basement, including the 4th and 5th, and to the mezzanine level for the Bridge. From the Energy Hall it only looks as though there's one lift, and you have to go behind it towards the groups entrance to find the other one. *Lift B on the plan*;
- **in the centre of the building**, just past the Exploring Space exhibition (which is quite dark), linking to the basement and floors 1 to 4. *Lift C on the plan*;
- **past Making the Modern World, and at the start of the Wellcome Wing (WW)**. *Lift D on the plan.*

There are some platform lifts providing access to various mezzanine levels (for example on the GF in Making the Modern World, and on Floor 3 to the walkway in the Flight exhibition), but these are not shown on the museum map.

The museum is effectively in two parts. The main floors, linked by the first three pairs of lifts you come to, and the semi-separate Wellcome Wing (WW) linked by the fourth pair of lifts (D) at the far end of the museum. At the beginning of the WW, which has step-free access from the GF, two lifts on the left give access to all the Wellcome floors (basement to 3rd floor). In the basement there's a ramped link from these lifts to the picnic area and the exhibits like The Garden and The Secret Life of the Home.

The **WW is physically separated from other parts of the museum on most floors** (see the museum map/plan). To make the link shown on the map as being on Level 3 you have to use the left-hand WW lift (D) which goes to a mezzanine on Level 2 (2M), and then use the ramp which takes you on to the main Level 3 'Flight' area. This is now indicated in the lift.

The **IMAX cinema** which is accessed from the GF by escalator has four chair spaces, reached via an internal lift, and it has an induction loop. Disabled walkers can ask for tickets in the same area/row as the wheelchair spaces, and then use the lift, thus avoiding the escalator.
The **Force Field** 'theatre' in the WW has a platform stairlift to bypass the +11, and there are chair spaces at the back. A chair user would be able to experience many of the effects, but not the jolting when the seats move suddenly.
We reckon that more than 98% of the floor space is accessible without steps.
One attraction where steps cannot be avoided is getting into the Simulator pods on the 3rd floor. On the 1st floor the glass bridge over the Energy Hall has a ramp at one end.

There are a good number of **wheelchair toilets (D70+ ST70+)** throughout the museum, which are reasonably well marked on the map. They are, however, slightly variable in terms of their accessibility in that although they just about meet our criteria D70 ST70, they only just do so, and several had big bins in them which could be a significant nuisance.
Several have BCF nearby (see the museum map). In some of those in the (new) WW, the door opens inwards, although they're all D70+ ST70+.
The wheelchair toilets are:

* **on the GF, past the café and behind the lifts (B), towards the Group entrance**. This one was absolutely stuffed with bins when we visited. There were four of them! There are two more **GF wheelchair toilets**, both with baby change facilities, on the right just past Space Exploration, and well signed, and another in the Wellcome Wing near the end on the left;
* in the **basement** there's an **adapted toilet (D70 ST60)** near the lifts from the WW (D). The ST space is restricted by the BC table. There's a **wheelchair toilet** near lifts C at the other end of the basement space;
* **on the 1st floor**, there's one near the Listening Post, and in the (separate) Wellcome Wing;
* **on the 2nd floor** it is between Mathematics and Ships, and in the (separate) Wellcome Wing;
* **on the 3rd floor** it is near Health Matters, and again in the (separate) Wellcome Wing.

The step-free access to the shop is to the right from the bottom of the ramp. There are two café's with movable chairs and tables on the GF, while the catering areas in the basement and on Level 3 are more suited to school parties having picnics. The museum exit on to Exhibition Road has a small [10cm] step.

Sir John Soane's Museum

13 Lincoln's Inn Fields, WC2A 3BP *Tel:* 020 7405-2107

website: www.soane.org

The house was left to the nation in 1837, with a stipulation that nothing should be changed. Full of artefacts and memorabilia, and of narrow doors and gaps, it is well worth a visit to step back into the dreamy and eclectic world of this great collector and architect. Visitors are required to put even quite small bags into plastic carriers to reduce the risk of inadvertent damage to objects inside the house.

There are two BB spaces on the east side of Lincoln's Inn Fields.

Because of the requirement not to change anything, providing 'access' has been a challenge.

The front entrance has +2+5+1 steps, and then 80% of the GF is flat. There are some narrow doorways, including one W52cm. The basement is −17 (winding), and the 1st floor +28.

However, there is now lift access to all three floors. The lift is well hidden and disguised, at the back of the house. The wheelchair route starts with +1 from the pavement, which can be ramped, and then there's a platform lift outside, to take you down to the basement level. The lifts are of value to many disabled walkers. Most of the museum can only be visited if a wheelchair user is able (and willing) to transfer to a narrow (W40) chair with small wheels, thus requiring a pusher. The chair is rather like those used to transfer people into a seat on an aircraft, although it has arms. It says on the website that "If a visitors' wheelchair is less than 71cm (28") wide, and shorter than 102cm (40"), they can access the Crypt area of the Museum and may be able to gain limited access to other floors". We haven't explored this in detail, but the provision of the lift will undoubtedly make a visit possible for many people. To facilitate use of the various lifts, visitors wanting to use them are asked to ring first, as this makes it easier to ensure that there is adequate staffing.

There is seating available in most of the rooms, and there's a **wheelchair toilet (D80 ST70)** with BCF in the basement.

Shakespeare's Globe Exhibition and Theatre

21 New Globe Walk, SE1 9DR *Tel:* 020 7902-1400 *BO:* 020 7401-9919

website: www.shakespearesglobe.com *e-mail:* info@shakespearesglobe.com

The theatre is a reconstruction of the open-air playhouse where Shakespeare worked. There are two BB spaces on New Globe Walk 40m from the theatre entrance.

Significant admission charge.

The exhibition entrance is on the riverside past the theatre and towards Tate Modern. Ramps bypass −7−3 steps in the ticket office area. A lift (D75 W110 L150) goes down to the huge 'Undercroft' beneath the theatre. There's an extensive and well presented exhibition covering both the theatre of

Shakespeare's time and the London in which he worked. There aren't many seats. Theatre tours start from here, and use a second lift (D100 W200 L200) to reach the theatre above.

There are **wheelchair toilets (D70+ ST70+):**
- near the first lift at the upper level:
- another on the bottom level: and,
- on the GF level near the shop and theatre foyer, where the tour finishes.

All the toilet doors are quite heavy to open.

Tate Britain

Millbank, SW1P 4RG

Tel: 020 7887-8888 *Textphone:* 020 7887-8687

website: www.tate.org.uk/visit/tate-britain *e-mail:* information@tate.org.uk

Located by Atterbury Street. When we visited, there was extensive refurbishment work going on, and parts of the gallery were closed. As a result we decided to include an updated write-up on our website. BB parking can be arranged and booked.

The main step-free access is down a slope in Atterbury Street to the LGF where there are some principal facilities. Alternatively it is step-free from street level via the Clore Gallery. Access will be step-free throughout, and there will be a number of accessible toilets.

Tate Modern

Bankside, SE1 9TG *Tel:* 020 7887-8888 *Textphone:* 020 7887-8687

website: www.tate.org.uk/modern *e-mail:* visiting.modern@tate.org.uk

The gallery showcasing post-1900 art is housed in a huge building that used to be a power station. There's a substantial development, taking in what were three big oil storage tanks located alongside the Turbine Hall. A new angular building is being constructed above the tanks, and the project was at an early stage when we visited.

The museum can be reached either from the south bank Thames Walk, or across the Millennium Bridge from St Paul's. Southwark tube station, which is on the 'accessible' JLE, is about 600m away.

Parking is restricted, but there are eleven BB spaces off Sumner Street at the south entrance to the building. During the development work the location of the BB spaces may change. The website says that 'reservation is essential', by ringing 020 7887-8888 or *e-mailing:* ticketing@tate.org.uk.

If you come from the riverside, there are two flat entrances. One is by the corner café, if you come from the west. The other is on the riverside if you come from the Millennium Bridge. Both are on the GF (Level 2). At the west end, off

Holland Street, there is a wide slope some 70m long down to the bottom level (level 1), with steps and a handrail down the right hand side. At this (basement) level, there are the ticket offices for special exhibitions, and just inside the doors to the left there is an **information desk**. You can get a gallery plan there, and an access leaflet. The plan takes a little getting used to.

The four lifts (D120 W150 L250) are in the middle of the building and go to all floors. They can get quite busy. There are escalators as an alternative.

Although step-free, the galleries are around 180m long and some 40m wide, so if you go to more than one level, there can be long distances involved as there is only one block of lifts in the main building. The new development alongside is an irregular cross between a rectangle and a pyramid. It has a 60m base, and will have eleven floors, separate lifts, and three step-free links across to the main building. The bottom galleries opened in 2012, but the extension will not be completed until 2015/16. It will double the exhibition space available. Additional accessible toilets will be included.

A new public walkway through the building will create a direct route between the heart of Southwark and the City. Two new public squares will be built to the south and west of the gallery and it is intended to generate connections with local audiences.

There are benches scattered throughout the galleries, and a valuable provision is that you can borrow stools which can be picked up from the concourses on levels 3, 4 and 5. Very useful if you don't want to stand for long periods.

There are many interesting and provocative exhibits, and increasing use will be made in the new galleries of live art, performance, installation and film. The turbine hall provides an enormous space for some innovative art expressions.

The main permanent collections are on floors 3 and 5, while the 4th floor often has special exhibitions. The descriptions of various exhibits are sometimes not designed for someone who is even slightly visually impaired, and some are not at a very friendly height for a chair user.

There are **wheelchair toilets (D80 ST80)** on most levels, adjacent to the main toilet blocks. The ST space was blocked by a large bin in most of them when we visited. There are also wheelchair toilets in the special exhibition areas, but these are very discreetly signed, and it's easiest to ask a staff member. Level 1 (the basement) has a *Changing Places* toilet with more extensive facilities than

V&A ground floor and basement plan
showing which floors the lifts go to

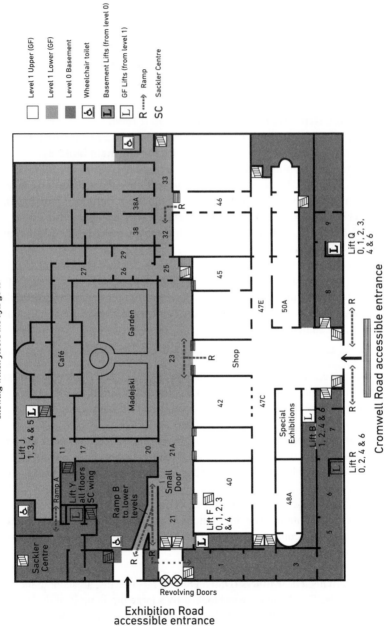

Level 1 Upper (GF)
Level 1 Lower (GF)
Level 0 Basement
Wheelchair toilet
Basement Lifts (from level 0)
GF Lifts (from level 1)
R ·····➤ Ramp
SC Sackler Centre

Sackler Centre

Lift J
1, 3, 4 & 5

Ramp A

Lift Y
all floors
SC wing

Ramp B
to lower
levels

Small
Door

Café

Garden

Madejski

Lift F
0, 1, 2, 3
& 4

Shop

Special
Exhibitions

Lift B
1, 2, 4 & 6

Lift R
0, 2, 4 & 6

Lift Q
0, 1, 2, 3,
4 & 6

Cromwell Road accessible entrance

Revolving Doors

Exhibition Road
accessible entrance

33
38A
38
29
27
26
25
23
32
46
45
47E
50A
8
9
42
47C
40
21A
21
20
17
11
1
3
5
6
7
48A

the usual accessible toilet, including a hoist, a bed and considerably more space. There's a baby care room facility in the toilets on level 1 and nappy-changing facilities in the toilet blocks on each floor

There are three cafés, on Level 2 (riverside), Level 4 and Level 7. In the one on Level 4 the counters are quite high. On the top floor, there's an outside balcony/ gallery giving some fine views back across the river towards the City. Note the accessible *Founders Arms* pub on the riverside nearby.

Victoria and Albert Museum

Cromwell Road, South Kensington, SW7 2RL
Tel: 020 7942-2000 *DisEnq:* 020 7942-2766 *Textphone:* 020 7942-2002
website: www.vam.ac.uk *e-mail:* disability@vam.ac.uk
Vast museum of Art and Design with 11km of galleries and literally thousands of exhibits, some of them very famous. The building measures about 250m along the Cromwell Road by 200m along Exhibition Road and the museum is on several floors. Collections cover furniture, jewellery, china, prints, drawings, sculpture and dress from Britain and all over the world. There is a broad division between the galleries devoted to art and design, and those concentrating on materials and techniques.
You might take advantage of the regular, free, guided tours and specialist talks. They do not provide audio-guides, probably because of the sheer size of the collection.
The museum has an ambitious ten-year development programme (FuturePlan) which involves progressive changes and occasional gallery closures. One of the first parts of this was the opening of the Sackler Centre for arts education in what was called the Henry Cole Wing (after the V&A's first director who was a driving force behind the great Exhibition of 1851). Many more details are provided on the website.

The Exhibition Road streetscape and the BB parking is described at the start of this chapter.
The main entrance in Cromwell Road is ramped with revolving doors at the top, bypassed by a central door for chair users and others, opened by pushing the large button. An entrance in Exhibition Road marked as being for schools and groups, provides an alternative step-free access some 30m to the left of the two (smallish) revolving doors. There's a third way in from the pedestrian tunnel leading to and from the underground station, but using this involves quite a number of steps.

Access around the museum is quite complicated and poorly signed but, with a little planning, you can reach most of the exhibition areas step-free. The split levels on the GF (level 1) and on level 3 can be slightly challenging. If you need help, ask a staff member. In some cases, it's essential to use the correct lift as some of the upper galleries are only on one side of the building.

Most London guidebooks will have a summary of what is where, and if you contact the museum, they will send you a detailed floor plan in advance. These can also be obtained from an information desk near either entrance.

Our GF plan is intended to help, and we will try to 'talk you through' the basic access details. You'll then have to make your own exploration.

If you're a first time visitor, there are several easily findable, accessible and interesting exhibitions on the GF (level 1).

Starting from the Cromwell Road (Grand) entrance, you are on Level 1. The foyer is spacious, but the GF involves a split level, and the whole of the area around the John Madejski Garden is lower than the front of the building (by −7/8 steps). There are two ramped routes to bypass the steps. The first is to go straight ahead through the Shop, and at the end there are ramps in both directions. There's a second ramped route via room 46.

An alternative route from the foyer to other parts of the museum is to use Lift B over to the left which goes to Levels 2, 4 and 6 on the left side of the upper galleries.

Starting from the 'accessible' Exhibition Road entrance, turn right past the information desk. Then the internal ramp (ramp B, see diagram) is on your left through a glass door. Go down the sloped corridor to the junction which is Y-shaped. If you turn very sharp right and go on downwards, it'll lead you to level 0 (the basement or LGF). If you then turn right at the door at the end you go to the **Sackler Centre**, or, if you turn left at the end of the ramp, to Galleries 1 to 7 via a further ramp bypassing −5 steps.

Alternatively, when you go down the first part of the ramp and come to the junction, if you go straight on, it leads you to a staff-only lift. If you go through the small (brown) door on the right of the lift, you come out on Level 1 near Gallery 21A in the lower section of the split-level floor. To get to the Cromwell Road entrance, go to Gallery 23, and use the ramps leading up through the Shop.

If you want to get orientated, to understand the museum layout and the link between the two entrances, then follow this route:

- go straight ahead from the foyer past the Grand entrance and through the Shop, the −8 steps at the end are ramped. Take the left turn into Gallery 23;
- from Gallery 23, go to 21A which has an open rectangular balcony in the ceiling. A little further along, in the wall on the right, there is a small door with a label *Ramp B to level 0 and 1*. Go through this door, and it gives you access to a split ramp (to the left). If you take the ramp upwards, it leads you to the Exhibition Road entrance (go right at the top of the ramp). If you take the ramp downwards, it leads either to Galleries 1 to 7 on Level 0 (if you turn left at the end) or to the Sackler Wing (if you turn right);
- alternatively, you can reach Level 0 and the Sackler Centre by using Ramp A from Gallery 11.

Ideally when you visit, you need to choose two or three areas which might be of particular interest. You can then work out how to get there, and check the way with a member of staff en route. The largest floors with galleries are levels 1 and 3, but there are important collections and facilities on all seven floors. The British Galleries are on levels 2 and 4 reached via 3 of the lifts (B, F, and R). On levels 0, 2, 4 and 6 most of the galleries in use are on the Cromwell Road side of the building. Level 5 houses a lecture theatre and seminar rooms.

The routes we describe should enable you to get to any part of the GF (level 1) where there are many interesting collections and displays.

Level 3 presents particular problems because there's a split level between galleries 111 and 107 with ±4 steps. To get to galleries 65 to 108, you need to use either lift F or J.

On the diagram, which is based around the GF (level 1), we have marked which lifts link to which floors.

To get to the other floors from the Cromwell Road entrance:

- Level 0 is reached using ramps A or B (through the Shop to the lower part of Level 1. Then go through the small door just past 21A, as described earlier for ramp B). Alternatively use lift F, or ramp A from Gallery 11;
- Levels 2, 4 and 6 on the left side of the building are reached using lift B;
- Level 0, 2, 3 and 6 on the right side of the building are reached using lift O;
- the largest part of Level 3 is reached from lifts J or F. The Cromwell Road side galleries are best reached using lift O, and there are ±4 steps between galleries 107 and 111;
- In the Jewellery galleries, 91-93, there's a platform lift (D80 L130) to enable visitors to get to the upper level;
- Level 5 has the lecture theatre which is normally reached via +21, although there is now lift access from lift J.
- Level 6 is reached using lifts B or O and is a floor where there is a link between the left and right sides of the main building when all the galleries are being used;
- the Sackler Centre where the information desk is on level O, is reached using ramps A or B, or via lift F (from level 1). There are two lifts (Y) in the centre which provide access from level O to all the other floors.

There are **wheelchair toilets (D70+ ST70+)** in the following places:

- on the GF (Level 1), off Room 33 and via ramp A at the far end of the café in the Sackler Centre. Both have BCF;
- on Level 0 (the basement), between the bottom of the big ramp, to the right towards the shop, where there are two wheelchair toilets with BC facilities just before the entrance to both the womens and mens. There are more wheelchair toilets in the Sackler Centre described above;
- on Level 2, left side, off Room 56, with BCF;
- on level 3 near lift J;

• on Level 4, left side, off room 123 and near lift R. With BCF.
The café/restaurants are in the Morris, Gamble and Poynter rooms (level 1).
The John Madejski Garden is a pleasant area for sitting outside in the summer, accessed step-free from gallery 23 on the lower part of level 1, or from the café area.

Wallace Collection

Hertford House, Manchester Square, W1U 3BN *Tel:* 020 7563-9500
website: www.wallacecollection.org *e-mail:* access@wallacecollection.org
Situated on the north side of Manchester Square, this is an extensive private art collection bequeathed to the nation by Lady Wallace in 1897.
A semicircular drive leads up to the entrance. There are two BB spaces (unmarked) on the side of the drive. It is advisable to phone and book in advance (*Tel:* 020 7563-9524). When you arrive, the staff just inside the entrance will show you where to park.
The entrance is ramped on both sides with automatic doors.
Folding stools are available to take around. Frequent tours. There is a braille map, and the audio guides have a T setting for those with a hearing aid. In addition, you can borrow a remote control device which opens some of the doors, for example to get to and from the lift. The control triggers a small circular sensor over some key doors, which are powered, and will open for you.
The lift (D80 W120 L155) goes to the LGF and 1st floors. Restaurant with ramped access on the GF towards the rear of the building. There are good floor plans on the website. The shop is on the LGF.
The **wheelchair toilet (D95 ST75)** and separate BCF are on the LGF underneath the restaurant.
Lecture theatre on the LGF with four chair spaces. An induction loop can be provided if you ask in advance.

Wellcome Collection

183 Euston Road, NW1 2BE *Tel:* 020 7611-2222
website: www.wellcomecollection.org *e-mail:* info@wellcomecollection.org
The Collection is a unique mix of galleries reflecting Sir Henry Wellcome's vision of a place where people could learn more about the development of medicine through the ages.
It is situated on the corner of Euston Road and Gordon Street. The building is quite compact, measuring about 75m by 30m. Access facilities are well described on the website.
A few BB spaces are available, but you need to book in advance. The CP entrance is on Gower Place which must be approached from Gordon Street. It is on the right, and you come first to the goods entrance, followed immediately by two silver lift doors. You use the one on the right. You can either use the intercom button on the wall or ring security (*Tel:* 020 7611-8532) to gain access. Drive into the lift, which will take you and your car down to the basement L1 where you

can park. It is step-free from here to the lifts. Note that Gower Place is inside the Congestion Zone.

The main entrance is on Euston Road about 30m from Gordon Street. There is a platform lift D80 L120) to bypass the +11 steps. **The building is step-free almost everywhere**, and there are four main lifts (D80 W130 L140) going to all floors. Platform lifts bypass any steps (for example to get into the auditorium on L1 in the conference centre).

The GF has an information desk, café and bookshop. It also has an exhibition hall. The main exhibition level is on the 1st floor. There are **wheelchair toilets** on almost every floor (L2, L1, GF, 1st, and 2nd). There are also BCF on the GF and 1st. On the GF the loos are located past the lifts and to the right just before the cloakroom.

Wellington Museum (Apsley House)

149 Piccadilly, W1J 7NT *Tel:* 020 7499-5676

The Duke of Wellington's former residence was known as *Number 1 London*, because it was the first building past the Knightsbridge tollgate. Wellington's descendants still live at Apsley House, but ten restored rooms are open to the public.

It is situated on the north side of the Hyde Park Corner roundabout, opposite the Wellington Arch, and somewhat isolated because of the swirl of traffic on almost all sides. Admission charge.

You can reach the house step-free across the roads from Grosvenor Place. The easiest alternative approach is from Hyde Park. Parking can be booked in the forecourt. The entrance has +7 steps then there are −9 to the lift (D85 W100 L105) which serves the other two floors. The main rooms are on the first floor and are step-free. In the basement there are −3 steps to a small gallery. Audio guides are available, and folding stools can be borrowed.

Places of Worship

London has an enormous number of historic and important places of Christian worship, of which we have only visited some of the more prominent ones. In addition, there have been many generations of Jewish people living in the city. It is now 'home' for an increasing number of Buddhists, Hindus and Moslems as well as those of other faiths. All need places where they can meet and worship. Many of London's churches were built with inherent architectural barriers of one kind or another, and our experience has been that in the past ecclesiastical authorities have been generally slow in providing ramps, lifts and accessible toilets. With encouragement from the DDA, many more places have provided step-free entry routes, and barriers to access have been removed. There are, of course, still some remaining challenges, and not everywhere can be made totally 'accessible' without disproportionate cost. Most places of worship provide an induction loop for their main activities, though often not for smaller meetings.

Westminster Abbey, Westminster Cathedral, St Paul's Cathedral, St James's Piccadilly and St Bartholomew-the-Great provide sharp contrasts in style and beauty, as do the Bevis Marks synagogue, the London Central Mosque, and the Swaminarayan Hindu Mission Temple. All are well worth visiting.

We will add to the list here as we visit more places, putting the details on our website under *Updated information*. This will be mainly sites of historic or architectural interest and importance.

If churches are your special interest, get a copy of *London's Churches and Cathedrals* by Stephen Humphrey (Author) and James Morris (Photographer), published by New Holland. Nearly 50 churches are described in detail, with some brilliant photos.

There's an interesting overview in *London's 100 best churches*, published in 2010, and with its own website *www.londons100bestchurches.co.uk*. While most of the churches are Anglican, 17 Roman Catholic ones are included, together with a Lutheran, Baptist and a Methodist chapel. There's also *The visitor's Guide to the City of London Churches* by Tony Tucker, published by The Horizon Press in 2010.

Apparently there were more than a hundred churches in London in the 16thC, of which 80 were destroyed in the Great Fire of 1666. Fifty-one were subsequently rebuilt under the direction of Sir Christopher Wren. More churches, some outside the City, were built in the Regency period, to designs by John Nash.

Note that some of the smaller churches are locked during the day, especially those in the city. If you want to see a particular church, it would be worth phoning in advance. *Friend's of the City Churches* have a useful website *www.london-city-churches.org.uk* which includes details about both services and opening times (where applicable). It does not include access details.

Reflecting the fact that both Londoners and visitors to the city have a wide variety of belief and practice, we have included descriptions of some of the more prominent mosques, synagogues and temples. Note also the Brahma Kumaris World Spiritual University, and the London Buddhist Centre which provide opportunities for joining in discussion and meditation. Both are described briefly. There's an extended list of places of worship in London on the website *www.4london.info/londoninformationplacesofworship.htm* and the list reflects the way in which various immigrant communities have established churches, mosques, synagogues and temples, in which to share worship and to provide a cultural meeting point.

Abbeys & Cathedrals

St Paul's Cathedral
The Chapter House, St Paul's Churchyard, EC4M 8AD
Tel: 020 7246-8350 *RecM:* 020 7246-8348
website: www.stpauls.co.uk *e-mail:* reception@stpaulscathedral.org.uk
Christopher Wren's masterpiece still dominates London's skyline. It is located on top of one of London's few hills, Ludgate Hill. It can be reached from the South Bank across the Millennium Bridge via a relatively gentle slope. Blackfriars is the nearest 'accessible' tube station, and Bank is at the end of the accessible DLR. Enquiries about parking for BB holders should be made to the Chapter House.

It is a church with a regular pattern of worship, and with some special events during the year for which you will need a ticket, often by invitation only.
The building is open for visitors almost every day, except Sundays.
Significant admission charge, except for services.
Access information is quite difficult to find on the website, but once on the page the information is good. It is found via: *Visits & Events* → *Getting here* → *Accessibility*
A considerable amount of work has been done to make the building more accessible, and this is discussed in the Spring 2010 edition of *Access by Design* published by the CAE.
The floor area of the cathedral is approximately 70m by 160m, and the crypt underneath covers some 30m by 100m. Following the audio-tour to all the commentary spots (CS) would involve a distance of roughly 500m.
The main west entrance has +10+14 steps.

A step-free way in is some 60m to the right of these stairs. Go along the south side of the cathedral, and find the door where the South Transept joins the Nave. To facilitate access, the area has been re-landscaped. This entrance is normally staffed from about 08.30 to 16.15, and the cathedral is staffed from 07.30 to 18.00. The ticket machine there only takes cards. If the door is shut, you can press the buzzer to contact a staff member to get into services taking place outside general visiting hours, although you may be wise to phone first *Tel:* 020 7246-8320.

A lift (D80 W130 L130) gives step-free access to both the crypt and the cathedral. This is staff operated, and there is good communication between staff members to ensure that someone can take you to the level you require. You may be issued with a special electronic fob/keypad to operate the lift, so that you don't have to ask every time you need to use it. An excellent facility.

The principal places where you should find a staff member to help are:
- just inside the door at street level;
- near the lift exit in the South Aisle of the cathedral; and,
- at what is called 'Crypt Gate' in the crypt. From the lift you turn left and left, towards CS13. There's a ticket check here, as entry to the café, restaurant, shop and toilets area is free, via −20 from the north side of the cathedral.

When we visited, there was a temporary ramp in place on the north side to facilitate improved access. This is particularly for groups who might include several, perhaps dozens, of wheelchair users. Proposals for a permanent stone structure require careful consideration and wide consultation. This was ongoing in 2012. The current temporary structure is intended to help the evaluation of the concept.

Groups should ask the Admissions Department *Tel:* 020 7246-8357, about using this.

On the **main cathedral floor** there is step-free access everywhere except to the Choir/Quire, where on the north side, there's a platform stairlift (W90 L110) to bypass +4, right by CS14. The lift can be self operated, or a staff member will help. It is fairly simple, although the controls are back to front from the aisle level. In the Quire there is −1 (unramped) to the choirstalls, but these are normally roped off. Behind the High Altar is the American Memorial Chapel. The current plan of this area in the *Visitor Information* leaflet doesn't show the access clearly, and it looks as though you can go from CS14, round past CS15 and into the South Quire Aisle, which you cannot do. The only step-free link between those Aisles is under the Dome.

A wooden structure with an altar has been placed under the dome, to bring the centre of worship nearer the congregation.

In the nave and transepts there are plenty of seats. There are also seats in various places in the Aisles, and throughout the crypt.

The crypt is reached using the lift (bypassing −38 from the main floor or −20 from outside). It contains a shop, restaurant and café. There are **wheelchair toilets (D80 ST75)** just inside the door of both mens and womens toilets. BCF are provided in the main toilet areas, but the one in the mens is very cramped and awkward, mainly because of the inward opening door.

You will find the tombs of Nelson and the Duke of Wellington in the crypt in a sunken area with −3 steps. If you go around the outside towards where CS2 is, there's a ramp down from both sides. Further on there is the Knights Bachelor and OBE Chapel at CS3. All can be accessed step-free.

On the north side is CS12, *Oculus*, described further below.

There are hundreds of narrow steps from the main floor to the various galleries: +257 to the Whispering Gallery, a further +119 to the Stone Gallery (outside), and then +152 to the Golden Gallery making a total of 528. Back in the days before health and safety dominated our thinking (many many years ago) the author remembers climbing a vertical ladder right up into the inside of the cross on top of the dome, and almost being blown away by the wind coming through the ironwork !

For those people who have difficulty climbing the stairs there's now "*Oculus: An Eye into St Paul's*", located in the crypt. *Oculus* is a 270deg (3-sided) film experience covering 1400 years of history. The chamber has four stone pillars in it and is just a space with no seating.

There are four short films, including a virtual 'fly-through' film of the dome. You can also see filmed views of the City from the outside galleries.

There's an induction loop covering the main part of the church, for services.

Southwark Cathedral
London Bridge, SE1 9DA *Tel:* 020 7367-6700
website: www.cathedral.southwark.anglican.org
e-mail: cathedral@southwark.anglican.org

The cathedral is situated beneath and to the SW of London Bridge. Though much restored, the building retains its traditional Gothic style. Shakespeare's brother Edmond is buried here. There are −22 steps down to the cathedral precincts from the bridge.

The entrance can be reached step-free from Borough Market, if approached from the SW corner of the church, along Cathedral Street by the junction with Winchester Walk. There's a ramp to the right to bypass −6. The entrance itself is step-free although there are some slightly difficult doors en route.

A great deal of thought has gone into making the facilities accessible, including the attached building on the north side.

Inside some 70% is step-free. The Ambulatory is reached via +1 + 3 on the right side. The first step is permanently ramped, and there are portable ramps available to get up the others. The shop and refectory on the north side are accessed via + 7 but with a platform lift (D120 L200) to bypass them. The platform lift has an unusual control system. There's a conventional wall button, but to open the door you need to press a release button and at the same time pull the bar on the top of the door. On arrival you need to use the release button on the outside of the door, and push at the same time (!).

Both the shop and café are step-free. The refectory/café is reached using a ramped passage outside the shop. It can also be approached step-free from Montague Close (approached from Tooley Street under the bridge), over a partly cobbled courtyard and a partly cobbled route. There's a large attractive area outside the refectory, with tables there during the summer.

Wheelchair toilet (D70+ ST70+ NKS) with BCF, near the top of the platform lift. A key can be borrowed from inside the bookshop. There's a second **wheelchair toilet (D70+ ST70+ NKS)** in the basement, reached by a lift (D70 W110 L140) next to the refectory. This also goes to upstairs meeting rooms. Induction loop in the church.

Westminster Abbey
The Chapter Office, 20 Dean's Yard, SW1P 3PA *Tel:* 020 7222-5152
website: www.westminster-abbey.org *e-mail:* info@westminster-abbey.org
The abbey church is used for many national occasions and royal events. It also has the tombs and monuments of hundreds of famous people.

It is a church with a regular pattern of worship, and there are some special events during the year for which you will need to get a ticket. The building is open for general visitors almost every day, except Sundays, when there are services. Significant admission charge, except for services. The College Garden is only open on certain days. Parking is sometimes available for BB holders, but you need to ring and ask. Westminster underground station about 500m away is 'accessible'.

The visitors entrance to the Abbey is approached from Parliament Square, alongside St Margaret's church, and through the North door. It is step-free. Some areas of the Abbey are unavoidably challenging and/or inaccessible, to wheelchair users - in particular the Lady Chapel, the Chapter House and the links between the Abbey church and the Cloisters. As a result, the Abbey offers free admission to wheelchair users, and to a companion.

While people can roam freely inside the Abbey, there is a well planned tour linked to an audio guide. If you want to be able to watch the videos while listening to the commentary, you can ask for a headset. On entry you get a map of the tour route with numbered commentary spots (CS). It takes you first to the west end of the church. After the grave of the Unknown Warrior, representing the fallen from the World Wars and other conflicts, it leads you down the centre of the Nave. You then go through the Quire and around the Ambulatory to Poets Corner. Several of the side chapels have 1 or 2 steps, and in some cases narrow entrances. To get to Henry VII's Lady Chapel there are 12+2+1 steps, which are wide and straight, with handrails.

The plan doesn't (currently) mark all the steps which you will encounter during a visit. In particular the −5 steps into the cloisters area, and the +5 to get back into the nave. Nor are the −3 into the Abbey Museum shown.

Once inside, much of the ground level is flat with occasional uneven surfaces over flagstones. The distance involved in a visit to the church is approaching 400m with a further 300m around the Cloisters. There are seats both in the main Nave and near Poet's Corner (where there are monuments to many of the countries greatest poets). Off Poet's Corner, there's a small toilet block, which includes a **wheelchair toilet (D85 ST120)** with BCF. It is located between CS18 and CS19 on the map.

The conventional route out takes you past the Coronation Chair and through the Great West Door where there are −2−1 steps with no handrails, followed by a cobbled area. A portable ramp is available. This route then leads through the shop. Alternatively, chair users can leave step-free via the North Door, where they came in.

There is, however, an additional area to visit, around the Cloisters. These lie along the south side of the Nave. The entry door is just past CS20. There are −5 steps, with handrails, from the doorway. If you are in an electric wheelchair, or with friends who cannot 'bump you down' those steps, then you will have to go outside. There's a slightly bumpy but step-free route through the Gateway off Broad Sanctuary, and into and through Deans Yard. This will add about 300 metres to the distance involved, and make the total something approaching a kilometre. You come back into the Cloisters, off which lie the Museum, Gardens and Café.

Disabled walkers might well like to borrow one of the wheelchairs available, in view of the distances involved, although they may be able to manage to steps into the Cloisters area.

Starting from the steps, going around the Cloister, you go first past the Chapter house which has +1(tiny)+2+7+1 steps to get in, with no handrails. At the bottom of the steps on the right is a door labelled 'Britains oldest door'. Further on is the Abbey Museum with −3 steps, and a handrail on one side only. Portable ramps are available to facilitate wheelchair access.

If the College Garden and Little Cloister are open, they are well worth a visit, and the route is step-free over some slightly bumpy surfaces. There are seats in the Garden.

The new *Cellarium Café* is off one corner of the Cloisters. Follow the signs, and you will find yourself at the top of −6 steps, with a lift immediately alongside (D80 W100 L130). The café is on two levels, level 0 and level 2 (used mainly at lunchtime). Along the corridor from the lift, at ground level, there's a spacious **accessible toilet** with BCF.

The conventional route for leaving is to go back into the Abbey Nave, via +5 steps, with handrails. Chair users can leave the Cloisters area via an exit leading back to Deans Yard, bypassing both the steps and the shop. Induction loop in the church for services.

Westminster RC Cathedral
Ashley Place, SW1P 1QW *Tel:* 020 7798-9055
website: www.westminstercathedral.org.uk *e-mail:* chreception@rcdow.org.uk
One of London's rare Byzantine buildings, its red-brick tower stands in sharp contrast to the nearby Abbey.
Entrance +4 steps, bypassed on both sides by gentle ramps. Flat inside to all the main areas. Numerous side chapels have +2, but a portable ramp can be made available if you ask one of the staff. The book and souvenir shop are step-free. The café in the crypt is only accessible via +2−19−1 steps but there are plenty of alternatives in Victoria Street or Victoria station.
When we visited there was an exhibition of cathedral treasures in the upper left hand balcony. This is either reached using +50 spiral steps, or by the lift (D80 W120 L140).
The lift goes to the top of the Tower. Visitors are warned that in the event of malfunction there are 307 steps to get down, but nobody is prevented from using it (an excellent attitude!). The views are interesting, but would be very limited for a chair user who cannot stand at all. This is because of the design of the tiny balconies with stonework some 120cm high, with small holes at an angle through which to see. It's not easy to think of any way of getting around this problem in an historic building.
There's an induction loop in the church.

Central Hall Westminster
Storey's Gate, SW1H 9NH *Tel:* 020 7222-8010
website: www.c-h-w.com *e-mail:* visitorservices@c-h-w.co.uk
Central Hall is the 'Cathedral' of Methodism, used on Sundays for worship and at other times for conferences, meetings and exhibitions. It was built more than a hundred years ago, with its huge Hall (for more than 2000 people) on the 3rd and 4th floors. It also houses administrative offices and about thirty meeting rooms. It measures some 50m square.
It is located opposite Westminster Abbey and alongside the Queen Elizabeth II Conference Centre.
There are some cobbled surfaces as you approach the hall. While it was clearly not built with 'accessibility' in mind, the management have gone to considerable lengths to ensure that disabled visitors can get almost anywhere. Using the website you can download floor plans, although these don't show the lifts and split levels very clearly.
The main entrance has +3+13 steps to a reception desk. There are then a

further +53 to the Hall. The steps can be bypassed by using the door at pavement level just to the left. This leads to two lifts (D80 W100 L200) which go to most floors, including the basement café and level 3 for the Hall. It does not provide a step-free route to some of the meeting rooms on level 2.

There's an alternative ramped entrance near the corner between Tothill Street and Matthew Parker Street. This leads to two other lifts, one somewhat smaller, and the other D100 W200 L400, giving access to other parts of the building.

Using the lifts, more than 95% of the building is step-free, although quite long distances may be involved. Two of the rooms on level 1 are accessed by a platform stairlift which bypasses +5 steps. The Broadbent room on the GF can be accessed using an open lift to bypass −3.

There are **wheelchair toilets**:

* on the LGF, near the café with a separate BCF;
* on the GF, accessed through the Broadbent room - and an **adapted toilet** (which is slightly smaller than our 'standard' size), near the Emmanuel room;
* on the 3rd floor to the left from the main lifts, and by the mens. With a BCF;
* on the 4th floor also to the left from the lifts and near the mens.

St George's RC Cathedral
Lambeth Road, SE1 7HY *Tel:* 020 7928-5256
website: www.southwark-rc-cathedral.org.uk
The cathedral, opposite the Imperial War Museum, was rebuilt after its destruction in World War II. Step-free entrance, then flat inside with plenty of space for chair users at the sides and front. Induction loop. There are toilets in the adjacent Amigo Hall.

Churches

All-Hallows-by-the-Tower
Byward Street, EC3R 5BJ *Tel:* 020 7481-2928
website: www.ahbtt.org.uk
An interesting and atmospheric church, offering the opportunity of doing some brass rubbing. Pepys watched the Great Fire from its tower. Recently built annexes called the Queen Mother's Building mean that there are three step-free entrances.
Entering via the main doors on the north side, there's a +1cm ridge, and a ramp with sharp turns, to bypass the −3 steps. Probably the easiest way in is from Byward Street, via a shallow 20m long ramp into *The Kitchen* café/restaurant, on the east (Tower) side of the church. From here it is ramped into the church, bypassing +2. On the south side from Tower Place, the first entrance involves +1+2 but if you go through the double wooden doors under an arch in the wall, there is a step-free route.

The **Brass Rubbing Centre** is a friendly spot inside, at the west end of the church, with tables at a suitable height for most chair users, and brasses mounted on mobile plinths which you can put on your knees. There are sections of the Undercroft with some Roman remains down −18 or −12.
Wheelchair toilet (D80 ST80) near *The Kitchen*, and just after the end of the ramp.

Brompton Oratory (The London Oratory)
Brompton Road, SW7 2RP *Tel:* 020 7808-0900
website: www.bromptonoratory.com
A quiet and attractive church with a stunning interior, located almost next to the V&A Museum.
Entrance +6+1 steps. If you go about 30m down the side of the church on the left, there's a ramp to an alternative entrance. If the door is locked, ask at the house, or ring the bell which is set in the wall by the drainpipe, and near the bottom of the ramp.
It is mainly step-free inside.

City Temple
Holborn Viaduct, EC1A 2DE *Tel:* 020 7583-5532
website: www.city-temple.com *e-mail:* enquiries@city-temple.com
The City's only nonconformist (Free) church with regular Sunday worship, and an international congregation. The building also provides a conference centre. It is located about 100m from Holborn Circus.
Entrance +3 steps, bypassed through a side door, normally locked. The GF contains the chapel, church and the hall. The church has mainly fixed pews/seats with a few wheelchair spaces at the back.
A lift (D85 W85 L185) goes to all the floors, which contain conference halls and meeting rooms. On floor −1 there are −6 steps to the two meeting rooms.
Wheelchair toilet (D80 ST80) with BCF down a twisty corridor on the 1st floor, reached by the lift.
There is an induction loop in the church.

St Bride's
Fleet Street, EC4Y 8AU *Tel:* 020 7427-0133
website: www.stbrides.com *e-mail:* info@stbrides.com
A Wren church with strong journalistic links, about 500m from St Paul's Cathedral. Fleet Street entrance +1 step, but there is level access if you come from Salisbury Court and go down St Brides Avenue. Flat inside with **wheelchair toilet (D75 ST100+)** with BCF in the office area which can be used on request. The crypt (−20 with further steps along the route) contains remnants of earlier churches on the site, and a section of Roman pavement.

St Clement Danes

Strand, WC2 *Tel:* 020 7242-8282
website: www.raf.mod.uk/stclementdanes
Another Wren church, best known for its oranges and lemons. Blitzed in World
War 2 and badly damaged, it has now been beautifully restored, and has become
the RAF church. It stands on an island in the middle of the Strand, just past
Aldwych.
Entrance +1 step with a portable ramp normally left in position. Step-free in the
main Nave inside. The balcony is +25, and crypt −22.

St Ethelburga's

78 Bishopsgate, EC2N 4AG *Tel:* 020 7496-1610
website: www.stethelburgas.org *e-mail:* enquiries@stethelburgas.org
Following its destruction in 1993 by an IRA bomb, the church has been
completely rebuilt. It is now a *Centre for Reconciliation and Peace* amongst
people from all faiths.
The entrance and floor area are all step-free.
Past the small garden is the *Bedouin Tent* where people of different faiths can
meet as equals, rather than as guests in each other spaces. This is the latest
stage in the development of St Ethelburga's. It provides a place for new types
of conversation, where people sitting as equals in a circle can discuss how
to understand their differences, and develop shared values and strategies for
collaboration in changing the world.
Wheelchair toilet (D75 ST85) at the far end of the building in the glass section
near the garden.

All Souls Langham Place

2 All Souls Place, W1B 3DA *Tel:* 020 7580-3522
website: www.allsouls.org *e-mail:* info@allsouls.org
Opposite Broadcasting House at the top end of Regent Street, the church is often
used as a recording studio. The +7 steps at the entrance can be bypassed by a
ramp on the left. Inside, a lift (D75 W110 L140) bypasses +3 into the church, and
also −18 to the lower floor which contains a meeting hall and an **adapted toilet
(D70 ST65)**. Induction loop in the church.

St Bartholomew-the-Great

West Smithfield, EC1A 7HW (parish office) *Tel:* 020 7606-5171
website: www.greatstbarts.com *e-mail:* admin@greatstbarts.com
Apart from the Tower Chapel, this is London's oldest church, with Norman arches
and a triforium. There are twelve BB spaces around the outside, near the hospital
entrance. Admission charge.
The main entrance is 50m along a passage at the end of Little Britain, just off the
West Smithfield roundabout. You go under an archway, and down a slight slope.

Immediately to your right is a ramp leading down into a grassed area, with some seats and shade. Potentially good for a picnic. As you go into the church there are two small steps −1[3cm]−1[4cm]. Level throughout with uneven surface, except for the Chapel (+1) where the video is shown, with +4 to an upper level.

The Cloister café/bar is just to the right of the entrance. **Tardis-type wheelchair toilet (NKS 24h)** on the West Smithfield roundabout just opposite the archway.

St Giles Cripplegate

St Giles Terrace, Fore Street, EC2Y 8DA   *Tel:* 020 7638-1997
website: www.stgilescripplegate.com
Milton's burial place. St Giles is situated in the middle of the Barbican development, and there are lifts to get down from the Podium level.
A ramp bypasses +2 steps at the entrance. Step-free inside.

St James's Piccadilly

197 Piccadilly, W1J 9LL   *Tel:* 020 7734-4511
website: www.st-james-piccadilly.org   *e-mail:* enquiries@st-james-piccadilly.org
On the south side of Piccadilly, opposite Swallow Street and about 200m from the Circus.

The poet and visionary William Blake was baptized here and it was supposedly Wren's favourite church. It has a lively and inclusive ministry, as you can see from the website.

There are −3 steps from Piccadilly into the churchyard, where small fairs are frequently held, and a further +2 into the church itself. Both these sets of steps are normally ramped. The ramp is W68 at its narrowest. The surface in the churchyard is slightly uneven.

There are +2+2 (not ramped) from Jermyn Street. Step-free inside the church to about 80%, although there are box pews (limiting where a chair user can sit for concerts) and there are steps up to the gallery.

The café, at the west end of the church, has +1 small step from the churchyard.

There's a **wheelchair toilet (D80 ST75 NKS)** with BCF by the Jermyn Street side. This is kept locked during the day, because of misuse, and the duty verger has the key. The NKS lock is normally operational when there are concerts or events.

The website is forthright about limitations of access to the Rectory, Church Hall and Garden, but says that *"We have plans to provide full access to all parts of the church. In the meantime we encourage anyone with limited mobility to contact us to discuss what provision can be made for specific events"*. A very friendly and positive attitude.

St John's Waterloo

Waterloo Road, SE1 8TY *Tel:* 020 7633-9819
website: www.stjohnswaterloo.org
Located on the big roundabout at the end of Waterloo Bridge. A ramp to the right
of the entrance bypasses +3 steps. Small threshold [±3cm] at the main entrance
door. Inside the church is largely step-free, and there's a **wheelchair toilet (D70+
ST70+)** towards the front on the left side.

St Lawrence Jewry

Gresham Street, EC2V 5AA *Tel:* 020 7600-9478
website: www.stlawrencejewry.org.uk
The church of the Corporation of London, on the corner of Guildhall Yard (see
Guildhall write-up in *Places of interest*). It has a fantastic ceiling.
Step-free entrance then flat throughout except for −2 to a small chapel. Induction
loop.

St Margaret's

Parliament Square, SW1P 3JX *Tel:* 020 7654-4840
website: www.westminster-abbey.org/st-margarets
The parish church of the House of Commons, where Sir Winston Churchill was
married.
The main entrance on west side has +3+1 steps. There's a permanent ramp at the
north entrance. You may have to ask the verger on duty to open the north door (or
you can ring in advance). Flat inside except for +1 to the information desk.

St Martin-in-the-Fields

Trafalgar Square, WC2N 4JJ *Tel:* 020 7766-1100
website: www.stmartin-in-the-fields.org *e-mail:* info@smitf.org
On the northeast corner of Trafalgar Square, at the bottom of St Martin's Lane.
Often called the *Parish church of London*, it has a fine spire and portico, and
dates from the 1720s.
**Its facilities have been extensively modernised, and wheelchair access has
been greatly improved.** In the main church building there are box pews, which
limits the number of places a wheelchair user can be accommodated. The gallery
can only be reached using about +30 steps.
While the main west entrance has a minimum of +5 steps, there is a permanent
ramp on the north side of the building (off St Martin's Place) leading to two
heavy doors controlled by a large 'push' button at the top. The doors then open
automatically.
Just inside these doors there's a platform lift (D80 L160), which bypasses the ±28
steps to and from the crypt.
Alternatively **there's a new circular lift (D100 diameter200) outside** under a
glass cupola and near the ramp. This leads to the **crypt** which contains a licensed

café, a shop, a brass rubbing centre and two **wheelchair toilets (D80 ST80)** both with BCF. In the café the surfaces are slightly bumpy as the flagstones and memorial tablets in the floor are very old. Brass rubbing is done on low tables which would be suitable for most chair users.

There's a second lower crypt area, accessed by another platform lift.

St Martin's hosts numerous concerts and events, in addition to the church services held there regularly. There are usually at least four wheelchair spaces at the concerts, at the front of the nave.

St Paul's Church, Covent Garden

Bedford Street, WC2E 9ED   *Tel:* 020 7836-5221
website: www.actorschurch.org

This is London's chief church for those in the theatrical profession. It backs on to Covent Garden, but has its entrance on the other side, from Bedford Street (via Inigo Place). Outside there is a quiet garden with a good number of seats, some shaded, and this provides a nice spot for a rest or a picnic.

Access to the church is via +4 steps, bypassed by a steepish ramp. Inside it is flat, with traditional box pews, an impressive elevated altar and many plaques commemorating famous actors.

Temple Church

Temple, EC4Y 7BB   *Tel:* 020 7353 3470
website: www.templechurch.com   *e-mail:* verger@templechurch.com

Temple Church lies just south of Fleet Street, and north of the Inner Temple Gardens. We approached it from Middle Temple Lane, which was blocked by big gates at the Fleet Street end, but there was a pedestrian bypass W68.

It is one of the most historic and beautiful churches in London. It was built by the Knights Templar. This order of crusading monks was founded to protect pilgrims on their way to and from Jerusalem in the 12thC, and the Round Church was consecrated in 1185. It has restricted opening hours, and you would be wise to check the website, or phone before visiting.

Access is from the south side via two sets of double doors, and chair users may have to get the other side opened in order to get in. The church is step-free, though there are sections in the nave with boxed pews.

Mosques, Synagogues, and Temples

As we said in the introduction to this section, both Londoners and visitors to the city have a wide variety of belief and practice. Visiting different places of worship provides a useful way of learning about what others believe and do.

We have included descriptions of some of the more prominent mosques, synagogues and temples which are readily open to the public. We also mention the Brahma Kumaris World Spiritual University, and the London Buddhist Centre which provide opportunities for joining in discussion and meditation. There are many more opportunities, and we hope to add some of these to our website in the future under *Updated information*.

London Central Mosque (Islamic Cultural Centre)
146 Park Road, NW8 7RG *Tel:* 020 7724-3363
website: www.iccuk.org *e-mail:* info@iccuk.org
A fine building with a bronze dome, SE of Regent's Park, by the junction with Hanover Gate. The website has the 'times for prayer', answers to basic questions about Islam, and a list of all the Mosques in London.
CP available for visitors, controlled by security gate, beside which is the pedestrian entrance. For the casual visitor it is almost certainly best to ring first and ask about parking.
There are +3 steps to the main square, bypassed by a ramp 15m away, along the left side. To the right of the main square is the reception to the mosque. Once inside, there is a bookshop to the right, and an enquiry desk to the left, as well as a prominent display, with clocks showing the five times of prayer - at dawn, noon, mid-afternoon, sunset and night. There's an excellent *Guided tour* booklet available at the desk. There is flat access to the bookshop, enquiry desk and main area of worship for men.

Visitors are allowed into the mosque even during the times of prayer, providing they show due respect and do not attract attention or get in the way.
10m in front of the main entrance are the Mosque doors. Inside these there is an uncarpeted (non-sacred) area where shoes must be removed before going on the carpet to pray. However, everything is visible from this area, including the fine carpet, chandelier and dome. Although women pray in a separate upper gallery, women visitors are allowed to look inside from this non-sacred area, provided they are suitably dressed. They are asked at the very least to cover their heads. Wheelchair users are allowed on to the carpet in the mosque if they want to pray.

For praying, the main GF part of the mosque is for men only. Women pray in an upper gallery. Both require *wudhu*, which is ritual washing before praying, principally of the feet.
There is a small lift (D75 W75 L100) which goes to the LGF, G and 1st floors to bypass the +20 steps to both the 1st floor gallery and the library and the −20 to the LGF.
The mens toilets and wudhu are on the LGF along with a café and restaurant, which has some excellent food. For disabled men there is a toilet available on the GF for washing. There is an unadapted womens toilet and wudhu on the GF.
There is a new administrative block, to the left of the security gate at the main entrance, contains a **wheelchair toilet (D85 ST110)** on the 2nd floor, to the left of the lift (D80 W100 L130).
The staff are friendly and welcoming, but it's a busy place.

Bevis Marks Synagogue
4 Heneage Lane, EC3A 5DQ (postal address only)
Tel: 020 7626-1274 (*info*) 020 7621-1188 (*office)*
website: www.bevismarks.org.uk
Built more than 300 years ago, it was located on a back alley as Jews were not
(then) allowed to build on the public highway. It was also built to look like a
church - from the outside - thus attracting less attention. The magnificent interior
is almost unchanged.
The main entrance is through the iron gates on Bevis Marks, halfway between
Heneage Lane and Bury Street. It is well hidden behind a modern building.
Admission charge, and limited times of opening. Listening to one of the
occasional tour commentaries is highly recommended.
**Entrance +2 steps, but there's a step-free route through a (fire exit) door at
the other end of the building, off Heneage Lane.** This route goes past a spot
W74. Male visitors are required to cover their head with a kippur, if they aren't
wearing a hat or cap. The main body of the synagogue has its original oak pews,
and is where the men sit for prayers. There's a gallery for women with +20, but
if this is a problem, women can sit in the main part of the synagogue. It is a very
atmospheric place.
In the attached hall for catering and for various events, there are −30 to a
basement level. There's a chair stairlift to bypass these (for people who can
transfer to a chair seat), and in the basement there's a **wheelchair toilet (D80
ST80).**

*Swaminarayan Hindu Mission (BAPS Shri Swaminarayan Mandir) Neasden
Temple*
105-119 Brentfield Road, NW10 8LD *Tel:* 020 8965-2651
website: www.mandir.org *e-mail:* info@mandir.org
A new and spectacularly beautiful building which is the largest Hindu temple
outside India. It is the first traditional temple in Europe and opened in 1995. It is
commonly known as the **Neasden Temple**. Visitors from all religions are made
very welcome.
It is located just off the North Circular Road in Neasden. Getting there by public
transport could be a bit of a challenge. Wembley Park is an 'accessible' tube
station, and Willesden Junction on the *Overground* is also 'accessible'. Both
are about 1.5km away, so it's a bus or taxi job. Getting back you would almost
certainly have to phone a cab (or pre-book a minicab).
There is parking in the school CP just across the road from the temple entrance,
with 9 BB spaces.
It is highly preferable (in terms of both understanding the work of the temple and
of seeing the shrines) to come during *Murti Darshan* between 09.00 and 11.00;
11.45 and 12.15 or 16.00 and 18.00. You might be wise to check the times.
Murti Darshan means being/sitting in the presence of a deity in the manifest form

of an image (Murti) - thereby coming to see and feel, and to be seen and touched by it, to exchange looks with it (the meaning of Darshan). This practice and language has similarities with the use of icons in the Eastern Orthodox Christian church.

Visitors are expected to dress modestly, and are not allowed to bring in bags, nor to take photographs. Security is quite tight, almost airport style, but more friendly.

A visit involves walking a total of something approaching 400-500m from the CP. From the courtyard where you come in there are +3 steps, bypassed on either side by a ramp. At the door there's the security check. After that, men go to the left to take their shoes off while women go to the right.

The toilets are by the entrance with a **wheelchair cubicle (D80 ST80)** with BCF in both the mens and womens loos. It was the third cubicle in the mens, and the door was unmarked when we visited. It also had no handle to assist opening. The entrance foyer is richly carved with soaring teak columns. There is a small but quite congested shop there. The way into the temple Mandir on the 1st floor is via the blue carpet to the left of the entrance. There is about 30m of gentle slope.

There's a well presented exhibition on *Understanding Hinduism* (small admission charge) which includes an excellent ten minute video about the building of the temple. You can time your visit to this to fit in with seeing the shrines, and we would recommend going round the exhibition first if possible.

A lift (D85 W105 L160) bypasses the ±27 steps to the Mandir which contains stunning white carvings, an amazing dome and the various sacred (and colourful) shrines.

There is much more information on *www.swaminarayan.org* which explains the origins of the Swaminarayan movement and its inspiration.

The **London Peace Pagoda**

On the riverfront in Battersea Park, it is a magnificent structure with gold tableaux depicting the birth, enlightenment, preaching and death of the Buddha. There are +14 steps to the walkway around it, but you can see perfectly well from ground level, and also from across the river.

To find out more about Buddhism, contact the:

London Buddhist Centre

51 Roman Road, Bethnal Green, E2 0HU *Tel:* 0845 458-4716

website: www.lbc.org.uk *e-mail:* info@lbc.org.uk

They provide drop-in meditation classes and introductory courses about Buddhism.

We were told that apart from one reception room which has a raised floor (with a portable ramp available) the entire place is wheelchair accessible. We were told that there are two accessible toilets, a lift to access the basement, and hearing enhancement systems at reception and in all the teaching rooms.

An interesting centre for meditation is the:
Brahma Kumaris World Spiritual University
Global Co-operation House, 65 Pound Lane, Willesden NW10 2HH
Tel: 020 8459-1400 *website:* www.bkwsu.org.uk *e-mail:* london@bkwsu.com
The international centre for Brahma Kumaris was opened in 1991. It is a
relatively modern movement originating from the 1930s with an emphasis on
meditation and spiritual development. The London HQ is located in a modern
office block in the NW.
Courses run daily, weekly, or more long term.
UGCP on Pound Lane with 22 spaces of which only 4 are not on a steepish
incline.
The main entrance and GF are flat. A lift (D80 W110 L130) gives step-free access
to all other floors. The seven floors contain numerous rooms, including a seminar
room and an auditorium.
Wheelchair toilet (D85 ST90) on the GF, and another **(D85 ST85)** on the 3rd
floor.

Shops

Among London's main attractions are the long streets full of shops, some of which are famous throughout the world. All of those listed here were visited during 2011. Our survey teams found that access to shops has improved considerably in recent years. In particular there are fewer split levels, more accessible toilets, and more BCF. However, few have textphone details on their website and there are still a small number with unexpected split levels. **Importantly, attitudes have changed, and staff members are more often understanding of special needs than was the case ten years ago.**

In this chapter we have concentrated mainly on the Oxford Street/Regent Street area, as well as including famous shops like Harrods, Harvey Nichols, Peter Jones and Fortnum and Mason. We have also included a few shops on Kensington High Street, and around Victoria. We have only visited and described a tiny percentage of London's shops, so please do not be limited by listings in this section. **Nearly all the big shops we have described have accessible toilets.** Access is generally good, although the majority of the big stores have central escalators. The lifts are less obvious and may even be slightly difficult to find. Signage is highly variable.

Most big department stores have a store guide/listing near the main entrance, or at the bottom of escalators, but these do not normally take account of access issues. A few have printed plans of the layout of each floor (which may be downloadable from their website), but these aren't always very clear or accurate. Departments are sometimes moved around without the list being amended. Sometimes you'll bump into some narrow gaps, especially when displays are being reorganised, and there are also occasional unexpected split levels with several steps between one level and another.

For shop locations, see the map, and note that the numbering along Oxford Street (which is very long) is shown. Shops get extremely busy, particularly during the whole of the Christmas period, and when there are sales. Car parking also gets more difficult then.
Near Oxford Street there are CPs with BB spaces and lifts, one attached to Selfridges, one behind Debenhams and one in Bryanston Street, near Marble Arch. The UGCP at Cavendish Square does not have lifts.

In the suburbs, there are many new and accessible shopping centres, with accessible toilets and BCF. We have included a brief description of the two Westfield shopping malls which opened recently.
In the suburbs, the Shopmobility schemes are of considerable importance. Each

is independently run and financed, but a central office coordinates information, and details can be found at www.shopmobilityuk.org. A list of the schemes in and around London in November 2011 is included at the end of this chapter.

Remember the **street and open-air markets** for shopping, which have, in principle, good access although they may be crowded, and in streets/areas with bumpy surfaces.

In the text, shops are listed in alphabetical order. Where there is more than one branch in the same area we have listed them together, but shown them separately on the map.

Debenhams

334 Oxford Street, W1C 1JG *Tel:* 0844 5616-161
website: www.debenhams.com
A large department store on six floors, located between Vere Street and Marylebone Lane. It measures about 30m by 70m, and has split levels on both the GF and LGF.
Step-free entrances from the Vere Street corner and the central doors from Oxford Street, but there are +2 steps from the Marylebone Lane corner and +3 from Henrietta Place.
The GF split level has ±5, bypassed by a platform lift (W80 L100) on the Marylebone Lane side, by the Staff Only doors. The main lifts (D80+ W160 L135+) go from the upper GF level at the back of the store towards Henrietta Place.
The basement/LGF split level with ±8 is also bypassed by a platform lift (W80 L100). **Wheelchair toilet (D85 ST90)** and BCF on the 3rd floor in the opposite corner of the shop from where the lifts are.
Although access has been improved with the provision of the platform lifts, the decision not to provide ramps remains disappointing, and it took a lot of pressure over a number of years to get anything at all done. The owners carried out a multi-million pound redevelopment, and access issues were clearly not a priority.

Fortnum and Mason

181 Piccadilly, W1A 1ER *Tel:* 020 7734-8040
website: www.fortnumandmason.com
One of London's traditional shops established more than 300 years ago with its own unique style. It sells a remarkable range of upmarket foods and other goods, and offers several opportunities for wineing and dining.
There are two step-free entrances from Piccadilly, avoiding steps at the entrances from Jermyn Street. All the floors are spacious, but most are carpeted. Three lifts give step-free access to all six floors. Curiously these aren't all the same size.

Two are wide but shallow (with L70) while the third (on the far left) is more rectangular, with L100, which would be easier for most chair users. A separate lift (D110 W140 L135) goes from the LGF to the 2nd floor. The upmarket St James's Restaurant on the fourth floor has step-free access.
The Fountain Restaurant is −12 steps from the GF, but only +1 from the entrance on the corner of Duke Street and Jermyn Street. **Wheelchair toilet (D100 ST80).** The Gallery Restaurant is +10 from the GF but step-free via a staff lift (D80 W120 L160). There are four more **wheelchair toilets**. All are spacious, but none are signed (except on the door). Staff members are very helpful, and will point you in the right direction:

- on the 1st floor **(D85 ST120)** to the right from the three lifts, and by a staircase;
- on the 2nd floor **(D80 ST100)** to the left from the single lift. There's a spacious BCF in the next room;
- on the 4th floor **(D80 ST110)** where the St James's Restaurant is
- on the LGF in the Wine Bar **(D85 ST80).**

Foyles
113-119 Charing Cross Road, WC2H 0EB *Tel:* 020 7437-5660
website: www.foyles.co.uk/book-shops-in-london
e-mail: customerservices@foyles.co.uk
A world-famous bookstore, which claims to have the widest range of titles of any bookshop in the UK. It also has a café, gallery and some in-store literary and music events.
Located on the corner with Manette Street.
Step-free entrance on Charing Cross Road. In Manette Street there is +1 step.
The shop is huge. It measures some 70m by 20m and is spread over five floors. There are two visible central lifts (D75 W90 L200) opposite the information desk that go to G, 1, 2, 3, but not B. A 'hidden' lift (D70 W100 L80) is situated in the stairwell around the right hand side of the information desk, this one allows access to all floors. The café on the 1st floor has a ramped entrance, and is then flat throughout. **Adapted toilet (D70 ST53)** doubling up with BCF, on the left hand side of the entrance of the café. Be warned that a considerable number of customers use this toilet, because it is convenient, even though there are clear signs asking people to use the toilets on other floors.

Hamleys
188-196 Regent Street, W1R 6BT   *Tel:* 0870 333-2455
website: www.hamleys.com
The world's largest toyshop is on seven floors. The shop is nearly always busy. There is flat access everywhere. It has central escalators. Two lifts (D105 W185 L145) on the left go to all floors. **Wheelchair toilet (D90 ST85)** on the fifth floor. Separate BCF alongside.

Harrods

87–135 Brompton Road, Knightsbridge, SW1X 7XL *Tel:* 020 7730-1234
website: www.harrods.com

A department store with a world famous reputation and an imposing facade.
It is said that you can buy anything - from a horse, to a house, to a hearse !
It is on the Brompton Road between Hans Crescent (which has been partially
pedestrianised alongside the store), and Hans Road. The SW1 postal boundary
goes all the way around the store. Valet parking is available.

The store is huge, and measures roughly 100m by 120m, spread over seven
floors. There are floor plans on the website, and printed plans are readily
available throughout the store. The various departments do move around, and we
were told that there's a new plan produced almost every month.

Harrods has a considerable problem in making the store fully and easily
accessible. It is a listed building resulting from combining two adjacent buildings
about a hundred years ago. There are a lot of level differences on most of the
floors, but fortunately, changing level is done mainly by ramps. There are,
however, some residual steps/split levels and the store plans do not (currently)
show where these are. You may therefore encounter some unexpected barriers.
Once inside, we found that the floor plans are quite difficult to follow, as they
don't show clearly enough where the through routes are, nor any of the internal
(or external) steps. In addition, it's easy to get slightly disorientated inside. Good
landmarks are the Egyptian Escalator, and the block of six lifts. **There seem to
be helpful staff everywhere. There are eleven different entrances:**

* **all those from the Brompton Road, from the pedestrianised Hans
  Crescent and from Basil Street, are step-free** (that is doors 3 to 10
  inclusive);
* down the Hans Road side there are +4 steps at door 2, a similar number just
  inside door 1 (though there's a platform lift to bypass these), and +3 at door
  11.

The main way of changing level is by escalator, but there are four groups of lifts,
although they're not always very easy to find !

The lifts are shown on the plans, and on the GF you can find them:

* by door 5, where there's a single express lift D90 W180 L250) going to
  floors LG/G/4 and 5. This is the only one going to the 5th;
* some little way in from door 3, where there are six lifts going to the floors
  from LG to the 4th;
* a little way in from doors 1 and 11 (but note the steps there) there are two
  lifts (D90 W250 L100) from the LGF to 4th, and these are the ones for
  getting to the LGF accessible toilet (see below);
* a little way in from door 10 there are two slightly smaller lifts going from the
  GF to the 4th.

When you're inside the shop, and on other floors, as we have said, the lifts can
be quite difficult to find. In addition, although many of the split levels in the shop

have been ramped, **there are some serious issues with steps**:
* just inside door 1 (although there's a well disguised platform lift); and,
* on both the 3rd and 4th floors, where you may have to go quite a long way around to bypass the steps.

It would be very helpful if these were shown clearly on the plan, together with the through routes on each floor. This would make moving around much easier, and we have suggested this to the management.

Note that at a number of the restaurants and café's the layout uses a bar with tall stools, not suitable for everyone. The best route to the Georgian Restaurant on the 4th floor (for a fancy afternoon tea among other things) is via the lifts near door 10.

There are several **wheelchair toilets**, though none are well signed:
* on the LGF, reached only by the lifts nearest doors 1/11. When we visited it was strictly only an **adapted toilet** as the ST space was restricted to W65 by the toilet roll dispenser on the wall. When we visited it was the other side of the Wines department;
* on the 1st floor near where door 3 would be, alongside a staff toilet (**D80 ST70**). Note that for the conventional mens and womens toilets in the middle of this floor there are steps (+3 or +2), and there are BCF by the womens;
* on the 2nd floor in the central area, not far from the six lifts, with a ramp to the accessible toilet which is by the mens;
* on the 4th floor, again in the central area, with a ramped accessible toilet by both the mens and the womens.

Harvey Nichols

109 Knightsbridge, SW1X 7RJ *Tel:* 020 7235-5000
website: www.harveynichols.com/stores/london
e-mail: contactknightsbridge@harveynichols.com
Exclusive store known particularly for ladies' outfitting. There are some general departments, together with a comprehensive food store and eating facilities on the 5th floor.

Located on Knightsbridge, and between Sloane Street and Seville Street and measuring just 50m by 50m, but on eight floors.

There's a step-free entrance from Knightsbridge, and two more from Sloane Street. Further down Sloane Street another entrance has +4 steps.

Visiting parts of the store is not as easy as perhaps it should be. The store guide listings are almost unreadable (because of the small font used). The building is bedevilled with split levels, particularly +4 steps to 25% of the GF, −1 and then −4 steps in either direction on level minus one, and ±lots of steps on level minus two. By contrast, most of the upper floors, including the 5th are step-free.

Signage is poor, and some of the staff don't seem to understand the question "How do I find the step-free route ?".

There are two lifts (D70 W120 L100) in the middle of the store and on the edge of the +4 split level. These go to all floors. In addition, there are two express lifts which only go from the GF to the 5th. These are in opposite corners of the store, and the one (D80 W130 L120) with step-free access is by the entrance from Sloane Street on the corner with Knightsbridge. The other one by an entrance from Seville Street involves ±3 steps (so be careful not to use this lift when you leave if steps are an issue).

On the 5th floor, part of the café area has movable chairs. The Yo! Sushi bar has one space where a chair user can slot in but it is very well hidden and is in the most difficult spot to get to. There's also a restaurant and bar nearby.

There's just one **wheelchair toilet (D80 ST75)** with BCF, and it's just outside the womens toilets near the bar on the 5th floor. For such a big store, this is a very minimal facility.

Hatchards

187 Piccadilly, W1J 9LE *Tel:* 020 7439-9921
website: www.hatchards.co.uk
e-mail: books@hatchards.co.uk

A smallish but well-stocked bookstore, the oldest surviving one in London, founded in 1797.

Located opposite the Royal Academy, and next to Fortnum's.

Flat entrance, and nearly all step-free, with a lift (D80 W105 L140) at the back of the store which goes to all five floors. On the 2nd and 3rd floors there are +2 steps to about 10% of the floor area.

Heals

196 Tottenham Court Road, W1T 7LQ *Tel:* 020 7636-1666
website: www.heals.co.uk

A store with a wide range of modern, designer and contemporary furniture and homewares. Located about 100m from Goodge Street tube station between Torrington Place and Alfred Mews.

Step-free at the entrance and throughout the store. Two lifts to the right from the entrance (D70 W105 L120).

Adapted toilet with BCF on the 1st floor, **(D80 ST70 but the inward opening door fouls the BC shelf behind it)**. To find it from the lifts, go forward about 20m, and then turn right.

House of Fraser

318 Oxford Street, W1C 1HF *Tel:* 0844 800-3752
website: www.houseoffraser.co.uk
e-mail: oxfordst@hof.co.uk

A department store situated between Chapel Place and Old Cavendish Street. It occupies an area of about 25m by 75m.

There's +1 (large) step at the entrance on the corner of Chapel Place, but the entrances from Old Cavendish Street are both step-free. Seven floors are reached via five lifts (D140 W170 L140) located on the Chapel Place side of the store. There's a **wheelchair toilet (D90 ST110)** and separate BCF on the 5th floor, on the Chapel Place side of the building.

House of Fraser
101 Victoria Street, SW1E 6QX *Tel:* 0844 800-3762
website: www.houseoffraser.co.uk
e-mail: victoria@hof.co.uk
This used to be known as the Army & Navy. Located by the junction with Artillery Row.
Step-free access from the entrances from Victoria Street, but +3 steps from Howick Place.
The store is flat throughout, and two lifts (D100 W200 L200) link all four floors (LG, G, 1st, 2nd). On the 2nd floor near the lifts, there's an **adapted toilet (D70 ST40)** and a basic BCF with no running water. The toilet was well adapted for a disabled walker but would be a challenge for a chair user.

John Lewis
300 Oxford Street, W1A 1EX *Tel:* 020 7629-7711
website: www.johnlewis.com
Large department store located between Oxford Circus and New Bond Street (or more specifically, Holles Street and Old Cavendish Street).
It is on seven floors with flat or ramped entrances. It measures about 80m by 80m and is step-free throughout. Floor plans (rather small) can be downloaded from the website, and these are good at showing the lifts and accessible toilets.
There are central escalators, together with eight lifts (D115 W180 L155). From the main entrance from Oxford Street, four lifts are some 20m inside, if you go straight. They are nearer the Old Cavendish Street side of the shop. The other set of four lifts are at the back of the shop near Cavendish Square.
There's a Brasserie and a Bistro on the 3rd floor with flat access, and a ramp in one to access the balcony.
There are **wheelchair toilets** (correctly called and signed 'accessible toilets') on the:
*   1st floor, by the lifts and stairs to Cavendish Square
*   2nd floor, by the lifts and stairs to Cavendish Square
*   3rd floor, by the lifts and stairs to Cavendish Square, and just outside the womens toilet
*   4th floor just outside the parents room which has BCF; and
*   5th floor also outside a parents room where there are BCF.

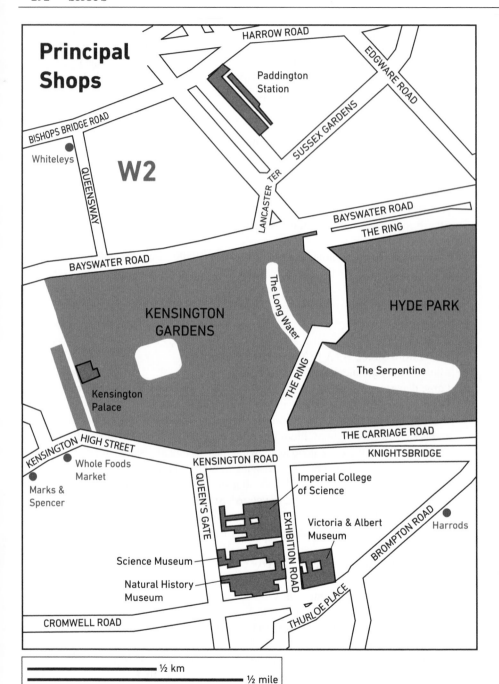

Principal Shops

HARROW ROAD

EDGWARE ROAD

Paddington Station

BISHOPS BRIDGE ROAD

SUSSEX GARDENS

Whiteleys

W2

QUEENSWAY

LANCASTER TER

BAYSWATER ROAD

THE RING

BAYSWATER ROAD

KENSINGTON GARDENS

The Long Water

HYDE PARK

THE RING

The Serpentine

Kensington Palace

THE CARRIAGE ROAD

KENSINGTON HIGH STREET

KNIGHTSBRIDGE

Whole Foods Market

KENSINGTON ROAD

Marks & Spencer

QUEEN'S GATE

Imperial College of Science

EXHIBITION ROAD

Victoria & Albert Museum

BROMPTON ROAD

Harrods

Science Museum

Natural History Museum

THURLOE PLACE

CROMWELL ROAD

½ km

½ mile

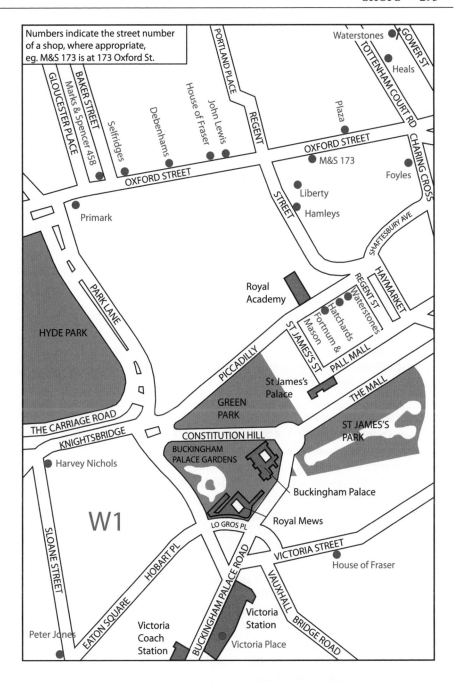

Numbers indicate the street number of a shop, where appropriate, eg. M&S 173 is at 173 Oxford St.

Liberty's

Great Marlborough Street, W1B 5AH   *Tel:* 020 7734-1234
website: www.liberty.co.uk
e-mail: londonstorecustomerservices@liberty.co.uk
A department store with wonderful character. Liberty designs and patterns are known the world over. Located just off Regent Street with its frontage starting at Kingly Street. It measures about 80m by 30m.
It is housed in a Tudor-style building with three atriums topped by glass lanterns. The central one has a series of magnificent oak panelled galleries.
There are three entrances. The one from the Kingly Street corner has +3 steps. The other two from Great Marlborough Street (GMS) are flat.
There's a store guide - which you would find useful if you are planning to look around several departments. When we visited, it was only easily available at the entrance from Kingly Street (with the steps).
The store is spread over six floors, and there are two pairs of lifts. The two larger ones (D100 W200 L200) are off the main central atrium and opposite the entrance from GMS. The smaller lifts which only take six people (D80 W120 L100) are located near the Kingly Street corner.
The store is flat throughout slightly cramped at times. The café on the 2nd floor has a ramped entrance.
There's a **wheelchair toilet (D80 ST80)** with BCF on the 4th floor. It is located on the Kingly Street side of the building by a big staircase. When exiting the central lifts, turn left, and go straight ahead.

Marks and Spencer (Kensington)

113 Kensington High Street, W8 5SQ   *Tel:* 020 7938-3711
website: www.marksandspencer.com
A large department store measuring about 40m by 70m on four floors. Located alongside the Kensington Arcade, outside High Street Kensington station.
It is step-free throughout. There are two lifts, both about half-way back in the shop on the left side. The smaller lift (D85 W105 L130) goes only to B/G/1st floor. The larger one (D130 W205 L245) also goes to the 2nd floor. There's a split level with ±3 steps on the 1st floor, bypassed by ramps alongside the escalators.
Wheelchair toilet (D85 ST105) and BCF on the 2nd floor, reached by turning left out of the lift, and then right, at which stage you'll see the signs.
A step-free exit/entrance on the GF leads to the station and into the Arcade.

Marks and Spencer (Pantheon)

173 Oxford Street, W1D 2JR   *Tel:* 020 7437-7722
website: www.marksandspencer.com
Large store measuring about 30m by 80m, located some 200m from Oxford

Circus towards Tottenham Court Road.

Step-free throughout via a single lift (D90 W130 L175) which is on the left about halfway down the store (on the GF).

There are **wheelchair toilets** and separate BCF:

* on the 1st floor on the opposite side of the building from the lift; and,
* on the LGF (the Food Hall). When you come out of the lift, turn right, right again after about 10m, and then they are signed.

Marks & Spencer (Marble Arch)

458 Oxford Street, W1C 1AP *Tel:* 020 7935-7954
website: www.marksandspencer.com

Large department store near Marble Arch, on the corner with Orchard Street. Has two entrances, one step-free from Oxford Street, and the other on the corner of Orchard Street with +2 steps.

It has five floors all accessed by two central lifts (D140 W190 L200) which are quite well hidden on the GF, but are near the escalators. The shop measures approximately 40m by 80m. There is step-free access throughout.

There are **wheelchair toilets**:

* in the basement, located in the far right corner of the store (from the lifts), and there are separate BCF;
* on the 3rd floor **(D90 ST80),** well hidden and almost opposite the lift exit, but go right, left and then left again.

Peter Jones

Sloane Square, SW1W 8EL *Tel:* 020 7730-3434
Textphone: 18001 + 020 7730 3434
website: www.peterjones.co.uk
customer services: 08456 049-049

Large John Lewis department store measuring about 100m long by 30m wide, with entrances on all sides. Most are step-free, including those from Sloane Square, Kings Road and Cadogan Gardens, but from Symons Street there are +2 steps. Most entrances have pairs of quite heavy double doors. Only the Kings Road entrance nearest Sloane Square has automatic doors.

Peter Jones has exceptionally helpful information for disabled shoppers on its website reached from the Home page, under Facilities and Catering on the side menu, then on the page headed Peter Jones Facilities, the fifth item is, Easier shopping for disabled customers. We summarise it here, because (compared with others) it's so good - providing a template for others to copy - BUT the page isn't easily found, even from the site Search facility.

Help with your shopping - just ask any of our staff, or contact our Personal Shopping Advisor in advance, on 020 7808-4201 or
email: PJ_personal_shopping@johnlewis.co.uk
Telephone shopping - Typetalk/Text Direct is available on 18001 + 020 7730 3434.
Hearing loops - please ask any of our staff for details about mobile hearing loops. Fixed loops are available at the Information Desk on the Ground floor and the Customer Service department on the Sixth floor.
Accessible parking - Kensington and Chelsea Council provides 2 spaces for BB holders in Cadogan Gardens, Kings Road end.
Accessible toilets - in the Basement, and on the Sixth floor near the restaurant.
Accessible fitting rooms - In Fashions, Lingerie and Menswear.
Wheelchairs for loan - For details please contact our Customer Collection Point on the Ground floor or ask any member of staff. To check availability please ring in advance.
Wide access lifts - available with access to all floors at the Sloane Square end of the shop.
Public telephone at accessible height - located at the Customer Collection Point on the Ground floor.
Large print or audio tape - please ask our staff if you need literature in alternative formats and we will do our best to provide it.

The store is huge, and spread over eight floors from the basement or LGF to the 6th floor.

Towards the Cadogan Gardens end there's a central open space with escalators going up in the middle, overlooked by surrounding balconies on each floor. There are two sets of lifts, both on the Kings Road side of the store. The first is more clearly visible, and from the Sloane Square entrance you'll find the four lifts (D135 W165 L145) on your left, just before the first Kings Road entrance. The second set of three lifts (D100 W115 L145) is more hidden, and they're alongside the other Kings Road entrance nearer to Cadogan Gardens. These do not go to the 6th floor.

The shop is step-free throughout.

There are **wheelchair toilets**:

• in the basement, using the Cadogan Gardens end lifts **(D90 ST100)** to the left coming out of the lifts
• on the 1st floor using the Sloane Square end lifts **(D85 ST80)** to the right coming out of the lifts
• on the 3rd floor to the right from the Sloane Square end lifts. In addition there's a parents room in the Nursery area with BCF, near the Cadogan Gardens end lifts

- on the 6th floor directly opposite the Sloane Square end lifts, **(D95 ST95)** with an inward opening door but a very large cubicle. There's a separate parents room with BCF nearby.

Plaza
120 Oxford Street, W1D 1LT   *Tel:* 020 7637-8811
website: www.theplazaoxfordstreet.co.uk
A small shopping centre in the shell of an old department store called Bournes. Step-free but slightly sloped main entrance. On two floors. The lift (D80 W80 L120) is on the left side of the building, and gives access to the Food Court on the 1st floor. Only about 20% of the seating is step-free and the rest involves +2 steps. The **wheelchair toilet (D85 ST90 NKS)** and separate BCF are on the 1st floor. From the lift, turn left, then left again, and they're about 15m more on your left.

Primark
499 Oxford Street, London W1C 2QQ   *Tel:* 020 7495-0420
website: www.primark.co.uk
Primark's largest store, near Marble Arch and measuring approximately 80m by 30m, located on the corner with Park Street. Flat entrances. On two floors, with two lifts (D90 W110 L175) located centrally at the back of the store. One was out of service when we visited. The store is very crowded and busy. There are no toilets for shoppers.

Selfridges
400 Oxford Street, W1A 1AB   *Tel:* 0800 123-400
website: www.selfridges.com
e-mail: customerservices@selfridges.com
One of London's biggest department stores. Each of the five floors measure roughly 180m by 80m. If you look up store location on the website you will find a good street plan for finding the CP and also the floor plans. Signage in the store is only moderately good, and is misleading in places. Copies of the floor plans are readily available, and although quite difficult to follow in any detail, they're better than nothing !
To get to the CP, use Wigmore Street, turn south into James Street, then right into Barrett Street, right again into Duke Street, then left into Edward Mews with the store on your left. Note that for the CP the Sat Nav code is W1U 1AT. Height restriction 2.3m. The CP is controlled by an attendant who will organise your parking when its busy, and BB holders can show their badge to enable their car to be parked conveniently. In 2011 the CP costs £7 for 2 hours and £23 for 8 hours, which is cheaper than other nearby CPs.
The seven storey CP has three lifts (D80 W130 L130) providing step-free access

to the shop from level G and level 3. Level 3, confusingly leads you to floor 2. There are entrances to the store on three sides, but the ones from Orchard Street are stepped (except into the Food Hall). There's a major difference in height/ level between Orchard Street and the main GF. At the central entrance on Oxford Street there are revolving doors, but there are conventional doors W80 on either side to bypass these. Other entrances have conventional doors. From the Food Hall, entered step-free on the Orchard Street side of the store, there is a minimum of –10 steps to get to the main floor level. These can be bypassed by using a platform lift (W80 L100), but this isn't well signed. There's a split level on the main GF involving +3 and –3–3 steps, all of which are bypassed by nearby ramps.

The main way of getting from floor to floor is by using the many escalators. The store has only two lifts (D120 W190 L150) located in the centre and near the main Oxford Street entrance. When we visited, one was out of action, resulting in quite long waits.

The café by the food hall and the restaurant by Duke Street have stepped access. The other seven eating places have flat access.

There are **wheelchair toilets** (most of which have nearby BCF, and all are unisex):

* on the LGF by the womens toilet on the Duke Street side of the store (the mens there has +4 steps)
* on floor 1 by the mens
* on floor 2 near the CP exit
* on floor 3 near the lifts, just outside the womens, and,
* on floor 4 just outside the womens, and again, near the lifts.

The toilets on floor 2 were very busy when we visited, and the quietest one was that on floor 4, but that'll vary from day to day.

Immediately opposite Selfridges main entrance on Oxford Street is a 24-hour Tardis-type **wheelchair toilet (D70+ ST70+ NKS)**, at the end of Balderton Street.

Victoria Place

115 Buckingham Palace Road, Eccleston Bridge SW1W 9SJ
Tel: 020 7931-8811
website: www.victoriaplaceshopping.com [not working when we went to press. We were told it was being revamped]

Two floors of shops and eating places built above Victoria Station with ramped access from Eccleston Bridge Road. From the station there appears to be only escalator access, but there is a lift (D110 W150 L220) to the first floor from halfway down platforms 13/14 (for the Gatwick Express). The platforms are open, so just walk or wheel down. At the upper level, you come out alongside the taxi rank, and to get to the shops, go a little way back (about 25m) along the rank and there are some doors on your left leading into the shops area. On the first floor, there's a good number of shops, virtually all with flat access. On the second floor there's a whole range of eating places including a number of fast food outlets, and a couple of restaurants. All have step-free access to some of their seating with movable chairs and tables. There are some places with high bar stools. On the 2nd floor, there's a **wheelchair toilet (D80 ST130 NKS).** Access to the second level is normally by escalator, but there is a service lift (D75 W100 L150) available. Use the intercom button at the bottom of the escalators (on the left) to contact security, or ask any shopholder to get hold of someone for you, and you'll be escorted to and from the lift.

Waterstones

82 Gower Street, WC1E 6EQ *Tel:* 0843 290-8351
website: www.waterstones.com
e-mail: enquiries@gowerst.waterstones.com
Europe's largest academic bookstore, located on the corner of Torrington Place. Two step-free entrances, and five floors of books. Two lifts (D80 W100 L135) one to the left of the Torrington Place entrance, and the other in the music section accessed from Gower Street. There's a café on the LGF, and there used to be an accessible toilet, but this has been taken out of use as it would have cost too much to refurbish.

Waterstones

203-206 Piccadilly, W1J 9HD *Tel:* 020 7851-2400
website: www.waterstones.com
A large bookshop located about 100m from Piccadilly Circus on the left, and past Eagle Place. At the entrance –5 steps are bypassed by a platform lift (D80 L120) to the right. On the GF there's a split level with –5 and a further –3 to the Jermyn Street entrance/exit. The –5 can be bypassed by using another platform lift, which also provides access to a small mezzanine.
All the other floors in the bookshop (floors 1 to 4) are accessed using the two central lifts (D75 W120 L140) from the GF. These provide the step-free link to the LGF with a café and a **wheelchair toilet** (which is protected by a keypad, so you'll need to get the number from a staff member).
The lifts also go to the 5th floor where there's a restaurant and bar, with a fine view from one end. There's another **wheelchair toilet (D80 ST100)** straight ahead from the lifts and just past the end of the bar on this floor.

Whiteleys

151 Queensway, W2 4YN *Tel:* 020 7229-8844
website: www.whiteleys.com
e-mail: info@whiteleys.com
Shopping and eating centre on three floors built in the shell of a once famous department store. The complex covers an area of approximately 150m by 50m. It contains a modern eight screen cinema.

The CP is approached off Queensway from Redan Place, and has ten BB spaces near the two entrances on the second floor. In 2011 it cost £1.50/h, and as it's a surface CP, it can accommodate vehicles up to 2.7m high.
There are three entrances from Queensway:
* one segment of the curved entrance at the Porchester end is step-free
* the middle entrance (where the lifts are) is step-free, and
* at the Redan end there's at least +1 small step [7cm].
There's flat/lift (D105 W200 L115) access inside. Note that there's a separate lift down to M&S from the CP. The site plans are good, but quite difficult to see from a chair users eyeline.
Shops are on the GF and 1st floors, the cinemas and restaurants are on the 2nd floor, while the 3rd contains offices. There's an easyInternet café on the 2nd floor. There are **wheelchair cubicles (D90 ST90)** and BCF in both the mens and womens toilets on the 2nd floor at the Porchester end of the building (at the opposite end from the cinema).

Whole Foods Market

The Barkers Building, 63-97 High Street Kensington, W8 5SE
Tel: 020 7368-4500
website: www.wholefoodsmarket.com
A huge market on two floors (GF/B), with a fascinating collection of cafés/bars on the 1st floor, housed in part of the old Barkers building. It measures about 40m by 50m and is located on the corner with Young Street.
It has a wide range of all kinds of organic and locally grown products, and the intention is to promote healthy eating. It had more than a hundred different olive oils - the largest collection that I've ever seen ! There was also a clear explanation of the outcomes for local communities in terms of health and education, from Fair Trade sales.
There are two lifts:
* a glass one (D90 W120 L300) near the centre of the store; and,
* an even larger one (D100 W200 L200) at the back.
The cafés/bars on the 1st floor have different styles, but all sell fast but wholesome food.
Much of the seating consists of high stools, but about 30% is at a conventional height with moveable chairs.
There are **wheelchair toilets**:
* on the GF at the back of the store, which includes BCF;
* on the 1st floor by the big lift at the back, where there are separate BCF in both the mens and womens areas.

The two Westfield malls

Two particularly big shopping malls opened during 2011 on either side of London, both with Shopmobility schemes. These are Westfield London at

Shepherd's Bush in the west, and Westfield Stratford City next to the Olympic Park at Stratford, in the east. Both have good adjacent bus stations. The Stratford one is linked to the accessible DLR, to the Jubilee line with many accessible stations and to NR services. The Shepherds Bush one has an accessible Overground station (but with a big step off the train).

They are significant because of their size and relative accessibility.

Westfield London

Ariel Way, Shepherd's Bush, W12 7GF *Tel:* 020 3371-2300
website: www.uk.westfield.com/london
e-mail: wlreception@westfield-uk.com

The Westfield shopping centre at Shepherd's Bush is huge.

The centre lies between Wood Lane and the West Cross Route spur to the A40, and between Shepherd's Bush tube station (where there's a new bus station) and White City tube (which also has a new bus station).

The Overground station is accessible by lift, but using the tube station involves escalators. It is regrettable that when the station exit was rebuilt to face Westfield no provision was made to incorporate a lift - presumably on the grounds of cost. When using Satnav, enter the postcode W12 7SL. The CP is off Ariel Way which is a new road (and roundabout) linking to Wood Lane on one side to the dual carriageway spur West Cross Route on the other. The UGCP can take 4500 cars on three levels with a height restriction of 2.15m. If you come by car then go to the Middle CP, where the Shopmobility desk is in Lift Lobby 2 at the end of Aisle 50 with 30 BB spaces. There is a substantial number of BB spaces on all levels, and the vacant ones are indicated by blue LED signs. To obtain four hours of free parking, BB holders need to go past the Shopmobility desk and get their ticket processed and stamped (Mon-Fri only). Alternatively there is a drop-off point on Westfield Way.

The centre covers an area measuring something like 600m by 400m with shops on two levels. It has several major department stores including Debenhams, Marks & Spencer and House of Fraser. It also has a wide range of restaurants, of upmarket shops and a multiplex cinema (Vue). In the middle of the main block there's a huge Atrium.

From an access viewpoint it's necessary to understand where the main blocks of lifts are, and where they go. There are plans at various places, and you can ask for a paper copy of the map/plan from the information points, and from the valet parking spot in Lift lobby 1 on the Middle level CP. You can also get one at the Shopmobility desk.

The information about the centre on the web is minimal.

There are **six wheelchair toilets** together with BCF on each main floor, and a *Changing places* facility by the *Shopmobility* office.

Westfield Stratford City

2 Stratford Place, Montfichet Road, Olympic Park, E20 1EJ *Tel:* 020 8221-7300
website: www.uk.westfield.com
e-mail: ukwscreception@westfield-uk.com
The Westfield shopping centre at Stratford is huge, measuring some 300m by
400m. It is on the edge of the Olympic park, between Stratford Regional and
Stratford International stations. It can be approached from the High Street side
via a long pedestrian bridge over the railway lines. Lifts bypass the steps. From
Stratford Regional station there are lifts to get directly to the shopping centre.
The three CPs have a total capacity for 5000 cars. CP A with nine levels is
entered from the A12 (follow the orange signs). It includes 14BB spaces near
the Shopmobility office (at the John Lewis/Waitrose end of the centre). CP B
is entered from the High Street and Warton Road, and CP C is entered from the
A112.
The centre is on four floors, but slightly bizarrely, the elevated level you reach
from the pedestrian bridge (over the railway) or from Stratford Regional station
is called the LGF. The other floors are the GF, 1st and 2nd, with shops and eating
places on most while the top floor has a multi-screen cinema with as many as 17
digital screens (contact Vue Tel: 08712 240240).
There are **wheelchair toilets** adjacent to the mens and womens toilets in three
blocks on each floor (LGF, GF and 1st). There are *Changing places* toilets (**NKS**)
in the middle of the avenue on the GF and 1st floors. If you need a key, contact a
staff member.
The website makes almost no reference to 'access' issues.

Shopmobility list

A Shopmobility scheme usually has an office with adjacent BB parking spaces,
and offers manual wheelchairs which can be borrowed or hired. Most also have
electric scooters which are particularly useful to elderly people who cannot walk
very far, or who find that carrying things is difficult. Some schemes can provide
volunteer escorts if necessary, some of whom are trained to guide people with
visual impairments. All require registration with proof of identity documents, and
for the scooters, some training is required before they can be used.
There may be an annual membership fee and/or a small hire charge each time
their equipment is used.
Opening times are variable, and depend both on demand, and on the availability
of staff. Opening is also dependent on the availability of volunteers, and of
finance. Some schemes open every day, others open for perhaps two or three days
a week.

They operate in areas where the local shopkeepers and/or shopping mall operators
provide much of the funding. However the nature of the shopping centre can vary
widely. For example:

- the Brent Cross centre is a separate 'dedicated' shopping mall, as are the two Westfield malls;
- in Ealing, the office is in a smallish covered mall while the main covered centre is across the road, and there's a whole range of shops along various surrounding streets;
- in Hounslow, the *Shopmobility* facility is in a new block next to a large Asda supermarket. The main covered mall is in the Treaty Centre about 500m away, and there are other shops in the High Street and elsewhere;
- in South Wimbledon the 'depot' for administering the hire of chairs and scooters is opposite an industrial estate, and the shops on Merton High Street are some 500m away.

Shopmobility schemes

We did a ring-around towards the end of 2011, and these were the ones we found and spoke to. Some of the numbers given will be where you can leave a message for them to ring back, if nobody is available to answer the phone at the time.

Bexley Heath, c/o The Bexley Accessible Transport Scheme
The Mall Shopping Centre (BHS End), The Broadway (off Albian Road),
DA6 7JJ *Tel*: 020 8301-5237
Brent Cross, Brent Cross Shopping Centre (by the North Circular Road),
Prince Charles Drive, Hendon, NW4 3FP *Tel*: 020 8457-4070
Bromley, The Glades CP (off Kentish Way), level 1 section B,
High Street, Bromley, BR1 1DN *Tel*: 020 8313-0031
Camden, Shopfront, 29a Pratt Street, NW1 0BG *Tel*: 020 7482-5503
Croydon, Whitgift CP (4th barrier along)
Wellesley Road, Croydon, CR0 2AG *Tel*: 020 8688-7336
Ealing, Units 19-20, The Arcadia Centre
Spring Bridge Road (off The Broadway), Ealing, W5 2ND *Tel*: 020 8579-1724
Edmonton, 4 Monmouth Road (end of Edmonton Green shopping centre),
Edmonton, N9 0LS *Tel*: 020 8379-1193
Enfield, Enfield Civic Centre, Silver Street, EN1 3XY *Tel*: 020 8379-1193 (it's a satellite scheme of Edmonton)
Epsom and Ewell, Ashley Centre CP, Ashley Avenue
Epsom, KT18 5BY *Tel*: 01372 727-086
Harrow and Wealdstone, 37 St George's Centre,
St Ann's Road, Harrow, HA1 1HS *Tel*: 020 8427-1200
Hillingdon, off Chippendale Waye, in the CP on 2nd floor,
Chimes Shopping Centre, Uxbridge, UB8 1GD *Tel*: 01895 271-510
Hounslow, Blenheim Centre, Prince Regent Road,
Hounslow, TW3 1NL *Tel*: 020 8570-3343
Ilford, Redbridge Disability Association, Exchange CP, The Exchange Mall
High Road, Ilford, IG1 1BY *Tel*: 020 847-6864

Kensington and Chelsea
Three days a week a truck with scooters will be at Queen's Gate, off Kensington Gore, near the Albert Memorial in Kensington Gardens. On the other days it will based at Kensington Town Hall and Sutton Estate, Chelsea.
Office and storage at: Westway Community Transport, 240 Acklam Road, W10 5YG *Tel*: 020 8960-9020
Kingston-on-Thames, Eden Walk CP, Union Street, KT1 1BL
Tel: 020 8547-1255
Lewisham, Unit 46/46A, The Lewisham Centre
Lewisham, SE13 7EP BB Parking on Rennell Street *Tel*: 020 8297-2735
Orpington, operated by VTB Mobility Limited,
266 High Street, Orpington, BR6 0NB *Tel*: 01689 837-800
South Wimbledon/Merton, operated by Scootability
High Path Resource Centre, 63 High Path, SW19 2JY *Tel*: 020 8648-1001/7727
Havering/Romford has two *Shopmobility* schemes operating quite near each other in different shopping malls
The Brewery, 1 The Brewery, Waterloo Road, RM1 1AU *Tel*: 01708 722-570
AND
Liberty Shopping Centre, RM1 3RL *Tel*: 01708 765-764
Sutton on Level 3 St Nicholas Centre CP
St Nicholas Way, Sutton, SM1 1AY *Tel*: 020 8770-0691
Walthamstow (CP off 45 Selborne Walk)
Selborne Walk Shopping Centre, Walthamstow, E17 7JR *Tel*: 020 8520-3366
Wandsworth, 45 Garratt Lane, SW18 4AD *Tel*: 020 8875-9585
Westfield London, Shepherds Bush (described above)
Tel: 020 3371-2401
Westfield Stratford City (described above)
Tel: 020 8221-7374

Entertainment

London offers an enormously diverse range of entertainment opportunities, including concerts of all kinds, theatre (both mainstream and fringe), cinema and comedy.

In previous editions of the guide we included an extensive section describing access to the various venues - including arts centres, cinemas and theatres.

Because fairly reliable information is now available elsewhere, we are only providing appropriate contacts, and a list (immediately below) of places where there are multiple venues with good access, and generally, nearby BB parking.

The O2 Arena is described in the chapter on *Places of interest.*

Because the book has grown so much, we are including descriptions on our website at *www.accessinlondon.org* of the access to:
*   the various South Bank venues;
*   the Barbican Centre;
*   Kings Place;
*   Stratford (with the Theatre Royal, the Stratford Circus arts venue and the Stratford East Picturehouse);
*   the Royal Opera House;
*   the London Coliseum; and,
*   the Royal Albert Hall.

Most of these meet the criteria above.

Gaining access to entertainment has become considerably easier over the years, although there's still room for improvement.

The DDA is something of a mixed blessing - mainly good, as it encourages people to do all kinds of things they would otherwise not have done, but it can be bad if it encourages the attitude "Well, we've met the required 'standard' (often poorly understood or explained)".

Widening the perception of 'access' to include provisions for those with hearing and visual impairments, and for those with learning difficulties is also a mixed blessing. The needs of those with a variety disabilities are, of course, of great importance. There is the need for loops or infra-red systems for hearing impaired people, and of BSL and other special performances. However, the inclusion of information on websites across all disabilities and the parallel extension of the training for 'Access information providers', means that much of the information is posted by someone who probably has no detailed understanding of what is involved. Even the people who answer a phone enquiry may/will have limited experience, and will be working from a 'script' on their computer screen. Most will, of course, be as helpful as they can.

A number of venues have *Access Membership Schemes* for booking 'accessible' spaces or seats, and people will need to negotiate directly with the individual venues if they want to join.
A relatively common concession in the price of entry is to include a free companion seat, as in many situations the disabled spectator is unable to get there/get in without a companion and facilitator. An example of this is the **Cinema Exhibitors Association Card**. It's a photocard renewed annually which (under certain conditions) gets your companion in free.
Contact the CEA at:
The Card Network, Network House, St Ives Way, Sandycroft, CH5 2QS
Tel: 0845 123-1292   *Textphone:* 0845 123-1297
website: www.ceacard.co.uk

The biggest ongoing challenge in relation to access to entertainment in central London is probably to do with parking and the transport system, together with the fact that some of the oldest venues were built long before 'access' was an issue.

Particularly for chair users, most venue managers now provide reliable data about the their facilities, and the person in the box office will probably be able to answer any queries accurately if you phone. That wasn't the case some years ago. There is nearly always provision for one or more chair users in the audience, generally with a nearby accessible toilet.
At some places the management want to maximise their revenue rather than provide the maximum number of chair spaces or the best view for a chair user. This may apply when it is necessary to remove a seat to accommodate a wheelchair.
Disabled walkers will have more difficulty in getting the information they may need, and hence appropriate seating. The data published in our earlier guides was insufficient in this respect anyway, and we don't have the necessary resource to make a comprehensive description for all of London's venues.
In many places, the best way for an ambulant disabled person to get an easily accessible seat is to book one which is on a level where there are wheelchair spaces. This should avoid internal steps, although it may be necessary to use a side entrance which might need to be specially opened. Note that most auditoriums have raked seating, with one or two steps between each row, and very few have handrails by these steps.

Cinemas
There are now a good number of cinemas with accessible screens throughout London, and we only mention here a few accessible multiplexes, some of which have adjacent parking.
There are ten Vue cinemas in London, see
www.myvue.com/vue-cinemas-in-london.

They include a cinema on Lower Regent Street with five accessible screens. Particular ones of interest with parking, include Westfield London (at Shepherds Bush), Westfield Stratford, and, further out, one at Acton. There are quite long distances between the parking and the cinemas at both Westfield centres.

There's the smaller and more compact Whiteleys complex in Queensway, with an attached MSCP, see *www.viewlondon.co.uk/cinemas/odeon-whiteleys-info-9223. html*.

If you require information regarding subtitles and audio description for cinemas visit *www.yourlocalcinema.com*.

Arts centres
The biggest centres are around the South Bank, and at the Barbican. All the venues there are basically 'accessible' but see *www.accessinlondon.org* for details.

On the South Bank, there's a whole variety, with the National Theatre complex, the British Film Institute centre and the concert halls known as the Southbank Centre, including the Festival Hall, Queen Elizabeth Hall and the Purcell Room. There is also the extensive London Wonderground which appears during the summer in temporary venues with sideshows, bandstands, food stalls, and sometimes roving performers. This is located between the Festival Hall and the London Eye.

The Hayward Gallery on the upper level, is described in the chapter on *Museums and galleries*.

The Barbican has, among other things, a concert hall, two theatres, three cinema screens a library and an art gallery.

All of these have relatively good, nearby/ish BB parking, and relatively good (if slightly confusing) access. If you're going to any of the venues for the first time, we suggest that you arrive there with plenty of time to spare, to allow for some 'exploration' !

There is a smaller arts centre at Kings Place, near St Pancras station, and several venues near to each other at Stratford. Parking is slightly more of a challenge but both are around 500m from an 'accessible' tube station.

Note also the generally excellent provisions made at the Royal Opera House, Covent Garden and those at the lower levels in the London Coliseum in St Martin's Lane. Parking near both of these can be a bit of a challenge.

Reliable information sources

For anyone with special needs, it is generally best to negotiate access with the venue management when booking. This is particularly true in places where seats have to be removed, which takes a little time. Fortunately for theatre going, the culture is such that booking in advance is quite normal. That is not quite so true for going to the cinema, where people are more used to taking decisions on the spur of the moment. However, the new multiplexes do offer disabled cinema goers much more choice about where they can go, and an environment where there are virtually no access difficulties.

Most venues provide for people who have impaired hearing. A good number of theatres now have infra-red systems and will lend you a headset, while cinemas tend to use induction loops.
There are occasional signed performances for deaf people; both SOLT and the venue concerned will have details.
For people who are visually impaired it is often best to sit at the front of the stalls. Chair users have to use the 'chair spaces' provided or transfer to a nearby seat.

Artsline have been information providers for more than thirty years, and now have an extensive database covering arts and entertainment venues. They have promoted the key message that access equals inclusion - which has been part of the Access Project (PHSP) *raison d'être* since the 1960s.
During this time, attitudes have changed enormously, and Artsline are partly a victim of their own success - in that because much of the information is now 'mainstreamed', it has become more difficult to fund their operation.
Their information is available online at: *www.artsline.org.uk* where there is a searchable database covering more than two thousand arts venues in London. Like that for Inclusive London (see below) it is not now consistently updated.

There's information in the **Direct Enquiries** directory at **Inclusive London** *www.inclusivelondon.com* but this is also not updated on a regular basis, and does not include a date when the information was last checked. It has a slightly eccentric listing under Entertainment, but it includes theatres and concert halls. The information is presented as a listing from a standard questionnaire, with no attempt at an intelligent description to make it easier to use.

Both the Artsline and Inclusive London information is presented in the form of a searchable database, now regarded as THE modern way to hold and provide data. Unfortunately, as is very common, there is no record of when the information was collected, nor whether it was supplied by the venue operator, or by an independent visitor. This (in our view) reduces its value, and there is a danger of old incorrect data lurking in the system, possibly for years.
With the Access Project data in the guide, it is at least clear when it was collected and published - and there's a page on our website for *Updated information.*

Shape Arts
Deane House Studios, 27 Greenwood Place, NW5 1LB
Tel: 020 7424-7330   *Textphone:* 020 7424-7368
website: www.shapearts.org.uk   *e-mail:* info@shapearts.org.uk
Shape is a disability-led arts organisation working to improve access to culture
for disabled people. It includes participation in a wide range of activities, mainly
in the London area.

Society of London Theatre (SOLT)
32 Rose Street, WC2E 9ET
Tel: 020 7557-6700   *Emergency helpdesk:* 08444 9999-999
website: www.solt.co.uk   *e-mail:* enquiries@soltukt.co.uk
SOLT is an organisation that represents the producers, theatre owners and
managers of the major commercial and grant-aided theatres in central London.
SOLT publish an excellent downloadable Theatre Access Guide - where they
have copied our style (from earlier editions), in providing information for both
chair users and disabled walkers about access to all parts of the theatre. It is
updated regularly.
SOLT do not, however, include information about the number of internal steps
involved in getting to a particular row of seats, nor of whether there might be
a handrail on the gangway. This would make the guide far too complicated,
but if you're booking seats, you need to ask when making a reservation. As we
said earlier, booking seats level with the wheelchair spaces, and using the same
entrance, should minimise the risk of encountering unexpected steps.
Visit the *www.officiallondontheatre.co.uk/access/* site, which also has
comprehensive lists of performances which are BSL interpreted, audio-described,
or captioned. They also list specially designed performances for people with
autism and other learning disabilities, under the Relaxed Performance Project.

Ticket agencies
**Some ticket agencies can book accessible seats/spaces, and the information
they provide can be generally helpful.** However, the person taking your call
when making a booking may never have been to the venue you want to visit.
We recently made enquiries from **Ticketmaster** about the accessible facilities
at Beating the Retreat on Horse Guards Parade in June. In the on-line section
relating to the event, we were offered the (slightly simplistic) choice between
various types of accessible seat:
*   wheelchair
*   mobility impaired
*   sight impaired
*   hearing impaired.
They have a dedicated phone line specifically for queries about accessible seating,
Tel: 0800 988-4440, and were helpful and reasonably informative when we spoke

to them. Mobility impaired walkers would have to say/explain in detail what they can do and what might be a challenge - like steps without a handrail, for example, or going a long way down a row past a lot of 'knees and bags' to get to a seat. The person taking the call said rather simplistically that a mobility impaired walker could sit anywhere they liked in the stands.

The other agencies that we looked at had no information on their website relating to booking accessible tickets.

At **Ticketline**, for example, you have to ring customer services *Tel:* 0844 888-4420, who may well refer you on to the venue involved.

At **eLondon tickets** you need to ring *Tel:* 020 7734-2088.

London Theatre Bookings *www.londontheatrebookings.com* advised us to go directly to each theatre to book an accessible seat/space.

The Really Useful Theatre group have a central booking system, *Tel:* 0844 412-4648 or *e-mail:* access@seetickets.com for booking accessible seats.

Sports grounds

researched and written by Alan Kerr
This chapter includes:
* an introduction, including information which is the same for virtually all the venues described
* detailed descriptions of the various sports grounds, some of which are used for concerts and other events
* a commentary with suggestions about how things need to change and progress
* contacts relating to participation in sport

As the guide was largely put together during the London Olympics year, this provided the background to an extended description of London's various sports grounds.

We have visited all the main venues for cricket, football, rugby and tennis, and collected the basic information about 'access'. Some of it was provided by the venues themselves, as it wasn't possible for us to test absolutely everything during our relatively brief visits.

We have, however, attended many events at lots of different venues over the years, including many of those described here. We have also talked to many people who use the various services and who have provided realistic feedback.
In this chapter, we have included the information available for hearing and/or visually impaired spectators, who have specific and clearly definable needs when attending events.

We unfortunately found that with a number of the venues, including several of the bigger ones, our phone calls and e-mails went unanswered. In many cases we had to be quite persistent before we managed to get through to someone who would really help with getting the information about access.

We have included a *Commentary*, AFTER **the detailed write-ups**
In this we assess some of the changes that are taking place, and make some suggestions for improving facilities in the future.
The organisation which is currently campaigning to improve attitudes and physical provisions at sports grounds, is:
Level playing field
The Meridian, 4 Copthall House, Station Square, Coventry, CV1 2FL
website: www.levelplayingfield.org.uk
Tel: 0845 230-6237 *e-mail:* info@levelplayingfield.org.uk
We hope that they will be able to take some of our comments and suggestions on board, and progress them in the future.

Information relating to nearly all the venues listed

Most of the grounds, particularly the football clubs, are located in built-up areas with residential streets all around, or they are in an industrial area. This makes coming by car and finding somewhere to park quite challenging at many of them.

Parking is slightly easier at places like Wembley, Twickenham and Wimbledon, though it is almost certainly wise to book a space in advance.

However you travel, you should arrive in very good time, possibly early enough to make use of the on-site food and drinks outlets, and the toilets. You may have to be patient after the event to wait until the bulk of the crowd has dispersed.

Much depends on whether you are a regular visitor who has found ways to 'manage' or if you're going to a venue for the first time, possibly for a one-off event. Much also depends on whether the venue is going to be full. The big events like cup games and internationals and also some concerts, will attract capacity crowds. Some grounds are full or almost full for most events.

Several venues do NOT have nearby 'accessible' tube or rail links, so you are reliant on finding parking OR on using buses or taxis or, possibly, being dropped off by someone who will then go and find somewhere to park. We have tried to recognise this in our descriptions, and have included detailed bus information - which we haven't done in the rest of the guide. Remember that if you plan to use a taxi at any stage, you will be paying for both distance travelled and the time taken. It is almost certainly worth getting there before the roads get clogged up, and getting out of the cab as soon as you're close enough, because otherwise the cost will increase sharply !

OF COURSE not all the grounds/venues are sold out for every event, and for some things it is quite easy to get tickets, and to get/book BB parking nearby, and/or to travel without encountering massive crowds.

In this chapter we refer to **accessible toilets**, as they have not all been seen and measured. Nearly all would meet our criteria for being a **wheelchair toilet** although this is slightly dependent on when they were installed, as the design criteria have changed and improved over the years. Most big venues use the **NKS** (RADAR) key, which can often be borrowed from a steward if you don't have your own. You will almost certainly find it easier to have your own key (see the section on Toilets under *Specialised information*). Where venues don't use the NKS, the toilets are often occupied by people who can perfectly well use the conventional facilities, so having the special key works well.

Information which applies to almost every write-up

In connection with going to see some of the big events, the main hurdles are:

- getting tickets in the first place, and ensuring that the seats/space you are allocated is easily accessible for you. Note that most on-line booking systems don't define 'access' in any meaningful way

- coping with the fact that there may be thousands of people wanting to arrive, and later to leave, all at about the same time. The roads around may be clogged up, with possible road closures, parking may be well-nigh impossible (unless booked in advance), and public transport is likely to be overloaded
- All the wheelchair spaces and designated ambulant disabled person seats provided, have provision for a companion to sit alongside, or in a few cases, behind. Various price concessions are offered, and commonly, one person comes in free, as a necessary carer/assistant. We discuss some of the effects of this in the *Commentary* at the end. Disabled supporters of soccer teams normally have to 'register' to qualify for the concessionary prices (see below)
- generally, powered wheelchairs and scooters should not exceed 120cm in length (including footplates) or 70cm wide
- nearly all spectators who want to come with an Assistance dog need to negotiate appropriate seating (or arrangements) by ringing in advance
- the information about what might be described as 'easy access' seats for disabled walkers is generally very poor, and this subject is discussed in the *Commentary* near the end of this chapter. Where a stadium has a lift or lifts, the possible choice of 'easy access' seats is greatly extended
- Stewards are much more helpful and better trained than they used to be. Most will be disability aware to an extent - and unless greatly overstretched, stewards should be willing to assist with information, and possibly in getting refreshments where this is difficult
- Many more induction loops have been introduced at ticket offices and catering outlets etc, but as we had no facility for testing these, we have not generally mentioned them
- The shops and megastores at all the venues will tend to be very crowded when there's a big match/event taking place

To 'register' as a disabled spectator at the football clubs, you generally need to be receiving:
- Disability Living Allowance, Attendance Allowance or Mobility Allowance;
- be Registered Blind or Partially Sighted;
- or provide a personal letter relating to your disability from a doctor or hospital specialist.
Being a BB holder is not a sufficient qualification for registration.

One recent change in attitudes which is to be welcomed is that venue and event managers are becoming slightly more aware of the needs of disabled walkers (ambulant disabled people). These are people for whom distance can be an issue, and steps/stairs, especially where there is no handrail provided. Some need more leg-room, perhaps because of arthritic joints.
The change hasn't yet got very far, and in our discussions and

correspondence with grounds there was little recognition of the fact that there are probably **5 to 10 times as many disabled walkers** as there are **wheelchair users.** The number is principally because there are more elderly people in the population such as those with arthritis, with Parkinson's or with a number of other conditions affecting mobility.

Based on recent experience, both at Wembley and Arsenal, they are not taken into account at the planning permission stages of new developments.

We explore these issues further in the *Commentary* near the end of this chapter with some specific suggestions about what might be done.

Wembley Stadium

Wembley Stadium, Harrow, HA9 0WS
(Postal address) PO Box 1966, Wembley Stadium, SW1P 9EQ
Tel: 0844 980-8001   *Fax:* 020 8795 5050   Disability Tickets via main ticket office
website: www.wembleystadium.com
For access information go to: *The stadium→Stadium guide→Accessible info*
Stadium tours *Tel:* 0844 800 2755 or book via the website
Ground capacity 90,000
There are spaces for 310 wheelchair users, well distributed around the stadium, and 100 enhanced amenity seats for ambulant disabled spectators, and those with Assistance dogs.
There are lifts throughout the stadium.

Ground description
The new Wembley Stadium was built on the site of the 1923 'Wembley' and was opened in 2007. It is used for major football matches (of various kinds) as well as for concerts and other events. It is dominated by the magnificent Arch which can be seen from the London Eye some 20km away. The stadium is located in a mixed industrial and retail park area, and the main pedestrian approach is from Wembley Park station along the elevated Olympic Way, which is on a podium leading to the north side of the stadium.

The stadium is huge, with a circumference of something like 1km. You need to take this into account and allow plenty of time to find where you go in, and how exactly you get to your seat/s. Inside there are more than 20 lifts and 30 escalators.

There are plenty of stewards on event days, who will assist if required both inside and outside the stadium.

Travel
There are three nearby stations: Wembley Park (UG), Wembley Stadium (NR)

and Wembley Central (UG & O). All, now, are 'accessible'.
There are also National Express Coaches that run services direct to the stadium
from >20 major towns and cities across the UK. Check *www.nationalexpress.com*
for further information and see write-up on coach travel in the *Getting around*
chapter.
Wembley Park (Jubilee & Metropolitan) is some 600m from the stadium. There
is step-free access between platforms and the street. On the Jubilee line you need
to be in the back coach for step-free transfer if coming from the JLE end. You
need the front coach if coming from Stanmore. Lifts provide access from the
Ticket Hall to Olympic Way.
Wembley Stadium (NR, Chiltern Trains) is about 750m from the stadium. It is
not normally staffed, and to ensure that the ramp is available *Tel:* 08456 005-165
in advance.
Wembley Central (Bakerloo, *Overground* and NR) is about 1.5km from the
stadium. There is now lift access to the Bakerloo and *Overground* platforms.
There is an accessible shuttle bus service on some event days between Wembley
Park Station and the Stadium which should be booked in advance by telephoning
020 8838-1353 or via *www.brentct.org.uk.*
Bus routes which go nearby include the:
18 from Sudbury to Harrow Road going along the A404 Harrow Road within
800m of the stadium
83 from Golders Green to Ealing Hospital going along Empire Way past
Wembley Stadium station
92 from Brent Park Ikea to Ealing Hospital going along Empire Way and then
Engineers Way with a stop by the Olympic Way <400m from the Stadium
182 from Hatch End to Brent Cross shopping centre going along Empire Way
past Wembley Stadium station
206 from Kilburn Park to Brent (The Paddocks) going along part of Engineers
Way with a stop by the Olympic Way <400m from the Stadium
223 from Harrow to Wembley Central station going along Empire Way past
Wembley Stadium station
224 from Brent to Wembley Stadium station
297 from Ealing Broadway to Willesden bus garage going along Park Lane and
Wembley Park Drive and past Wembley Park station, all just over 1km from the
stadium
Parking
The stadium has two huge official CPs with good provision for BB holders at
a discounted cost. Places can be booked in advance and going via the Stadium
website, you reach the contractor CSP (Combined Service Provider) at
www.gotocsp.com. You can only make advanced bookings on-line but we were
told that there is usually adequate space, and it is possible to pay on arrival. The
lack of a pre-booking phone line is of concern, as not everyone is 'on-line'. From
the BB spaces in the official CSP CP, there are lifts to take you up to the podium

level, though there may be long queues to use these.
As with other big venues holding events, there are a number of independently
run CPs nearby. These include those run by *www.stadiumcarparks.com Tel:*
0845 834-0210 and *www.waspparking.com*, and there will be others. The CPs
tend to open 3 hours before the event, and to close down an hour after it finishes.
The WASP CP said that they don't have specific BB spaces, but have on many
occasions accommodated customers needing space for wheelchairs and vehicle
ramps.
**For the big events, to get a space and also just to find your CP, get there
early**. From the motorway and from the North Circular Road, you are likely to
have to follow a busy and crowded one-way system to get to the CP entrance. If
you overshoot, it can be a long way round to get back in the queue, so go gently
and don't rush when you're nearly there.

Tickets for disabled spectators

There are two types of ticket at Wembley, and these are for General Admission
GA (with >70,000 seats) and Club Wembley (with 17,000 seats, including boxes),
which are bought on a 10-year license basis.
GA tickets are distributed according to the policy of the event organiser (eg the
Football Association, Football League, Rugby Football League, concert promoter
etc). For inter-club football games, tickets will be handled by the participating
clubs. You therefore need to contact your club's Disability Team or their ticket
office, making your access needs such as step-free access to seating, extra leg-
room or a wheelchair space, absolutely clear.
It is worth mentioning that if you have vertigo, some of the seating could be
unacceptably high up, particularly at level 5.
For music events, the tickets will be sold by a variety of outside agencies. It is
essential that you make your needs known when you book tickets. Many agencies
have specialist teams that deal with disabled clients, but some will have less
understanding or local knowledge.

Spaces for wheelchair users

There are 310 wheelchair spaces, all with a companion seat alongside. They are
spread out around the stadium. Their location on levels 1, 2 and 5 is shown on
the stadium plans on the website. Powered wheelchairs and scooters should not
exceed 120cm in length (including footplates) or 70cm wide. There are no storage
facilities.

Entrances for wheelchair users

The appropriate entrance will be shown on your ticket. They are well signed, and
located near lifts that take you to the upper levels.

Ambulant disabled spectators

Wembley has 100 what it calls 'enhanced mobility seats' for people who are
able to walk but have limited mobility or are visually impaired. There are spaces
for people who bring an Assistance dog (with two dog "toilets" on the outside

concourse on the podium on Level 1). Being a brand new stadium, slightly more leg-room has been provided, and there are some seats which can be accessed via just +3 steps, with a handrail. You will need to ask for these specifically. Because there are some lifts, there will be a good number of 'easy access' seats, but these have not been properly recognised.

Visually impaired spectators

An event commentary is provided via headsets that can be booked in advance by e-mailing *accessforall@wembleystadium.com*. Football matches have a full commentary.

Hearing impaired spectators

All the information desks have induction loops.

Catering

There are 688 food and beverage service points. Each has a position for disabled customers.

Toilets

There are >2,500 toilets on all levels, including 147 **accessible toilets (NKS)**. There's a *Changing places* facility on Level 1 of the internal concourse, Block 104 **(NKS)**.

Stadium store

The shop in located on Level B1 by the East Ticket Office and is reached via a flight of stairs in the north of the stadium in front of the main reception. The shop is accessible via the Olympic Way ramp or via lift 5 on non-event days. When there's an event, there are alternative outlets within the stadium.

Stadium tours

These take place during the day when there are no major events taking place (see the website) and that they can easily be made step-free by the use of various lifts. The approximate distance involved from the ticket office is about 750m, and remember that you need to add the distance from the Green CP, or from Wembley Park station.

CRICKET

Lord's

Lord's Cricket Ground,
St John's Wood, NW8 8QN *Tel:* 020 7616-8500
website: www.lords.org
For access information go to: *Lord's→Visitors with disabilities*
e-mail: reception@mcc.org.uk
Ticket office *Tel:* 020 7432-1000 *e-mail:* ticketing@mcc.org.uk
Tours *Tel:* 020 7616-8595 *e-mail:* tours@mcc.org.uk
Ground capacity 28,800
There are dozens of wheelchair spaces, and lifts in the Grand Stand and Mound
Stand.

Lord's is widely regarded as the home of cricket and is owned by the Marylebone
Cricket Club. It is also the home of Middlesex County Cricket Club, the England
and Wales Cricket Board, and the European Cricket Board.
It is also the base for the MCC Cricket Academy, The MCC Library and the MCC
Museum that exhibits the Ashes Urn and the Wisden Trophy.
Ground description
The ground is in a residential area quite near Regent's Park. The area around is
generally flat. The ground which has stands going all the way round, has been
mostly rebuilt since 1987. Only the Pavilion and Allen Stands are older. During
major matches the upper tier of the Allen Stand is treated as an extension of The
Pavilion and is therefore open only to members.
There is a good plan of the ground on the website (under *Lord's→Lord's map*).
Travel
The nearest 'accessible' tube stations are KingsX/St Pancras, and Green Park, and
both are about 4km away. The nearest station is St John's Wood in Wellington
Road, just over 1km from the ground. However, access to the platforms is via
escalators or about 100 steps.
The bus routes passing nearby include the:
6 from Willesden bus garage to Aldwych
13 from Golders Green to Aldwych
46 from Lancaster Gate to Farringdon
82 from North Finchley to Victoria
98 from Willesden bus garage to Holborn
113 from Edgware to Marble Arch
139 from West Hampstead to Waterloo (which is 'accessible' on both NR and the
JLE)

189 from Brent Cross to Oxford Circus (and goes near Marylebone NR station)
274 from Lancaster Gate to the Angel Islington, and
414 from Maida Vale to Putney Bridge.
Parking
There is no parking available at the ground. Passes for setting down and picking up can be issued. Contact the MCC Club Facilities Department on *Tel:* 020 7616-8653 for information about nearby car parking.
On major match days there is a park & ride scheme from a nearby CP, usually at Quintin Kynaston School, Marlborough Hill, NW8, but we haven't managed to establish whether the vehicles used are 'accessible'.
There is a UGCP in Kingsmill Terrace, NW8 6AA with 200 spaces, just over 1km from the ground. On match days there is a flat fee for entry. Height limit 2m.

Tickets for wheelchair users
Applications must be made through the MCC Ticket Office.
Spaces for wheelchair users
There are three areas/enclosures - in front of the Mound and Warner Stands, and in the rear of the (covered) lower Grand Stand. The front areas have movable seating, and are on the grass. The Grand Stand area has' fixed/allocated' spaces with an adjacent seat for a companion.
Entrances for wheelchair users
For the Mound Stand use the East Gate. For the Warner and Grand Stands use the Grace Gate. Both are on St John's Wood Road. Using the North Gate in Wellington Place is another option.
Ambulant disabled spectators
Ambulant spectators should make their requirements known when booking. The Ticket Office has identified seats where there are few steps en route, and easy access to toilets.
Visually impaired spectators
A commentary is provided for every major match. Headsets are available from the Head Steward's Office at the back of the Mound Stand (*Tel:* 020 7616-8592 to book).
Hearing impaired supporters
An induction loop in the Grand Stand links in to the Radio5 live commentary on matches.

Catering
The Extra Covers Food Area has level access and the Lord's Tavern Bar and Brassiere (by the Grace Gate) are reached via ramps. There are ramps to reach the bars in the Grand Stand. There are also various food outlets around the ground.
Toilets
There are six **accessible toilets (NKS)**, all on the GF at the:
Pavilion (by the North Door entrance); Mound Stand; Warner Stand; North Clock

Tower; Grand Stand East; and Grand Stand West.
Club shop
There is a large shop located to the right of the East Gate in St John's Wood Road. Step-free.
Ticket office
There are daily ticket outlets by the North Gate in Wellington Place and another one by the Grace Gate. Disabled spectators are recommended to get their tickets in advance to ensure that they are seated somewhere that meets their needs.
Tours
The stadium tours are accessible although they involve something like 1km distance. There is lift access in the Pavilion, The Media Centre and The Grand Stand, and, if it's not being used for a function, the famous *Long Room* is included in the tour.

The Oval

The (Kia) Oval
Surrey County Cricket Club, Kennington, SE11 5SS
Tel: 0844 375-1845 (*& Ticket Office*)
website: www.kiaoval.com *e-mail:* enquiries@surreycricket.com
For access information go to: *Tickets→Accessibility (on the menu at the bottom)*
DisEnq: 020 7820-5735 *e-mail:* dda@surreycricket.com
Tours *Tel:* 020 7820-5750 *e-mail:* enquiries@surreycricket.com
Ground Capacity 23,000
There are nearly 40 spaces for wheelchair users, and the following Stands have a lift: OCS, Bedser, Pavilion and Lock&Laker.

Ground description
The Oval has been a cricket ground since 1845. It is the home of Surrey County Cricket Club and is a regular Test Match venue. It is located near the Thames in a heavily built-up area which is generally flat. There has been an ongoing rebuilding plan since 2002.
It hosts a variety of matches and events, some of which are sold out a long time in advance.
Travel
The nearest 'accessible' station is Waterloo, with NR and the JLE, or Westminster on the District line. Both are nearly 2.5km away. The nearby Oval and Vauxhall stations both have a substantial number of steps.
The bus routes in the area include the:
3 from Crystal Palace to Oxford Circus;

59 from Streatham Hill to Kings Cross;
133 from Streatham to Liverpool Street;
159 from Streatham to Paddington Basin
all of which come up the Brixton Road and past Kennington within about 500m from the ground. The 59 also goes past Waterloo station while the 133 goes past London Bridge.

In addition, the **333** from Tooting Broadway to Elephant and Castle, comes up the Clapham Road, and past Kennington Park within about 300m of the ground.

Parking
There is some BB parking available for 'lesser' fixtures at the Oval if booked well in advance. Contact: *DDA@surreycricket.com*. Street parking is very restricted.

Tickets for wheelchair users
Applications should be made through the Ticket Office *Tel:* 0844 375-1845.

Spaces for wheelchair users
Due to the recent major rebuilding in the ground there are 39 spaces for chair users that are scattered all around. These include 28 in the uncovered enclosures in Blocks 1, 12, 13 and 20; covered balconies in the OCS Stand and some in the Pavilion Terrace for Members.

Entrances for wheelchair users
The entrances are clearly signposted all around the ground.

Ambulant disabled spectators
The Ticket Office has identified areas of the ground where there are limited steps and easy access to the toilets.

Visually impaired spectators
There is a commentary provided via Radio London Online. The public address system gives updates of key moments and scores from other matches.

Hearing impaired spectators
There are induction loops in a number of the stands. Check when booking.

Catering
There are a wide range of food outlets around the ground, many with lowered counters and induction loops. Staff are willing to help if necessary.

Toilets
There are a good number of **accessible toilets (NKS)** distributed throughout the ground. These include - the Lock & Laker Stand (GF); The Pavilion (GF front, 2nd & 3rd floors); Bedser Stand (GF & 1st floor); and more than ten in the OCS Stand on various floors, and off the Concourse.

Club shop
There is a large shop with onsite parking on non-match days via either the Hobbs or the Alec Stewart Gates.

Ticket office
The Ticket Office is located by the Hobbs Gate

Stadium tours
Stadium tours can be step-free, and involve a total distance of about 800m, starting from the Hobbs Gate.

FOOTBALL

All the grounds have an official website, but the presentation of information about access and about ticketing for people with disabilities is highly variable. This is partly because each is designed by a different web designer, with no particular understanding of, or focus on, the needs of disabled spectators.
As with all venues, on major event days, get there early. For big matches, surrounding roads may be closed as much as an hour before kick off. They may remain closed until the bulk of the crowd has left.

Arsenal (in the Premiership in 2012/13)

Arsenal FC, Emirates Stadium, Highbury House, 75 Drayton Park, Islington, N5 1BU
Tel: 020 7619-5003 Ticket Office *Tel:* 020 7619-5000 *Fax:* 020 7704-4161
website: www.arsenal.com *e-mail:* contactafc@arsenal.com
For access information go to: *The club→Disabled supporters* and/or to: *Emirates stadium→Disabled access on non-match days*
Disability Tickets (via main ticket office) 020 7619-5050
e-mail: disability@arsenal.co.uk Stadium Tours *Tel:* 020 7704-4504
Arsenal Museum *Tel:* 020 7704-4507

Ground Capacity 60,361
Space for 241 wheelchair users
There are lifts all around inside the ground.

Ground description
The Emirates Stadium opened in 2006. It was designed in the same way as the new Wembley, and disabled spectators are spread out around the ground with lift access to the upper levels. It is located on a former industrial estate and between two rail lines going north which merge just before Finsbury Park station. There are houses on all the other sides. It is only about 0.5km away from the old ground at Highbury.
The new stadium sits on a podium above ground level, with lift access to all the main areas. There are two long ramps for getting up on to the podium. One is to the right of *The Armoury* (Megastore) and the flight of 40 steps, by the

roundabout between Hornsey Road and Benwell Road. The other is from Drayton Park, near Martineau Road, via a bridge over the railway line. The other bridge from Drayton Park nearer Arsenal tube station involves ±50 steps.
From ground level, there is lift access to the podium via the Media Entrance, which is to the left of *The Armoury*, mentioned above.

Travel
Apart from using buses and taxis, the Emirates Stadium is difficult to get to for those with mobility problems, although BB holders may be able to park nearby, if they're lucky (see below).
The nearest tube stations (Arsenal, Highbury & Islington and Finsbury Park) all involve between about 25 and 40 steps. Caledonian Road on the Piccadilly line is the nearest 'accessible' station. It is nearly 1.5km away. Upper Holloway on the *Overground* is around 2km and is also 'accessible'.
The website has particularly useful bus maps under *Tickets/Getting to Emirates*, with both a local and area map as separate pdfs.
Numbers **4, 19** and **236** stop on Highbury Grove
The **4, 153, 271** and **393** all stop on Holloway Road by the junction with Liverpool Road.
The **29, 253, 254** and **259** all stop on the Seven Sisters Road.

Parking
There are 100 BB spaces within the stadium. Most are reserved for season ticket holders but it is worth asking the Disability Team in case there is an available space. Street parking is strictly controlled, but BB holders can park in residential and meter bays without time restriction IF they can find a space. There are a number of schools in the area that provide parking facilities without pre-booking. If you want to find/book somewhere, *www.stadiumcarparks.com* may be able to help, or possibly *www.parkatmyhouse.com/uk* though any CP is likely to be some way away. *http://en.parkopedia.co.uk/parking/info/parking_by_emirates_ stadium/* had helpful and realistic advice.

Tickets for wheelchair users
Disabled supporters must register with the Club to get tickets, and book through the Disability Team. The form filling and procedures take a little while. Away supporters must book through their own club.
Spaces for wheelchair users
The 241 wheelchair spaces are located on the Club/Lower/Upper Level Tiers. 12 spaces are for Away fans. All the Boxes are 'accessible' but for wheelchair users the view is poor, as they have to stay at the back.
According to the *Level Playing Field* website, there are about 70 wheelchair spaces available on a match by match basis.
Entrances for wheelchair users
There are accessible entrances all around the Stadium at Podium Level. There is a way in from street level via the Media Entrance to the left of the Ticket Office and

Armoury Shop. There are 8 lifts to take supporters to the Upper Tiers (including Club and Box Levels).

Ambulant disabled spectators
Disabled walkers can use either the standard turnstiles, or the designated 'disabled persons' entrances that are clearly signed. Ask a steward if you require assistance. If you are arriving at the ground from Drayton Park the first access point to the Podium Level has two flights of stairs, so go down further to the large concrete Arsenal sign opposite Martineau Road where there is step-free/ramped access.

Visually impaired spectators
There is a commentary during the matches for visually impaired supporters; contact the Disability Team for further details on how to access it. In addition Arsenal produces an audio copy of the match day programme which is available from the Disability Team.

The Emirates Stadium has a toilet for Assistance Dogs located near the Arsenal Museum at the northern end of the Podium Level.

Hearing impaired supporters
The Stadium has induction loops at various customer contact points such as the Ticket Office, shops, Museum and Receptions along with the conference areas and meeting rooms.

Catering
All bars and food outlets have lowered counters that are suitable for wheelchair users, staff will assist if necessary although this will be more problematic during busy periods such as just before kick - off and half time.

Toilets
There are 113 **accessible toilets (NKS)** spread around in the stadium, including a *Changing places* facility in Block 48 on Club level.

Club shop
There are two Club Shops at the Stadium; *The Armoury* and the *All Arsenal Store* on Drayton Park. *The Armoury* is located on the Hornsey Road side of the Stadium and is the most accessible as it is all on one level unlike the *All Arsenal Store* where there is a platform lift down to the Supporters Support Centre where tickets for the museum can be booked.

Ticket office
The main ticket office by the Armoury is accessible with lowered counters and induction loops.

Tours
Arsenal offers both self-guided tours, with an audio guide - and what are called Legends Tours, where you are taken around by an ex-player, and possibly a very famous one. The tours and the museum are all step-free (some of it via internal lifts). The total distance involved is something over 1km if you include the museum. There are, however, places where you can sit and relax en route, and

you might give the museum a miss.
The Museum is in a building at the north end of the podium.
Note that if you come by car there may be quite a long walk/wheel to get to the
tours entrance. The museum is in a separate building off the podium near the
stepped footbridge to Drayton Park. The museum is accessed from the podium
via a lift and has an **accessible toilet**. It is probably worth booking your tour in
advance.

Brentford (in League One in 2012/13)

Brentford FC, Griffin Park, Braemar Road, Brentford, TW8 0NT
Tel: 0845 3456-442 *Fax:* 020 8568-9940 *e-mail:* enquiries@brentfordfc.co.uk
website: www.brentfordfc.co.uk *e-mail:* tickets@brentfordfc.co.uk
For access information go to: *Tickets→Disabled facilities*
Ground Capacity 12,763
There are 12 wheelchair spaces (which need to be booked in advance).
Note that on match days, general entry is by cash only, paid at the turnstiles.

Ground description
Brentford's stadium is located in a flat, residential area, and built on the site of
a former brewery. It claims to be the only ground with a pub on every corner.
The Braemar Road Stand has been renamed as the Bees United Stand, but is still
referred to by its original name. None of the stands has a lift.
Travel
There are two 'accessible' stations which are relatively near: Brentford (NR,
<1km), and Acton Town (District and Piccadilly), ~2km. Neither has a black cab
rank, but both have minicab offices. The Brentford one is up on the bridge, some
400m away.
Nearby bus routes include the:
267 which goes from/to Hammersmith bus station, with good 'accessible' tube
links.
65 from Ealing Broadway to Kingston, via Richmond, which is an 'accessible'
station (NR and District line).
Both the **E2** and **E8** go within 500m, on the Boston Manor Road.
Parking
Street parking only. There's a pay and display CP off Layton Road. The
surrounding roads aren't closed before or after matches.

Tickets for wheelchair users
Chair users should apply in advance, as there are only 12 spaces.

Spaces for wheelchair users
The spaces for both "home" and "away" supporters are in the SW corner of the Bees United Stand, level with the pitch, and close to the players' tunnel.
Entrance for wheelchair users
The entry is clearly signed in Braemar Road.
Ambulant disabled spectators
Should contact the Ticket Office to discuss their access needs.
Visually impaired spectators
There are 14 seats in the Bees United Stand where a commentary is provided via headsets. Book in advance.
Hearing impaired spectators
There are no specific facilities for those with hearing impairment.

Catering
There are refreshment facilities in the concourse in the Bees United Stand behind the wheelchair spaces.
Toilets
There are two **accessible toilets** by the catering facilities in the Bees United (Braemar Road) Stand concourse.
Ticket office and Club shop
This is located in Braemar Road.

Charlton Athletic (in the Championship in 2012/13)

Charlton Athletic FC, The Valley, Floyd Road, Charlton, SE7 8BL
Tel: 020 8333-4000 *Fax:* 020 8333-4001 *Textphone:* 020 8333-4094
Ticket office *Tel:* 0871 226-1905 *Textphone:* 020 8333-4093
e-mail: tickets@cafc.co.uk
website: www.cafc.co.uk *e-mail:* disability@cafc.co.uk (though not for ticket enquiries)
For access information go to: *Fans→Disabled supporters.* The DLO is contacted via the main club number.
Ground capacity 27,111
Includes 96 wheelchair spaces (8 in the away end)

Ground description
The Valley is in a residential area, about 1km SW of the Thames Barrier. The area around the ground is, as the stadium name suggests, quite hilly. Floyd Road leading up to Charlton Church Road is particularly steep. Note that you cannot walk all around the ground, and there are pedestrian routes on only three sides. Three of the stands have a lift, the East, North and the West.

Travel
Charlton NR station is less than 500m away, and is 'accessible' with a lift on the London bound side, and step-free access to Troughton Road on the other. There's an **accessible toilet NKS** on the platform with the lift. Southeastern Trains come from London Bridge.
North Greenwich tube station on the JLE is more than 3km away, but with good bus links. These include the **161, 472, 486**, all of which go along the Woolwich Road, to the north of the ground, and the **422** which goes along The Village, further to the south.
Other bus routes along the Woolwich Road include the **177**, and the **180**. The **380** goes close to the ground down Charlton Church Lane, while the **53**, the **54**, and the **486** all go to the south through The Village.
Parking
The Club has two CPs, with about 40 BB spaces. *Tel:* 0871 226-1905 to see if there's a spare space. 2 BB spaces are kept for Away fans. Additional spaces may be available at the Fossdene School, Victoria Way, SE7 7NQ nearly 1km away. Landsdowne Mews (off Charlton Lane) has a number of unreservable BB spaces. Parking in the streets around the stadium is strictly controlled. There are road closures on match days.

Tickets for wheelchair users
Booked through the Ticket Office. Away supporters must book through their own club.
Spaces for wheelchair users
There are spaces on top of the North Stand (level 4) in both the East and West corners, reached via lifts. Spaces are available at pitch-side on the West Stand, and at the back of the East Stand. There are 7 spaces in the away end, in the Jimmy Seed (South) Stand. All are under cover except for the pitch-side seating. The location of these spaces is shown in yellow on the Ground Plan on the website (which is well hidden under *Club→The Valley* where there's a link right at the bottom of the page).
Entrances for wheelchair users
All are clearly signed, but you need to know which side of the ground you are going to. The entrance to the West Stand is at the southern end. To get into the East Stand, go via Landsdowne Mews, which is up a hill at the SE corner. This leads to a long ramp up to the spaces. The North Stand spaces are reached via lifts on the east and west corners, and the away end via a gate by the main turnstiles in Valley Grove, with step-free access to the mid-tier seating.
Ambulant disabled spectators
There are 12 seats in the West Stand for home supporters with further seating in rows A and C that are step-free in the lower tier. In the Jimmy Seed stand away supporters should ask for row P which is also step-free. The lifts in the North Stand should provide easy access to more rows of seats.

Visually impaired supporters
12 headsets with a commentary are available, and should be booked in advance.
Hearing impaired supporters
No facilities were noted.

Catering
There is a trolley service for the West Stand pitch-side spectators, but there'll be more choice in the concourse, reached via the Press Room by turnstile 22. Just go straight through. On both corners of the North Stand, a staff member will get drinks etc from the concourse on level 2.
Toilets
There are eight **accessible toilets (NKS)** - by the entrance to the West Stand (2), the top corner of the East Stand, next to the main toilets in the Jimmy Seed Stand, and by the lifts in both corners of the North Stand (2 each)
Club shop
The Charlton Superstore is by the NW corner, with D85 and step-free throughout.
Ticket office
Located in the West Stand to the left of the main entrance with 'accessible' windows.

Chelsea (in the Premiership in 2012/13)

Chelsea FC, Stamford Bridge, Fulham Road, SW6 1HS
Tel: 0871 984-1955 *Ticket Office:* 0871 984-1905
DisEnq: DLO 020 7915-1950 *Fax:* 020 7565-1462
e-mail: disability@chelseafc.com
website: www.chelseafc.com
For access information go to: *Tickets→Disabled tickets→Disabled supporters FAQ* which we were assured will tell you everything you need to know (Hmmmm...!)
Ground capacity 41,841
There are 110 spaces for wheelchair users, including 10 for away fans.
Both the East and West Stands have a lift.

Ground description
The Stamford Bridge site has been completely redeveloped and includes a hotel, a museum and a music venue, as well as the rebuilt stadium. It is in a high density residential area, and although relatively flat, there are some quite steep short slopes that run along the East Stand towards the Museum entrance.

Travel

The nearest 'accessible' station is Fulham Broadway (District) about 500m away with a big step on/off the train. Earls Court (District and Piccadilly) is about 2km away. West Brompton on the *Overground* is just under 1.5km via the Brompton Cemetery, or nearer 2km via North End Road.

Buses which all go past the ground include the:

14 from Putney Heath to Warren Street, and via Green Park tube station

211 from Hammersmith bus station to Waterloo station (both with 'accessible' tube links)

414 from Putney Bridge to Maida Vale

Note that there are road closures near the ground, but our informant was reluctant to tell us what exactly is involved. We suspect that the Fulham Road will be closed outside the ground with traffic re-routed via King's Road.

Parking

Parking is extremely difficult. There is limited parking at the stadium (*Tel:* 020 7915-2981 to enquire about space) and very limited Pay&Display street parking.

Tickets for wheelchair users

It appears that tickets are issued only to registered disabled members. To apply for membership, contact the club by either an e-mail to *disability@chelseafc.com* or via *Tel:* 020 7915-1950 requesting an application form. Proof of disability is required. There seem to be three schemes, Season tickets (with tickets for all the matches); Match Membership (applying to come to specific matches) and Rota Membership, whereby you are allocated tickets for matches on a rota basis. All these tickets are free, including those for a companion (see general comments in the introduction to the chapter).

Away supporters need to apply for a space through their own ticket office.

Spaces for wheelchair users

Most of the spaces are pitch-side in the West Stand but there are a couple of areas that are elevated in the corner of the East Stand.

Entrances for wheelchair users

These are clearly marked for both home and away supporters.

Ambulant disabled spectators

Chelsea have a similar registration procedure for ambulant disabled supporters as for wheelchair users. For those needing a PA to accompany them, and/or an Assistance dog, they must advise the Club when registering. People may also have specific needs like more leg-room, proximity to a toilet, and step-free or nearly step-free access.

Certain spectators will qualify for with them of any specific access needs to ensure that they are allocated suitable seats. There are some relatively easy access seats near the chair spaces. For disabled walkers applying for tickets through the Ticket Office, note that there are lifts in some of the stands, but you may need to ask for a lift pass. Then you can request a seat accessed by a minimum number of steps, and/or near a toilet etc.

Visually impaired spectators
There are headsets available that supply commentaries, reserved using the *DisEnq* contacts. They work all over the ground.

Hearing impaired spectators
There is an induction loop in the West Stand for announcements.

Catering
The main concourses all have refreshment concessions that are 'accessible'.

Toilets
There are **five accessible toilets (NKS)**. 3 are in the West Stand concourse, 1 in the East Stand and 1 outside the Megastore. Make sure that you bring your own RADAR key.

Club shop
The Chelsea Megastore is on the SW corner of the stadium with a short walkway from the entrance to the site on the Fulham Road. It is step-free.

Ticket office
Located at the Shed End, to the right of the Megastore.

Crystal Palace (in the Championship in 2012/13)

Crystal Palace FC
Selhurst Park Stadium, Whitehorse Lane, Crystal Palace, SE25 6PU
Tel: 020 8768-6000 *Fax:* 020 8771-5311 *Ticket Office:* 0871 2000-071
website: www.cpfc.co.uk *e-mail:* boxoffice@cpfc.co.uk
For access information go to: *Tickets→Disabled information*
DisEnq: 020 8768-6080 (for Special Needs Coordinator SNC)
Ground capacity 28,309
There are 56 wheelchair spaces.
None of the stands has a lift.

Ground description
The stadium is located in a residential area and has been partially updated with two newish stands. The area is hilly in places with a steepish slope, for example, on Whitehorse Lane.

Travel
The nearest 'accessible' station is East Croydon, just over 4km away. The nearer stations at Norwood Junction, Selhurst and Thornton Heath, all involve access difficulties. The Tramlink stops are all more than 2.5km away.

A number of bus routes that run close to the stadium including the:
50 from Croydon to Camberwell, via Whitehorse Lane, about 500m away

X68 from West Croydon to Russell Square (with limited stops). It stops some 250m away

75 from Croydon to Lewisham stops some 250m away

157 from Morden to Crystal Palace bus station via Park Road

196 from Elephant & Castle to Norwood Junction which is about 800m away

198 from Thornton Heath to Shrublands, with a stop some 500m away

312 from South Croydon bus garage to Norwood Junction (800m) , via East Croydon station

468 from Croydon to Elephant & Castle via Tramlink stops including Wellesley Road. It goes along Whitehorse Lane and stops some 250m away

Parking

Parking around the ground is difficult. There are some "pay and display" areas with a limit of up to 4 hours. Make sure that you check the parking regulations. There's a CP for the Sainsbury's in Whitehorse Lane with some BB spaces, but it gets filled up very quickly.

Tickets for wheelchair users

Book via the SNC *Tel:* 020 8768-6080 or e-mail *boxoffice@cpfc.co.uk.*

Spaces for wheelchair users

There are 28 spaces for home supporters in the Holmesdale Road Stand and a further 28 for away supporters in the Arthur Wait Stand. Both areas are pitch-side and slightly elevated.

Entrances for wheelchair users

There is an entrance half way along the Holmesdale Road Stand at Gate 1. Away fans should head for Entrance 6 near the turnstiles at the corner of the Arthur Wait and Croydon Advertiser Stands.

Ambulant disabled spectators

Contact the SNC giving the necessary information about your needs (for example if you find steps difficult, or you need extra leg-room etc). This is important as both the Arthur Wait Stand and the Main Stand have wooden seats with little leg room. Another factor, particularly in the Arthur Wait Stand, is that it is not steeply banked so supporters tend to stand until ordered to sit down by officials and if you are at the back apparently the roof overhang obscures the view along with the occasional pillar.

Visually impaired spectators

There are 20 seats for visually impaired supporters with headsets providing a radio commentary.

Hearing impaired supporters

There is no induction loop but the SNC can assist with seating and advise on radio coverage.

Catering
The refreshment facilities are in the Holmesdale Road Stand. Getting there and back at half-time can be a major challenge !
Toilets
There are **four accessible toilets**, two by Gate 1 in the concourse of the Holmesdale Road Stand **and another two** behind the wheelchair spaces in the Arthur Wait Stand. None require a RADAR Key, so they tend to be used by non-disabled supporters, and are not strictly monitored by stewards.
Club shop
Located in the corner between the Croydon Advertiser and Main Stands. It has a ramp to bypass the −3 steps to get in.
Ticket office
This is situated by the club shop and is readily 'accessible'.

Fulham (in the Premiership in 2012/13)

Fulham FC
Craven Cottage, Stevenage Road, SW6 6HH
Tel: 0843 208-1222 *Fax:* 0870 442-0236 (Motspur Park)
Ticket Office: 0843 208-1234
website: www.fulhamfc.com *e-mail:* enquiries@fulhamfc.com
On the website the information for disabled visitors is quite difficult to find, and it is under *Tickets→Booking tickets FAQ*, and a long way down the page you find *Disabled fans*
DisEnq: 020 8336-7477 for the DLO *e-mail:* disability@fulhamfc.com
Ground capacity: 26,600
There are 40 wheelchair spaces, 9 of which are for away supporters.

Ground description
Craven Cottage is located alongside the Thames and the original cottage (a royal hunting lodge with a 300-year history) has been incorporated into the ground. The area around is flat and is entirely residential. A riverside development is planned, to increase the ground capacity to 30,000, and this will include a lift and some more wheelchair spaces. The Club is unusual in that it has a 'neutrals' area at the Putney end, although this is without 'accessible' seats.
Travel
The nearest 'accessible' tube station at Hammersmith is just over 2km away. This has its 'accessible' bus station on top. It is on the District, Piccadilly and H&C lines, but there are big steps into and out of most of the trains. Fulham Broadway (District) is also 'accessible' and is about the same distance away. Putney Bridge station is the closest, but has >40 steps.

The buses which go down the Fulham Palace Road some 500m away, include the:

74 from Putney to Baker Street, past Earls Court station

220 from Wandsworth to Willesden Junction via Hammersmith bus station

430 from South Kensington to Roehampton

The **424** goes from Putney, across the bridge and around Fulham, past the Town Hall and along Lillie Road to the ground. It will stop a little way short on match days.

The **190**, **211** and the **295**, go along Lillie Road within about 1.2km from the ground.

Parking

Parking is strictly controlled on match days and there are road closures on match days.

The Club provides a limited amount of BB parking, booked in advance with the DLO. This is at the Fulham College Boys School, in Kingwood Road, SW6 6SN. There is a fully accessible shuttle bus to get to and fro on matchdays.

Tickets for wheelchair users

These are booked through the ticket office for 'registered' disabled supporters.

Spaces for wheelchair users

There are spaces at either end of the lower Johnny Haynes stand (11 in Block KL and 6 in Block AL). There are 14 spaces in Block S of the Riverside Stand, and 9 at the Putney End (Block P7) for away supporters. All are approached step-free from ground level.

Entrances for wheelchair users

For Block KL use the Cottage Main Gate, for Block AL use Gate 50 and for Block S use the Riverside Gate. Away supporters should head for Gate 1.

Ambulant disabled spectators

Block KL is the area that is best for ambulant disabled spectators as there is step-free access to the front, and an accessible toilet close by. There are other seats at the front which can be reached step-free.

Visually impaired spectators

Headsets are available with a match commentary. Book through the DLO.

Hearing impaired spectators

There is an induction loop in the main reception of Craven Cottage and at all the catering outlets. At the time of our visit there were two members of staff who could use BSL so ask a steward if you need to contact them. As with all organisations staff come and go, so check with the DLO to find out if they are still available.

Catering

There are fixed and mobile catering facilities around the stadium, some with accessible counters.

Toilets
There are **accessible toilets (NKS)** by all the disabled spectators' areas.
Club shop
The main club shop is at 959 Fulham Road, SW6 5HY, some distance from the
ground and towards Putney. It has steps to get to both upper and lower levels. A
second store at Craven Cottage also has steps to its lower level. On matchdays
there are two mobile units which are more accessible.
Ticket office
Located by the Cottage.

Leyton Orient (in League One in 2012/13)

Leyton Orient FC, Matchroom Stadium, Brisbane Road, Leyton, E10 5NF
Tel: 0871 310-1881 *Fax:* 0871 310-1882 *Ticket Office:* 0871 310-1883
website: www.leytonorient.com
For access information go to: *Fans→Disabled Supporters*
Tel: the DLO via the main number (0871 310-1881), but as the club is quite
small, this isn't always answered, so you may have to be persistent
e-mail: info@leytonorient.net
Ground capacity: 9,271
There are 61 wheelchair spaces. None of the stands has a lift.

Ground description
The Matchroom Stadium is located in a residential area with narrow surrounding
streets with room for only one vehicle to pass when cars are parked on opposite
sides of the road. Three sides of the ground have been rebuilt since 1999 leaving a
modern compact stadium. The area around is fairly flat.
Travel
The nearest 'accessible' station is Stratford, about 2km away. This is the biggest
accessible hub in London with step-free links between NR lines, the DLR, JLE
and Central line. The nearest underground station is Leyton, but this involves
nearly ±30 steps.
**There are a number of bus links with stops less than 600m away. Two are
from Stratford station:**
The **97** and **158**, both go from Stratford bus station
The **69** goes from Canning Town to Walthamstow with nearby stops
The **308** goes from Clapton to Wanstead with a stop at Oliver Road
Parking
There are 3 BB spaces in Club's CP reservable in advance through the DLO.
There are 2 BB spaces in Brisbane Road near the junction with Windsor Road
and at least two more in Windsor Road. Note that Buckingham Road which runs
along the South Stand has no vehicular access.

Tickets for wheelchair users
Booked through the Ticket Office *Tel:* 0871 310-1883 or by contacting the DLO
Spaces for wheelchair users
There are 23 spaces in the West Stand and 16 in the North Stand. The 22 spaces in the East Stand are generally for away supporters, but sometimes these spaces are shared
Entrances for wheelchair users
The gate in Brisbane Road by Turnstile A provides a step-free route to the East Stand concourse and to the North Stand. The other entry point is the ramped entrance in the SE corner of the ground.
Ambulant disabled spectators
There are a number of seats close to the wheelchair spaces that can be reached with a minimum number of steps, and you can ask to be allocated one of these when you book.
Visually impaired spectators
Guide Dogs are welcome but contact the DLO in advance so that arrangements can be made.
Hearing impaired spectators
There were no facilities at the time of our visit but we were told that they are planning to install an induction loop at one of the ticket office counters.

Catering
The facilities are quite close to the seating areas but do not have dedicated counters for disabled spectators. but stewards are willing to help if required.
Toilets
There are two **accessible toilets**.
Club shop
The club shop is part of the West Stand in Oliver Road has a ramped access.
Ticket office
Located in Oliver Road next to the Club Shop.

Millwall (in the Championship in 2012/13)

Millwall FC, The New Den, Zampa Road, SE16 3LN
Tel: 020 7232-1222 *Ticket office:* 020 7231-9999 *Fax:* 020 7231-3663
website: www.millwallfc.co.uk
For access information go to: *Tickets→Disabled info*
e-mail: tickets@millwallplc.com
DisEnq: 020 7740-0512 or *e-mail:* gray@millwallplc.com
Ground capacity 20,146
Space for 78 + 17 wheelchair users
There's a lift in both the East and West stands.

Ground description
The New Den was completed in 1993 so it is a modern stadium where disabled access has been considered during the building process. It is located between two railway lines that run to London Bridge. The area around is fairly flat.

Travel
The club is particularly difficult to get to using accessible transport. At the nearby stations like South Bermondsey and New Cross Gate there are steps. The nearest 'accessible' stations are Canada Water and New Cross, both 2 to 3km away, while London Bridge is even further.

The only bus to go past the ground is the P12 which goes from Surrey Quays Shopping Centre via Canada Water station to Peckham and Honor Oak Park

Other bus routes getting within 1.5km of the ground, include the:

21 goes from Lewisham, some 300m from New Cross station, and, later, via London Bridge station. It goes along the Old Kent Road about 750m from the ground,

47 from Shoreditch to Catford, going past London Bridge and Canada Water stations, and getting within just over 1km, at Surrey Quays station

53 from Whitehall to Plumstead, via Westminster

171 from Holborn to Bellingham, gets within 1.5km

172 from St Paul's to Brockley Rise, via Waterloo station

177 from Peckham to Thamesmead goes within 1.5km, past New Cross and Deptford DLR stations

188 from Russell Square to North Greenwich station, via Waterloo and Canada Water stations, and then through Greenwich

Parking
There are 10 BB spaces available disabled home supporters and 1 for an away supporter. Reserve in advance through the DLO.

Tickets for wheelchair users
Tickets should be booked in advance although it is often possible just to turn up on the day. Contact the DLO for further information.

Spaces for wheelchair users
There are 78 spaces for both home and away supporters in the West Stand, plus 17 spaces at pitch level for away supporters at the front of the lower North Stand. This area is not covered and you risk getting hit by wayward shots at goal !

Entrances for wheelchair users
There are two entrances at Gates W1 and W14. There is a lift available to the right of Gate W1, and to the left of Gate W14. Access to the lower North Stand is through Gate W1.

Ambulant disabled spectators
If you make your needs clear, you can be allocated 'easy/easier access' seats near where the lifts can take you.

Visually impaired spectators

If visually impaired supporters sit in the disabled area of the West Stand they can bring an assistant free of charge. There are no facilities for guide dogs at the time of writing. Millwall is experimenting with supporters using their own headsets to listen to the commentary running from the Club's website.

Hearing impaired spectators

There are induction loops at designated windows at the ticket office.

Catering

Refreshments are available through the concessions on the ground and upper tier concourses.

Toilets

There are **three accessible toilets**, at each end of the wheelchair platform in the West Stand, with the third one in the corner between the West and North Stands for supporters in the Lower North Stand.

Club shop

The shop is in Bolina Road, close to the West and North Stand. It has step-free access.

Ticket office

The Ticket Office has counters with induction loops and ones at a suitable height for wheelchair users.

QPR (in the Premiership 2012/13)

Queens Park Rangers FC, Loftus Road Stadium, South Africa Road, W12 7PJ

Tel: 020 8743-0262   *Ticket Office:* 08444 777-007   *Fax:* 020 8749-0994

website: www.qpr.co.uk

For access information go to: *Tickets→Disabled tickets*

DLO contact *e-mail:* jond@qpr.co.uk

Ground capacity 18,682

There are 24 wheelchair spaces. None of the stands has a lift.

Ground description

The Loftus Road Stadium is small and compact, and located in a flat residential area. The advantage of such a small ground is the proximity to the pitch for all the fans which helps build 'atmosphere'. The stands are of traditional design with relatively few seats accessible without steps.

Travel

The nearest 'accessible' stations are at Wood Lane (H&C) and Shepherds Bush (*Overground*) 1to1.5km away. Hammersmith (District, Piccadilly and H&C) is just under 3km, while Willesden Junction (*Overground* and Bakerloo) is about

4km away. There are nearly 30 steps at the nearest station at White City.
From Hammersmith you could take the H&C line to Wood Lane (which is just
under 1km from the ground) or take one of several buses, or even take a taxi to
close to the ground.
The new Westfield Shopping Centre which is a major bus terminus and has a
large CP with multiple BB spaces, is about 1 to 1.5km away.
**Nearby bus routes include those along the Uxbridge Road; along Wood
Lane; and going to Westfield:**
Two bus routes (the 228 and 283) go past the ground, but are diverted on match
days. Many more go close, on the Uxbridge Road, or on Wood Lane.
72 from Roehampton to East Acton,via Hammersmith
95 from Southall to Shepherds Bush station, past White City station
207 from the Hayes bypass to White City, along the Uxbridge Road, to Loftus
Road
220 from Wandsworth to Willesden Junction, via Hammersmith
228 from Maida Vale to the Central Middlesex Hospital, down Ladbrook Grove,
and via Shepherds Bush station, down South Africa Road, past the stadium (see
above comment)
237 from Hounslow to the White City bus station
260 from Golders Green to White City, via the Uxbridge Road, stopping at Loftus
Road
272 from Chiswick to Shepherds Bush Green via White City station
283 from Barnes to East Acton via Hammersmith (see above comment)
C1 from Victoria to White City bus station
Parking
There may be some limited parking at the stadium with up to 6 BB spaces.
Contact the DLO. Because the area is a CPZ and is almost entirely residential,
parking nearby is difficult. The Westfield shopping centre is a possibility, though
it is nearly 1.5m away.

Tickets for wheelchair users
Tickets should be booked through the ticket office. To 'register' and qualify for
the concessionary rate, contact the DLO. Away supporters should apply through
their own club.
Spaces for wheelchair users
There are 24 spaces in the Paddocks in the South Africa Road Stand, East (Block
GL) and West (Block AL), as well as some in the Ellerslie Road Stand (Block X).
3 spaces in the Ellerslie Road Stand are allocated to away supporters.
Entrances for wheelchair users
These are clearly marked for both home and away supporters along the entrances
in South Africa Road.
Ambulant disabled supporters
There are very few seats in the stadium that can be reached without going up

steps, and because of when most of the stands were built, the leg-room available in most of the seats is quite restricted. There is a row of step-free seats in the West Paddock (Row A), though they are very low down.

If you are in receipt of certain DWP benefits, and need someone to be with you to get in and out safely, then you may qualify for the same concessions as those available to wheelchair users.

Visually impaired supporters

There are 10 headsets providing a commentary, bookable in advance for use in the Ellerslie Road Stand

Hearing impaired supporters

There were no facilities noted at the time of our visit.

Catering

There are +4 steps from the Paddock areas to where refreshments can be purchased. In the Ellerslie Road Stand there is level access.

Toilets

There are two **accessible NKS toilets** , one in the South Africa Road concourse and the other in the Ellerslie Stand near the School End.

Club shop

The club shop is on South Africa Road near the School End. It is step-free.

Ticket office

The main office in the South Africa Road has +2 steps. On matchdays there are several windows accessed from the pavement, near the Club Shop.

Tottenham Hotspur commonly called Spurs (in the Premiership 2012/13)

Tottenham Hotspur FC, Bill Nicholson Way, 748 High Road, N17 0AP
Tel: 0844 499-5000 *Fax:* 020 8365-5005 *Textphone:* 0844 4777-462
Ticket Office: 0844 844-0102
website: www.tottenhamhotspur.com
For access information go to: *The stadium (on the bottom line menu)→Fans with disabilities DisEnq:* 020 8365-5161
e-mail: support@tottenhamhotspur.com
Ground capacity 36,240
There are 51 wheelchair spaces.
Only the North Upper Stand has lift access for spectators. Other lifts in the East and South Stand are only for the caterers, and the one in the West Stand goes only to the corporate areas.

Ground description

At the time of writing plans are in an advanced stage to build a new stadium with a capacity of around 56,000 on the site of the existing ground and on industrial land to the north. This would enable the club to improve its provisions for disabled spectators, particularly for disabled walkers. It is in a flat, largely residential area.

Spurs have a particularly well expressed policy relating to concessions for disabled spectators. It is "Supporters with disabilities, wheelchair user or ambulant, are required to pay the normal admission charges. Should they require the assistance of a PA, then the PA will be admitted free of charge".

Travel

The nearest 'accessible' stations are **Tottenham Hale** on both NR and the Victoria line, which is about 2km away, and **Northumberland Park** (NR Greater Anglia Trains from Liverpool Street) which is just over 500m away. White Hart Lane NR station which is some 400m away has ±>40 steps to/from the elevated platforms.

The bus routes that go past the ground on the High Road are the number:

149 from London Bridge to Edmonton Green

259 from Kings Cross to Edmonton Green

279 Manor House station to Waltham Cross, and the

349 from Stamford Hill to Ponders End

Bus routes that go within about 600m of the ground are the:

123, 243 and **W4** which both go along Birch Grove

341 from Waterloo station to Glover Drive, and the

W3 Finsbury Park via Alexandra Park to Northumberland Park station.

Unfortunately the buses passing Tottenham Hale are the **123** and the **W4** which only go part way to the ground.

Parking

The Club has just 13 BB parking spaces in their Paxton Road and West Stand CPs, which cannot be reserved. The CPs are closed an hour before kickoff. In the residential streets around, there's a CPZ preventing non-residents from parking on matchdays, although an exception is made for BB holders. It says on the club website that the CPZ finishes at 16.30 over weekends and bank holidays and at 20.30 on a weeknight, so it seems that the concession for BB holders for 3 hours parking should generally be sufficient. Check with the club if you're in doubt, but we were told that people have had no problems with BB parking.

Tickets for wheelchair users

All registered disabled supporters are able to bring an assistant with them.

For home tickets contact the DLO *Tel:* 020 8365-5161.

For away tickets, complete the online application form and email it to *support@tottenhamhotspur.com*.

Spaces for wheelchair users
The North Stand has 29 spaces in the lower tier, pitch-side and 6 in the upper tier. There are 16 spaces in the South Stand lower tier, of which away supporters have 5 spaces pitch-side.

Entrances for wheelchair users
The entrances are clearly marked from the Main Gate and around the stadium.

Ambulant disabled spectators
There are 8 designated seats in the North Stand lower tier for ambulant supporters, a further 10 in the South Stand and 17 in the West Stand lower tier. These areas provide step-free access using the same routes that chair users would follow ie bypassing the turnstiles and the steps, and see the note above on concessionary entry for a PA if needed.

Visually impaired spectators
The club provides a commentary via 22 headsets, booked in advance using *DisEnq*. Visually impaired supporters can sit anywhere, but would almost certainly prefer an 'easy access' seat.

Hearing impaired supporters
The ticket office has an induction loop and the club has a Textphone (see above).

Catering
The main concourses in the lower tiers of the North, South and West Stands all have 'accessible' refreshment concessions.

Toilets
There are six **accessible toilets (NKS)**. They are located close to the disabled seating areas. Four are in the North stand and two in the South Stand by the away end.

Club shop
The Megastore is fully accessible, as are the mobile units around the ground.

Ticket office
The Ticket Office located in Park Lane is 'accessible'.

West Ham (in the Championship in 2012/13)

West Ham United FC, The Boleyn Ground, Upton Park, Green Street, E13 9AZ
Tel: 020 8548-2748 Disability Tickets via main ticket office
Tel: 0871 222 2700
Fax: 020 8548-2757 (Disabled supporters only)
website: www.whufc.com
For access information go to: *Tickets→Disabled and visually impaired supporters*
DisEnq: 0845 217-1332 (for the DLO)
e-mail: disabledinfo@westhamunited.co.uk
Ground capacity 35,303
Space for 111 wheelchair users. There are lifts in three stands, Alpari (which was called Dr Martens), Bobby Moore and Centenary.

Ground description

The current stadium is located in a residential area just off the A124 Barking Road. The club has been playing there for more than 100 years. It lies between East and West Ham in an area called Upton Park - which is fairly flat. It is not possible to walk all the way around the ground because Priory Court is next to the Centenary Stand.

The club seems to have the opportunity to move to the Olympic Stadium in 2016, but at the time of writing this may still be subject to legal challenge from other clubs.

Travel

The nearest 'accessible' tube station at East Ham is about 1.5km away where lifts bypass the ±28 steps. Canning Town is also 'accessible' but is just under 3km away, and is on both the JLE and DLR. West Ham is slightly further. The nearest tube station is Upton Park, some 500m away, but with ±30 steps.

There are bus links from both Canning Town and East Ham. From Canning Town you can take a **5, 147** or **330**. From East Ham you can take a **104** or **376**. There's also the **104** from Stratford which has 'accessible links' to NR trains, the Central line, JLE and DLR.

Parking

There are 13 BB spaces on match days, usually all taken by season ticket holders. Away supporters should contact the DLO. The alternative is street parking but watch for match day and resident's bays restrictions. There is a drop off point for disabled passengers by the Alpari Stand.

Tickets for wheelchair users

Contact the DLO to register. The process can take four weeks. Proof will be required; a copy of the DWP letter confirming receipt of the high level of the mobility component of Disability Living Allowance is acceptable.

Spaces for wheelchair users

There are 111 wheelchair spaces, located in most parts of the ground with the exception of East Stand. There is lift access to reach the upper levels in all three stands, and ramps for the lower levels. The 6 away spaces are in the upper Centenary Stand.

Entrances for wheelchair users

The entrance points are clearly signed with entry points on Castle Street for the Bobby Moore Stand and the adjacent Alpari Stand. To get to the other end of the Alpari Stand and the Centenary Stand head for the left hand turret on the Alpari Stand. For pitch-side seats in the Dr Martens Stand head for Turnstile 38 where there is an adjacent entrance.

Ambulant disabled spectators

There are some 400 seats provided for ambulant disabled supporters, these are situated in both the Alpari Stand upper and lower tiers and the Bobby Moore lower tier. Lift passes are available by emailing *disabledinfo@westhamunited. co.uk* or from the Ticket Office.

This is a far better provision than that at most other clubs !

Visually impaired spectators

A commentary is provided through 22 headsets that should be booked in advance by emailing disabledinfo@westhamunited.co.uk. The headsets can then be collected from the Main Ticket Office on match days. Guide dogs are welcome in the stadium but you need to contact the club first to make appropriate arrangements.

Hearing impaired spectators

As well as one at the main Ticket Office, there is an induction loop in the main stadium to broadcast emergency messages.

Catering

There are dedicated refreshment facilities in the concourse of all the Stands.

Toilets

There are **twelve accessible toilets (NKS)** by all the designated disabled areas. On the upper levels the toilets are near the lifts. In the Alpari Stand lower they are in entrance tunnels.

Club Shop

The Club Shop is in the Alpari Stand by the left hand tower. The shop is step-free and there is plenty of room to move around although on match days it does get very busy.

Ticket Office

The Ticket Office is to the left of the Club Shop and has designated windows with induction loops and one lower accessible counter.

RUGBY

Twickenham

Twickenham Stadium, Whitton Road, Twickenham, Middlesex, TW2 7BA
Run by: **Rugby Football Union,** Rugby House, Rugby Road, Twickenham,
TW1 1DS
Tel: 020 8892-2000 *Fax:* 020 8892-9818
website: www.rfu.com/TwickenhamStadium
For access information go to: *Home page→Disabled access*
and via: *Tickets→Disabled ticketing (which includes booking BB parking)*
DisEnq: Tel: 0871 222-2017 (option 4) *e-mail:* disabledaccess@therfu.com
There's a variety of ways of obtaining tickets for different events. Some
accessible spaces/seats are booked via Ticketmaster 0844 847-2492, others are
obtained in ballots
Ground capacity 82,000
There are 336 wheelchair spaces, 272 at pitch-side and 64 in upper covered
terraces
Membership of the England Rugby Supporters Club or of a rugby club should
increase your chances of getting tickets for international matches

---

Ground description
The stadium is in a residential area in an outer London suburb just off the A316.
It was rebuilt between 1991 and 2005 and is an enormous structure with 7 lifts, 6
sets of escalators and 6,400 steps. It is used for international rugby matches and
big football games, as well as for concerts and other events.
On non-match days visitors gain access through to the Stadium via Gate F by the
Ticket Office on the SE corner in Rugby Road.
Travel
Since the parking provisions are good (see below) many disabled spectators come
by road.
Twickenham station (NR) is some 900m away. The nearest 'accessible' station
at Richmond (NR and District line) some 3km away. On matchdays there's an
'accessible' bus link to the ground.
There are National Express Coaches that run services direct to the stadium from
>20 towns and cities across the UK. Check *www.nationalexpress.com* for further
information, and see our write-up on coach travel in the *Getting around* chapter.
Buses that pass near the ground (within about 500m) include the:
267 Hammersmith (an 'accessible' station) to Fulwell
281 Hounslow to Tolworth
481 West Middlesex Hospital to Kingston

681 Hounslow to Teddington
Other bus routes pass through Twickenham centre, more than 1km away.
Note that the description of Twickenham on the National Rail Station Search website has been misleading and inaccurate for several months.
It said "Twickenham is fully accessible to wheelchair users. Access to platforms 4 and 5 is via a staff-operated stair lift. Please ask a member of staff for assistance. Access to platform 3 (for stopping services to London Waterloo and all Waterloo bound services on match days) is via the car park - please approach staff at the main entrance who will be happy to assist you."
The CP is in fact the other side of Platform 2, and the only access to any of the platforms is via about 25 steps.
When we rang NR Enquiries, they got through directly to the station, and we were told that access to and from platforms 2/3 was (for a wheelchair user) by using a Scalomobile-type tracked machine. It needs to be charged and operated by a trained member of staff. There is no direct access from the CP.

Parking
Parking is inevitably strictly controlled when there are big events, but there are a substantial number of BB spaces which can be reserved in advance. The North and West CPs are in the stadium grounds, and the Tesco CP is only 100m from the NW corner of the stadium.
Reservations can be made via the RFU eTicketing website, or by going to the RFU website and downloading a "Disabled Car Parking Form". If you have a problem, contact *carparking@therfu.com*. Even if you have a reserved spot, you're advised to get there early, as otherwise you may finish up further away, and using an unsigned and slightly uncertain route (a comment based on experience !).

Tickets for wheelchair users
The booking system varies, depending on the type of event. For International rugby matches the tickets are largely allocated via ballots for rugby club and England Rugby Supporters Club members. Each successful applicant for a wheelchair space will receive two tickets plus a CP place. For other rugby matches go to the Stadium's website where Wheelchair and Non-Wheelchair (Easy Access) booking forms can be downloaded.
For concerts and other events, the Stadium uses Ticketmaster to organise bookings.

Spaces for wheelchair users
There are a total of 336 spaces available with 272 at pitch-side and a further 64 in covered terraces.

Entrances for wheelchair users
There are clearly signed level entrances all round the stadium with lifts to the upper levels.

Ambulant disabled spectators
There are some 7,000 easy access seats for people who find stairs difficult to manage. They can be booked through the stadium for rugby matches, and via Ticketmaster for other events. This includes seats which can be reached step-free, some that can be reached via steps tthat have a handrail and some that have more leg room.
This sounds like the very best such facility that we have come across at any ground.
Visually impaired spectators
Visitors to events who wish to bring Guide Dogs must advise the stadium in advance using the *DisEnq* contacts.
Hearing impaired spectators
There are 100 seats that are linked to the hearing loop system for commentaries. Headsets can be booked in advance by emailing *disabledaccess@therfu.com*.

Catering
There are dedicated bars for disabled people at all the corners of the stadium with lowered counters; they tend to get crowded as they also are by the thoroughfares to reach the concessions outside which tend to be in portable, caravan style, outlets. Those concessions generally offer very little in the way of access but the staff are usually helpful and will come out to help pass food/drink etc.
Toilets
There are 13 **accessible toilets (NKS)**, including 2 in both the SE and NW corners, 1 each in the SW and NE, 3 in each of the corner terraces and 1 in the West terrace.
Rugby Store
The shop is located on the SW corner of the Stadium, and is step-free. It has a small CP with BB spaces approached from Whitton Road, and the main West CP is nearby. You buy tickets there for the Stadium Tour and for the Museum.
Stadium tours
The tours start at the Rugby Store, and end by the Museum. They involve a total distance of approaching 1km (including getting back to the store).
Museum
The Rugby Museum is in the East Stand, with lift access. Tickets are purchased in the Rugby Store. The Museum is split over two floors, with lift access. It has an **accessible toilet** on the upper level.

Ticket Office
The Ticket Office is located on the SE corner of the Stadium, and has lowered counters and an induction loop.

TENNIS

Wimbledon

The All England Lawn Tennis and Croquet Club
Church Road, Wimbledon SW19 5AE
Tel: 020 8946-2244 for ticket information, 020 8971-2473 for ticket enquiries
and 020 8944-1066 for other business
website: www.wimbledon.org
The Ground Capacity is enormous, and play takes place on about twenty
courts. Spectators can also view the Big Screen from the hill. There are
four 'show' courts with more then 30,000 seats - on Centre (15,000), No 1
(10,000), No 2 (4,000) and No 3 (2000).
There are 28 wheelchair spaces on Centre Court, Court 1 has 40 spaces, No 2
has 20 and No 3 has 10.

The world's most famous tennis tournament takes place here for two weeks
towards the end of June, and there are other smaller events on the site during the
year.

An unusual feature at Wimbledon is that some of the seats on the show courts are
sold 'on the day', and people queue, often overnight, to have a chance of buying
these tickets. See the notes below about the availability of wheelchair spaces, and
the procedures for anyone who is mobility impaired, as the normal route from
the overnight camping area and for day entry tickets is via a bridge over the road,
with approximately ±30 steps.

The nearest 'accessible' stations are Southfields (District line, 1.5km) and
Wimbledon just over 2km away, which is a junction for NR trains, the District
line, and Tramlink. Getting on and off the NR and District line trains involves a
big step, but Tramlink is accessible - see the chapter on *Getting around*. There's
an 'accessible' bus service to and from Southfields. If you have a problem
walking long distances, it's probably worth taking a taxi, and getting dropped off
outside one of the gates – and using a cab to get back afterwards. A good pick-up
point for getting home is the rank just to the left of Gate 13 as you come out.
Car parking in the area around the club is inevitably strictly controlled. Many
local people rent out their front gardens for parking during the tournament
fortnight. There is a drop-off point by gate 19 next to CP4 behind Court 1 and at
the top of the hill.
There is no on-site parking, but BB spaces are available in CP8 opposite Gate
4 on Church Road. There are also spaces in CP6 a little further on. You almost
certainly need to reserve a space in advance. The parking is in the grounds of the
local Golf Club, so the paths and surfaces are roughish. If you don't have a BB

space by the entrance, there are golf buggies to help disabled walkers to get back to near the road, if you ask.

There are nine parking bays for electric scooters by the debenture lounge at Centre court, and scooters must enter the grounds through gate 4 off Church Road.

The grounds are triangular in shape, and measure over 700m down two of the sides and nearly 200m across the base, so it's quite large. Along the Church Road side, the ground is only very gently sloping, but **there's a substantial hill**, as you go past No 1 Court up towards the Aorangi Terrace picnic area. This is better known to some as Henman Hill or more recently (2011) as Murray Mound. During the tournament, the whole Terrace gets very busy with tens of thousands of fans watching matches on the big screen, generating huge amounts of movement.

No 1 Court nestles into the hillside, and there is step-free (though sloped) access around the Aorangi Terrace side, but some steps as you go towards the Church Road side. To get to and from the lower parts of the site there's a sloped path between courts 18 and 19, and going downwards, a chair user would need to follow the North Concourse and then go past Fred Perry's statue to get to the flatter part of the site. There are ±32 steps at the end of St Mary's Walk at one corner of Centre Court if you were to go straight ahead.

To illustrate the steepness of the hill, from the top of the sloped path between courts 18 and 19, if you go straight ahead up the other part of St Mary's Path, there are +16+16+16+7 steps - so it's quite a climb and that's after the ±32 mentioned earlier !

The part of the grounds where Nos 2 and 3 Courts hae been built and past the outside courts to the South Concourse is nearly flat, as are the paths past the Museum and around the lower parts of Court No 1 on the Church Road side.

There are a small number of 'show' courts which will host the most prestigious matches. On all of these you have to book in advance to get a place. Only Centre Court has a potential cover/roof in the event of rain. Early on in the tournament, many of the matches are played on courts 4 to 19, and it's possible to get really close to the action, although you'll almost certainly have to be patient waiting for a slot or a spot from which you can get a good view. You can see matches between Juniors, and between Veterans on these outside courts, and sometimes these are exciting and closely fought.

The site is very 'open' so roaming around and taking in the atmosphere - possibly stopping to have some strawberries and cream, can be as much a part of the day out as watching tennis.

There's a good plan/map available which show the step-free routes around the site, and you would do well to get hold of one of these in advance. The standard *Easy access guide* has a small plan, but a double size one (which is much clearer) is available if you ask. This guide covers most of the basic information you need, and is very well put together. It does not, however, explain the topography of the site, and the effects of No 1 court "nestling into the hillside" as we have described it. Although the site is quite large and confusing, particularly when there are thousands of people there, there is a small army of well trained people wandering around with a sign over their heads saying 'information'. We found that they were both helpful and knowledgeable.

The provisions for disabled spectators are fairly minimal. The number of chair users who can get tickets is tiny. Even on the brand new No 1 court there are only forty spaces for disabled people amongst some 10,000 spectators. As there is little or no provision for disabled walkers (for example to enable them to book the more easily accessible seats) the 40 seems fairly minimal, and there are only 28 spaces on the Centre Court whose capacity is 15,000. We understand that there are some difficult compromises to be made, and that there are commercial considerations affecting policy. However the official guidelines for new stadia being built suggest a minimum of 100 spaces for chair users in a 10,000 seater stadium - and **there seem to be NO proper guidelines yet covering provisions for disabled walkers**. Nearly all the seats involve stepped access, and generally there are quite a lot of steps. Little thought has been given to allocating those seats which do not involve many steps to disabled walkers. If you're successful in the ballot (see below) you can request seating reached by a minimum number of steps, and, possibly in an aisle seat if getting past other people (and their bags etc) might be difficult. Be specific if steps are a challenge, but don't imply that you're a 'Health and Safety' risk !
If you do manage to come, you'll be well looked after.

Getting hold of tickets is a chancy process. Many go to corporate entertainers, others are distributed through tennis clubs, and finally, there is an annual ballot for seats on the show courts. There is a separate ballot for the chair spaces.
To apply, write to the Ticket Department, POB 98, Church Road, Wimbledon SW19 5AE by the previous December marking both the letter and envelope 'Wheelchair'. You first have to write in to get an Application Form, and this must be done before December 15th. The closing date for applications using these forms is December 31st. Even if you don't have a ticket, chair users and other disabled people can join the *Queue* 'on the day' in Wimbledon Park, across the road from the main Club grounds. If anyone has difficulty getting from the *Queue* to the Search Tent prior to ground entry, then one of the Stewards will take them by buggy. There are some ground entry tickets, and in the earlier parts of the tournament, there is a small allocation of wheelchair spaces for people in the *Queue*. there are unreserved chair spaces on courts 6, 13, 14, 15, 16, 17, 18 and 19, but most of these courts will not feature the 'big name' players, though you may well get to see some interesting tennis, including veterans matches and mixed doubles. You may have to queue for several hours – but you'll catch

something of the atmosphere, even if you only go and watch the big video screen on Henman Hill, and have some strawberries ! There is a reduced entry charge after 5pm.

There are unreserved viewing areas on courts 6 (grass sloped area), 13, 14, 15, 16, 17, 18 and 19. All are courtside and are accessed step-free. There is also a step-free route to courts 3,4,5,6,7,8,9 and 10. The main area of the **Aorangi Picnic Hill** has steep ramped access at its north end near to gate 19.

Tickets for wheelchair users
Getting hold of tickets is a chancy process, explained above. There is a separate ballot for the wheelchair spaces. To apply, write to the Ticket Department, POB 98, Church Road, Wimbledon SW19 5AE, marking both the letter and envelope 'Wheelchair'.
You first have to get an Application Form, and this needs to be done before December 15th. The closing date for applications using these forms is December 31st.
Even if you don't have a ticket, chair users and other disabled spectators can join the *Queue* 'on the day'.
It is impossible to prebook tickets since almost all show court tickets are issued by ballot. If it were possible, best seats would be: Centre: Row Z step free, back row B use lift by gate 5 for chair users area (see earlier); Court One: 4 to row J at SW corner (if chair users access is used), +10 to row R (public staircases).

Spaces for wheelchair users
There are 28 on Centre Court, 20 of which are at the top level (so you get something of a birdseye view), 5 are courtside NE and 3 are courtside SE.
No 1 Court has 40 spaces, has 20 in the East and 20 in the West.
No 2 court has 20 spaces in the South, and No 3 has 10 spaces in the West.
Entrances for wheelchair users
All are fairly clearly defined and marked. There's a lift up to the top level on Centre Court.
Ambulant disabled spectators
Very few provisions have been made for disabled walkers. About the only thing that you can do is to request an appropriate seat allocation (saying clearly what you need, and why) if you are successful in the Ballot.
Visually impaired spectators
No special provisions have been made, although Assistance Dogs are welcome, provided they stay with their owners and do not block evacuation routes.
Hearing impaired spectators
No special provisions have been made. On court there's a visual display on the scoreboard.

Catering
There is a wide variety of catering facilities all around the site which as far as we could see were all sensibly accessible. At certain times, particularly when a match ends on one of the big courts, they can become very crowded.

Toilets
There are a good number of **accessible toilets and cubicles (NKS)** around the site. All are clearly marked on maps and operate with RADAR keys, and several are around No 1 court. Those that we saw were all D70+ ST70+.

Museum
The museum is on two levels with lift access. It is step-free throughout. There are also site tours lasting about an hour and a half, which should almost certainly be pre-booked. Entrance through Gate 4. Significant admission charge.
During the Championships entry to the Museum is from inside the grounds.

Ticket Office
This is approached from Gate 3 if you have queued up to purchase tickets on the day - having joined *The Queue*.

Commentary

'Access' is a question of design and of physical provision, AND it involves the ticketing process, which is increasingly inflexible with the growth of computerisation. When you ring, it is becoming more and more difficult to speak to a person, and even more difficult to find (and get through to) a person who will understand what you are needing. Most of the sports grounds described here have a *Disability enquiry* telephone line, so that detailed issues can be tackled. However, too often this means leaving a voicemail message, which may or may not be replied to. The allocated staff member may be working only part-time on access issues.
Very few of the stadia offer the service of a *Textphone* number, which is particularly disappointing.

The design of stands and stadia
Football (and other spectator) stadia are nearly all built with so-called Stands on four sides of the pitch, court or track, where the action takes place. To enable a lot of spectators to have a good view, the seats can be quite steeply raked, and the steepness often increases as you get further away from the pitch/area of action. This was very noticeable at the Olympic venues, as it is at the Dome/O2 Arena. The easiest place to provide wheelchair spaces and access for ambulant disabled people, is at ground level - but the view is not very good, as it's so low down. At football matches you're at increased risk of having a ball flying very fast in your direction ! In some stands, even quite new ones, there can be problems with sightlines from upper levels - particularly if other spectators stand up, thus blocking the view of anyone who cannot stand, and usually at crucial stages of the game.

The conventional design has always been to provide access into the lower parts of a Stand by providing a flight of stairs taking spectators into a middle level (often about a third of the way up), so that to find their seats from there, people either have to go down some more steps, or to go up. The initial stairs will almost certainly have handrails, whereas the steps leading to the rows of seats probably have no further supports.

Where there are two or even three levels in a single Stand (like the North Bank at the Manchester United ground), the same principle applies to the upper levels. At the highest level there are nearly 200 steps before you reach the middle of the section where you may be seated !

Because of this methodology, which has been, and still is, widely used, the number of seats that can be reached via a limited number of steps (say <5), is very small indeed. It depends on whether there are access routes at ground level to the front (lowest levels) of the Stands OR on whether there is a lift giving step-free access to intermediate levels.

Virtually no grounds clarify such issues on their websites, nor even in the comments and information we have managed to glean from discussing our write-ups with the DLOs at grounds. We found when making enquiries that even the Ticket Office does not always have details of the lifts.

Wheelchair users

The provisions for wheelchair users have undoubtedly improved, even though many spaces at football grounds are uncovered at pitch-side, with a somewhat restricted view. More needs to be done, especially when new stadia or stands are built. This is tending to happen, as with the new Arsenal stadium, at Wembley, and with the riverside stand planned at Fulham.

Disabled walkers

What seems to be almost completely lacking is an understanding of the needs of the substantial number of disabled walkers, and a way of identifying and codifying their requirements.

The number of (generally older) spectators who have difficulties is growing. They may have a hassle with:

• walking long distances
• steps (especially when there is no handrail or support)
• lack of leg-room (particularly for those with arthritis)
• getting along a row of seats to get to a seat some distance along it, as there is no support

They may also need an aisle seat so that they can more easily slip out to go to the toilet.

These are NOT people who 'need' a companion, who have an Assistance dog, or who are in receipt of DWP benefits. Many, however, might have a BB, although not all. ALL however have genuine needs relating to their disability.

The concept of 'Easy access' seats

Seats, for example aisle seats, and the one alongside, which have <5 steps from the level reached using the standard stairs with handrails, or a lift, might be designated as 'easy access' seats. These might then be sold only to those on the 'easy access' register.

The stands which have a lift can potentially offer a much wider range of 'easy access' seats, and in our enquiries that was one of our questions.

To their credit, some stadia have thought about this, and the possibility of asking for an 'easy access' seat already exists, for example at Twickenham and at West Ham FC where the choice available to disabled walkers seems to be particularly good.

Note what happened at the Olympics

We were pleased to see in the Ticketing Application for the Olympics and Paralympics that when applying for a standard seat, it was possible to register additional accessibility requirements such as:

- seats close to the action, for visually impaired people;
- seats with a direct view of a video screen for people who are deaf or have impaired hearing;
- seats for people who cannot manage many steps, at the back or the front of a stand;
- seats for people who need to be on the end of a row.

What the Olympics Ticketing office said was that "If your application for tickets is successful, we will do all we can to ensure you and your party are allocated seats which suit your needs."

This is a great potential advance for disabled walkers, as more Stands have lifts, and as those in the ticket office take note of their additional needs. We hope that our proposals included here to enable disabled walkers to register their need for an 'easy access' seat will be taken forward and acted on.

Provisions at stadia for disabled people so far

Virtually all the football clubs require disabled spectators to 'Register' as Disabled Supporters, for the concessionary facilities available (including wheelchair spaces and seats for ambulant disabled people who need a companion or Assistance dog).

What they say is something like

"The Club reserves the right to check a person's eligibility under the DDA .

"The Club will use a system of concessionary ticket prices tailored to its disabled supporters. "Concessions are not based on impairment type but recognise that some disabled supporters have a restricted choice of viewing in the stadium and/ or could not attend a match without personal support."

The whole thrust of the approach adopted by clubs to providing facilities for disabled spectators is dominated by the need to:

- satisfy the requirements of the DDA, and
- to protect themselves against misuse of the concessions offered to disabled

supporters, both those who use a wheelchair and disabled walkers.
What the approach does NOT do is to facilitate people who are not in receipt of Attendance Allowance, or similar DWP support, in being able to book, pay full price for, and get to the most appropriate seats or spaces.
It doesn't seem/appear to be friendly to the occasional disabled visitor - for example, what if I have a friend from Canada staying who is a wheelchair user, and we might want to buy tickets without worrying too much about the free carer/companion concession ?
I might have some difficult in booking a space.
Similarly there are a huge number of people who may have difficulty getting to the ground, and who might use a wheelchair to make the journey possible - but while they don't need a wheelchair space they DO need access to a seat with a minimum number of steps en route, and they may need a storage place for their chair.
There can be a MAJOR distortion in the 'market', because of the well meaning provision of concessionary, or even free places. Having taken advantage of such provisions for many years, those getting them may be very reluctant to share things around.
It seems to us that the principle should simply be that IF someone needs a PA/companion to enable them to get there and get in, then the PA should get in free. Others with real 'access' needs should be able to get appropriate seats, but without any price concession.
Price concessions are a great and well intentioned gesture, but are quite likely to result in maximum benefit to a small group of people - who will get in quickly when applications open AND, when consulted, will vote for continuing the scheme ....

We queried the relatively small number of 'easy access' seats provided at the new Wembley Stadium where there are 310 wheelchair spaces but only 100 enhanced amenity seats for disabled walkers.
When asked about the fact that there are probably to 10 times as many disabled walkers in the population as wheelchair users, the Wembley management said that "at the time of the 2002 planning permission, the numbers of facilities were thought to meet the needs of disabled spectators".

Participation

One of the hoped-for outcomes from the Paralympics, was a growth in opportunities for participation. If you want to join in some sporting activities, you need to look first at what is available nearby, probably in your borough. We provide here a few points of contact to help your search.

English Federation Of Disability Sport,
SportPark, Loughborough University, 3 Oakwood Drive, Loughborough, LE11
3QF *Tel:* 01509-227-750 *Fax:* 01509-227-777
website: www.efds.co.uk

Interactive is an organisation promoting inclusion in sport *"To create a society
where being active is an intrinsic part of a disabled person's life, and disabled
people are at the heart of sport in London."*
Unit 2B07, London South Bank University, Technopark, 90 London Road, SE1
6LN *Tel:* 020 7717-1699
website: www.interactive.uk.net *e-mail:* info@interactive.uk.net

There is also **Get active London** who have an extensive web-based resource, but
no address or phone number. They present a wide range of links, though many are
for able-bodied people rather than those with disabilities.
website: www.getactivelondon.com *e-mail:* info@getactivelondon.com
The resource is based around five **Pro-active London Partnerships** which work
to increase participation in sport and physical activity in different areas.
You can find out more at *www.pro-activelondon.org.*

Special Needs Kids is a nationwide online information and guidance resource,
see: *www.special-needs-kids.co.uk/Disabled-Sports.htm*
e-mail: enquiries@special-needs-kids.co.uk

For those with a learning disability, see:
www.enabledlondon.com/default/52.healthLiving/gym and there's **The UK
Sports Association for People with Learning Disability (UKSA)**
12 City Forum, 250 City Road, EC1V 2PU
Tel: 020 7490-3057 *Fax:* 020 7251-8861
website: www.uksportsassociation.org *e-mail:* info@uksportsassociation.org

Access Sport was founded in 2004 to give more children, particularly in
disadvantaged areas, access to a wide range of quality local sport.
3 Durham Yard, Teesdale Street, E2 6QF *Tel:* 020 7993-9883
website: www.accesssport.org.uk *e-mail:* info@accesssport.co.uk
It launched its Disability Legacy Project in 2011, helping to ensure that there is
a lasting positive effect from the London 2012 Games. The aim of the project is
to have equipped five mainstream sports clubs with the skills and resources to be
inclusive of more disabled young people.

If you want to take a sport very seriously, then there's the
British Paralympic Association
Room 514, Impact House, 2 Eldridge Road, Croydon CR9 1JP
website: www.paralympics.org.uk

Recommended itineraries

We have identified some connected areas, where there are a number of varied and interesting sights. You will find accessible toilets *en route,* (see the *Good loo guide*).The majority of the places mentioned are described in detail in the guide. You will need to study a map, because only you know what sort of distances you can cope with. It is of course difficult to represent everyone's interests, and you'll have your own ideas about what you want to see. You might, for example, want to go shopping, which we haven't covered here. Also, where you go will be affected by where your accommodation is, and how easily you can get around on public transport, by cab or by car.

We hope that with the judicious use of other guides, you can plan your visit to make the most of your time and resources, doing the things of most interest. You will find an extended version of this chapter on our website.

The Barbican & St Paul's

A varied group of sights is centred on the Barbican area. Parking is possible at the Barbican Centre, or you might be able to reserve a space at the Museum of London. Within 500m of the Barbican Centre are St Bartholomew-the-Great and St Giles Cripplegate churches and the Museum of London. There are accessible toilets in the Barbican Arts Centre and in the Museum of London. Postman's Park offers a possible shady picnic spot, although a good number of office workers will probably have the same idea. A little further afield are the Guildhall, the Clock Museum and further again, St Paul's Cathedral. There's a step-free link from St Paul's across the river using the Millennium Bridge, which joins up with the next itinerary.

The Riverside Walk along the South Bank

This now stretches from County Hall and the London Eye, under Waterloo, Blackfriars, Southwark and London Bridges right along to Tower Bridge. It covers a distance of something just over 2km, so it may be necessary to split it into two, three or even four sections. Relatively nearby is the JLE with 'accessible' stations at Waterloo, Southwark and London Bridge. Parking is possible near the Festival Hall, or under the National Theatre.

Places to visit in both Southwark and Lambeth, include:

- Tower Bridge and HMS Belfast;
- the Shard, Southwark Cathedral and the London Bridge Experience & London Tombs (three very contrasting venues !);
- Vinopolis, and The Anchor pub;
- Shakespeare's Globe Exhibition and Theatre, together with Tate Modern:
- the Oxo tower, National Theatre, British Film Institute Southbank cinemas, Festival Hall complex, Hayward Gallery, and towards Waterloo, the IMAX

cinema (a huge collection of venues);
* the London Eye, London Dungeon and the London Aquarium.
The construction of the pedestrian bridges at Hungerford Bridge and the
Millennium Bridge has made access to and from the north and south banks of the
Thames much easier.

Westminster to Piccadilly

Westminster to Piccadilly is another area containing, again, a wide variety of
sights. Parking is possible on the South Bank. One way of getting quite close is
to come in by train to Charing Cross. If you decide to take in the whole area, St
James's Park provides a good place for a rest or a picnic. Places to visit include:
* around and near Parliament Square are the Houses of Parliament, the
  Supreme Court, Westminster Abbey, Central Hall Westminster and the
  Churchill War Rooms;
* Whitehall is full of government buildings, there are a number of memorials
  and military statues, including Britain's primary war memorial.
* around Trafalgar Square are the National Gallery, St Martin-in-the-Fields
  church and crypt, and just to the north is the National Portrait Gallery;
* from there you can either go up Haymarket or Regent Street to get to
  Piccadilly Circus.

A river trip to Greenwich

A river trip is an ideal way to see London. Starting points include the
Embankment and Westminster piers on the north side of the river and the Festival
pier on the south side. Depending on the tide, there is steepish ramped access and
a good number of the boats operating are now 'accessible'.
The trip enables you to see much of central London in a really relaxed way,
and Greenwich has some amazing buildings, as well as the park and National
Maritime Museum.

A walk through the parks

If you want a relaxing walk or wheel, then a route starting somewhere in Hyde
Park, going past the Serpentine to Hyde Park Corner, and then on through Green
Park and St James's (past Buckingham Palace) will keep you in the 'countryside'
for quite a long time. En route you can visit the Wellington Arch, and at the end
you can go and visit places round Trafalgar Square, or around Westminster.

Canary Wharf and the Museum in Docklands

A surprisingly different and varied day out can be had in the newly developed
Docklands area. There is ample parking in the MSCP on Hertsmere road to the
north of Canary Wharf and there are 'accessible' train connections via the JLE
and/or DLR to Canary Wharf. There is a big shopping complex in the centre of
Canary Wharf, and the Museum in Docklands tells an interesting story.

The good loo guide

This chapter brings together the information we have on accessible toilets/loos in central London, which is scattered through the guide, and relates them to a map. There are a few in the list that are not mentioned elsewhere in the text. To be accessible, there are three major criteria, which are that:

* the toilet can be reached step-free;
* the cubicle is large enough for a chair user, and should have support rails and lever taps etc; and
* it should be open/available, or use the NKS lock, and not in a building where there is an admission charge or restricted admission.

Accessible toilets may be in an area where there is a small fee to pay to get in, usually of 20 to 50p. The majority of accessible toilets are free to access, and use the NKS lock. However, charging a fee is becoming more common, particularly at railway stations, so carrying a small number of 10p, 20p, and 50p coins, is a good defensive strategy.

We strongly recommend that you get an NKS key, as this will open a large percentage of accessible loos in both in London and elsewhere. A key can be obtained from a number of places, see page 23. It costs less than £10, including postage. The Disability Rights UK store will also have the *National Key Scheme Guide* listing over 4000 NKS toilets around the country.

Tardis toilets

In the text we have referred to *Tardis* toilets, which may be slightly confusing for some people - so we ought to explain further.

The reference and description is for a public toilet, usually located on a pavement in the street, and often with a wheelchair sign on top. The ones we list are permanent installations, and are all wheelchair accessible.

They are entered by paying a small fee (commonly 20-50p) or by using a RADAR NKS key, in which case they are free. They are usually available 24/7. The designs vary, and they might be best described as 'compact'. They have a time limit on use, and when someone leaves and closes the door, there is a preprogrammed cycle for self cleaning.

The *Tardis* is a time machine and spacecraft, used in a very well known science fiction television series about 'Doctor Who'. It looks like a 1960s-style London police box, and there's a similarity with both the shape and location of the accessible pavement toilets.

Hence the (possibly confusing) description !

We have highlighted public accessible toilets that are available 24 hours of the day, such as the 'Tardis' toilets found on some pavements **by putting them in bold** in the listing.

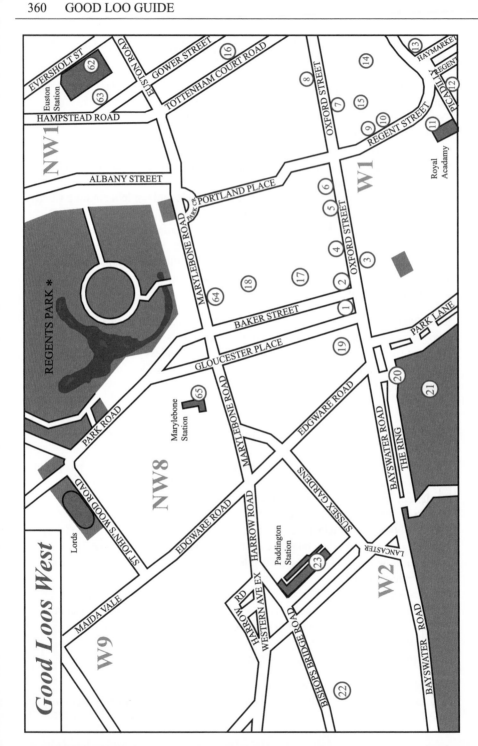

Good Loos West

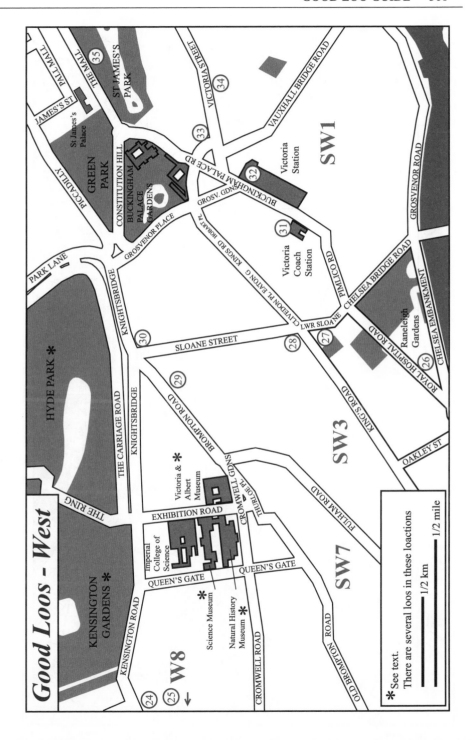

Good Loos - West

W8

SW1

SW3

SW7

HYDE PARK *

KENSINGTON GARDENS *

Victoria & Albert Museum *

Science Museum *

Natural History Museum *

St James's Palace

GREEN PARK

BUCKINGHAM PALACE GARDENS

Victoria Station

Victoria Coach Station

Ranelagh Gardens

Imperial College of Science

* See text.
There are several loos in these loactions

1/2 km
1/2 mile

PALL MALL
THE MALL
ST JAMES'S PARK
JAMES'S ST
VICTORIA STREET
VAUXHALL BRIDGE ROAD
PICCADILLY
CONSTITUTION HILL
BUCKINGHAM PALACE RD
GROSV. GDNS
GROSVENOR PLACE
GROSVENOR ROAD
PARK LANE
KNIGHTSBRIDGE
KINGS RD EATON G CLIVEDON PL
HOBART PL
PIMLICO RD
CHELSEA BRIDGE ROAD
LWR SLOANE
CHELSEA EMBANKMENT
SLOANE STREET
ROYAL HOSPITAL ROAD
THE CARRIAGE ROAD
KNIGHTSBRIDGE
BROMPTON ROAD
KING'S ROAD
OAKLEY ST
THE RING
CROMWELL GDNS
CROMWELL RD
EXHIBITION ROAD
THURLOE PL
FULHAM ROAD
QUEEN'S GATE
QUEEN'S GATE
KENSINGTON ROAD
CROMWELL ROAD
OLD BROMPTON ROAD

24
25
30
29
28
27
26
31
32
33
34
35

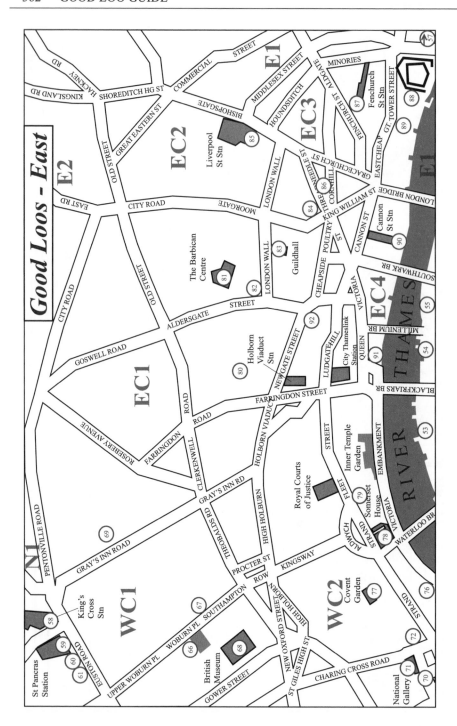

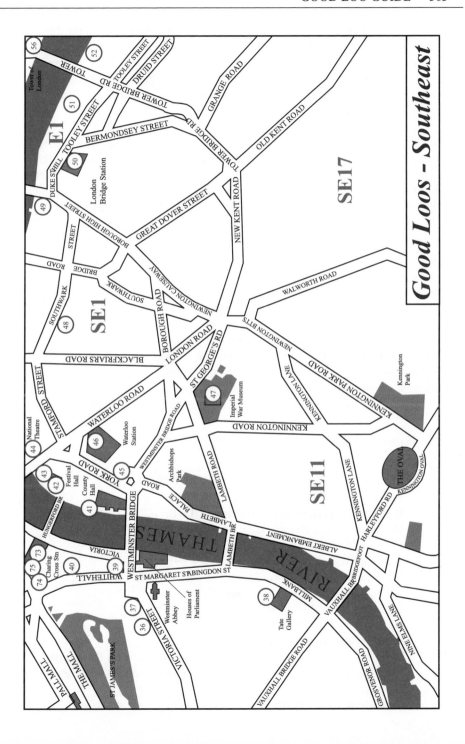

Good Loos – Southeast

364   GOOD LOO GUIDE

We have also **put in bold** other toilets that can be accessed for most of the day such as those in shops, museums and rail stations. Those in pubs and hotels are slightly less 'public', and you may feel obliged to buy a drink if you want to use one, but if your need is urgent, they can be really useful. Pubs can get extremely crowded at certain times, as can fast food outlets such as *Burger King, Costa Coffee* and *McDonald's*.

The *Good loo guide* covers the central London area, and is split up according to postal districts. If you don't happen to know which postal district you are in, then it is normally written on street name signs, for example, Oxford Street W1. There is more information on our website, including a listing of pubs with accessible toilets in some central areas, such as Covent Garden, Whitehall, and on the South Bank.

Changing places
website: www.changing-places.org
The **Changing Places Consortium** has launched a campaign on behalf of people who cannot use standard accessible toilets. This includes adults needing an incontinence pad change, people with profound and multiple learning disabilities and their carers, and many other disabled people.
There is a need for publicly accessible toilets with enough space and the right equipment, including a height adjustable changing bench and a hoist.
We are fully supportive of this initiative, and have included information in our write-ups, in the listing here, and in a supplementary list at the end of the chapter.

The good loo list
W1
1	**Marks & Spencer (Marble Arch)**, see page 295
2	**Selfridges**, Oxford Street, see page 297
3	**Balderton Street, opposite Selfridges, Tardis toilet (NKS, 24 hrs)**
4	**Debenhams**, 334 Oxford Street, see page 286
5	**House of Fraser**, 318 Oxford Street, see page 290
6	**John Lewis**, 300 Oxford Street, see page 291
7	**Marks and Spencer (Pantheon)**, 173 Oxford Street, see page 294
8	**Plaza**, 120 Oxford Street, see page 297
9	**Liberty's**, 210/220 Regent Street, see page 294
10	**Hamleys**, 188 Regent Street, see page 287
11	**Royal Academy**, Piccadilly, see page 252
12	**Waterstones**, 203 Piccadilly, see page 299, together with **Hatchards**, 187 Piccadilly, see page 290, and **Fortnum & Mason**, 181 Piccadilly, see page 286
13	**Trocadero**, Coventry Street and Shaftesbury Avenue, see page 181

14	**Broadwick Street**, 50m west of the junction with Wardour Street. **Tardis toilet NKS**
15	**Photographers Gallery**, 16 Ramillies Street, see page 251
16	**Heals**, 196 Tottenham Court Road, see page 290
17	**Wallace Collection**, Manchester Square, see page 264
18	**Paddington Street opposite Luxborough Street**, in a corner of Paddington Street Gardens, **wheelchair toilet (D80 ST80)** with separate BCF
19	**Thistle Inn Marble Arch**, Bryanston Street, see page 47
20	**Marble** Arch, in the ramped subway which runs from Speakers Corner (by the park), under the roundabout to the west side of Edgware Road. **Wheelchair cubicles (D85 ST75) in both womens and mens**.

W2

21	**Hyde Park and Kensington Gardens** see page 192, with a loos list on page 196. Note those at the Serpentine Gallery, Kensington Palace and by the restaurants
22	**Whiteleys**, 151 Queensway see page 299
23	**Paddington Station**. There's a 24-hour **accessible toilet (NKS and *Changing Places*)** by the end of platform 12, see page 135

W8 *(Both are just off the map)*

| 24 | **Marks and Spencers**, 113 Kensington High Street see page 294 |
| 25 | **Copthorne Tara Hotel** see page 70 |

SW3

| 26 | **National Army Museum**, Royal Hospital Road see page 244 |

SW1

27	**Saatchi Gallery**, see page 252
28	**Peter Jones**, Sloane Square see page 295
29	**Harrods**, Brompton Road, Knightsbridge see page 288
30	**Harvey Nichols**, 109 Knightsbridge see page 289
31	**Victoria coach station** see page 140
32	**Victoria station** see page 138, and **Victoria Place** see page 298
33	**Bressenden Place**, at the junction with Victoria Street. **Tardis toilet NKS**
34	**House of Fraser**, 101 Victoria Street see page 291
35	**St James's Park**, see page 189
36	**Central Hall Westminster**, Storey's Gate, see page 273, and there's another **outside the QE2 Conference Centre**, opposite Westminster Abbey
37	**The Supreme Court**, see page 190
38	**Tate Britain**, Millbank, see page 258
39	**By Westminster Pier** the **wheelchair toilet (NKS)** by Westminster Bridge can be approached step-free from the Embankment, alongside the

Pier OR from the ticket hall level of Westminster station via Exit 1. It is at the bottom of a flight of stairs from the Bridge.

40   **Banqueting House**, Whitehall see page 182

SE1

41   **London Eye**, Jubilee Gardens, see page 166
42   **Royal Festival Hall,** has accessible toilets on most floors, and is open all day. There's one at riverside level on the same side as the Hayward Gallery by the JCB lift
43   **British Film Institute** has an accessible toilet off the main foyer, accessed by a platform lift. There's another reached from the riverside, going through the café and turning left
44   **National Theatre.** Extensive development is under way, and the current GF accessible toilet is past the main bar at Lyttleton Stalls level. See the website for updates
45   **The three hotels** near the southern end of Westminster Bridge, numbered 35 on the hotels map, see pages 64/65
46   **Waterloo station** see page 136
47   **Imperial War Museum**, Lambeth Road, see page 240
48   **Holiday Inn Express Southwark**, see page 62
49   **Southwark Cathedral**, Borough High Street, see page 270
50   **London Bridge station**, see page 138
51   **City Hall**, see page 160, with a *Changing places* facility
52   **Design Museum**, Shad Thames see page 236
53   **Gabriel's Wharf**, next to the *Studio Six* pub see page 161, and the **Oxo Tower**, see page 168
54   **Tate Modern**, Bankside which has a *Changing places* facility see page 258, and the *Founders Arms* pub on the riverside
55   **Shakespeare's Globe**, 21 New Globe Walk see page 257, and the *Anchor* pub see page 159

E1

56   **Tower Hotel**, St Katharine's Way see page 59
57   **Dickens Inn**, St Katharine's Way see page 154

N1

58   **Kings Cross station**, York Way, with a *Changing places* facility, see page 133

NW1

59   **St Pancras station**, see page 134
60   **British Library**, 96 Euston Road, see page 231
61   **Euston Road** by the corner with Chalton Street. **Tardis toilet NKS**
62   **Euston station**, see page 135
63   **Ibis Hotel**, Euston, see page 57

64   **Marylebone Road,** 50m west of Madame Tussauds. **Tardis toilet NKS**
65   **Marylebone station,** see page 133

WC1

66   **Russell Square,** by the corner of Bernard Street and Southampton Row. **Tardis toilet NKS**
67   **Double Tree by Hilton,** 92 Southampton Row, see page 52
68   **British Museum,** Great Russell Street, see page 232
69   **Holiday Inn Bloomsbury,** 1 Kings Cross Road, see page 52

WC2

70   **Trafalgar Square.** There are two **accessible toilets (NKS)** in the square, level with the fountains and to the left of the café. **See also 71to75,** all of which are very close
71   **National Gallery,** see page 246; and the **National Portrait Gallery** see page 245, both reached from the north side upper level of the Square
72   **St Martin-in-the-Fields church,** see page 278
73   **Charing Cross station,** see page 138
74   **Waterstones,** at the end of the Strand, Trafalgar Square. Step-fee entrance from the Strand. **Accessible toilet** (D80 ST80) with BCF on the 1st floor, reached via the lift.
75   **Charing Cross Hotel,** Strand, see page 54
76   **Victoria Embankment,** 50m east of Embankment station (D80 ST80 NKS) with a *Changing places* facility
77   **Covent Garden** see page 174
78   **Somerset House,** which can be accessed from the Strand or from the Embankment, see page 178
79   **Aldwych,** on the south side of the Strand some 50m from the junction with Arundel Street. **Tardis toilet NKS.**

EC1 and EC2

80   **West Smithfield,** near the market, and by the UGCP entrance on the roundabout. **Tardis toilet NKS**
81   **The Barbican Centre,** see page 151
82   **Museum of London,** London Wall, see page 243
83   **Guildhall,** Gresham Street, see page 151
84   **Bank of England Museum,** see page 230
85   **Liverpool Street station,** see page 136

EC3 and EC4

86   **Royal Exchange,** see page 154
87   **Fenchurch Street station,** off the ground level concourse by the lift, approached from Fenchurch Place, **NKS,** see page 132
88   **Tower Hill,** Petty Wales, behind the Visitor Centre, see pages 156/7
89   **All-Hallows-by-the-Tower,** Byward Street see page 274

90   **Cannon Street station**, see page 138
91   **Blackfriars station**, see page 134
92   **Paternoster Square** (on the north side of St Paul's Cathedral). Paternoster Lodge is a redbrick office building by the archway leading to the cathedral. **Two wheelchair toilets (D75 ST 75 NKS)** in the basement, reached by lift (D75 W100 L125). Open most days, but not in the evenings

Changing places toilets

There are an increasing number of *Changing places*, see their website for an updated list. It includes five in the new Queen Elizabeth Olympic Park. Some are included on our map.

When we went to press, there were *Changing places* at:
- **Victoria Embankment Gardens** (no 76 on the map)
- the **Houses of Parliament**, close to the Central Lobby, see page 185
- **Great Ormond Street Hospital**, WC1N 3JH, on the GF, main site, (off the Southwood to Variety Club Building link corridor)
- **Tate Modern** (no 54 on the map)
- **Kings Cross station**, see page 133, (no 58 on the map)
- **Barbican Centre**, located within the Beech Street cinema complex (Cinemas 2&3) which is separate from the main centre and next to Exhibition Hall 1
- **Pancras Square Leisure Centre**, 5 Pancras Square, N1C 4AG, on the LGF
- **Paddington station**, see page 133, (no 23 on the map)
- **City Hall**, see page 160, (no 51 on the map)
- **Arsenal FC Emirates stadium**, see page 324
- **Westfield London (Shepherds Bush)**, level −2 off the UGCP and by the *Shopmobility* office, see page 301
- **O2 Arena**, on Level 1 by Block 106. Access is by electronic card, obtainable from the customer service desk, see page 172
- **Westfield Stratford**, on both GF and 1st floor, see page 302
- **Wembley stadium**, on Level 1, internal concourse, by Block 104, **(NKS)** see page 316
- **Kew Gardens**, by the Brentford Gate, see our website
- **ExCel London**, at the east end on the GF, see page 171

In the **Queen Elizabeth Olympic Park**, there are *Changing places* at:
- the **Podium** (by the **Orbit**), no 4 on the QE map
- the **Aquatics Centre**, no 5 on the QE map
- the **Copper Box Arena**, no 9 on the QE map
- **Timber Lodge**, no 11 on the QE map
- **The Lee Valley Velopark**, no 13 on the QE map

See *www.queenelizabetholympicpark.co.uk*

Index